Applications
of Nonverbal Communication

Edited by

Ronald E. Riggio
Claremont McKenna College

Robert S. Feldman
University of Massachusetts, Amherst

The Claremont Symposium
on Applied Social Psychology

2005

LAWRENCE ERLBAUM ASSOCIATES, PUBLISHERS
Mahwah, New Jersey   London

Lawrence Erlbaum Associates, Inc., Publishers
10 Industrial Avenue
Mahwah, New Jersey 07430

Cover design by Kathryn Houghtaling Lacey

Library of Congress Cataloging-in-Publication Data

Claremont Symposium on Applied Social Psychology (2003)
   Applications of nonverbal communication : edited by Ronald
   E. Riggio, Robert S. Feldman.
      p. cm.
Includes bibliographical references and index.
ISBN 0-8058-4334-5 (cloth : alk. paper)
ISBN 0-8058-4335-3 (pbk. : alk. paper)
1. Nonverbal communication—Congresses. I. Riggio, Ronald E.
   II. Feldman, Robert S. (Robert Stephen), 1947– . III. Title.
P99.5.C58   2003
302.2'22—dc22

                                        2004050673
                                        CIP

Books published by Lawrence Erlbaum Associates are printed on acid-free paper, and their bindings are chosen for strength and durability.

Printed in the United States of America
10 9 8 7 6 5 4 3 2 1

Applications
of Nonverbal Communication

THE STAUFFER SYMPOSIUM ON APPLIED PSYCHOLOGY AT THE CLAREMONT COLLEGES

This series of volumes highlights important new developments on the leading edge of applied social psychology. Each volume focuses on one area in which social psychological knowledge is being applied to the resolution of social problems. Within that area, a distinguished group of authorities present chapters summarizing recent theoretical views and empirical findings, including the results of their own research and applied activities. An introductory chapter frames the material, pointing out common themes and varied areas of practical applications. Thus each volume brings together trenchant new social psychological ideas, research results, and fruitful applications bearing on an area of current social interest. The volumes will be of value not only to practitioners and researchers, but also to students and lay people interested in this vital and expanding area of psychology.

Series books published by Lawrence Erlbaum Associates:

- *Reducing Prejudice and Discrimination*, edited by Stuart Oskamp (2000).

- *Mass Media and Drug Prevention: Classic and Contemporary Theories and Research*, edited by William D. Crano and Michael Burgoon (2002).

- Evaluating Social Programs and Problems: Visions for the New Millennium, edited by Steward I. Donaldson and Michael Scriven (2003).

- *Processes of Community Change and Social Action*, edited by Allen M. Omoto and Stuart Oskamp (2004).

- *Applications of Nonverbal Communication*, edited by Ronald E. Riggio and Robert S. Feldman (2005).

Dedication

This book is dedicated
to Robert Rosenthal and Paul Ekman,
for their pioneering work
that inspired much of this research.

Contents

ॐ ॐ

Preface:
Applications of Nonverbal Communication

Each and every day, in every social interaction, we communicate our feelings, attitudes, thoughts, and concerns nonverbally. Nonverbal communication is used to convey power and status, it is used to express love and intimacy, it is used to communicate agreement, to establish rapport, and to regulate the flow of communication. Nonverbal communication is pervasive, ongoing, and it is part of virtually every human endeavor.

The scientific study of nonverbal communication began more than 125 years ago, with the pioneering work of Charles Darwin and his book, *The Expression of the Emotions in Man and Animals* (1872). A check of the PsycINFO database (beginning coincidentally in 1872) shows nearly 20,000 entries with the subject heading "nonverbal." However, despite this long and rigorous line of research, we still are quite limited in our ability to apply much of this research to important "real world" settings. Much of what researchers have discovered about nonverbal communication remains in professional journals, read and studied only by other researchers of nonverbal communication.

This volume provides a much-needed bridge between the research on nonverbal communication and the application of these research findings. In this volume, some of the leading researchers in the field apply their work to understanding nonverbal communication processes in hospitals and clinics, in courtrooms and police stations, in the workplace and in government, in the classroom, and in everyday settings. It explores nonverbal communication in public settings, in intimate interpersonal relationships, and across cultures. It is our hope that practitioners of all types, from healthcare workers, to law enforcement specialists, to teachers to managers and government leaders, will find the information contained in this volume useful for improving their professional and everyday communication.

The editors of this volume would like to express thanks to the team that helped organize and host the 20th Annual Claremont Symposium on Applied Social Psychology that was the beginning of this project—Lynda Mulhall, Paul Thomas, Stuart Oskamp, and Sandy Counts. The Symposium was supported by Claremont Graduate University, Claremont McKenna College, the Kravis Leadership Institute, and associate sponsors from Harvey Mudd College, Pitzer College, Pomona College, and Scripps College. A special thanks to President Steadman Upham of Claremont Graduate University. Sandy Counts, Lynda Mulhall, Carli Straight, Yoonmi Kim, and Erin Smith were instrumental in helping with the preparation and production of this volume.

—*Ronald E. Riggio*
Claremont, California

—*Robert S. Feldman*
Amherst, Massachusetts

Introduction to Applications of Nonverbal Communication

Ronald E. Riggio
Robert S. Feldman

Few topics encompass such a rich and broad area of investigation as nonverbal communication. Researchers in fields as diverse as psychology, ethology, communication studies, sociology, anthropology, and neuroscience have all made important contributions to our understanding of the way that humans communicate nonverbally.

Yet frequently the applied implications of such research have gone ignored, unstated, or unelaborated. In part, this lack of attention to applications is a function of the kind of work carried out by nonverbal communication researchers. Such work is often very precise and exacting, employing a "microscopic" approach to studying human social behavior that is driven by theoretical questions. For example, to a nonverbal researcher, a smile is not necessarily a smile, as work on the distinction between felt, or Duchenne, smiles and feigned smiles has illustrated so compellingly (Woodzicka & LaFrance, chap. 7, this volume). Likewise, the nonverbal communication scholars who have made use of Paul Ekman's FACS, facial coding system (Ekman 1978), are able to determine that a particular photograph does or does not contain a genuine, felt expression of anger or sadness.

Although this concern with precision has produced an extensive body of significant findings, it has a downside. Specifically, scholars of nonverbal behavior are often reluctant to generalize their typically laboratory-based research findings to real-world, everyday behavior. However, it is the precision of their work that also makes nonverbal communication research so valuable—both to researchers in related areas, and to practitioners.

Similarly, although the recent surge of research on emotion has led to significant increases in our understanding of the phenomenon, emotion researchers have not always made the connection between their work and the role played by nonverbal behavior in their communication. And even when emotions researchers venture into applied territory—such as the work on emotional intelligence, or EQ—they may not make the connection to basic research on nonverbal communication of emotion.

The other side of the coin is the willingness of non-researchers to make claims and offer pronouncements that have little, if any, connection to the research on nonverbal communication. For example, some authors have claimed that they will teach you *How to Read a Person Like a Book* (Nierenberg & Calero, 1991), to *Never Be Lied to Again* (Lieberman, 1998), and *How to Understand People and Predict Their Behavior Anytime, Anyplace* (Dimitrius & Mazzarella, 1999). Such claims are often wildly exaggerated. Research shows that nonverbal behavior is far too complex to make such blanket statements, and we simply do not yet know enough to be able to do any of these things very accurately and consistently.

Yet, the dissemination of unsupported "facts" about the practice of nonverbal communication is widespread, despite the lack of a firm research foundation for the suggestions found in the popular literature. Communication professionals abound who will train politicians to be more effective and charismatic, who will use nonverbal cues to select sympathetic jurors or prepare witnesses to appear more credible. There is an entire industry around the nonverbal detection of lies, and physicians and business managers are taught to focus on nonverbal communication in order to make them more empathic. At the process level, clinicians realize that nonverbal behavior is useful in both diagnosing, and to some extent, in treating troubled marriages and family relationships, although their work may not have firm empirically-grounded support.

The sheer magnitude of work involving nonverbal behavior in everyday life—even if much of this work is not supported by research—suggests the importance of identifying research-based solutions to everyday problems. This book is intended to help bridge the gap between the research conducted by scholars of nonverbal communication and those who seek to use nonverbal communication in practice.

THE CURRENT VOLUME

The chapters in this volume represent the outgrowth of the 2003 Claremont Symposium on Applied Social Psychology. The Symposium brought together many of the leading researchers in nonverbal communication, who had the opportunity to present and share their research and to interact with one another. They later summarized their work as the chapters of the current book. The basic intent of the book is to present the practical applications suggested by research in non-verbal communication, as well as to also highlight the limitations— noting where we simply do not yet know enough to safely and fully inform practice.

What are some of the general lessons found in this volume? Several broad conclusions emerge:

- First, *there is no dictionary of nonverbal communication.* Given the great range and variety of nonverbal cues, only very few are "translatable" into their verbal counterparts. These few would include certain "universal" basic expressions of emotions (i.e., happy, sad, angry, etc. facial expressions; see Ekman & Friesen, 1975), and *emblems*—specific gestures designed to substitute for words or phrases (Johnson, Ekman, & Friesen, 1975). Yet, even in terpretation of these small groups of nonverbal cues may vary from culture to culture (especially true for gestures; e.g., the thumb and forefinger gesture to symbolize "OK" in the U.S. is considered an obscene gesture in other countries), and there is controversy over the universality of facial displays of emotion (see Russell, 1995).

- *Context matters.* One of the reasons that nonverbal communication is difficult to translate consistently is that the meaning of specific nonverbal cues can vary depending on the context. Nowhere is this made more apparent than in this book's chapters on nonverbal communication in health care and in the courtroom (Martin & Friedman, chap. 1; Searcy, Duck & Blanck, chap. 3). Similarly, on a molar level, Matsumoto and Yoo's chapter (chap. 11) on culture makes clear the central role that culture plays in determining the meaning of a particular nonverbal behavior.

- *Individual differences matter.* Clearly there are significant individual differences in people's abilities to convey (encode), interpret (decode), and regulate their nonverbal behavior (Riggio, 1992). Several chapters in this book focus on these individual differences, and they have important implications for understanding clinical populations (Philippot, et al., chap. 2), for understanding the effectiveness of political leaders (Goethals, chap. 5), and for exploring individuals who are extraordinary detectors of others' deceptions (O'Sullivan, chap. 11).

- *Expectations affect interpretation of nonverbal behavior.* Another important lesson is the critical role of interpersonal expectations. This has two aspects. First, our expectations concerning characteristics and qualities of others can be subtly communicated via nonverbal cues and can impact their behavior. Such expectancy effects, also known as the "Rosenthal effect," in honor of nonverbal scholar, Robert Rosenthal, have been most clearly applied to understanding how teachers can influence students' performance (but has applications to many other settings, as well), are outlined in Chapter 7. However, expectations can also affect how the same nonverbal display is interpreted by others in the social setting, as demonstrated by Woodzicka and LaFrance's (chap. 8) work on how certain nonverbal cues can be completely misinterpreted in the workplace.

* *Nonverbal communication patterns are not immutable.* Several of the chapters bring home the point that nonverbal communication patterns have the potential to be altered through training and therefore made more adaptive. For example, Philippot et al.'s work (chap. 2) illustrates the importance of nonverbal behavior in a psychotherapeutic context, while the clear implication of Noller's research (reported in chap. 9) is that a couple's nonverbal behavior can be enhanced.

THE CONTENTS OF THE BOOK

This book is divided into four parts. The first part looks at health applications of nonverbal communication and includes Martin and Friedman's overview of applications of nonverbal communication to medical health care settings. The second chapter looks at a more specific area in clinical mental health (Philippot, et al.), demonstrating that deficits in nonverbal communication can underlie relationship dysfunctions. Nonverbal applications to mental health is a very large area of study, and the topic of a recent collection, *Nonverbal Behavior in Clinical Settings* (Philippot, Feldman, & Coats, 2003).

The second part of the book looks at legal and political applications of nonverbal communication, and features a chapter on nonverbal communication in the courtroom (Searcy, Duck, & Blanck), and Vrij and Mann's overview of how law enforcement officials use nonverbal communication to detect deception. The section also features Goethal's recent work on how nonverbal communication plays a role in the perceived effectiveness of political leaders.

Part III of the book examines the role of nonverbal communication in business and education. In Chapter 6, Riggio provides an overview of the ways in which nonverbal communication impacts on the world of business and industry. Woodzicka and LaFrance (chap. 7) discuss a series of elegant experiments that investigate sexual provocation in workplace settings. Turning to the realm of education, Harris and Rosenthal (chap. 8) summarize the results of scores of studies that look at teacher nonverbal behavior, providing a compelling illustration of the role it plays in the classroom.

The final part of the book looks at social and cultural issues involving nonverbal behavior. Noller, Feeney, and Roberts (chap. 9) examine the ways that couples' use of nonverbal behavior varies over the course of their relationship. In Chapter 10, O'Sullivan examines the detection of deception, considering why some individuals are so much better than others at identifying others' lies. Finally, the book ends with Matsumoto and Yoo's chapter (chap. 11), which presents a compelling argument for the importance of cultural factors in nonverbal behavior.

A FINAL WORD

We see this book as an initial step in illustrating the ways that nonverbal behavior relates to a broad swathe of everyday life. But it is merely a beginning. More basic researchers studying nonverbal behavior need to specifically address the implications of their basic research to everyday problems. Similarly, practitioners who advocate using nonverbal behavior to address real-world situations need to be certain to embed their work in the context of the research base addressing nonverbal communication. Without such efforts, those in both camps will be unable to achieve the full potential of their work.

REFERENCES

Dimitrius, J. E., & Mazzarella, M. (1999). *Reading people: How to understand people and predict their behavior, anytime, anyplace.* New York: Ballantine.

Ekman, P. (1978). *The Facial Action Coding System.* Palo Alto, CA: Consulting Psychologists Press.

Ekman, P., & Friesen, W. V. (1975). *Unmasking the face: A guide for recognizing emotions from facial clues.*

Johnson, H. G., Ekman, P., & Friesen, W. V. (1975). Communicative body movements: American emblems. *Semiotica, 15,* 335–353.

Lieberman, D. J. (1998). *Never be lied to again: How to get the truth in 5 minutes or less in any conversation or situation.* New York: St. Martin's Press.

Nierenberg, G. I., & Calero, H. H. (1991). *How to read a person like a book.* (rev. ed.), New York: Pocket Books.

Noller, P. (1984). *Nonverbal communication in marital interaction.* Oxford: Pergamon Press.

Philippot, R., Feldman, R. S., & Coats, E. J. (Eds.). (2003). *Nonverbal behavior in clinical settings.* New York: Oxford University Press.

Riggio, R. E. (1992). Social interaction skills and nonverbal behavior. In R.S. Feldman (Ed.), *Applications of nonverbal behavioral theories and research.* (pp. 3–30). Hillsdale, NJ: Lawrence Erlbaum Associates.

Russell, J. A. (1995). Facial expressions of emotion: What lies beyond minimal universality. *Psychological Bulletin, 118,* 379–391.

I

Health Applications

✺ 1 ✺

Nonverbal Communication and Health Care

Leslie R. Martin
La Sierra University

Howard S. Friedman
University of California, Riverside

Health and illness are complex, socially influenced concepts and understandings that rely heavily on communication. Nonverbal communication—the use of dynamic but non-language messages such as facial expressions, gestures, gaze, touch, and vocal cues—is especially important when emotions, identities, and status roles are significant, as well as in situations where *verbal* communications are untrustworthy, ambiguous, or otherwise difficult to interpret (DePaulo & Friedman, 1998). The importance of nonverbal cues is thus central in the health arena. Health care providers need accurate information from their patients regarding the type and duration of their symptoms; the frequency and validity of health-relevant behaviors; reactions to illness and treatment; and the probabilities associated with future behaviors. Patients, however, may be unable to report this information, and they may be motivated to conceal or misinterpret certain symptoms or behaviors, and to overestimate the likelihood of adherence to their medical regimens.

From the patient's perspective, transactions in a health care setting are often confusing and intimidating. The medical encounter represents a unique social situation, with one person holding most of the power, knowledge, and prestige and the other disclosing personal details about him- or herself, often while scantily dressed and experiencing considerable anxiety about the symptoms that precipitated the visit. The information that patients receive from health care providers

3

may be difficult to understand due to technical language or jargon, as well as the stress of the situation. Further, the health recommendations that are made or prescribed may seem confusing, daunting, or unreasonable.

Patients and providers share the common goal of improving patient health, but often have different communicative styles, bodies of knowledge, and philosophical perspectives. In many cases, there are no simple ways to decide if one is healthy or ill, as people vary markedly in their pain perceptions, their genetics, their motivations, and their behavioral reactions to physiological states. Rather, health and illness are often socially negotiated states. Further, there are very few areas of health care that do *not* involve extensive face-to-face interactions. As models for understanding health and illness have moved steadily away from traditional mechanical, biomedical approaches and toward the biopsychosocial model (Engel, 1977), increasing emphasis has been placed on treating the person within this complex system, rather than trying to isolate one particular part of the whole. Thus, with the importance of effective communication now recognized, efforts to enhance interactions and negotiations between patients and health care workers have increased steadily over the past two decades (Hall, Harrigan, & Rosenthal, 1995; Roter, 2000).

This chapter focuses on the nonverbal elements of communication within a health care setting. Because nonverbal behaviors are often more subtle and abstruse than verbal behaviors, they tend to be poorly understood. And, the challenges associated with measuring and interpreting nonverbal cues make research in this area difficult. Despite the challenges, a body of literature on nonverbal communications in health care settings has accumulated. The present chapter will briefly review this literature beginning with nonverbal cues that are transmitted from patients to providers and the ways in which health care providers interpret and understand these communications, followed by an overview of nonverbal transmissions of information from health care providers to patients and the ways in which these are utilized. We will then focus more specifically on identifying elements of good nonverbal communication, and ways in which these can be increased to improve both the patient-provider encounter and patient health outcomes. Finally, measurement limitations, innovations, and current trends in this important sub-field of Health Psychology will be addressed.

PATIENTS' NONVERBAL COMMUNICATION

Thoughtful attention to the unspoken details of patients' presenting complaints has been a component of diagnosing and treating illness for centuries, especially when the physician had few diagnostic tests available. Hippocrates urged the practitioner to first focus on the patient's face, and the face-to-face clinical intake or diagnostic interview has become the cornerstone of modern diagnosis (Friedman, 1982). In theory, computerized questionnaires and blood analysis could go a long way toward initial diagnosis but, in practice, the value of complex, difficult-to-specify information gleaned from a face-to-face interview remains central.

An experienced clinician gains many insights from the gestalt (configural) view of a patient. Pallor, weakness, tenderness, restricted movement, emotion, breathing changes, voice tones, perspiration levels, and so on may paint an informative picture. Further, many particular nonverbal diagnostic techniques also have been uncovered or documented. Patients' nonverbal behaviors may be the best means for physicians' detection of pain levels (Craig, Prkachin, & Grunau, 2001). Nonverbal cues can often be a good indicator of psychopathological comorbidity, an important issue as depression is increasingly recognized as relevant to many illnesses. Nonverbal cues are essential to diagnosing syndromes such as the Type A Behavior Pattern (e.g., involving explosive speech and glaring facial expressions; Chesney, Ekman, Friesen, Black, & Hecker, 1990; Hall, Friedman, & Harris, 1986) and related unhealthy patterns of hostility.

Facial expressions can yield important information about an individual's true physical or emotional state but are also most subject to distortion. The neural pathways for volitional facial expression are at the cortical level, whereas subcortical areas govern spontaneous expressions (Rinn, 1991). Thus, a patient might consciously exhibit a pleasant expression while reassuring the doctor that "the pain is better … " but unknowingly contradict this with an involuntary expression of pain seconds later. An astute observer will note this discrepancy and probe for further details (e.g., Quill, 1989). Although the face is thus a common place to look for nonverbal information, people are also likely to take this into account when consciously trying to hide something or convey a different emotion than is truly felt. We learn to closely monitor and control our facial expressions (Ekman & Friesen, 1969). Therefore, other nonverbal channels, such as speech patterns, gestures, or posture should not be ignored. Because we may be less practiced in controlling non-facial cues, these areas can be valuable sources for detecting nonverbal "leakage" (DePaulo & Friedman, 1998; Friedman, 1982).

In addition to leaking information about their current states through nonverbal channels, patients may also exhibit behaviors that carry a particular message about their desires or needs within the medical encounter itself. Patients who behave submissively (using passive voice tone, making little eye contact, holding the body with a closed posture) and who talk less are lowering their own likelihood for involvement in the medical care process (Kaplan, et al., 1989; Patterson, 1983). A patient's desire for involvement may be expressed by leaning toward the doctor, making eye contact, smiling, nodding, and otherwise being both facially and vocally expressive (Coker & Burgoon, 1987). When met with resistance from the physician, a patient might pause in speaking until the doctor appears attentive, interrupt, lean further toward the physician, or fail to make eye contact with the doctor as she or he exits, binding the physician to the encounter or signaling nonadherence (Patterson, 1983).

Physicians who are sensitive to the nonverbal cues of their patients may obtain a more accurate view of the patients' needs (physical, social, and emotional). The importance of physician skill in decoding nonverbal cues to patient satisfaction was first demonstrated by the positive relationship of physicians' scores on the Profile of Nonverbal Sensitivity (PONS; Rosenthal, Hall, DiMatteo, Rogers, & Archer, 1979) to their patients' levels of satisfaction with care received (DiMatteo, Friedman, & Taranta, 1979). This study suggested that doctors who are better able to read the nonverbal cues of their patients might be better equipped to meet their patients' needs.

PHYSICIANS' NONVERBAL COMMUNICATION

Patients often seek clues to their own health status or judge the quality of their care by the nonverbal behavior exhibited by their doctors (e.g., DiMatteo & DiNicola, 1982; Friedman, 1982; Roter & Hall, 1992). Most patients report that they want to be involved in their own care and health-decision making, and although the level of desired involvement does vary, many patients say that they would like to receive more information and be more involved than they are (e.g., Blanchard, Labrecque, Ruckdeschel, & Blanchard, 1988; Faden, Becker, Lewis, Freeman, & Faden, 1981; Strull, Lo, & Charles, 1984). The information that patients glean from nonverbal channels supplements the information that is given to them verbally, and is important because patients often are ill-equipped to judge the technical quality of care received or to understand the complexity of their technical diagnosis. So, they may rely instead on the interpersonal quality of care. In some cases, such as in cases of life-threatening diseases, patients may have reason to disbelieve what their health care providers say to them, or may think that they are receiving less than the full truth regarding their health, and in these cases nonverbal expressions also become highly salient.

Power and Status

The difference in power and status between physicians and patients may contribute to increased patient attention to physicians' nonverbal cues (Fiske, 1993; Friedman, 1982). In addition to being knowledgeable, expert physicians have inherently higher status than patients and this status differential is reinforced by having patients come to the territories (offices) of physicians, by control over time (appointments), by dress (physicians in white coats versus patients in gowns), and by voice tones. Physicians further communicate power by touching the bodies of patients (including intimate places). Even though such examinations are for instrumental (task) purposes, they also carry socioemotional implications as patients react. Indeed, skilled physicians often employ this power differential to encourage the healing process. The "healing touch" as well as the nonverbal encouragement and positive expectations of a high-status physician can help encourage, motivate, and reassure a distraught or confused patient.

Health care providers nonverbally communicate not only their own internal states, but also their preferences for how the medical encounter ought to proceed. Physicians who behave in a hurried manner convey the expectation that patient involvement is not important, whereas doctors who match their patients' affiliative behaviors demonstrate their expectation that their patients will be involved in the medical care process (Buller & Street, 1992; Lepper, Martin, & DiMatteo, 1995; Svarstad, 1974). Other behavioral clues that patients are not invited to participate in their own care include: longer speaking turns, interruptions of the patient, more pauses, sitting or standing with a backward lean, looking at (or writing in) the chart during patient speech, and more use of social touch which reinforces the difference in status between patient and physician (Fisher, 1983; Patterson, 1983; Street & Buller, 1987, 1988; West, 1984).

Nonverbal communication by the health care provider can be related to patient outcomes. For example, patient anxiety, recall, and perceptions of severity were shown to increase with the apparent anxiety of the oncologist who communicated their mammogram results (Shapiro, Boggs, Melamed, & Graham-Pole, 1992). Nonverbal behaviors (such as head nodding, forward lean, uncrossed legs and arms, direct body orientation, arm symmetry, and gaze that is appropriate to the situation and not overly intense) may be significantly associated with patient outcomes such as satisfaction, understanding, and lowered anxiety (Beck, Daughtridge, & Sloan, 2002).

These effects of provider nonverbal communications on patient outcomes can be long lasting. A study of the nonverbal behaviors of physical therapists indicated that even over a several-month follow up period, distancing (not smiling, looking away from the client) was strongly associated with decreases in both physical and cognitive functioning, whereas facial expressiveness (nodding, smiling, and frowning) was linked to improvements in functioning (Ambady, Koo, Rosenthal, & Winograd, 2002).

LEARNING TO COMMUNICATE NONVERBALLY

Certain medical educators now advocate rapport-building and partnering within the health care encounter (Barnett, 2001; Novack, Volk, Drossman, & Lipkin, 1993; Roter & Hall, 1992; Simpson, Buckman, Stewart, Maguire, Lipkin, Novack, & Till, 1991; Zinn, 1993). As of 2004, mandated by the board overseeing the United States Medical Licensing Examination, medical students have to pass a clinical skills examination, essentially a test of successful "bedside manner." But, to what degree are the components of high quality rapport or facilitative style teachable? What exactly is bedside manner, and is it reasonable to assume that it can be learned?

Bedside manner refers broadly and informally to the interpersonal behaviors shown by a physician or other health care provider, especially those that foster trust and a sense of well-being in patients. Hippocrates (1923 translation) noted that through "contentment with the goodness of the physician" a patient in perilous condition might nevertheless recover. In addition to some of the nonverbal behaviors outlined above that might facilitate an interpersonal connection between patient and physician, bedside manner also includes the psychosocial elements of empathy (sensitivity and emotional connection to another person; Rogers, 1951) and rapport (synchrony of interactants' behaviors, mutual positive feelings, and mutual attentiveness; Tickle-Degnan & Rosenthal, 1990).

Empirical evidence suggests that at least some of these processes occur unconsciously. One recent study demonstrated that facial mimicry, measured by electromyographic activity as participants viewed pictures of happy and angry faces, corresponded more closely to self-reported emotional experience in individuals with high empathy (Sonnby-Borgstrom, 2002). Another study exposed participants to happy or angry facial pictures in very brief flashes, so that participants were not consciously aware of them, and found that both negative and positive emotional reactions could be facially evoked without the participants' knowledge or recognition of them (Dimberg, Thunberg, & Elmehed, 2002).

Despite such findings of the importance of the individual and the overall context, the empirical evidence also suggests that health professionals can learn to effectively engage their patients in positive interchanges and health-building partnerships (Fallowfield, Jenkins, Farewell, Saul, Duffy, & Eves, 2002; Langewitz, Eich, Kiss, & Woeessmer, 1998; Seeman & Evans, 1961a, 1961b; Smith, Lyles, Mettler, Marshall, et al., 1995). These studies show that improving the physician-patient partnership is not simply a matter of teaching doctors to speak more clearly and avoid jargon. A wide range of competencies, including nonverbal competency, can be learned with practice, and these skills are *not* habits that accrue naturally over time, without intervention (e.g., Fallowfield, et al., 2002). Data also point to the importance of learning the *appropriate* behaviors and style, however, because what seems intuitively sensible may not be valid. For example, the common advice that patients should be offered alternative courses of treatment as a way of partnering with them may backfire; one study showed that patients who were offered more alternatives did not feel that their physicians facilitated their involvement in care (Martin, Jahng, Golin, & DiMatteo, 2003). This same study showed that some other typically suggested physician behaviors, such as using warm and friendly tones and speaking to the patient as an adult, were related in the expected ways to patients' perceptions of being invited to participate in their own care. A review of nonverbal behavior in patient-provider interactions indicated that not talking too much, and instead listening closely, is generally viewed as helpful in building rapport (Hall, Harrigan, & Rosenthal, 1995). But, although this may be true on average, it is also clear that the effectiveness of this rapport-building tool can vary across situations. For example, in interactions where the doctor and/or patient is male, interruptions by either party are negatively associated with patient satisfaction, perhaps because they foster or indicate dominance or competition. But, in female-female dyads, interruptions tend to relate to greater patient satisfaction, maybe because they indicate enthusiasm or collaboration (Hall, Irish, Roter, Ehrlich, & Miller, 1994). Other nonverbal cues, such as touch and eye contact, are also highly context dependent (Larsen & Smith, 1981; Davidhizar, 1992). Thus, training systems and strategies that aim to increase partnership-skills must pay careful attention to the types of situations in which these skills will be used, and would do well to teach a flexible system of responses, rather than striving for increases or decreases in absolute numbers of particular nonverbal behaviors (Lee, Back, Block, & Stewart, 2002).

MEASUREMENT OF NONVERBAL BEHAVIOR IN PATIENT-PRACTITIONER INTERACTIONS

A great deal of the literature on physician-patient communication has focused primarily on verbal aspects of the interchange (Buller & Street, 1992), often using such measures as the Roter Interaction Analysis System (RIAS; Roter, 1991) or the Verona Medical Interview Classification System (Verona-MICS; Del Piccolo, Saltini, Cellerino, & Zimmermann, 1998). These systems, despite their emphasis on providing a standard, reliable, and valid documentation of the encounter are often also able to provide good information regarding the affective (emotional and motivational) elements of interactions. The RIAS, in particular, has demonstrated sensitivity to emotional facets of physician-patient communication and is flexible enough to be useful across a wide range of age, gender, and cultural groups (Hall, Horgan, Stein, & Roter, 2002; Roter, 2000; Roter & Larson, 2002).

Despite mounting evidence regarding the broad utility of some of the most popular medical interaction coding systems, researchers who are interested in nonverbal aspects of communication often rely more on global assessments of the encounter, as assessed by raters, because these potentially allow for even greater integration of subtle nuances that are difficult to otherwise operationally define. Many of the global ratings are judged from audio-recorded encounters, and while certain elements of nonverbal communication can be assessed from audiotape (e.g., voice tone, inflection, rate, volume, and number of interruptions), how well these really reflect the overall nonverbal character of the encounter is unclear.

A comprehensive study (Riddle, Albrecht, Coovert, Penner, Ruckdeschel, Blanchard, Quinn, & Urbizu, 2002) addressed this issue by assessing whether ratings were different when coders viewed videotaped information vs. heard only the audio portion of the videotape. The Moffitt Accrual Analysis System (MAAS; Albrecht, Blanchard, Ruckdeschel, Coovert, & Strongbow, 1999), designed for use with video, and the RIAS (Roter, 1991), designed for use with audio, were used for ratings. Results indicated that the measures were almost identically reliable, but the ratings themselves were not equivalent—relational communication information was coded differently according to the type of data (audio vs. video) used, with different factor structures emerging from exploratory factor analyses of both the RIAS and the MAAS. In each instance, the video-based factor analyses accounted for a greater proportion of variance, and were more consistent with theoretical predictions than were the audio-based factor analyses. These researchers argue that, despite the cost and intrusiveness of videotaping, serious consideration should be given to the types of information that can be obtained from video vs. audio-tapes, and selections should be made with the understanding that these two forms of recording will not subsequently be coded in the same way.

Does this mean that techniques, such as the MAAS, which were designed for use with videotaped data should become the gold standard for analysis of interpersonal interactions? The findings by Riddle and colleagues (2002) do not establish that the video-based scoring system is a better tool, nor have problems arisen in previous studies that have used the RIAS with videotaped data (e.g., Roter & Larson, 2000; Roter & Larson, 2002). Instead, these results suggest that the goals of each study must be clearly defined and that, having weighed the merits and shortcomings of each methodological approach, the most appropriate form of data collection for addressing those particular questions or goals should be selected. Many tools exist for assessing nonverbal decoding skills (e.g., the PONS), encoding skills (e.g., the Affective Communication Test, ACT; Friedman, Prince, Riggio, & DiMatteo, 1980) and elements of the interaction itself (e.g., RIAS, MAAS, Verona-MICS). Together, these instruments provide the means for assessing much of the complexity inherent in the physician-patient interchange.

THE NEXT STEPS FOR NONVERBAL RESEARCH AND PRACTICE IN HEALTH CARE

Over the past 25 years, there has been a swell of interest in nonverbal communication within the medical encounter on the part of both researchers and clinicians. Much of the research literature is still non-experimental, however, and this limits the conclusions that can be drawn about causal relationships between nonverbal behaviors and outcome variables. The field is now at the point of beginning to aggregate data from disparate studies in order to discern patterns of physician and patient nonverbal behaviors that "work" within the encounter, as well as those that seem problematic. Systematic reviews and meta-analyses of physician-patient interactions are providing a clearer picture of which communicative elements tend to be most powerful, how they are typically perceived, and how they are related to patient outcomes although the numbers of nonverbal studies included in such integrative reviews is typically small (e.g., Beck, Daughtridge, & Sloane, 2002; Hall, Harrigan, & Rosenthal, 1995; Ong, de Haes, Hoos, & Lammes, 1995; Stewart, 1995; Stewart, Brown, Boon, Galajda, Meredith, & Sangster, 1999). For example, Beck and colleagues (2002), in their review of studies on primary care physician-patient communication from 1975-2000 found only eight studies of nonverbal communication that met their inclusion criteria. Nonverbal behaviors associated with positive outcomes included physician head-nodding; forward lean; direct body orientation; arm symmetry; uncrossed legs and arms; and less mutual gaze. Negative outcomes were associated with indirect body orientation; backward lean; more patient gaze toward the physician; crossed arms; and more frequent touch (Beck et al., 2002). Such findings are in line with what is known more generally about successful nonverbal communication in social interaction. Thus, with better understanding of nonverbal expressions and communications within their particular contexts, it is very possible to develop useful programs for training health care interactants (professionals and patients) to promote positive outcomes. Of course, ongoing experimental testing will help insure that conclusions regarding efficacy will be optimally valid.

In addition, future research should continue to validate the associations of nonverbal expression to health and illness using innovative strategies such as comparing various bodily and facial movements with states of health; and studying nonverbal behaviors as they relate to brain and other physiological activation (with PET scans, fMRIs, pupil dilation, heart rate, blood pressure, and galvanic skin responses). Such psychophysiological and social neuroscience research will yield additional clues to what has been termed the "self-healing personality" (Friedman, 1991, 1998). The term self-healing personality refers to a healing emotional style involving a match between the individual and environment, which allows for physiological and psychosocial homeostasis, through which good mental health promotes good physical health. Self-healing individuals share certain personality characteristics, find themselves in environments that match their individual style, experience healthy social interactions and life paths, and often reflect a certain nonverbal style as well. Self-healing people tend to smile naturally—movements of the eyes, eyebrows, and mouth are synchronized and unforced. Their gestures are smooth and tend to expand out from the body; they are not likely to make aggressive gestures, and tend not to fidget. These individuals not only walk smoothly, they also talk smoothly, showing fewer speech disturbances and more modulated tones. Their voices are also less likely to change in tone under stress. And, there are exceptions to these rules. A single nonverbal cue cannot tell us much by itself. Still, substantial valid information about a person's emotional style can be obtained from just a short episode of social interaction, as has been powerfully demonstrated by the work on "thin slices" of expressive behavior (e.g., Ambady & Rosenthal, 1992; 1993). These studies have shown that even very short (6 to 30 second) episodes of expressive behavior are strongly related to important outcomes and are highly accurate. This is why a careful intake interview can be so valuable to the health care professional who knows what to look for, and why that first encounter is so important to the subsequent health of the relationship.

Nonverbal emotional styles are not easily or directly changed. As expressive products, however, they reflect elements of perception, coping, and person-environment match that *can* be altered with time and effort. Changing emotional responses to make them health promoting involves changing the habits and social environments from which they derive (Friedman, 1991). As small changes in habits are made and as individuals engage in social interactions that encourage the personal qualities they hope to achieve, movement toward self-healing will be evident in their nonverbal expressions. A biopsychosocial model suggests that health care providers can gain better understanding of their patients from interpreting nonverbal emotional expressions, and can also foster self-healing by encouraging small but consistent changes in social environments and behaviors (Friedman, 1993).

In medical interactions, as with all social encounters, participants function together to determine outcomes. As such, each individual shares responsibility for these outcomes and plays a role in defining the reality of the encounter. Individual components of communication can be uninformative or even misleading when viewed in isolation, but when placed in a larger context, embedded within the elements that precede and follow them, meaningful patterns emerge and subtle nuances yield rich insights.

REFERENCES

Albrecht, T. L., Blanchard, C. G., Ruckdeschel, J. C., Coovert, M., & Strongbow, R. (1999). Strategic physician communication and oncology clinical trials. *Journal of Clinical Oncology, 17*, 3324–3332.

Ambady, N., Koo, J., Rosenthal, R. R., & Winograd, C. H. (2002). Physical therapists' nonverbal communication predicts geriatric patients' health outcomes. *Psychology and Aging, 17*, 443–452.

Ambady, N., & Rosenthal, R. (1992). Thin slices of expressive behavior as predictors of interpersonal consequences: A meta-analysis. *Psychological Bulletin, 111*, 256–274.

Ambady, N., & Rosenthal, R. (1993). Half a minute: Predicting teacher evaluations from thin slices of nonverbal behavior and physical attractiveness. *Journal of Personality and Social Psychology, 64*, 431–441.

Barnett, P. B. (2001). Rapport and the hospitalist. *American Journal of Medicine, 111*, 31S–35S.

Beck, R. S., Daughtridge, R., & Sloane, P. D. (2002). Physician-patient communication in the primary care office: A systematic review. *Journal of the American Board of Family Practice, 15*, 25–38.

Blanchard, C. G., Labrecque, M. S., Ruckdeschel, J. C., & Blanchard, E. B. (1988). Information and decision-making preferences of hospitalized adult cancer patients. *Social Science and Medicine, 27*, 1139–1145.

Buller, D. B., & Street, R. L. (1992). Physician-patient relationships. In R. S. Feldman (Ed.), *Applications of nonverbal behavioral theories and research*. Hillsdale, NJ: Lawrence Erlbaum Associates.

Chesney, M. A., Ekman, P., Friesen, W. V., Black, G. W., & Hecker, M. H. (1990). Type A behavior pattern: Facial behavior and speech components. *Psychosomatic Medicine, 52*, 307–319.

Coker, D. A., & Burgoon, J. K. (1987). The nature of conversational involvement and nonverbal encoding patterns. *Human Communication Research, 13*, 464–494.

Craig, K. D., Prkachin, K. M., & Grunau, R. V. E. (2001). The facial expression of pain. In D. C. Turk & R. Melzack (Eds.), *Handbook of pain assessment* (2nd ed., pp. 153–169). New York, NY: Guilford.

Davidhizar, R. (1992). Interpersonal communication: A review of eye contact. *Infection Control in Hospital Epidemiology, 13*, 222–225.

DePaulo, B. M., & Friedman, H. S. (1998). Nonverbal communication. In D. T. Gilbert, S. T. Fiske et al. (Eds.), *The handbook of social psychology*, Volume 2 (4th ed., pp. 3–40). Washington, DC: American Psychological Association.

Del Piccolo, L., Saltini, A., Cellerino, P., & Zimmermann, C. (1998). *Verona Medical Interview Classification System Manual*. Verona: University of Verona, Italy.

Dimberg, U., Thunberg, M., & Elmehed, K. (2002). Unconscious facial reactions to emotional facial expressions. *Psychology and Aging, 17*, 443–452.

DiMatteo, M. R., & DiNicola, D. D. (1982). *Achieving patient compliance: The psychology of the medical practitioner's role*. Elmsford, NY: Pergamon Press.

DiMatteo, M. R., Friedman, H. S., & Taranta, A. (1979). Sensitivity to bodily nonverbal communication as a factor in practitioner-patient rapport. *Journal of Nonverbal Behavior, 4*, 18–26.

Ekman, P., & Friesen, W. V. (1969). Nonverbal leakage and clues to deception. *Psychiatry, 32*, 88–106.

Faden, R. R., Becker, C., Lewis, C., Freeman, J., & Faden, A. I. (1981). Disclosure of information to patients in medical care. *Medical Care, 19*, 718–733.

Fallowfield, L., Jenkins, V., Farewell, V., Saul, J., Duffy, A., & Eves, R. (2002). Efficacy of a Cancer Research UK communication skills training model for oncologists: A randomized controlled trial. *Lancet, 359*, 650–653.

Fisher, S. (1983). Doctor talk/patient talk: How treatment decisions are negotiated in doctor/patient communication. In S. Fisher & A. Todd (Eds.), *The social organization of doctor-communication*. Washington, DC: Center for Applied Linguistics.

Fiske, S. T. (1993). Controlling other people: The impact of power on stereotyping. *American Psychologist, 48*, 621–628.

Friedman, H. S. (1982). Nonverbal communication in medical interaction. In H. S. Friedman & M. R. DiMatteo (Eds.), *Interpersonal issues in health care*. New York: Academic Press.

Friedman, H. S. (1991). *The self-healing personality: Why some people achieve health and others succumb to illness*. New York: Henry Holt.

Friedman, H. S. (1993). Interpersonal expectations and the maintenance of health. In P. Blanck (Ed.), *Interpersonal Expectations: Theory, Research, and Application* (pp. 179–193). England: Cambridge University. Press.

Friedman, H. S. (1998). Self-healing personalities. In H. S. Friedman (Editor-in-Chief), *Encyclopedia of Mental Health, 3* (pp. 453–459). San Diego, CA: Academic Press.

Friedman, H. S., Prince, L. M., Riggio, R. E., & DiMatteo, M. R. (1980). Understanding and assessing nonverbal expressiveness: The Affective Communication Test. *Journal of Personality and Social Psychology, 39*, 333–351.

Hall, J. A., Friedman, H. S., & Harris, M. J. (1986). Nonverbal cues and the Type A behavior pattern. In P. Blanck, R. Buck, & R. Rosenthal (Eds.), *Nonverbal communication in the clinical context*. Penn: Pennsylvania State University Press.

Hall, J. A., Harrigan, J. A., & Rosenthal, R. R. (1995). Nonverbal behavior in clinician-patient interaction. *Applied and Preventive Psychology, 4*, 21–37.

Hall, J. A., Horgan, T. G., Stein, T. S., & Roter, D. L. (2002). Liking in the physician-patient relationship. *Patient Education and Counseling, 48*, 69–77.

Hall, J. A., Irish, J. T., Roter, D. L., Ehrlich, C. M., & Miller, L. H. (1994). Satisfaction, gender, and communication in medical visits. *Medical Care, 32*, 1216–1231.

Hippocrates. (1923 translation). *Volume II: On decorum and the physician* (W. H. S. Jones, Trans.). London: William Heinemann.

Kaplan, S. H., Greenfield, S., & Ware, J. E., Jr. (1989). Assessing the effects of physician-patient interactions on the outcomes of chronic disease. *Medical Care, 27*, S110–S127.

Langewitz, W. A., Eich, P., Kiss, A., & Woeessmer, B. (1998). Improving communication skills—A randomized controlled behaviorally oriented intervention study for residents in internal medicine. *Psychosomatic Medicine, 60*, 268–2276.

Larsen, K. M., & Smith, C. K. (1981). Assessment of nonverbal communication in the patient-physician interview. *Journal of Family Practice, 12*, 481–488.

Lee, S. J., Back, A. L., Block, S. D., & Stewart, S. K. (2002). Enhancing physician-patient communication. *Hematology, 1*, 464–483.

Lepper, H. S., Martin, L. R., & DiMatteo, M. R. (1995). A model of nonverbal exchange in physician-patient expectations for patient involvement. *Journal of Nonverbal Behavior, 19*, 207–222.

Martin, L. R., Jahng, K. H., Golin, C., & DiMatteo, M. R. (2003). Physician facilitation of patient involvement in care: Correspondence between patient and observer reports. *Behavioral Medicine, 28*, 159–168.

Novack, D. H., Volk, G., Drossman, D. A., & Lipkin, M., Jr. (1993). Medical interviewing and interpersonal skills teaching in US medical schools. *Journal of the American Medical Association, 269*, 2101–2105.

Ong, L. M., de Haes, J. C., Hoos, A. M., & Lammes, F. B. (1995). Doctor-patient communication: A review of the literature. *Social Science and Medicine, 40*, 903–918.

Patterson, M. L. (1983). *Nonverbal behavior: A functional perspective.* New York: Springer-Verlag.

Quill, T. E. (1989). Recognizing and adjusting to barriers in doctor-patient communication. *Annals of Internal Medicine, 111*, 51–57.

Riddle, D. L., Albrecht, T. L., Coovert, M. D., Penner, L. A., Ruckdeschel, J. C., Blanchard, C. G., Quinn, G., & Urbizu, D. (2002). Differences in audiotaped versus videotaped physician-patient interactions. *Journal of Nonverbal Behavior, 26*, 219–240.

Rinn, W. E. (1991). Neuropsychology of facial expression. In R. S. Feldman & B. Rimé (Eds.), *Fundamentals of nonverbal behavior.* Cambridge, MA: Cambridge University Press.

Rogers, C. R. (1951). *Client-centered therapy.* Boston, MA: Houghton-Mifflin.

Rosenthal, R., Hall, J. A., DiMatteo, M. R., Rogers, P. L., & Archer, D. (1979). *Sensitivity to nonverbal communication: The PONS test.* Baltimore, MD: The Johns Hopkins University Press.

Roter, D. L. (1991). *The Roter Method of Interaction Process Analysis: RIAS Manual.* Baltimore, MD: Johns Hopking University Press.

Roter, D. L. (2000). The enduring and evolving nature of the patient_physician relationship. *Patient Education and Counseling, 46*, 243–251.

Roter, D. L., & Hall, J. A. (1992). *Doctors talking with patients/patient talking to doctors: Improving communication in medical visits.* Westport, CT: Auburn House.

Roter, D. L., & Larson, S. (2000). Use of RIAS as a video-based interactive tool for self-assessment, feedback and evaluation of the medical interview. Paper presented at the International Conference on Health Communication, Barcelona, Spain, September, 2000.

Roter, D. L., & Larson, S. (2002). The Roter Interaction Analysis System (RIAS): Utility and flexibility for analysis of medical interactions. *Patient Education and Counseling, 46*, 233–234.

Seeman, M., & Evans, J. W. (1961a). Stratification and hospital care, Part 1: The performance of the medical intern. *American Sociological Review, 26*, 67–80.

Seeman, M., & Evans, J. W. (1961b). Stratification and hospital care, Part 2: The objective criterion of performance. *American Sociological Review, 26*, 193–204.

Shapiro, D. E., Boggs, S. R., Melamed, B. G., & Graham-Pole, J. (1992). The effect of varied physician affect on recall, anxiety, and perceptions in women at risk for breast cancer: An analogue study. *Health Psychology, 1*, 61–66.

Simpson, M., Buckman, R., Stewart, M., Maguire, P., Lipkin, M., Novack, D., & Till, J. (1991). Doctor-patient communication: The Toronto consensus statement. *British Medical Journal, 303*, 1385–1387.

Smith, R. C., Lyles, J. S., Mettler, J. A., Marshall, A. A., et al. (1995). A strategy for improving patient satisfaction by the intensive training of residents in psychosocial medicine: A controlled, randomized study. *Academic Medicine, 70*, 729–732.

Sonnby-Bergstrom, M. (2002). Automatic mimicry reactions as related to differences in emotional empathy. *Journal of Cognitive Neuroscience, 14*, 1158–1173.

Stewart, M. A. (1995). Effective physician-patient communication and health outcomes: A review. *Canadian Medical Association Journal, 152*, 1423–1433.

Stewart, M. A., Brown, J. B., Boon, H., Galajda, J., Meredith, L., & Sangster, M. (1999). Evidence on patient-doctor communication. *Cancer Prevention and Control, 3,* 25–30.

Street, R. L., & Buller, D. B. (1987). Nonverbal response patterns in physician-patient interactions: A functional analysis. *Journal of Nonverbal Behavior, 11,* 234–253.

Street, R. L., & Buller, D. B. (1988). Patients' characteristics affecting physician-patient nonverbal communication. *Human Communication Research, 15,* 60–90.

Strull, W. M., Lo, B., & Charles, G. (1984). Do patients want to participate in medical decision making? *Journal of the American Medical Association, 252,* 2990–2994.

Svarstad, B. L. (1974). The doctor-patient encounter: An observational study of communication and outcome. Unpublished doctoral dissertation, University of Wisconsin, Madison.

Tickle-Degnan, L., & Rosenthal, R. R. (1990). The nature of rapport and its nonverbal correlates. *Psychological Inquiry, 1,* 285.

West, C. (1984). *Routine complications: Troubles with talk between doctors and patients.* Bloomington, IN: Indiana University Press.

Zinn, W. (1993). The empathic physician. *Archives of Internal Medicine, 153,* 306–312.

❧ 2 ❧

Facial Expression Decoding Deficits in Clinical Populations with Interpersonal Relationship Dysfunctions

Pierre Philippot
Céline Douilliez
University of Louvain at Louvain-la-Neuve, Belgium

Thierry Pham
Centre de recherche en défense sociale, Tournai, Belgium

Marie-Line Foisy
Charles Kornreich
Free University of Brussels, Belgium

The existentialist French philosopher, Jean-Paul Sartre is famous for his statement "Hell is the others." This pessimistic stance is actually an "a contrario" claim that the secret of happiness rests, at least partly, in the way we relate to others. At an even more basic level in our social species, interactive adjustment to and coordination with others are central to our survival. Successful interaction, adjustment, and coordination with others depend upon many emotional processes, and more specifically on emotional communication and coordination. A failure to adequately communicate one's emotional and motivational state and/or to accurately perceive the internal state of others is likely to result in interpersonal and personal problems. This notion is supported by theories and empirical data relating nonverbal social skills and more general social competence, or psychopathology (e.g., Perez & Riggio, 2003).

Indeed, several lines of research have demonstrated that the capacity to accurately decode facial expression is an acquired skill that develops

17

until adolescence (Gross & Ballif, 1991). Further, this skill is related to more general social skills in adults (Patterson, 1999) as well as in children (Philippot & Feldman, 1990). Poor skills in decoding emotional facial expression have been related to clinical conditions as various as depression (Bouhuys, 2003), alcohol dependency (Philippot, Kornreich & Blairy, 2003), or schizophrenia (Kring & Earnst, 2003). However, the causal direction of this relation remains an open issue: Are some clinical conditions a consequence of a basic emotional deficit, such as a deficit in decoding nonverbal expression of emotion, or is this latter deficit the consequence of the clinical condition?

One can speculate that many interpersonal problems might result from a deficit in decoding facial expression, whatever the direction of causality with clinical conditions. The most obvious problem is the difficulty in identifying the internal states of others: their desires, emotions, or intentions. Such information is essential for the understanding of others, of the meaning of their behavior in general as well as during social interaction. Relating to someone whose intentions and emotions are obscure is virtually impossible. Further, such a decoding deficit may make more likely the occurrence of interpretation bias, that is, erroneously attributing a given emotion to someone. For instance, people fearing social rejection might erroneously attribute contempt to people with whom they are interacting; A neutral face in this case might be misperceived as expressing non-interest, rejection, or even despise. Such hypothetical bias might surely impact on the behavior of socially anxious individuals. This resulting behavior is likely to be perceived as awkward by their interaction partners. A social distance would thus be created and would result in effective social distance, ultimately confirming the fear of the socially anxious.

Another, more subtle, problem might result from a deficit in decoding facial expression. According to the self perception theory of Bem (1972), the way we perceive ourselves depends to a significant extent on how we imagine that others see us. In other words, the perception of ourselves results in part from how others do react to us. It follows that misinterpreting others' behavior and attitude toward us, including misinterpreting their facial expression when they are interacting with us, might result in the construction of an inaccurate social self, and ultimately in a biased view of ourselves. For instance, a socially anxious individual erroneously decoding contempt in the faces of people with whom they are interacting, might end up believing that they are contempt deserving persons.

Thus, a deficit or a systematic bias in decoding facial expression might result in personal as well as in interpersonal difficulties. Some clinical populations seem to be particularly exposed to such problems. From the examples given above, it appears that social phobics are likely candidates for presenting systematic biases in the way they process facial expressions of others. To the opposite of the continuum, psychopaths, characterized by a lack of empathy and perverse interpersonal relationships

(Hare, 1998), might be particularly insensitive to the affective signal communicated via nonverbal behaviors. People suffering from a dependency to alcohol are renown to present important difficulties in their social and intimate relationships, difficulties that are often related to the regulation of frustration and anger (Sferrazza, Philippot, Kornreich et al., 2002). They might thus also present difficulties in understanding accurately the desires and intentions of others toward them. Other clinical populations, such as individuals suffering from paranoia may also be suspected of presenting deficits in the decoding of emotional expression. Indeed, for all these populations, a sound theoretical rationale can be constructed to support the notion that a nonverbal deficit might constitute a maintenance factor for their clinical condition. Similarly, for all the clinical conditions mentioned above, this notion is supported by a strong conviction of clinicians working in the field.

The aim of the present contribution is to examine the empirical evidence for a nonverbal deficit in three clinical populations that are especially characterized by difficulties in interpersonal relationships: social phobia, psychopathy, and alcohol dependence. For each population, we will review experiments from our and others' laboratories with three questions in mind: What do we know about potential nonverbal deficits or bias in that population that could be applied and used by practitioners?; What are the myths that need to be dispelled?; What are the current limitations of the area?

Before addressing these questions, we need to distinguish among the different types of deficits and biases that might be encountered. First, one should differentiate between deficits in the evaluation of the intensity of the emotion conveyed by the face, and the accuracy of the emotion attributed. In other words, one can over- or under-estimate the intensity of an emotion that is present on the face of the interaction partner; For example, the psychopath can underestimate the intensity of the sadness or distress expressed by the "interaction partner". In this case, we will speak of evaluative deficit in intensity. We will speak of evaluative deficit in accuracy in the case of a general poor performance in the identification of the emotion conveyed by the face. This situation must be distinguished from the situation in which one wrongly and *systematically* attributes an emotion X to a face, while it is actually emotion Y that is expressed. In this latter case, we will speak of evaluative bias. Finally, an attentional bias consists in the fact that the perception threshold for certain facial expression is lower than for others. For example, socially anxious individuals might have their attention more readily attracted to faces expressing rejection than to other faces.

SOCIAL ANXIETY

The study of biases and deficits in the processing of interpersonal information has generated a wealth of research in anxiety in general (e.g., Williams, Watts, MacLeod & Mathews, 1999) and in social anxiety in particular (Clark & McManus, 2002). Most of this research focuses on attentional biases. Surprisingly little research has been devoted to evaluative biases and deficits, despite a strong belief in the clinical world that socially anxious individuals over-estimate threat in social signals (e.g., Beck, Emery & Greenberg, 1985).

In their cognitive-motivational model of anxiety, Mogg and Bradley (1998) have articulated attentional and evaluative biases. Their model relies on two different systems: The Valence Evaluation System and the Goal Engagement System. The Valence Evaluation System assesses the stimulus threat value according to the relevance of the stimulus to the person's preoccupation and learning experiences. The Goal Engagement System orients allocation of attention as a function of the output of the former system. If a stimulus in the environment is evaluated as threatening, the Goal Engagement System interrupts ongoing activities and orients attention toward the threat stimulus. This model postulates that attentional biases in anxious individuals result from a negative and unbalanced appraisal of social situations (Mogg & Bradley, 2002).

Attentional Biases

A wealth of studies has evidenced an attentional bias in the processing of threatening stimuli by socially anxious individuals (see Musa & Lèpine, 2000, for review). However, the direction of these attentional biases is the object of a controversy. On one hand, several cognitive models of anxiety (e.g., Mogg & Bradley, 1998; Williams et al., 1999) propose that anxious individuals preferentially attend to threatening information (Beck, Emery, & Greenberg, 1985).

Different studies have demonstrated such a vigilance bias towards threat words by social phobics (Asmundson & Stein, 1994; Maidenberg, Chen, Craske, & Bohn, 1996; Mattia, Heimberg, & Hope, 1993). Some authors have criticized the use of words to measure response to social cues (Chen, Ehlers, Clark, & Mansell, 2002): Responses to words would index worry rather than actual response to social stimuli. However, the same findings have been replicated with more ecological material—faces—by socials phobics (Gilboa-Schechtman, Foa & Amir, 1999) and in non-clinical samples with high fear of negative evaluation (FNE, Watson & Friend, 1969; Mogg & Bradley, 2002).

On the other hand, some researchers predict the opposite attentional bias. Clark (1999) has proposed that avoidance of threatening information may play an important role in the maintenance of social anxiety. For instance, actively avoiding social stimuli (e.g., faces) constitutes a form of cognitive escape from anxiety-provoking situations for social phobics (e.g., avoiding looking at others' faces makes conversation less likely; Clark & Wells, 1995). Studies using probe detection tasks found that social phobics (Chen et al., 2002) and socially anxious individuals (Mansell, Clark, Ehlers, & Chen, 1999) avoid emotional (negative and positive) faces.

In an attempt to reconciliate these divergent findings, Amir, Freshman and Foa (2002) have proposed a two-stage model of information processing. According to this view, anxious individuals would show an initial hypervigilance for threat-relevant stimuli. This hypervigilance would be the consequence of automatic processes, and it could be observed without conscious perception of threat-relevant information (Mogg & Bradley, 1999). However, at further and less automatic stages of information processing, people would actively turn away from threatening information. Thus, this model postulates a dynamic shift of attention allocation from initial threat hypervigilance to later threat avoidance. For instance, while speaking to other people, socially anxious individuals would have their attention automatically attracted to frowns more readily than would non-anxious individuals. Because of this perception bias, socially anxious individuals are likely to automatically over-activate a state of social anxiety. However, as soon as a frown was detected, they would turn their attention away from it—and, more generally, from others' faces—to avoid the threatening stimulus and the discomfort associated with it. Unfortunately, in doing so, they are likely to maintain their anxiety: Not only are they likely to behave socially inappropriately, but they will also be unable to determine whether the frowns were a sign of actual social threat or, for instance, simply a sign of perplexity.

Two studies (Amir, Freshman, & Foa, 2002; Amir, Mc Nally, Riemann, Burns, Lorenz & Mullen, 1996) manipulating strategic control in the Stroop task suggest that social phobics are able to modulate their attention to threat using strategic processes. However, this "vigilance-avoidance" hypothesis was not supported in a non-clinical sample of anxious individuals (Mogg, Bradley, de Bono, & Painter, 1997).

In an experiment using the dot prime paradigm (Mogg, Philippot, & Bradley, 2003), we examined the time course of attentional biases for faces in order to test the "vigilance-avoidance" hypothesis. Social phobics and matched controls achieved a probe detection task with facial expressions as stimuli. In order to observe if the focus of attention changed over time, the stimulus duration was manipulated (either 500 ms or 1250 ms). It was predicted, and observed, that social phobics initially focus their attention on the threatening face, but that this attentional bias rapidly disappears. In contrast, non-phobics showed the opposite pattern. Similar results, using a different paradigm (homograph paradigm) were reported by Amir, Foa, and Coles (1998). They fit nicely with our prediction of an initial automatic vigilance for threatening information, followed by a protective voluntary attempt to redirect attention away from the threatening stimulus.

Evaluative Deficits and Biases

In the previous section, we have stressed the strong belief that attentional biases result from evaluative biases. However, few studies have tested this hypothesis. In a study by Merckelbach, Van Hout, Van den Hout, & Mersch (1989), social phobics and controls had to evaluate angry, neutral, and joyful faces with respect to their pleasantness. Contrary to the cognitive-motivational model's prediction (Mogg & Bradley, 1998), no differences were observed between the two populations.

We recently replicated this intriguing result (Douilliez & Philippot, 2003): Socially-anxious and control participants were asked to evaluate the threatening value of fearful, joyful, and neutral faces. In addition, we extended the study to other types of stimuli: words and pictures, of which we manipulated valence and social relevance. Our rationale was that faces are potent innate stimuli (Öhman & Soares, 1993), and, as such, the processing of faces should not be influenced by social anxiety. In contrast, words and scenes depicted in the pictures require an interpretation and can therefore be affected by experience, including social anxiety. As predicted, replicating Merckelbach et al. (1989), no differences between anxious individuals and controls were observed for the evaluation of faces. In contrast, anxious individuals evaluated negative pictures and words as more threatening, compared to evaluations by normal controls.

A possible explanation to the limitations of the study of Merckelbach et al. (1989) as well as our studies is that prototypical facial expressions were used, displaying full-blown emotions. These extreme stimuli have not only little ecological validity, but they are also easy to decode and the use of such a material is likely to produce ceiling effects (Hess, Blairy, & Kleck, 1997). To avoid ceiling effects and to use a material reflecting real life expressions, we designed a study in which stimuli varied in emotional intensity (Philippot & Douilliez, 2003). Specifically, a series of emotional facial expressions constructed by Hess and Blairy (1995) was employed in which two actors portray five emotions (happiness, anger, sadness, disgust and fear) at four intensity levels (0%—i.e., neutral, 30%, 70%, 100%). These stimuli were presented in a random order on a computer screen. Finally, to increase the sensitivity of our measures, participants rated each facial expression on 7-point scales for a large profile of eight emotions (happiness, sadness, fear, anger, disgust, surprise, shame, and contempt).

This decoding task has been proposed to 17 out-patients diagnosed with social phobia according to DSM IV criteria, to 17 out-patients diagnosed with another anxiety disorder (agoraphobia, general anxiety) according to DSM IV criteria and to 41 controls who were matched for sex, age, and level of education. The analysis of the data revealed no differences among the three groups in terms of intensity ratings, accuracy or systematic biases, nor in their estimation of the difficulty of the task.

In conclusion, even if the "vigilance-avoidance" model of anxiety is not fully supported in social anxiety, initial attentive biases toward threatening stimuli, including real life information such as facial expressions, are supported by a wealth of empirical studies. However, socially anxious individuals do not seem to over or under-estimate the intensity of an emotion present on the face, and they identify accurately the emotions conveyed by the face. Moreover, the evaluative biases are less likely to generate attentional biases than hypothesized by Mogg and Bradley (1998). Clearly, further research is needed to investigate the possibility of implicit as well as of explicit evaluative biases in the socially anxious and to examine the relationship between possible evaluative biases and attentional biases.

ALCOHOL DEPENDENCE

As suggested in the introduction, in their daily functioning, alcoholics are confronted with severe interpersonal problems (Duberstein, Conwell, & Caine, 1993), including the use of violence (Myers, 1984). Alcoholics seem to have difficulties dealing with negative emotions, and especially with anger (Marlatt, 1979). This observation has inspired clinicians to design and evaluate communication training programs in the treatment of alcoholism. For instance, Monti et al. (1990) have compared the effectiveness of different treatment groups for alcoholic men. In a Communication Skills Training (CST) condition, participants were taught communication skills and interpersonal problem solving skills. In a Cognitive Behavioral Mood Management Training (CBMMT) condition, participants were taught how to control their desires to consume alcohol in difficult situations. The results showed that all treatments had a positive impact on social skills and on reducing anxiety in participants. CST was somewhat superior to CBMMT in this respect, attesting to the importance of communication deficit in alcoholics' problems. Moreover, participants in the CST condition drank less alcohol up to six months after treatment than participants in the CBMMT condition. In sum, this study suggests that emotion communication plays a very important role in the problems to which alcoholics are confronted.

We directly addressed the question of communication problems in alcoholism in a study focusing on emotion communication within couples with an alcoholic member (Sferrazza et al., 2002). Both wife and husband independently completed a questionnaire addressing the type, intensity, rumination about, and control of emotion, first for themselves, then for their spouses, and finally for what they believed their spouses were perceiving about their own (respondent's) emotion. Both partners from twenty-five alcoholic couples and twenty-five matched control couples participated in this study. Overall, the results showed marked differences in emotional experiences and expression between alcoholic couples and control couples. Interestingly, there were very few differences between the alcoholic member of the couple and his or her spouse. Specifically, alcoholic couples reported experiencing more intense emotions in general, and in particular for anger, guilt, sadness, anxiety, shame, and disgust. Interestingly, while alcoholics and their spouses reported to feel more guilt, they attributed more anger to their partner. Alcoholic couples also reported less emotional control. When they spoke about their emotion, they felt more discomfort, they did not know how to react and how to express themselves, and did not feel understood. They also attributed more negative and less positive effects to their emotional expression. Thus, compared to matched controls, both members of couples with an alcoholic member reported more intense and negative emotions, difficulties in expressing and controlling their emotions, and negative consequences of their emotional expression.

These observations are suggestive of an important deficit in emotion communication in alcoholics' families. The importance of communicative aspects in alcohol problems is further documented by the effectiveness of treatments focusing on communication training. Based on these observations, we developed the hypothesis that alcoholics suffer from deficits in nonverbal communication. There are several empirical arguments suggesting such deficits. Some arguments pertain to the immediate effects of alcohol, while others are related to the effect of alcohol dependency.

Regarding the immediate effects of alcohol, it has been well demonstrated that alcohol impairs higher cognitive functioning and that this impairment impacts on several emotional processes (Lang et al., 1999). For instance, emotional appraisal appears to be impaired. This produces consequences both for the type of emotion that is experienced and expressed, and for the way nonverbal cues of emotion are decoded. Quite obviously, evaluative deficits in accuracy are expected when under the influence of alcohol. Second, alcohol changes expectations and self perception (Cooper, Frone, Russell, & Mudar, 1995). When intoxicated, men are likely to behave more aggressively (Keane & Lisman, 1980), to express more anger nonverbally, and to interpret others' nonverbal cues as indicating provocation or threat (evaluative bias). Other reasons to suspect a nonverbal deficit are related to consequences of alcohol dependency. Alcoholics have difficulties dealing with negative emotions, especially with anger and frustration (Marlatt, 1996). They report more problems expressing their emotions and more negative consequences of such expression. A large part of emotion communication relies on nonverbal cues, and as social competence and harmonious functioning require the mastery of nonverbal communication, the problems of alcoholics in solving interpersonal conflicts and in communicating their emotions are suggestive of a nonverbal deficit.

Based on these considerations, we propose that alcoholics are characterized by specific deficits in the decoding of nonverbal cues of emotion: They should over-perceive negative displays in others, especially those related to anger and frustration (evaluative bias). They should also be less accurate in general (evaluative deficit in accuracy). We further propose that this nonverbal deficit impairs alcoholics' social competence. They would be more likely to find themselves in interpersonal conflicts, and more importantly, in such situations they would misattribute anger and hostile feelings to their partners. This would diminish alcoholics' capacities to react efficiently and to find a constructive solution to the conflict that would remain unresolved. Alcoholics would then turn to alcohol as a coping strategy (although a faulty one).

The use of alcohol as an avoidant coping strategy is likely to maintain interpersonal problems and even to increase them. A first positive feedback loop would be created: increased interpersonal tension would result in increased alcohol consumption, feeding back into the interpersonal tension. Further, as alcohol intoxication diminishes nonverbal decoding capacity, a second feedback loop would be created: alcohol intoxication would lead to more nonverbal impairments, the latter nourishing interpersonal tension, which then results in more alcohol consumption. This process is illustrated in Fig. 2.1.

We now turn to empirical evidences pertaining to facial expression decoding in alcoholics. Indeed, despite the importance of the question both from a clinical and from a theoretical perspective, few empirical studies have investigated nonverbal decoding skills in alcoholics. To our knowledge, the first experimental investigation of facial expression in alcoholics has been conducted by Oscar-Berman and colleagues (Oscar-Berman et al., 1990). They compared alcoholic Korsakoff patients, non-Korsakoff alcoholics, and non-alcoholic controls regarding their ability to identify and recognize emotional material, including facial expressions. They observed that alcoholic Korsakoff patients and non-Korsakoff alcoholics attributed more emotional intensity to facial expressions than controls (evaluative deficit in intensity). Further, the ability to match facial expressions with written labels was determined by the interaction between experimental group and age of the subject. Unfortunately, Oscar-Berman and colleagues did not specify nor interpret this interaction. Similarly, they did not explore alcoholics' accuracy in the decoding of facial expression.

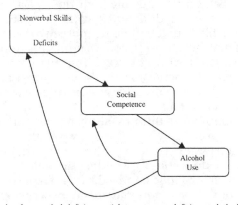

Fig. 2.1. The cycle of nonverbal deficits, social competence deficits, and alcohol consumption.

In order to further document possible biases or impairments in the way alcoholics interpret emotional facial expression, we started a systematic research program in our laboratories. In the first study (Philippot et al., 1999), we addressed three questions. First, we wondered whether we could replicate the observation of Oscar-Berman et al. (1990) that alcoholics over-attribute emotional intensity to facial stimuli. Second, we examined whether alcoholics are less accurate than non-alcoholics in recognizing the type of emotion portrayed by a facial expression. Third, we asked if alcoholics show systematic biases in interpreting facial expression. In other words, do they tend to misattribute some types of emotion more than others?

We used exactly the same procedure as the one described for the study on social phobia in the preceding section (Philippot & Douilliez, 2003). The decoding task was proposed to 25 inpatients diagnosed with alcohol dependence according to DSM III-R criteria and to 25 controls who were matched for sex, age, and level of education. Inpatients were in their third week of detoxification process and were not receiving any psychotropic drugs at the time of assessment. The results demonstrated that alcoholics suffer from several deficits in the interpretation of emotional facial expressions. First, compared to controls, they overestimated the intensity of the emotion conveyed by facial expressions, thereby replicating the observation of Oscar-Berman et al. (1990) with full-blown expressions and extending it to expressions of moderate and weak intensity and even to neutral faces: Alcoholics tend to perceive more intense emotion than controls in the faces of their interaction partners, even if no emotion is expressed.

Second, alcoholic participants misinterpreted facial expressions more than controls: They were more likely to believe that someone presenting a happy face was actually in a negative mood. They further tended to misattribute negative expressions (except for fear). For disgust, they presented a systematic bias, attributing to their interaction partners' emotions of anger and contempt, two emotions typical of interpersonal conflict. Finally, despite their poor performance, alcoholics did not report more difficulties with the decoding task than controls. It is thus likely that they do not perceive their deficit in the decoding of emotional facial expression. In sum, this first study portrays alcoholics as living in a world in which they perceive more emotional signals from their interaction partners, emotional signals that they tend to misinterpret with a negative and hostile bias, without noticing their deficits in this domain.

Alcoholic participants in this first study were inpatients at the end of the detoxification process. We do not know whether they already presented a facial expression decoding deficit before they became dependent on alcohol nor do we know whether the deficit is maintained in long-term abstinent alcoholics. Indeed, two interpretations of the deficits in the decoding of emotional facial expressions observed by Philippot et al. (1999) can be made. On the one hand, the deficits might be the consequence of a general neurocognitive deterioration caused by alcohol that is known to impair multiple functions in chronic alcoholics. As most of these cognitive impairments remit with long-term abstinence, one would expect the deficits in the decoding of facial expression to be alleviated with long-term abstinence (Mann, Günther, Selter, & Ackerman, 1999). On the other hand, emotional decoding deficits in alcoholics might be related to fundamental impairments that would precede the onset of alcohol dependency. Indeed, social skills deficits in alcoholics seem to be present before the onset of alcoholism (Rosenthal-Gaffney et al., 1998).

Following this question, we designed a second study (Kornreich et al., 2001b) in which we compared the performance of abstainers (former alcoholics, abstinent for at least several months) with the performance of recently detoxified alcoholics in the facial expression decoding task. If it could be shown that there are no differences between these two populations, such an observation would rule out the possibility that the deficits are a consequence of a general cognitive deterioration alleviating with abstinence. The analysis of the data revealed that, while some nonverbal impairments were no longer present in abstainers, others persisted. Specifically, the over-attribution of emotional intensity to facial expression was not observed in abstainers. Similarly, the mis-interpretation of happy and sad faces shown by recently detoxified alcoholics was not present in abstainers. However, their decoding accuracy deficit still persisted for anger and disgust facial expressions: For these emotions, there were no differences between recently detoxified and abstinent alcoholics.

Overall, this pattern of results suggests that different facets of alcoholics' nonverbal impairments are determined by different processes. Some decline with time. Others seem to persist long after alcohol detoxification, like the misinterpretation of some negative emotions. However, it remains to establish whether these deficits were present *before* the onset of alcohol dependency. Indeed, the fact that they remain, even years after the recession of alcohol abuse, does not imply that they are pre-existing or independent from alcohol abuse.

Another question that needs to be addressed is whether the precise nonverbal deficits that we have observed in alcoholics are specific to the alcoholic population (Sher, Trull, Bartholow, & Vieth, 1999). To partially answer this question, we replicated our first study, with two non-alcoholic control groups, one with psychopathology (i.e., obsessive compulsive disorder, OCD) and one with no psychopathology (Kornreich et al., 2001a). We chose an OCD control group because alcoholism and OCD display symptomatic similarities but do not share common etiologies. Indeed, several investigators have noted similarities between urges and desires to drink heavily and obsessive-compulsive disorders (Anton, Moak, & Latham, 1995; Caetano, 1985; Edwards & Gross, 1976; Modell, Glaser, Cyr, & Montz, 1992). Furthermore, the life-time risk for obsessive compulsive disorder among close relatives of alcoholics is 1.4 percent, which does not support the existence of a common genotype for the two disorders (Schuckit et al., 1995). It seemed therefore relevant to use an obsessive-compulsive sample as a control group with psychopathology.

We used the same procedure as in our former studies, but with a restricted set of stimuli, given the (obsessively) long response time of participants with OCD. Twenty-two outpatients suffering from obsessive-compulsive disorder according to the DSM IV were recruited in a general hospital out-patient department. They were matched for age, sex, and educational level with 22 volunteers with no psychiatric record and 22 inpatients diagnosed with alcohol dependence according to DSM IV criteria who were at the end of their detoxification process. The results of Study 1 were replicated: Recently detoxified alcoholics attributed more emotional intensity to facial stimuli, were less accurate in identifying the emotion portrayed, and did not report more difficulties in the decoding task. The patients with OCD, however, did not differ from the normal controls. This observation supports the conclusions of our study comparing controls, anxious, and socially anxious outpatients—a study that had observed no differences among the three groups. Thus, the facial expression decoding deficits observed in alcoholics could not be found in OCD patients, or in another clinically anxious population. The social isolation and stigmatization shared by these conditions is thus unlikely to account for the nonverbal deficits observed in alcoholics.

This procedure was replicated in a study in which we compared post-cure groups presenting a dependency to opiate, to both opiate and alcohol, to alcohol only, and controls. The results indicated that participants who presented a dependency to alcohol only, and to both opiate and alcohol had the worst accuracy scores. Opiate only dependent participants were more accurate that the latter, but still not as accurate as controls. It thus seems that alcohol dependency has a particularly pronounced effect on the accuracy of facial expression decoding. At the least, these results demonstrate that the deficits we evidenced in alcoholics are not ubiquitous in psychopathological populations. Still, more investigations are needed to establish how specific these deficits are, and how they relate to conditions of substance dependence and to the social exclusion often accompanying these conditions.

Above, we defended the notion that the impairments shown by alcoholics in the recognition of emotion from nonverbal cues might generate interpersonal difficulties. These conflictive social relations might increase the probability of alcohol abuse. Alcohol intoxication might in turn impair the capacity of alcoholics to accurately interpret others' internal states from their nonverbal behavior. They would then fall in a vicious circle, leading to more interpersonal conflict and to more alcohol consumption.

If this hypothesis is correct, the deficit in nonverbal decoding observed in alcoholics should be accounted for by their deficit in interpersonal relations. To examine this possibility, we conducted a fourth study in which we replicated the procedure of Study 3 with 29 recently detoxified alcoholics and 29 controls matched for age, sex and educational level. In addition, we administrated to all participants the Interpersonal Problem Inventory of Horowitz et al. (1988). This scale comprises 127 items assessing six domains of potential interpersonal difficulties: assertiveness, sociability, submissiveness, intimacy, excessive self-control, and excessive self-responsibility. Once again, the results indicated that alcoholics were less accurate in decoding facial expression, that they attributed more emotional intensity to the facial stimuli, but that they did not report more difficulties with the task than the control participants. As expected, alcoholics reported more interpersonal difficulties for all domains (excepted for self-control). We then examined whether the nonverbal decoding deficits of alcoholics were still statistically observable after partialling out the variance accounted for by their interpersonal difficulties. The ANCOVAs revealed that alcoholics and controls were no more different in terms of nonverbal decoding accuracy, after partialling out the variance accounted for by interpersonal difficulties. This latter observation suggests that the relationship between nonverbal deficit and alcoholism is mediated by interpersonal problems and tension.

In conclusion, it appears that chronic alcoholics present three deficits in the interpretation of facial expression. First, they over-estimate the intensity of the emotion felt by their interactant. Second, they decode facial expression less accurately than controls; they might also present a systematic bias in the over-attribution of anger and contempt, but we did not replicate this finding in all our studies. Third, alcoholics are not aware of their nonverbal deficits. This pattern of deficits seems specific to alcoholics, although more research is needed regarding this point. These deficits are enduring, as abstinent alcoholics present the same pattern of deficits with the exception that they no longer over-estimate emotional intensity. Finally, these nonverbal deficits are related to interpersonal difficulties, which act as a mediator between nonverbal deficits and alcohol abuse.

Introducing this section, we have demonstrated that alcoholics tend to generate tension and conflict when interacting with others, including their close relatives and family members. Furthermore, alcoholics present special difficulties in dealing with anger and frustration, two feelings that are often generated by interpersonal tension and conflicts. Difficulties in dealing with and expressing these feelings are the best predictors of relapse (Marlatt, 1979). In other words, relapse prevention programs should focus on teaching alcoholics appropriate coping strategies and expression modes in situations in which they feel angry and/or frustrated.

Some research suggests that communication deficits, especially those relating to emotion, might be central in the deficient coping strategies used by alcoholics. The mechanism that we propose is that because of their inability to correctly read others' emotional states, alcoholics generate interpersonal tensions and are less well-armed to solve these tensions constructively. Further, to avoid feelings of helplessness generated by their inability to solve these situations, alcoholics turn to alcohol consumption as a coping strategy. They thus initiate two positive feedback loops. Alcohol intoxication first aggravates interpersonal tensions and second depletes the already limited nonverbal skills. This suggests that training programs, aimed at developing nonverbal sensitivity in alcoholics, should decrease interpersonal tension, increase appropriate coping skills, and consequently decrease alcohol consumption and relapse. Such training programs should especially focus on emotional intensity, and expression of emotion related to interpersonal tension such as anger, contempt, and disgust.

PSYCHOPATHY

One of the defining characteristics of psychopathy is the lack of empathy. One may thus suspect psychopaths of paying little attention to the emotional state of others, especially to states of distress, fear, or sadness. In this perspective, one might expect a poor performance for the decoding of facial expression of emotion in psychopaths, especially for distress, fear, or sadness. On the other hand, psychopaths have also been portrayed as having a "superficial charm" and as being skilled manipulators. In this perspective, one would expect better performance in the decoding of facial expression in psychopaths than in controls. Which of these two plausible but contradictory hypotheses is best supported in the literature?

While several studies have provided consistent evidence of deficits for psychopaths in processing verbal emotional material (Williamson, Harpur, & Hare, 1990, 1991), thereby supporting the former hypothesis, evidences are much less consistent regarding nonverbal material. Actually, most studies that examined the meaning attributed to facial features did not observe differences between psychopaths and non psychopaths. For instance, Day and Wong (1996) observed hemispheric asymmetric differences between the two groups in a tachitoscopic task involving emotional words, but not in a similar task involving emotional faces. Likewise, Richell, Mitchell, Newman, Leonard, Baron-Cohen, and Blair (2003) did not observe differences between psychopaths and non psychopaths in a task requiring the identification of mental states from photographs of the eye region alone. In contrast, Stevens, Chapman and Blair (2001) reported that children with psychopathic tendencies were impaired in the recognition of sad and fearful faces, but not of angry and happy faces. However, the samples were small ($n = 9$ for each group). Further, this observation was not replicated in adults samples by Kosson, Suchy, Mayer, and Libby (2002) who reported that psychopaths' deficits were specific to the classification of disgust faces only when participants were required to use their left hand (i.e., in conditions designed to minimize the involvement of left-hemisphere mechanisms). Further, in that study, psychopaths were unexpectedly observed to be *better* at decoding anger when relying on left-hemisphere resources (when using their right hand).

To account for these discrepancies, authors often evoke the lack of sensitivity of the nonverbal tasks used (relying on full-blown facial expression) as well as the fact that some studies did not distinguish among the emotion tones of facial expressions presented (Kosson et al., 2002). To overcome these weaknesses, we recently conducted a study in which we compared criminal psychopaths and non psychopaths among inmates of a Belgian state prison and of a high security forensic treatment facility. We used our highly sensitive nonverbal decoding task described in the preceding sections of this chapter (e.g., Philippot & Douilliez, in prep.; Philippot et al., 1999) and we further compared these criminal groups to men with no history of psychiatric disorder and with no criminal history. The analyses revealed that there were no differences between groups regarding the intensity of any emotion they attributed to the facial stimuli (no evaluative deficit in intensity), nor regarding the type of emotion they attributed to neutral faces. However, both criminal groups were less accurate than the controls, especially for fear and disgust. Further, psychopaths were less accurate than controls for anger, and non psychopathic criminals were less accurate than controls for sadness. These effects were not affected by entering Education as a covariate (the controls were significantly more educated than the criminals). Finally, differences appeared in the difficulty participants reported for the decoding task. Controls tended to report *more* difficulties than psychopaths, especially for weak intensity stimuli. Further, both criminal groups reported fewer difficulties than controls for decoding angry and sad faces. In sum, although both criminal groups reported fewer difficulties in decoding facial expression of emotion, they were less accurate, especially for negative emotions. Importantly, no differences were observed between the two criminal groups in any dimension of the decoding task.

In conclusion, the psychopathic deficit consistently observed in the processing of emotional verbal material is not replicated with nonverbal material. From the available evidence, one can conclude that if such a deficit exists, it should be highly specific and/or of weak intensity. Indeed, psychopathy is a rare syndrome resulting from a very complex combination of subtle deficits (Halle, Hodgins, & Roussy, 2000). We suggest that faces are basic social stimuli that require little to no reflexive processes to be decoded. However, the understanding of verbal material requires more elaborated processes. The latter would be impaired in psychopaths, but not the former. It is intriguing to notice that the same pattern of results and rationale does apply to social phobics, whose social impairment (lack of assertiveness and irrational social fear) is in many respects opposite to the social impairment of psychopaths (narcissism and total absence of social fear).

CONCLUSIONS AND DIRECTION FOR FUTURE RESEARCH

In this chapter, we have presented several lines of research investigating how the interpretation of facial expression of emotion might be altered by clinical conditions characterized by difficulties in interpersonal regulation. Specifically, we studied social anxiety, alcohol dependency, and psychopathy. For each condition, a logical rational could be formulated to support the notion that deficits in facial expression decoding were to be expected. Further, for each of these pathologies, there exists a strong clinical belief in the existence of bias or of deficit in the interpretation of others' emotional signals, and foremost of facial expression. As we have demonstrated, these beliefs were in some cases myths, but in other cases reality.

The more surprising case is the one of social phobia. For this anxiety disorder, there is strong evidence of attentional biases in general, and of evaluative biases for affective words specifically. However, despite a strong belief and theoretical claim of the opposite, the evaluative bias for facial expression in social phobics turned out to be a myth. Although one cannot capitalize on the null hypothesis and absence of differences, the lack of any differences between socially anxious individuals and non anxious in many different studies strongly suggests that if an evaluative bias exists, it should be at the least modest and of very little clinical significance. Similar conclusions could be made as regards to psychopaths. However, studies focusing on possible attentional biases are still to be done to obtain a fuller picture of how this specific population processes nonverbal emotional information.

Finally, the case of alcoholism is much better documented regarding emotion facial expression recognition. We have reviewed ample and consistent evidence of interpretation biases and deficits in accuracy and evaluation of the intensity of facial expression. More research is needed to determine whether this profile of nonverbal decoding deficits is proper to alcoholism, or if it might also be found in other conditions related to substance dependence. We also need to investigate the possibility of attentional bias in alcoholics, especially for faces expressing rejection and contempt. Still, the corpus of research presented in this chapter is suggestive of many paths that can be directly exploited by clinicians, as the ones specified at the end of that section.

Still, in closing this chapter, we want to stress that the future of the field is not only dependent upon "more research," a common conclusion in many chapters! In our view, this area suffers from an important limitation of a basic theoretical nature: We urgently need a model specifying the processes involved in the decoding of facial expression of emotion. Indeed, despite three decades of intense empirical research on facial expression decoding, we are still uncertain about the processes implicated in the perception of emotional facial expression, and we ignore how affective meaning is attributed to faces. The little theoretical basis we have is that different processes are active in the recognition of faces as compared to those implicated in the interpretation of facial expression. Having a theoretical model of the processes involved in the decoding of facial expression would offer a basis to infer hypotheses regarding which processes should be preserved and which one would be impaired in given pathologies. On this basis, one could predict the profile of decoding performances for given clinical conditions.

As in many areas of psychology, clinical research may help in the elaboration of such a fundamental model. Indeed, showing consistencies in the association or dissociation of some performances and deficits in given clinical conditions suggests that these performances are underlined by similar or different processes. For instance, we demonstrated that alcoholics' over-estimation of emotional intensity in faces disappears with long term abstinence, while the interpretation biases remain. This observation is suggestive that these two facets of the interpretation of emotional facial expression are supported by different processes. Similar inferences can be made from the observation that social phobics and psychopaths present biases in the processing of emotional verbal material, but not of nonverbal material.

It is our hope that the clinical work presented in this chapter, and the one that is forthcoming, will prove useful in the endeavor of building a basic model of the decoding of facial expression of emotion.

ACKNOWLEDGMENTS

The writing of this chapter has been facilitated by grants from the "Fonds National de la Recherche Scientifique de Belgique" 8.4512.98 and 3.4609.01. The authors appreciate helpful comments of Christopher Long on earlier drafts of this paper. Correspondence regarding this chapter should be addressed to Pierre Philippot who is at Faculté de Psychologie, Université de Louvain, place du Cardinal Mercier, 10, B-1348 Louvain-la-Neuve, Belgique. Electronic mail may be sent via Internet to Pierre.Philippot@psp.ucl.ac.be Recent updates of our research can be found on Internet : www.ecsa.ucl.ac.be/personnel/philippot/

REFERENCES

Amir, N., Freshman, M., & Foa, E. (2002). Enhanced Stroop interference for threat in social phobia. *Journal of Anxiety Disorder, 16*, 1–9.

Amir, N., McNally, R. J., Riemann, B. C., Burns, J., Lorenz, M., & Mullen, J. T. (1996). Suppression of the emotional Stroop effect by increased anxiety in patients with social phobia. *Behaviour Research & Therapy, 34*, 945–948.

Anton, R. F., Moak, D. H., & Latham, P. (1995). The Obsessive Compulsive Drinking Scale: A self-rated instrument for the quantification of thoughts about alcohol and drinking behavior. *Alcoholism: Clinical and Experimental Research, 19*, 92–99.

Asmundson, G. J. G., & Stein, M. B. (1994). Selective processing of social threat in patients with generalized social phobia: Evaluation using a dot-probe paradigm. *Journal of Anxiety Disorders, 8*, 107–117.

Beck, A. T., Emery, G., & Greenberg, R. L. (1985). Cognitive structures and anxiogenic rules. In A. T. Beck, G. Emery, & R. L. Greenberg (Eds.), *Anxiety disorders and phobias* (pp. 54–66). New York: Basic books

Bem, D. J. (1972). Self-perception theory. In L. Berkowitz (Ed.), *Advances in experimental social psychology* (pp. 1–62). New York: Academic Press.

Bouhuys, A. L. (2003). Ethology and depression. In P. Philippot, E. J. Coats & R. S. Feldman (Eds.). *Nonverbal behavior in clinical context*. New York: Oxford University Press.

Caetano, R. (1985). Alcohol dependence and the need to drink: A compulsion. *Psychosomatic Medicine, 15*, 463–469.

Chen, Y. P., Ehlers, A., Clark, D. M., & Mansell, W. (2002). Patients with social phobia direct their attention away from faces. *Behaviour Research & Therapy, 40*, 677–687.

Clark, D. M. (1999). Anxiety disorders: Why do they persist and how to treat them. *Behavior Research and Therapy, 37*, 5–27.

Clark, D. M., & MacManus, F. (2002). Information processing in social phobia. *Biological Psychiatry, 51*, 92–100.

Clark, D. M. & Wells, A. (1995). A Cognitive model of social phobia. In R. Heimberg, M. Liebowitz, D. A. Hope, & F. R. Schneier. *Social phobia: diagnosis, assessment and treatment* (pp. 69–93). New York: Guilford Press.

Cooper, M. L., Frone, M. R., Russell, M., & Mudar, P. (1995). Drinking to regulate positive and negative moods: A motivational model of alcohol use. *Journal of Personality and Social Psychology, 69*, 990–1005.

Day, R., & Wong, S. (1996). Anomalous perceptual asymmetries for negative emotional stimuli in the psychopath. *Journal of Abnormal Psychology, 105*, 648–652.

Douilliez, C., & Philippot, P. (2003). Biais dans l'évaluation volontaire de stimuli verbaux et non-verbaux: Effet de l'anxiété sociale. *Revue Francophone de Clinique Comportementale et Cognitive.*

Duberstein, P. R., Conwell, Y., & Caine, E. D. (1993). Interpersonal stressors, substance abuse, and suicide. *Journal of Nervous and Mental Disorders, 181*, 80–85.

Edwards, G., & Gross, M. M. (1976). Alcohol dependence: Provisional description of a clinical syndrome. *British Medical Journal, 1*, 1058–1061.

Gilboa-Schechtman, E., Foa, E. B., & Amir, N. (1999). Attentional biases for facial expressions in social phobia: The face-in-the-crowd paradigm. *Cognition and Emotion, 13*, 305–318.

Gross, A. L., & Ballif, B. (1991). Children's understanding of emotion from facial expressions and situations: A review. *Developmental Review, 11*, 368–398.

Halle, P., Hodgins, S., & Roussy, S. (2000). *Revue critique des études expérimentales auprès de détenus adultes: Précision du syndrome de la psychopathie et hypothèses développementales.* Septentrion: Presses Universitaires de Lille.

Hare, R. D. (1998). Psychopathy, affect and behavior. In D. J. Cooke, A. E. Forth, & R. D. Hare (Eds.), *Psychopathy: Theory, research and implications for society* (pp. 105–137). Boston: Kluwer Academic.

Hess, U., & Blairy, S. (1995). *Set of emotional facial stimuli*. Montréal, Canada: Department of Psychology, University of Quebec at Montréal.

Hess, U., Blairy, S., & Kleck, R. E. (1997). Intensity of emotional facial expression and decoding accuracy. *Journal of Nonverbal Behavior, 21,* 241–257.

Horowitz, L. M., Rosenberg, S. E., Baer, B. A., Ureno, G., & Villasenor, V. S. (1988). Inventory of Interpersonal problems: Psychometric properties and clinical applications. *Journal of Consulting and Clinical Psychology, 56,* 885–892.

Keane, T. M., & Lisman, S. A. (1980). Alcohol and social anxiety in males: Behavioral, cognitive and physiological effects. *Journal of Abnormal Psychology, 89,* 213–223.

Kornreich, C., Blairy, S., Philippot, P., Dan, B., Foisy, M. L., Le Bon, O., Pelc, I., & Verbanck, P. (2001a). Impaired emotional facial expression recognition in alcoholism compared to obsessive compulsive disorder and normal controls. *Psychiatric Research, 102,* 235–248.

Kornreich, C., Blairy, S., Philippot, P., Hess, U., Noël, X., Streel, E., Le Bon, O., Dan, B., Pelc, I., & Verbanck, P. (2001b). Deficits in Recognition of emotional facial expression are still present after mid to long-term abstinence in alcoholics. *Journal of Studies on Alcohol, 62,* 533–542.

Kosson, D. S., Suchy, Y., Mayer, A. R., & Libby, J. (2002). Facial affect recognition in criminal psychopaths. *Emotion, 2,* 398–411.

Kring, A. M., & Earnst, K. S. (2003). Nonverbal behavior in schizophrenia. In P. Philippot, E. J. Coats, & R. S. Feldman (Eds.). *Nonverbal behavior in clinical context.* New York: Oxford University Press.

Lang, A. R., Patrick, C. J., & Stritzke, W. G. K. (1999). Alcohol and emotional response: A multidimensional-multilevel analysis. In K. E. Leonard & H. T. Blane (Eds.), *Psychological theories of drinking and alcoholism* (2nd. ed., pp. 328–371). New York: Guilford Press.

Maidenberg, E., Chen, E., Craske, M., Bohn, P. et al., (1996). Specificity of attentional bias in panic disorder and social phobia. *Journal of Anxiety Disorders, 10,* 529–541.

Mann K., Günther, A., Stetter, F., & Ackerman, K. (1999). Rapid recovery from cognitive deficits in abstinent alcoholics: A controlled test-retest study. *Alcohol and Alcoholics, 34,* 567–574.

Mansell, W., Clark, D. M., Ehlers, A., & Chen, Y. P. (1999). Social anxiety and attention away from emotional faces. *Cognition and Emotion, 13,* 673–690.

Marlatt, C. A. (1979). *Alcohol use and problem drinking: a cognitive behavioral analysis.* New York: Academic Press.

Marlatt, G. A. (1996). Taxonomy of high-risk situations for alcohol relapse: Evolution and development of a cognitive behavioral model. *Addiction, 91* (suppl.), S37–S49.

Mattia, J. I., Heimberg, R. G., & Hope, D. A. (1993). The revised Stroop color-naming task in socials phobics. *Behavior Research and Therapy, 31,* 305–313.

Merckelbach, H., Van Hout, W., Van den Hout, M. A., & Mersch, P. P. (1989). Psychophysiological and subjective reactions of social phobics and normals to facial stimuli. *Behaviour Research and Therapy, 27,* 289–294.

Modell, J. G., Glaser, F. B., Cyr, L., Montz, J. M. (1992). Obsessive and compulsive characteristics of craving for alcohol in alcohol abuse and dependence. *Alcoholism: Clinical and Experimental Research, 16,* 272–274.

Mogg, K., & Bradley, B. P. (1999). Some methodological issues in assessing attentional biases for threatening faces in anxiety: A replication study using a modified version of the probe detection task. *Behaviour Research and Therapy, 37*, 595–604.

Mogg, K., & Bradley, B. P. (2002). Selective orienting of attention to masked threat faces in social anxiety. *Behaviour Research and Therapy, 40*, 1403–1414.

Mogg, K., & Bradley, B. P. (1998). A cognitive-motivational analysis of anxiety. *Behavior Research and Therapy, 36*, 809–848.

Mogg, K., Bradley, B. P., de Bono, J., & Painter, M. (1997) Time course of attentional bias for threat information in non-clinical anxiety. *Behaviour Research and Therapy, 35*, 297–303.

Mogg, K., Philippot, P., & Bradley, B. (2003). Selective attention to angry faces in a clinical sample with social phobia. *Journal of Abnormal Psychology, 113*, 160–165.

Musa, C. Z., & Lépine, J. P. (2000). Cognitive aspects of social phobia: a review of theories and experimental research. *European Psychiatry, 15*, 59–66.

Myers, T. (1984). Alcohol and violence: Self-reported alcohol consumption among violent and nonviolent male prisoners. In N. Karsner, J. S. Madden, & R. J. Walker (Eds.), *Alcohol-related problems*. Chichester: Wiley.

Öhman, A., & Soares, J. J. F. (1993). On the automatic nature of phobic fear: Conditioned electrodermal responses to masked fear-relevant stimuli. *Journal of Abnormal Psychology, 102*, 121–132.

Oscar-Berman, M., Hancock, M., Mildwordf, B., Hutner, N., & Altman-Weber, D. (1990). Emotional perception and memory in alcoholism and aging. *Alcoholism: Clinical and Experimental Research, 14*, 384–393.

Patterson, M. L. (1999). The evolution of a parallel process model of nonverbal communication. In P. Philippot, R. S. Feldman, & E. J. Coats (Eds.), *Nonverbal behavior in social context*. New York: Cambridge University Press.

Perez, J. E., & Riggio, R. E. (2003). Nonverbal social skills and psychopathology. In P. Philippot, E. J. Coats, & R. S. Feldman (Eds.), *Nonverbal behavior in clinical context*. New York: Oxford University Press.

Philippot, P., & Feldman, R. S. (1990). Age and social competence in preschoolers' decoding of facial expression. *British Journal of Social Psychology, 29*, 43–54.

Philippot, P., & Douilliez, C. (2003). *The decoding of facial expression of emotion in social phobics is not impaired*. Manuscript in preparation.

Philippot, P., Baeyens, C., Douilliez, C., & Francart, B. (2003). Cognitive regulation of emotion: Application to clinical disorders. In P. Philippot & R. S. Feldman (Eds.), *The regulation of emotion*. New York: Lawrence Erlbaum Associates.

Philippot, P., Kornreich, C., & Blairy, S. (2003). Nonverbal deficits and interpersonal regulation in alcoholics. In P. Philippot, E. J. Coats, & R. S. Feldman (Eds.), *Nonverbal behavior in clinical context*. New York: Oxford University Press.

Philippot, P., Kornreich, C., Blairy, S., Baert, Y., Den Dulk, A., Le Bon, O., Verbanck, P., Hess, U., & Pelc, I. (1999). Alcoholics' deficits in the decoding of emotional facial expression. *Alcoholism: Clinical and Experimental Research, 23*, 1031–1038.

Richell, R. A., Mitchell, D. G. V., Newman, C., Leonard, A., Baron-Cohen, S., & Blair, R. J. R. (2003). Theory of mind and psychopathy: Can psychopathic individuals read the "language of the eyes"? *Neuropsychologia, 41*, 523–526.

Rosenthal-Gaffney, L., Thorpe, K., Young, R., Colett, R., & Occhipinti, S. (1998). Social skills, expectancies, and drinking in adolescents. *Addictive Behaviors, 23*, 587–599.

Schuckit, M. A., Hesselbrock, V. M., Tipp, J., Nurnberger, J. I., Anthenelli, R. M., & Crowe R. R. (1995). The prevalence of major anxiety disorders in relatives of alcohol dependent men and women. *Journal of Studies on Alcohol,* *56*, 309–317.

Sferrazza, R., Philippot, P., Kornreich, C., Tang, C., Noel, X., Pelc, I., & Verbanck, P. (2002). Dysfonctionnement relationnel au sein des couples alcooliques. *Alcoologie et Addictologie, 24*, 117–125.

Sher, K. J., Trull, T. J., Bartholow, B. D., Vieth, A. (1999). Personality and Alcoholism issues methods and etiological processes. In K. E. Leonard & H. T. Blane (Eds.), *Psychological Theories of Drinking and Alcoholism* (2nd ed.). New York: Guilford press.

Stevens, D., Chapman, T., & Blair, R. J. R. (2001). Recognition of emotion in facial expressions and vocal tones in children with psychopathic tendencies. *Journal of Genetic Psychology, 162*, 201–211.

Watson, D., & Friend, R. (1969). Measurement of social-evaluative anxiety. *Journal of Consulting and Clinical Psychology, 33*, 448–457.

Williams, J. M. G., Watts, F. N., MacLeod, C., & Mathews, A. (1999). *Cognitive psychology and emotional disorders* (2nd ed.). Chichester, UK: Wiley.

Williamson, S., Harpur, T. T., & Hare, R. D. (1990). *Sensitivity to emotional polarity in psychopaths.* Paper presented at the 98th Annual Convention of the American Psychological Association, Boston.

Williamson, S., Harpur, T. T., & Hare, R. D. (1991). Abnormal processing of affective words by psychopaths. *Psychophysiology, 28*, 260–273.

II

Applications to Law and Politics

❧3❧

Communication in the Courtroom and the "Appearance" of Justice

Michael Searcy
Steve Duck
Peter Blanck
University of Iowa

When the jury revealed its verdict on Charles Ingram, he made no response other than pursing his lips and slightly shaking his head. But his wife reached down and took her husband's hand. Whittock also made no response when he too was found guilty but kept his hands clasped on the table in front of him. Later when the jury returned with its verdict on Diana Ingram her appearance remained unchanged but her husband once again slightly shook his head. *The Times* [of London] 7 April 2003.

INTRODUCTION

It has long been known that non-typical verbal *and* nonverbal behaviors by a defendant or witness in a criminal or civil case often are interpreted by judges and juries as evidence of guilt or untrustworthiness (Blanck, Rosenthal, & Cordell, 1985). The behaviors known to be associated with a lack of credibility and dishonesty are the shifty eye, shuffling feet, hesitancy in tone of voice, lack of expected emotion, and inconsistencies among verbal and nonverbal messages (Hickson, Stacks, & Moore, 2003).

Outside of the courtroom, however, these same non-typical verbal and nonverbal behaviors, even produced by these same individuals, may be interpreted as eccentric, humorous and perfectly appropriate in their context. This simple observation frames the core message of this chapter: specifically, interpretations of verbal and nonverbal be-

41

havior must be considered relative to their social context (Duck, 1998; Searcy, 2003), and it is this comparison that makes behavior "appropriate" or "inappropriate" (Duck & Vandervoot, 2002).

The core message alerts us to two basic contentions regarding verbal and nonverbal communication (henceforth: NVC), whether observed macroscopically or microscopically:

1. they evidence part (and sometimes the majority) of their meaning by placement in social context, and,

2. by definition, they convey meanings that are non-intrinsic and hence are disputable by reference to context.

Within these premises, this chapter explores how the social context of the courtroom (for purposes of illustration) establishes expectations—that is, learned or instinctual rules of communication—against which specific micro and macro manifestations of verbal and nonverbal communication are assessed. The courtroom is a strongly defined context: It is orderly and the assessments relevant therein concern the meaning of verbal and nonverbal messages as these cast light on issues of truth, falsehood, guilt, or liability specifically.

The courtroom's social dynamics, what Blanck and his colleagues (1985) described as "the appearance of justice," are established for one reason: For the orderly and just determination of guilt or not, civil liability or not. To reach the ultimate conclusions about guilt or liability, and their mediators such as defendant or witness trustworthiness, truthfulness, and culpability, trial judges and jurors assess both the written trial record and the participants' verbal and nonverbal behavior in that "tight" context.

Previously, researchers have given little weight to the role of this tight context in influencing interpretation of NVC or verbal messages and, conversely, have too freely assumed that rules governing NVC and verbal messages in everyday life can be projected unaltered into such contexts (Hickson, Stacks, & Moore, 2003). Indeed, whereas much work has assessed the social impact of NVC and verbal cues against each other (Keeley & Hart, 1994), little study has examined NVC trans-contextually, an approach this chapter attempts to further.

COURTROOM CONTEXT AND COMMUNICATION

Interpersonal communication researchers have shown that the ways people process and interpret verbal and nonverbal messages are influenced importantly by broad elements of "social context" (Knapp & Hall, 2002). For instance, "self-disclosure" is now recognized as a contextually dependent transaction (Dindia, 2000), rather than the one-sided expression of inner thought as it was portrayed previously (Jourard, 1971). Indeed, the meaning of self-disclosure in a particular social context often is less psychologically expressive than, say, educational and instructive, by exposing lessons learned (Spencer, 1994).

Similarly, micro-momentary nonverbal behaviors, such as eye movements or head nods, long have been known to be capable of conveying different meanings; for example, a stare may be a welcoming sign of approval or a threatening signal of hostility (Argyle, 1967). Recent efforts have noted that it is the social context provided by circumstances and accompanying interpersonal cues that enables an observer to attribute meaning appropriately (Knapp & Hall, 2002).

Within the spectrum of the social stage, the courtroom provides a unique context and hence, we argue, *disables* certain ordinary sorts of attribution of meaning about observed cues and behavior. The courtroom is a context where pleasure and sociability are irrelevant and determination of criminal guilt or civil liability, or the lack thereof, is the prescribed focus for jurors and judges. The outcome-driven process, particularly where the presented evidence is finely balanced or confusing to lay jurors, often depends on their determinations of witness credibility. Yet, the unfamiliar legal context does not necessarily reflect similar determinations in other contexts of everyday life where conversation may offer "testimony" of one kind or another upon which judgments are made of other people.

The physical organization of the courtroom context is highly unusual compared to most everyday settings (Duck, 1998). Likewise, the sequencing of communicative interactions is circumscribed by procedural rules—direct versus cross-examination, objections to speculative statements, and so on. The nature of the controlled interaction further is atypical in that amounts of self-disclosure are unusually high, even required by probing questions in which a witness may be required to answer, and sometimes even with only a "yes" or "no."

In addition, challenges to courtroom statements are formal, rather than indirect or polite, truthfulness is prescribed by oaths, and familiar processing of communicative information is replaced with prescribed ritual—"The jury is to disregard that statement." In the courtroom, then, the contextually forced and definitional focus on persuasive credibility gives verbal and nonverbal utterances more weight, as compared to typical conversation with intimates or strangers.

However, the courtroom context also *enables* attributions about certain performances. Clearly, not all players in the trial drama are informed equally about the context and its parameters and processes. The courtroom "regulars"—judges and trial lawyers—learn to expect and use contextual cues; for instance, highlighting to the jury the inconsistency in a witness's nonverbal and verbal behavior. These deviations from what may be expected as normal or "reasonable" in this context are sometimes read by lawyers as "leaking" or "oozing" guilt, culpability, or dishonesty (Searcy & Duck, 2003).

Lawyers also understand that jurors and most witnesses are acting in an unfamiliar and stressful context, while facing unfamiliar forms of prescribed interactions, with dramatic legal consequences. For such non-repeat courtroom players, critical evaluations of courtroom behavior (for instance, in the assessment of witness credibility) necessarily are based on expectancies formed elsewhere in life.

Previous analysis of NVC in the courtroom has not been grounded sufficiently in analysis of these unequally enabled and disabled operations of the social environment (Searcy, 2003). Thus, behavior that is acceptable for some actors in a social, familiar setting often is unusual and notable in the courtroom trial context and vice versa. Violations of normative (contextual) expectations in NVC, therefore, mark the courtroom witness as deviant, to be vigilantly observed (so a lawyer might say) for other signs of lack of credibility. However, the standards of contextual expectancy by jurors and trial lawyers may be grounded in different bases (Duck, 2003).

Contextual expectancy violations take at least two forms in the courtroom: those attaching to regular performers (lawyers, judges, expert witnesses, court officers), and those attaching to the irregulars (lay witnesses, defendants). A lay witness's violation of courtroom evidentiary rules may excite—or even require—comment by the "regulars" (e.g., formal objection); and violation of the contextual normality in that individual's communicative performance (e.g., nervous nonverbal behaviors) can be presented as evidence of guilt or culpability when the defendant is testifying, or a lack of credibility when a fact witness is testifying. Examination of the NVC of these participants in the courtroom as compared to other everyday life contexts enables analysis of that tight context in the interpretation of communicative information.

Jurors further bring to the courtroom their intuitive expectations about the ways in which ordinary people manifest guilt. Often, the jury's collective judgment of guilt in a criminal trial is a report that the defendant "performed" nonverbally when testifying in a way that was consistent with expectations surrounding the presence of guilt.

Unlike jurors, regular courtroom performers conform to a different set of expectations. Trial judges, as all persons do, hold expectancies about the new players, particularly the defendant. Yet, improper beliefs and expectations for guilt in a criminal trial, if manifested in a judge's nonverbal behavior, may warrant reversal and judicial disqualification (Blanck, 1993).

Describing the relationship between the defendant's criminal background and the judges' expectancy, Blanck noted:

> This relationship describes how a judge's expectations for trial outcome may be predicted solely from the background variables of the trial participants. The results suggest that judges' beliefs about trial outcomes are related to defendants' criminal histories in predictable ways. For example, judges usually expect a guilty verdict when defendants have serious criminal histories and expect innocent verdicts when defendants do not have serious criminal histories. (Blanck, 1991, p. 8)

So too, trial attorneys take care to observe the demeanor of potential jurors during the selection process and attempt to predict ("expect") the attitudes of those jurors toward the case.

In the evaluation of communication in the courtroom, then, two sets of norms of context first must be explicated (courtroom; everyday), and then differentiated. We add, "differentiated," because not only must the courtroom be differentiated from everyday life context, but also the expectations for performers in the courtroom differ by design, as they also do in other settings.

In early studies, Blanck et al. (1985) examined the importance of such verbal and nonverbal behaviors in the courtroom. We now review that work from a new perspective, by examining aspects of the differentiated courtroom context that affect credibility determinations by judges, jurors, lawyers, witnesses, and other participants that may otherwise be attributable to NVC studied in isolation.

The next part of this chapter examines contextual expectancy in the courtroom, as indicated by courtroom design and prescribed rules of interaction. Thereafter, we explore how NVC conforms to the normative expectations in the courtroom, and the impact of that determination on the evaluation of the credibility and probative value of the testimony presented.

We attempt to build on, and to develop, the pioneering work of Rosenthal and his colleagues (see, e.g., Harris & Rosenthal, chap. 8, this volume), which elegantly explores the verbal and nonverbal mediators of social expectancies and outcomes, as we draw out new implications of contextual expectations in the courtroom specifically. We also remind readers of seminal work by Martin Orne (1962) on "demand characteristics," and develop his approach (which was specific to situational and procedural effects in the social scientific experiment) by making new applications of that concept to the courtroom context.

EXPECTANCY VIOLATION THEORY

Robert Rosenthal and his colleagues consistently have shown that people develop expectations for social and cultural interactions and outcomes—appropriate eye gaze, proximal distance between interactants, touching, vocalics (including speech rate, volume, pitch, tone, etc.) (see Harris & Rosenthal, chap. 8, this volume). These expectations often are mediated through NVC alone.

Violation of contextual expectancies (whether cultural or interpersonal) leads to heightened awareness, and arousal, suspicion and so on, of the particular behavior or communicative act. These "violations" distract from the normal course of interaction in everyday life and likely influence an individual's (or groups of individuals as in a jury) responses to the verbal and nonverbal behaviors as a positive or negative "violation response." The degree of response may lead the observer (i.e., judge or jury in the courtroom) to be suspicious of the underlying motives for the violation. Indeed, in the courtroom, many trial lawyers and expert witnesses have become used to manipulating such distractions, to emphasize or de-emphasize trial facts so that the result is helpful to their side, or at least not helpful to the opposing side.

Studies show that there are cultural norms of appropriateness, and within a given culture there exist norms for personal space, expressivity and emotional NVC (for a review see Knapp & Hall, 2002). These interpersonal and cultural expectancies have a range of tolerance levels. Violations of behavioral norms often are expressed as exceeding the range of observer normalcy in context, previous experiences, and status (Burgoon & Jones, 1976).

Burgoon and her colleagues (Burgoon & Buller, 1994; Burgoon, Buller, Ebesu, & Rockwell, 1994; Burgoon, LePoire, & Rosenthal, 1995; Burgoon, Stern, & Dillman, 1995) argue that normative "expectancy" is central to the understanding of the evaluation of NVC. By "expectancy," these researchers mean communicative behavior, verbal and nonverbal, that one regards as normative in a given social context.

These researchers suggest that reactions to an unexpected communication by another arouse observers to direct attention to the social status of the communicator. In this model, individuals favor high status and disfavor low status persons to differentiate their appraisal of the appropriateness of communication. Low status violators are perceived negatively, whereas high status ones are not (Burgoon, 1983). In addition, higher status communicators are given broader latitude before censure, in ways reminiscent of "idiosyncrasy credits" granted to leaders who violate group norms.

Burgoon and her colleagues predict that the degree to which observers evaluate social interactions positively or negatively is mediated by *communicator reward valence* (Burgoon, Stern et al.,1995). Reward valence is the net social, or other, costs and benefits to the individuals involved, and assessment of character traits associated with future interactive involvement.

In the courtroom, individuals of high status (such as judges and lawyers) may be perceived by witnesses and jurors as behaving appropriately to the context even when they violate everyday expectancies. Observers or raters (in this context, jurors) readily evaluate low status individuals as not holding such favor (in this context, defendants and witnesses), less optimistically and attribute ulterior motives not within the range of acceptable contextual involvement.

Burgoon's model is useful for the analysis of courtroom communicative dynamics where status differences are marked. Her model focuses attention on the differentiation that similar communicative behaviors evince by different status performers. The same nonverbal act may hold different meaning in varying contexts depending upon one's status in the proceedings. Therefore, generalizations about "the role" or "the meaning" of NVC in the courtroom should be treated with circumspection because the same behavioral act may be interpreted differently depending on the communicator's perceived role in courtroom process.

CONTEXT AND EXPECTANCY VIOLATION IN THE COURTROOM

The courtroom dynamic is, by definition, driven by tight formal procedures and role expectancy. The primary and regular actors in the courtroom (judges, jurors, lawyers, court officers) follow prescribed behavior, especially as compared to the non-repeat players (fact witnesses, defendants, jurors). In addition, expectations by non-regular actors are influenced by exposure to television courtroom channels and popular dramas.

Yet, the popular view that courtrooms are places of high drama and unfolding excitement rarely is validated by the average trial, but nevertheless is a likely expectation by jurors. The strong influences of such juror baseline expectancies require assessment. Non-regular player baseline contextual expectancies are important to the courtroom communicative process, particularly when a jury's role is to differentiate credible from not credible behavior.

A further influence that differentiates expectancies of participation in courtroom interaction is found in environmental spatial cues. The physical layout of the courtroom is indicative of certain formal expectations. In the United States, defense and prosecution (or plaintiff) counsel each sit positioned in equal but separate relation to the judge, and apart from the jury and judge.

By contrast, for instance, in Chinese criminal courtrooms (where the defendant is always *a priori* presumed guilty), the prisoner occupies a central position, with participants arranged in circular format around him or her. The physical layout of the Chinese courtroom marks accepted structures and habits of interaction that differ from those in the United States and establish different expectations about the relative positions of defendant (and defendant's lawyers) and court officers. Chang (2003, November) notes that:

> The physical setting conditions and contextualizes verbal interactions, renders them meaningful, and most importantly, reflects and enacts cultural meanings .... Defendants are seated (or stand) almost in the center of the square or circle, closer to the defense lawyer's seat .... Such a circular arrangement makes a spectacle of defendants. What is more, it facilitates interrogations of defendants who, being in the middle of a circle, are able to be face-to-face with either prosecutors or the presiding judge. ... Public prosecutors sit behind a desk similar to that of the judges, but not as high. The defendants, in contrast, sit on ordinary chairs or stand in the middle of the trial area. [All] participants including judges, public prosecutors, defense lawyers, and defendants were provided with loudspeakers ... [but] defendants had to use their biological voice. (Chang, 2003, November)

The contextual setup of the Chinese courtroom establishes expectancies about guilt, roles, and the purpose of the trial as a public re-education of a miscreant. Likewise in the United States, the courtroom formal setup conveys messages about the nature of roles and expectations. The judge, having the highest position, is in charge of interaction, takes a moderating and leading role, and may interrupt anyone at any time. Court officers seek permission from the judge to interrupt other participants.

The U.S. courtroom layout indicates the theoretical equivalence of the prosecuting and defending counsel by placing them at equal distances from the judge. In jury trials, the jury box has its place alongside the proceedings. The jurors are *spectators* at the proceedings, much as a crowd views a football game or as bystanders watch a car accident on the street. Yet, the jury is asked to gain its perspective during the public deliberation of events. Powers of active participation are reserved to the jury, although suppressed by judges so that the regular players may expedite the proceedings.

Witnesses have their place in the courtroom, not only in physical placement but also in question format. Witnesses assume a spotlight position and rarely are invited to offer a narrative of events that is not interrupted, guided, or challenged by the principal players in ways that would violate normal expectancies if they occurred in everyday life conversations. Also, in everyday life an acknowledged expert or knowledgeable account provided outside of the courtroom usually is acquiesced to without demur. Within the courtroom, such expectations are turned.

Those with expert knowledge take the stand outside of their familiar environment, the trappings of their expertise and the deference that it normally affords them. Their accounts, expertise, and abilities to assess facts are challenged so that the familiar rug of their own professional stature may be pulled from under them. Experts are judged as much from their ability to stand up to lawyers (their comportment as "experts"), as for their opinions in ways that, for example, a testifying physician would not be challenged in the medical examination room when delivering an opinion to a patient.

Sequences of presentation of information also are atypical in the courtroom. Participants face scrutiny in question-and-answer formats that violate daily conversational interaction within the social context outside the courtroom. Witnesses are not allowed to challenge the form of questions. They are sequestered and are not able to place what other witnesses have said in court during their own narrative contexts since those comments were not heard. Objections are permitted in the courtroom about a comment or viewpoint from a witness from the lawyers or the judge, but not from other people who may have grounds for challenging the claims.

For regular players, expectancies therefore are consistent with behavior in the courtroom. Courtroom theater is their normal social context. However, it is in a jury trial (a relatively infrequent occurrence in the U.S. system of justice) that non-repeat lay players decide the fate of a defendant while in a context that, by its physical setup and routine, represents a violation of daily interactive expectations.

COMMUNICATION, BEHAVIOR EXPECTATIONS, AND NORMS IN THE COURTROOM

Although we and others have systematically studied the "appearance of justice" and NVC in the courtroom (Blanck, 1993; Blanck & Rosenthal, 1992; Blanck et al., 1985), this early work has not adequately been developed to consider the differentiated expectancy norms that "irregulars," such as jurors and lay witnesses, bring to the courtroom context. These non-regular participants process messages presented in an environment that embodies violations of normal everyday contextual expectations.

As suggested, one illustrative dimension of normal everyday life communication is frequency of "self-disclosure" behavior. Self-disclosure has been examined for its effects on interpersonal relationships, but nevertheless accounts for a relatively small percentage (about 2% overall) of relational communication (Dindia, 2000; Dindia & Fitzpatrick, 1989). Still, self-disclosure communication has a strong impact on interpersonal relationships. Self-disclosure, as it may occur in the courtroom, however, whether verbal or nonverbal, is proportionally more frequent in the process and deemed significant, despite the fact that it most likely results from a lawyer's trial strategy rather than arising spontaneously.

NVC that violates expectancies likewise is relatively rare in influencing trial outcomes and jury decision-making. However, as Blanck and his colleagues have found (1985), when such communicative behavior occurs, it may be as impactful as self-disclosure within relationships. Indeed, the term "thin slices" of NVC has been used to describe activities that are short, usually de-contextualized, segments of nonverbal behaviors that have a measured impact on social outcomes (Ambady, Bernieri, & Richeson, 2000; Ambady, Hallahan, & Conner, 1999; Ambady, Hallahan, & Rosenthal, 1995; Ambady & Rosenthal, 1992; Bond, Jr. et al., 1992). When the thin slices are re-placed in context, however, their effects become less predictable and robust, in much the same way that intense scrutiny of anatomy is necessary to medicine but does not predict tendencies to healthy activity. When studied as "pure" events, the impact of these thin slices may be exaggerated.

What then of pure (or even impure) NVC that is de-contextualized not from other cues, as in the above research, but from the "normal" social context itself? There is no universal definition across individuals, cultures, and contexts of the interpretation of human communicative behavior. A dictionary of NVC skills and behaviors does not exist. The task for jurors, unfamiliar with the social context of a courtroom, then, is to use normal expectation strategies in an unfamiliar and contrived context.

Undoubtedly, in special contexts other than the courtroom, defined and specific behavioral and communicative expectations apply. Doctors, for example, have few, or only implicit, protocols (Duck, 1998)—although there has been a movement between innovative medical schools and communication departments to create explicit protocol—for dealing with patients in various contexts (Galvin, Bylund, & Brommel, 2004; see also Friedman & Martin, chap. 1, this volume). An oncologist treating a cancer patient does not enter a consultation wearing a Hawaiian shirt when about to discuss the gravity of chemotherapy treatment with a critically ill patient. Nor does the oncologist show up to her six-year old child's birthday party wearing clinical theater gear.

Violations of expectations at the child's birthday party are created by the gravity expressed in the clothing, while similar expectations are violated when child birthday party clothing is worn during a patient consultation. The same sorts of nonverbal violations affect other social contexts—student-teacher, therapist-patient, manager-employee scenarios (Rosenthal, 2002). Thin slices of behavior outside the contextual scenario convey meaning only because they represent violations of expectancy. Within the course of everyday interpersonal relationships, they do not; but they do depend for that label on their conformity with social norms.

Of course, cultural norms affect such contextual expectancies (for a review, see Matsumoto, chap. 11 and Philippot, chap. 2, this volume). By definition, a culture has norms of expectation for everyday NVC and other forms of behavior. People interacting in a different culture may be aware of "being in a special environment," but are not always clear on what is expected of them. The manner in which due solemnity is "performed" at weddings varies by culture and often violates an outsider's norms for that behavior.

Although these other everyday contexts have sanctions for inappropriate behavior (Duck & Vandervoot, 2002; Vandervoot & Duck, 2003), the courtroom is unusual in that sanctions on communicative violations, normal in the individual's personal context, may be grave. Not only do they lead to unwelcome decisions of extreme impact, such as a guilty verdict or liability, but also they can lead to other restraints on life, liberty and property.

As experiencing a different culture, the non-regular participant enters the courtroom with norms and expectations formed in contexts outside of the courtroom environment. In what ways do the roles of "juror," "judge," "counselor," and others operate as fulfillments of expected behavior? Each participant in the courtroom follows prescribed social expectations. The courtroom code of conduct and guidelines about demeanor are set out publicly. Professional players in the context follow written advice explicitly outlining many of the "rules" of the game and the expectations in place for attorneys and judges (Caughfield, 2001; Milford, 2001).

Other rules are presumed for this context, such as those relating to civil demeanor in the courtroom, constituting behavior of respect and dignity to not be found "in contempt" of the court. Procedural guidelines are specific, such as the direction to witnesses to take an oath to tell the truth, the witness chair as the focus of attention, and the respectful standing as the judge enters and leaves the courtroom.

Additionally, the judge is expected to provide localized rules and instruction to the new players with respect to behavior and communication in his or her courtroom. This may be in the form of jury instructions (Blanck et al., 1985), sequestering the jury members during the trial from influences while deliberating, and the format in which juries may request access to previous testimony for reaching their decision.

However, a person's expectancies about NVC are not easily rewritten. Although jurors may become accustomed to them during long trials, witnesses have less time to do so. Non-regular courtroom players process information presented while operating in a context that differs from daily interaction expectancies. Yet, they must show the appearance of understanding immediately the context in which they have been placed. Typically, there are no explicit prescriptions for new courtroom players (however, some judges initially explain the trial proceedings), with the exception that one should not be contemptuous of the court or disrespectful, and that rules about testifying under oath apply.

In a criminal trial, a defendant's appearance and NVCs may become relevant only in the light of "contextual appropriateness," even if that context embodies expectancies that violate a person's normal expectations for comportment (e.g., wearing a suit may be uncomfortable and nonverbally disruptive for people used to wearing overalls). Contextual appropriateness is an important moderating factor when jurors evaluate defendant credibility, for instance when testifying. The defendant may express high status via professional business dress (prison dress typically is not permitted as it is discriminatory in this effect) that may lead to the appearance of high credibility (Lefkowitz, Blake, & Mouton, 1995).

Some courts have required disruptive criminal defendants to wear shock belts (belts which deliver 50,000 volts of electricity to the wearer) or to be gagged with duct tape as a result of continual outbursts (Administrative Office of Courts, 2002; *Juan Rodriguez Chavez v. Janie Cockrell*, 2002). Where such extreme constraints are imposed on disorderly defendants, contextual information is bound to impact jurors' individual and collective evaluation of defendant credibility.

Because the courtroom environment violates the expectations of daily codes of interaction, jurors' evaluative judgments regarding the credibility of others—witnesses and defendants—are disadvantaged. Some research has concluded that in such a foreign environment, new players benefit by "disregard[ing] witnesses' faces if they want to maximize their ability to detect deception, or just wear a blindfold and listen closely" (Saks, 1997, p. 12).

Jurors are aroused when expectancies are violated and make evaluative judgments about the credibility of those presenting messages. The regular players in the context recognize that "[a]s advocates, our nonverbal communications in the courtroom convey powerful messages whether we like it or not. So we must devote some of the same care that we put into presenting the law into presenting ourselves" (Milford, 2001, p. 4).

In sum, jurors as non-repeat players are not accustomed to the courtroom environment. More than this, the courtroom is a place where expectations for the normal flow of interaction are disturbed. Conversation is not on equal terms—one person (lawyer) frames the issues that the other (witness) answers within the frames of reference set by the questioner. Jurors operate in a tight context where their social expectancies are violated. They are required to reach judgments about the credibility and demeanor of witnesses and defendant, while having to negotiate evaluations of each other primarily during the deliberation phase. The courtroom setting emphasizes consistency and clarity. In daily life, words are not always consistent with behavior and lucid in ways that remove doubt about meaning and intent.

COURTROOM EXPECTANCY VIOLATIONS AND PERCEIVED CREDIBILITY

To this point, we have suggested that there is communication distortion, by design, in the courtroom environment. Moreover, the sense of discomfort in nonprofessional players is exaggerated with heightened states of arousal concerning violations of contextual expectancy. A witness who is inarticulate and confused likely is twisted into calamity by the activities of the lawyers (Duck, 1998). Furthermore, many people are made uncomfortable by wearing formal clothes and some unpracticed at sitting at a desk or on a chair for several hours on end.

We suspect, however, that a witness's communicative agitation (verbal and nonverbal) leads jurors to read discomfort about the testimony offered. This cycle, in turn, creates further disconcert in the behavior of the unpracticed performer (witness) that lead jurors to question the credibility of the testimony. Research on determinations of credibility in the courtroom illustrates this chain of events (Blumenthal, 1993; Kassin, 2002; Rand, 2000), but generally has not considered fully violations of contextual expectations.

How does a juror determine witness credibility when observing a staged interview in which questions are controlled by regular players? Determining credibility (truthfulness) of individuals outside of context is difficult. In terms of nonverbal interpretation, six general emotional expressions have been identified across context and culture: happiness, anger, disgust, sadness, surprise, and fear (Ekman, 2001; Ekman & Friesen, 1969; Fiedler & Schenck, 2001; Izard, 1971; Knapp & Hall, 2002).

The determination of credibility (conversely deception) often is read in the facial expression of fear. One is said to "leak" clues to deception when the "fear of getting caught" is displayed on the face and interpreted as an indicator of guilt. However, in the absence of an acute conscious or obvious sense of guilt about lying, using NVC alone to determine witness credibility is difficult (Ben-Shakhar & Furedy, 1990; Hollien, Geison, & Hicks, 1987; http://antipolygraph.org).

When a non-regular player is placed in a context with high stakes such as in the courtroom, the fear of the foreign context confounds the perceiver's (a juror's) evaluations. Consistency of behavior is expected even in foreign environments, not only between the outward manifestations and a person's inner orientations or feelings, but also between intrapersonal states of the individual, such as love and horror.

Thus, spouses are supposed to indicate horror at learning that their partner has died and lack of such emotion is suspicious, as for example in the case of William Wallace in England in the 1930s, on whom suspicion fell *because* he showed no emotion when informed that his wife had been murdered. This fact figured largely in the prosecution's argument that such a response would be appropriate only in someone who already knew she was dead. The defense case that Wallace was a "practicing stoic," for whom the display of emotion was anathema, did not sway the jury, but did influence the Appeals Court who overturned his conviction.

Issues of credibility further are expressed and perceived as communicative consistency or inconsistency (Blanck & Rosenthal, 1992). Behavior is examined closely when NVC is inconsistent with the perceiver's expectations, and inconsistent with the baseline of verbal (or other nonverbal) behavior established by the defendant or the witness during the entire course of a trial (Blanck, 1993). Awareness is heightened when a defendant or witness acts unusually from her baseline, not necessarily because of guilt but perhaps because of a rushed lunch during trial recess.

Internal behavioral consistency has been examined also through the physiological perspective relative to the polygraph. Analysis of the physiological aspects of the polygraph suggest that research is not robust to justify adequate establishment of baseline behavior to compare slices of behavioral response to conclusively determine truth telling or the practicing of deception (Ben-Shakhar & Furedy, 1990; Dollins, Cestaro, & Pettit, 1998; Elaad, 2003; Holden, 2001; Lykken, 1981; *The polygraph and lie detection*, 2003). These and other conclusions have supported the general inadmissibility of polygraph results in court. However, the average person on the street is required to serve on a jury and make such determinations about deception and credibility based on their own baseline comprehension of an environment out of usual context.

The courtroom, however, is not an easy venue to explore the expectancy range of a target person's behaviors and communicative styles. In the courtroom, the brevity of the encounters is an integral component of the imposition of generalized contextual expectations. The fact that a witness is habitually cool and aloof alone will not be the basis for making judgments about the meaning of observed coolness and aloofness when presenting testimony in the case. Rather, the perceived aloofness likely is judged as meaningful relative to the standard of the population as a whole, and the credibility or value of the testimony rests on that generalized assessment, not on a particularized one.

Moreover, NVCs are not the only basis for the credibility attribution. Attorneys review and take evidence (e.g., depositions, documents, emails, and so on) from witnesses and defendants months before trial with the sole strategy of later "catching" those same individuals in apparent inconsistencies of communication when testifying during the trial. When individuals testifying in court make statements different from previous ones, the popular question becomes whether the witness was "lying" earlier or now during the examination at the trial. More seriously, increasingly attorneys videotape deposition testimony so that witness NVC may be compared and scrutinized at trial.

TOWARD A UNIFIED UNDERSTANDING OF COMMUNICATION IN THE COURTROOM

Four Core Themes For Researchers

This chapter has identified four core themes toward the development of a unified understanding of communication in the courtroom.

First, by examining the courtroom dynamic as a "tight" social context with a unique set of expectancies, we attempted to expand the interpretative power of NVC in the courtroom.

Second, by differentiating the prescribed roles of courtroom actors, we illustrated the relativity of NVC and the importance of contextual forces in interpretation. This observation has obvious implications for assessment of trial judges' NVC, as distinct from lay witnesses' NVC.

Third, by attending to jurors' expectancies about NVC in context, we provide enhanced perspective on forces related to juror deliberations.

And, fourth, by stressing the contextual interpretation of courtroom NVC, future researchers and practitioners may attend with increasing frequency to the social nature of judgments about NVC in the courtroom, rather than primarily to micro aspects of the individual cognitive process.

We next address these issues in more detail.

We have described how social context, exemplified by the courtroom illustration in this chapter, profoundly influences interpersonal verbal and nonverbal communication styles, requirements and expectancies. Contextual, expectancy and communicative factors combine to provide meaning to the courtroom experience, and ultimately, influence the outcome. However, we have shown how these forces impact regulars and non-repeat courtroom players differently.

Repeat and novice courtroom players are surrounded by different weightings of their NVC that differentially affect conclusions about credibility. We have emphasized that study of interpersonal communication in a broader social context should include variables such as the actor's placement within the social context, group affiliations, personal and physical appearance, perceived communicative competency, social background, perceived social status, and so on.

The more subtle analysis of the courtroom context also should consider the ways in which novice players (e.g., jurors or witnesses) adapt to aroused expectancy violations of their "normal" everyday experiences. The differences between everyday life norms and courtroom contextual norms must be examined to accurately assess the meaning and role of NVC to trial behavior and outcome.

In addition, it is necessary to identify systematically individual differences in juror abilities to adjust contextual expectations to the courtroom, and hence to assess others' behaviors as a violation of expectancy (e.g., a credibility determination based on a self-disclosure in the courtroom). One practical implication of this idea is that, in choosing jurors, trial lawyers should be cognizant of a juror's ability to transfer or moderate expectancies from everyday life to the courtroom. Thus, jurors' expectancies of everyday life may corrupt their assessment of a defendant's behavior as a "self-fulfilling prophecy" in a way that maximizes suspicion at, rather than explaining the underlying contextually-driven dynamic of, irregular NVC, unless court officers (such as judges and attorneys) stress the need to differentiate by context.

Another byproduct of a more subtle approach to the assessment of NVC in the courtroom is enhanced attention to jurors' individual differences in abilities to recognize the relevance, or irrelevance, of everyday context in making judgments in the courtroom context. In particular, this issue is relevant when, following our argument, the jury deliberation is seen as a *social* process of judgment about normative expectations, and hence a process where relationships between jurors' and their individual assessments of one another affect the outcome.

Moreover, because a juror's skill to evaluate trial performance is a function of an ability to transfer expectancies from everyday life to courtroom situations, these same skills likely affect individual juror and collective group evaluations of defendant and witness credibility. These social processes in jury deliberation certainly are influenced by relationship formation (Duck, 1998) through which jurors mold their communication.

In past studies, many of the factors identified and highlighted in this chapter have not been adequately examined; one important factor being that the deliberative process in a jury is essentially a communicative relational group task and not simply a cognitive, information-processing task (Duck, 1998). Thus, in the course of trials, jurors form real and notional relationships, based on judgments about authority, intelligence, credibility and trustworthiness of their fellow jurors. These relations fill a tight social context in which the evaluations of information and judgments are made during the deliberative process. As in the other judgments, these interpersonal determinations are based on NVC cues and contextual influences.

Future research, therefore, needs to consider how such relational contexts affect the jury's deliberative process. A unified approach to study of courtroom communication suggests that it is important not only to evaluate individual jurors' weightings of expectancy violations, but also the ways in which they communicate their different judgments and discuss standards of assessment with the other jurors. This, of course, is the essence of the relational process.

Searcy has articulated one example of such a relational process in Social Problematic Integration Theory (SPIT; Searcy, 2003). SPIT theorizes that messages are received and integrated in groups through socially-based working metaphors that are adopted for group operation and context. Groups such as families operate in a "team" metaphor and pull together during crisis. Likewise, organizations such as businesses operate within a "corporate" metaphor and deliberate by cutting to the profit margin.

Future study may examine how social group metaphors and context position the jury to resolve the case at hand by adopting particular modes of relational attitudes in their deliberations, as well as the impact of NVC and contextual expectancies on courtroom dynamics. Study of group processes of integration and deliberation likewise may be helpful in understanding individual differences in NVC judgments in the courtroom.

The social and communicative factors we have described in this chapter certainly have differing degrees of importance or "weighting" to social interaction; and they are subject to the perceiver's evaluation of importance placed on them, as well as factors subject to direct relevance in the event being questioned. In Fig. 3.1 we identify many of such factors useful for future study.

In a jury deliberation, by way of illustration, the factors identified in Fig. 3.1 register in the jurors' minds before an evaluation occurs. The jury delib-

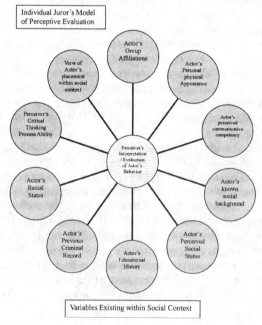

FIG. 3.1

eration that follows is a collective process to reach consensus on decision about guilt or liability, and then perhaps sentencing or monetary award. These deliberations are regarded as based on the rational processing of information—for examples, note the explications of functional theory (Hirokawa, 1983; Hirokawa & Rost, 1992; Hirokawa, DeGooyer, & Valde, 2000), or the Vigilant Problem Solving model (Janis, 1989)—as most social psychological models of decision-making are cognitively-based. Nevertheless, other social contextual features affect the jury deliberation process, such as the Constraints model articulated by Janis (1989).

Because observers (and video cameras) are not allowed in the jury deliberation room as common practice, an understanding of the social processes occurring behind the closed doors is as important as a check on trial fairness, juror training and satisfaction with the process, and so on (in addition to the legally proscribed appeals process). However, in the absence of randomized "trial" experimentation (which is not possible), it is difficult for researchers to ascribe causal relationships among the factors we have identified. Social science researchers and others will need to continue the examination of context and NVC in the courtroom, and their impact on "the appearance of" justice and on actual justice. The possible ramifications of not conducting such analyses are too dire to be overlooked.

Four Implications For Practitioners

There are other practical implications of our analysis here worth noting. First, expert analysis of NVC in the courtroom must be differentiated such that cues are interpreted contextually and not absolutely: Those behaviors that indicate bias (or lack of credibility) in a witness may not indicate bias in a trial judge.

Second, trial lawyers preparing a witness to testify would be well served to explain the contextual tightness of the courtroom, particularly in regard to its impact on verbal and nonverbal behavior.

Third, trial judges charging their juries should be aware of their contextual expectancies, and alert juries to their effects and to their differences from everyday life expectancies.

Fourth, those experts who study (and try to predict) the jury deliberation process may be advised to pay increased attention to evaluation of contextual violations and their importance to assessment of the "appropriateness" of NVC in the courtroom.

CLOSING

To the extent that social science research is helpful, it may play an active role in understanding the force of context in the courtroom, as we have outlined in this chapter. Whether instructing a jury or monitoring a lawyer who is examining a witness, our system of justice requires that trial judges eliminate reasonably contextual and actual bias so as to offer the parties the appearance of a fair hearing.

Social scientists have a remarkable opportunity to help ensure that trial fairness occurs, in large part by identifying ways to selectively remove bias (to the extent possible) through scientifically applied methods of voir dire and jury selection (Kressel & Kressel, 2002), witness preparation (Boccaccini, 2002), and juror deliberation processes (Pritchard & Keenan, 2002; Saks, 1997; Williams, 1997). Such uses of social science in law can help to ensure actual and perceived fairness in our system of justice.

REFERENCES

Administrative Office of Courts. (2002, July 8). *Judicial Rules and Procedures: Criminal Rule 2.* Retrieved March 1, 2003 from http://www.alacourt.org/Publications/Rules/Criminal/rule09-2.htm

Ambady, N., Bernieri, F. I., & Richeson, L. A. (2000). Towards a histology of social behavior: Judgmental accuracy from thin slices of the behavioral stream. In M. P. Zanna (Ed.), *Advances in Experimental Social Psychology* (pp. 201–272). Boston: Academic Press.

Ambady, N., Hallahan, M., & Conner, B. (1999). Accuracy of judgments of sexual orientation from thin slices of behavior. *Journal of Personality and Social Psychology, 77,* 538–547.

Ambady, N., Hallahan, M., & Rosenthal, R. (1995). On judging and being judged accurately in zero acquaintance situations. *Journal of Personality and Social Psychology, 69,* 518–529.

Ambady, N., & Rosenthal, R. (1992). Thin slices of behavior as predictors of interpersonal consequences: A meta-analysis. *Psychological Bulletin, 11,* 256–274.

Argyle, M. (1967). *The psychology of interpersonal behaviour.* Harmondsworth, UK: Penguin Books.

Ben-Shakhar, G., & Furedy, J. J. (1990). *Theories and applications in the detection of deception: A psychophysiological and international perspective.* New York: Springer-Verlag.

Blanck, P. (1991). What empirical research tells us: Studying judges' and juries' behavior. *American University Law Review, Winter,* 2–24.

Blanck, P. D. (1993). Calibrating the scales of justice: Studying judges' behavior in bench trials. *Indiana Law Journal, 68*(4), 1119–1198.

Blanck, P. D., & Rosenthal, R. (1992). Nonverbal behavior in the courtroom. In R. Feldman (Ed.), *Applications of nonverbal behavioral theories and research* (pp. 89–115). Hillsdale, NJ: Lawrence Erlbaum Associates.

Blanck, P. D., Rosenthal, R., & Cordell, L. H. (1985). The appearance of justice: Judges' verbal and nonverbal behavior in criminal jury trials. *Stanford Law Review, 38*(1), 89–164.

Blumenthal, J. A. (1993). A wipe of the hands, a lick of the lips: The validity of demeanor evidence in assessing witness credibility. *Nebraska Law Review, 72,* 2–44.

Boccaccini, M. T. (2002). What do we really know about witness preparation? *Behavioral sciences and the law, 20*(1–2), 161–189.

Bond, C. F., Jr., Omar, A., Pitre, U., Lashley, B. R., Skaggs, L. M., & Kirk, C. T. (1992). Fishy-looking liars: Deception judgment from expectancy violation. *Journal of Personality and Social Psychology, 63*(6), 969–977.

Burgoon, J. K. (1983). Nonverbal violations of expectations. In J. Wiemann & R. P. Harrison (Eds.) *Nonverbal Interaction* (pp. 77–111). Beverly Hills, CA: Sage Publications.

Burgoon, J. K., & Buller, D. B. (1994). Interpersonal deception: III. Effects of deceit on perceived communication and nonverbal behavior dynamics. *Journal of Nonverbal Behavior, 18*(2), 155–184.

Burgoon, J. K., Buller, D. B., Ebesu, A., & Rockwell, P. (1994). Interpersonal deception: V. Accuracy in deception detection. *Communication Monographs, 61*, 303–325.

Burgoon, J. K., & Jones, S. B. (1976). Toward a theory of personal space expectations and their violations. *Human Communication Research, 2*, 131–146.

Burgoon, J. K., LePoire, B. A., & Rosenthal, R. (1995). Effects of preinteraction expectancies and target communication on perceiver reciprocity and compensation in dyadic interaction. *Journal of Experimental Psychology, 31*, 287–321.

Burgoon, J. K., Stern, L. A., & Dillman, L. (1995). *Interpersonal adaptation: Dyadic interaction patterns*. New York: Cambridge University Press.

Caughfield, L. E. (2001). Credibility. *Litigation, 27*(4), 2–8.

Chang, Y. (2003). *Who speaks next? Discourse Structure as persuasion in Chinese criminal courtrooms*. Paper presented at the annual conference of the National Communication Association. Miami Beach, Florida, November.

Dindia, K. (2000). Self-disclosure, identity, and relationship development: A dialectical perspective. In K. Dindia & S. Duck (Eds.), *Communication and personal relationships* (pp. 147–162). New York: John Wiley & Sons, Ltd.

Dindia, K., & Fitzpatrick, M. A. (1989). *Self-disclosure in spouse and stranger dyads: A social relations analysis*. San Francisco: International Communication Association.

Dollins, A. B., Cestaro, V. L., & Pettit, D. J. (1998). Efficacy of repeated psychophysiological detection of deception testing. *Journal of Forensic Science, 43*(5), 1016–1023.

Duck, S. W. (1998). *Human relationships* (3rd ed.). London: SAGE Publications Ltd.

Duck, S. W. (2003). *A new model of interpersonal influence in juries (and trials)* [SCIPI]. Paper presented to the Annual Convention of American Society of Trial Consultants, Reno, NV, June.

Duck, S. W., & VanderVoort, L. A. (2002). Scarlet letters and whited sepulchers: The social marking of relationships as "inappropriate." In R. Goodwin & D. Cramer (Eds.), *Inappropriate relationships: The unconventional, the disapproved, and the forbidden* (pp. 3–24). Mahwah, NJ: Lawrence Erlbaum Associates.

Ekman, P. (2001). *Telling lies: Clues to deceit in the marketplace, politics, and marriage*. New York: W. W. Norton and Company.

Ekman, P., & Friesen, W. V. (1969). The repertoire of nonverbal behavior: Categories, origins, usage, and coding. *Semiotica, 1*, 49–98.

Elaad, E. (2003). Is the inference rule of the "control question polygraph technique" plausible? *Psychology, Crime & Law, 9*(1), 37–47.

Fiedler, K., & Schenck, W. (2001). Spontaneous inferences from pictorially presented behaviors. *Personality and Social Psychology Bulletin, 27*(11), 1533–1546.

Galvin, K. M., Bylund, C. L., & Brommel, B. J. (2004). *Family communication: Cohesion and change* (6th ed.). Allyn & Bacon/ Longman, Inc.

Hickson, M., Stacks, D. W., & Moore, N. J. (2003). *Nonverbal communication: Studies and applications*. Los Angeles, CA: Roxbury.

Hirokawa, R. (1983). Group communication and problem-solving effectiveness II: An exploratory investigation of procedural functions. *Western Journal of Speech Communication, 47*(Winter), 59–74.

Hirokawa, R., & Rost, K. M. (1992). Effective group decision making in organizations: Field test of the vigilant interaction theory. *Management Communication Quarterly, 5*(3), 267–288.

Hirokawa, R. Y., DeGooyer, D. H., & Valde, K. (2000). Using narratives to study task group effectiveness. *Small Group Research, 31*(5), 573–591.

Holden, C. (2001, 9 February). Polygraph Screening: Panel seeks truth in lie detector debate. *Science, 291*, 967.

Hollien, H., Geison, L., & Hicks, J. W., Jr. (1987). Voice stress evaluators and lie detection. *Journal of Forensic Sciences, 32*(2), 405–418.

Izard, C. E. (1971). *The face of emotion*. New York: Appleton-Century-Crofts.

Janis, I. L. (1989). *Crucial decisions: Leadership in policymaking and crisis management*. New York: The Free Press.

Jourard, S. M. (1971). *The Transparent Self* (rev. ed.). New York: Van Nostrand Reinhold.

Juan Rodriguez Chavez v. Janie Cockrell, Director, Texas Department of Criminal Justice, Institutional Division, United States Court of Appeals: Fifth Circuit (2002).

Kassin, S. M. (2002). Human judges of truth, deception, and credibility: Confident but erroneous. *Cardozo Law Review, 23*(Feb), 2–7.

Keeley, M., & Hart, A. (1994). Nonverbal behavior in dyadic interaction. In S. W. Duck (Ed.), *Dynamics of relationships [Understanding relationships 4]* (pp. 135–162). Thousand Oaks: SAGE.

Knapp, M., & Hall, J. (2002). *Nonverbal communication in human interaction* (5th ed.). London: Wadsworth.

Kressel, N. J., & Kressel, D. F. (2002). *Stack and sway: The new science of jury consulting*. Boulder, CO: Westview Press.

Lefkowitz, M., Blake, R. R., & Mouton, J. S. (1955). Status factors in pedestrian violations of traffic signals. *Journal of Abnormal and Social Psychology, 51*, 704–706.

Lykken, D. T. (1981). *A tremor in the blood: Uses and abuses of the lie detector*. New York: McGraw-Hill Book Company.

Milford, L. S. (2001). Nonverbal communication. *Litigation, 27*(4), 2–9.

Orne, M. (1962). On the social psychology of the psychological experiment: With particular reference to demand characteristics and their implications. *American Psychologist, 17*, 776–783.

The polygraph and lie detection. (2003). Washington, DC: National Research Council. Committee to review the scientific evidence on the polygraph. Division of behavioral and social sciences and education. The National Academies Press. Retrieved December 1, 2002 from http://antipolygraph.org

Pritchard, M. E., & Keenan, J. M. (2002). Does jury deliberation really improve jurors' memories? *Applied Cognitive Psychology, 16*(5), 589–601.

Rand, J. W. (2000). The demeanor gap: Race, lie detection, and the jury. *Connecticut Law Review*, *33*, 2–61.

Rosenthal, R. (2002). Covert communication in classrooms, clinics, courtrooms, and cubicles. *American Psychologist, 57*(11), 839–849.

Saks, M. J. (1997). What do jury experiments tell us about how juries (should) make decisions? *Southern California Interdisciplinary Law Journal, Fall*, 1–38.

Searcy, M. A. (2003). *Social problematic integration theory (the spit model): Taking the cognitive theory of problematic integration into close family communication* (paper presentation). Omaha, NE: Central States Communication Association.

Spencer, E. E. (1994). Transforming relationships through ordinary talk. In S. W. Duck (Ed.), *Understanding relationship processes 4: Dynamics of relationships*, (pp. 58–85). Newbury Park: SAGE.

VanderVoort, L. A., & Duck, S. W. (2004). In appropriate relationships and out of them: The social paradoxes of normative and non-normative relational forms. Forthcoming in G. A. Allan, J. Duncombe, K. Harrison, & D. Marsden (Eds.), *The State of Affairs*. Mahwah, NJ: Lawrence Erlbaum Associates.

Williams, S. M. (1997). *Narrative rationality in jury decision-making*. Unpublished Dissertation, University of Iowa, Iowa City.

❧ 4 ❧

Police Use of Nonverbal Behavior as Indicators of Deception

Aldert Vrij*
Samantha Mann
University of Portsmouth

People rely on various sources of information when they form impressions about others. They could pay attention to various characteristics of the target person, such as gender (Hall & Carter, 1999; Stangor, Lynch, Changming, & Glass, 1992), age (Hargie & Tourish, 1999; Hummert, 1999), race (Brown, 1995; Ruby & Brigham, 1996), dialect (Giles & Johnson, 1986; Giles & Powesland, 1975; Street & Hopper, 1982), dress (Vrij, 1993), clothing (Frank & Gilovich, 1988; Vrij, 1997), and facial appearance (Bull & Rumsey, 1988). They also could examine what people actually say (speech content, Krauss & Chiu, 1998; Steller & Köhnken, 1989) or observe their behavior (DePaulo & Friedman, 1998). In this article we primarily focus on the impact of nonverbal communication on impression formation. Nonverbal behavior does not only include body language, such as movements people make, smiling, gaze behavior, etc., but also vocal characteristics, such as speech rate, speech pauses, uhms and ers, pitch of voice, etc. In addition, we primarily focus on a specific area within impression formation, which is the judgment about whether or not someone is lying (we will use the words deception and lying interchangeably). As Horvath, Jayne and Buckley (1994) pointed out, making judgements about the veracity of statements is an important aspect of police work.

*Correspondence should be addressed to: Aldert Vrij, University of Portsmouth, Psychology Department, King Henry Building, King Henry 1 Street, Portsmouth, PO1 2DY, United Kingdom or via email: aldert.vrij@port.ac.uk . Our studies concerning real life police interviews which are discussed in this article (Mann, Vrij, & Bull, 2002, in press) were sponsored by the Economic and Social Research Council (Grant R00429734727).

We first address the question of whether people pay more attention to speech content or nonverbal communication when they form impressions of others. We do not consider the other characteristics (age, gender, etc.) as researchers typically just focus on speech content and nonverbal communication when addressing this issue. This does not mean that the other characteristics do not play a role in impression formation. On the contrary, in our research, for example, conducted in the Netherlands (Vrij, 1993), we found that Dutch police detectives take into account the way people are dressed when making veracity judgments. They judged people as more suspicious when they were untidily dressed. We will see that the impact of nonverbal communication and speech content on impression formation is situation dependent, and that in some circumstances police officers primarily rely upon nonverbal displays. Reasons for this will be discussed.

Given the fact that nonverbal behavior plays a role in determining whether someone is lying or not, we then move on to the question of how suspects and people in general actually behave when they are lying. This section shows that no single cue to deception, such as Pinocchio's growing nose, exists, but that some behaviors are more indicative than others.

In the third section of this article we discuss how police officers and people in general think liars behave. We will see that police officers think that several behaviors are associated with deception, however, many of those beliefs are in fact nondiagnostic. An important reason why police officers hold incorrect beliefs will be discussed, as well as the negative consequences that may arise from these incorrect views. We will show that certain groups of people are in a disadvantageous position, and readily make a suspicious impression on police officers because they naturally show the behavioral patterns police officers typically think liars display.

The fourth section of this article answers the question of how good police officers are at detecting truths and lies. Unsurprisingly, given the fact that they hold incorrect views about how liars behave, this section reveals that errors in veracity judgments are often made. However, there are individual differences and some police officers seem to be better lie detectors than others. We will also discuss whether any relationship exists between accuracy in detecting truths and lies and the cues police officers say they pay attention to while attempting to detect these truths and lies. Given the fact that lie detectors are often inaccurate, we discuss in the fifth, and final, section some thoughts regarding possibilities for future research in improving people's ability to detect deceit.

RELATIVE IMPACT OF SPEECH CONTENT AND NONVERBAL COMMUNICATION ON IMPRESSION FORMATION

Mehrabian and his colleagues (Mehrabian, 1972; Mehrabian & Ferris, 1967; Mehrabian & Wiener, 1967) were among the first researchers to examine the relative impact of speech content and nonverbal communication on impression formation. The experiments were ingenious. A target person expressed an opinion in different ways and participants were asked to give their impressions about what that person's true opinion actually was. Sometimes the speech content and nonverbal communication of that target person were consistent (both positive, both neutral, or both negative), and sometimes inconsistent (speech content was positive, nonverbal communication was negative, etc.). On the basis of a series of experiments, Mehrabian concluded that nonverbal communication had a substantially larger impact on forming impressions of others than speech content.

However, the relative impact of speech content and nonverbal communication depends on the situation. For example, the knowledge of the lie detector will influence how that person will interpret a situation. In one real life case (*The Independent*, Friday 20 July 2001, p. 3) Jeffrey Archer, a British politician, asked three journalists to leave his hotel room during a political party conference while he took a call from the Prime Minister. Another politician who saw the three journalists pacing up and down the corridor asked them what they were doing. He immediately realized that Archer had lied to the journalists and could not be speaking to the Prime Minister on the phone, because he knew that the Prime Minister was sitting on the conference platform at that very moment. In another real life case (Mann, Vrij, & Bull, 2002), police officers asked a man who was suspected of murder about his whereabouts on a certain afternoon. The man explained in detail that he visited a market in a village near his home. The police detectives knew that this was a lie because, unknown to the suspect, the market had been cancelled on that particular day. In both examples by paying attention to the speech content the lie detectors compared what was known with what the target person said, and discovered that the person was lying. Also, when police officers hear different statements from the same person about a topic, or different statements from different people about a topic, they primarily tend to focus on speech content, checking for consistency between the different statements (Granhag & Strömwall, 1999, 2000, 2001a, b; Strömwall, Granhag, & Jonsson, 2003). Hence, police officers believe that there is a relationship between consistency and veracity (Akehurst, Köhnken, Bull, & Vrij, 1996; Granhag & Strömwall, 1999; Greuel, 1992; Strömwall & Granhag, 2003). More specifically, they believe that consistent statements are likely to be truthful and inconsistent statements are likely to be deceptive. However, the limited research in this area has shown that there is no such link between consistency and veracity, or at least, if there is a link, it is more likely to be in the opposite direction. Granhag, Strömwall and Reiman (2002) found that lying pairs (i.e., two people lying in collusion) were more consistent than truth telling pairs, and that single liars and single truth tellers were equally consistent over time.[1]

There is evidence that in situations where there is no information to check and only one statement is made, police officers, like the participants in Mehrabian's experiment, primarily pay attention to nonverbal communication when forming an impression (Greuel, 1992; Rozelle & Baxter, 1975; Vrij, Foppes, Volger, & Winkel, 1992; Walkley, 1985; Waltman, 1983). Meissner and Kassin (2002) pointed out that in Florida, Tom Sawyer, believed to be innocent but accused of sexual assault and murder, became a prime suspect because he appeared embarrassed and his face flushed during an initial interview (see Ofshe, 1989, for a detailed description of the Tom Sawyer case). According to Kaufmann, Drevland, Wessel, Overskeid, and Magnussen (2003), judicial decisions are sometimes based on nonverbal communication, even when available evidence points in the other direction. They describe a Norwegian court trial in which (p. 2) "although the circumstantial evidence of guilt was strong, the defendant (a financial adviser) was acquitted partly because ... his nonverbal behavior was confident without evasive eye movements of any sort."

There are several reasons why in these circumstances people rely so much on nonverbal behavior. First, it might be more revealing than speech (DePaulo & Kirkendol, 1989; Vrij, 2000a). There are automatic links between strongly felt emotions and certain behaviors (Ekman, 1985), whereas there are no such links between emotions and speech content. Anger, for example, results in several cues, including narrowing of the lips. This might well give a lie away if an angry person denies being angry. Also, we are more practiced in using words than in using behavior (because we exchange information predominantly via words), and this practice makes perfect. The fact that words are more important than nonverbal behavior in the exchange of information makes people also more aware of what they are saying than of how they are behaving. Suspects during a police interview will probably know and remember most of what they have said. However, it will be more difficult for them to indicate exactly how they behaved, that is, which hand movements they made, what their voice tone was like, etc. Being aware of one's own behavior is essential when effectively controlling behavior. This requires not only being aware of one's behavior when trying to control it but also knowing the behavior one normally exhibits. Finally, although people can refrain from speech, they can't be silent nonverbally. Suppose a suspect realizes during his police interview that the police know more that he thought they did about his involvement in the crime. This probably implies that he will have to give a different story from that which he had planned to tell. Verbally he can afford a little rest to think of an appropriate response in this awkward situation. Nonverbally, however, there is no possibility of taking a rest. He will display behavior throughout the entire interview, even when he remains silent, and the police officers can observe and interpret this behavior.

Second, sometimes there is little speech content to rely upon because the person just says a few words or just a couple of sentences. In such situations an observer has almost no other choice than to examine someone's behavior.

Third, people may not know which verbal cues to pay attention to even when the target person speaks substantially. In our opinion, speech content can reveal a deception if only observers knew what to pay attention to. Our own research has consistently shown that more accurate truth/lie decisions can be made when both speech content and nonverbal behavior are taken into account instead of just speech content or just nonverbal communication (Vrij, Edward, Roberts, & Bull, 2000; Vrij, Akehurst, Soukara, & Bull, 2003; Vrij & Mann, in press). Also, Porter and his colleagues pointed out that verbal cues have clear potential in deception detection (Porter & Yuille, 1995, 1996; Porter, Yuille, & Birt, 2001; Porter, Yuille, & Lehman, 1999). See Vrij (2003) for a recent review of verbal indicators of deceit.[2]

The Behavior of Liars

DePaulo, Lindsay, Malone, Muhlenbruck, Charlton, and Cooper (2003) and Vrij (2000a) recently reviewed over 100 scientific studies regarding nonverbal indicators of deceit. Perhaps the main finding was that no single behavioral response was uniquely related to deception. In other words, a straightforward giveaway cue, similar to Pinocchio's growing nose, does not exist. However, the reviews also demonstrated that some behaviors are more likely to occur during deception than others, perhaps depending on three processes that a liar may experience: emotion, content complexity, and attempted behavioral control (DePaulo, Stone, & Lassiter, 1985; Vrij, 2000a; Zuckerman, DePaulo, & Rosenthal, 1981).[3, 4] The mere fact that a person is lying will not result in any particular behavior, but liars might be nervous (emotional), might have to think hard to come up with a plausible and convincing answer (content complexity), or might try to control their behavior in order to give a credible impression (attempted behavioral control). The six behaviours, which, according to the literature reviews, are to some extent associated with deception, can all be explained with these processes. The reviews revealed that liars tend to speak with a *higher pitched voice* which might be the result of arousal experienced by liars (Ekman, Friesen, & Scherer, 1976). However, differences in pitch between liars and truth tellers are usually very small and therefore only detectable with sophisticated equipment.[5] Also, sometimes liars' *voices sound more tense* than truth tellers' voices, another result of arousal. The results concerning *speech errors* (word and/or sentence repetition, sentence change, sentence incompletions, slips of the tongue, and so on) and *speech hesitations* (use of speech fillers such as 'ah', 'um', 'er' and so on) show a conflicting pattern. In most studies an increase in such errors (particularly word and phrase repetitions) and hesitations have been found during deception. This increase might have been the result of liars having to think hard about their answer. Alternatively, the increase might be the result of nervousness. In some studies, however, a decrease in speech errors and speech hesitations occurred. There is some evidence that variations of lie complexity are responsible for these conflicting findings (Vrij & Heaven, 1999). Lies that are difficult to tell result in an increase in speech errors and speech hesitations (in line with the content complexity approach), whereas lies that are easy to tell result in a decrease in speech hesitations and speech errors (in line with the attempted control approach).

Liars tend to make *fewer illustrators* (hand and arm movements designed to modify and/or supplement what is being said verbally) and *fewer hand and finger movements* (non-functional movements of hands and fingers without moving the arms) than truth tellers. The decrease in these movements might be the result of lie complexity. Cognitive load results in a neglect of body language, reducing overall animation (Ekman & Friesen, 1972). Ask people what they ate three days ago, and observe their behavior while they try to remember. Most people will sit still while thinking about the answer. The decrease in movements might also be the result of an attempt to control behavior. Liars may believe that movements will give their lies away, and will therefore move very deliberately and tend to avoid any movements which are not strictly essential. This may result in an unusual degree of rigidity and inhibition (i.e., an overcompensation of behavior), because people normally make movements which are not essential (DePaulo & Kirkendol, 1989). Finally, the decrease in movements might be the result of lack of emotional involvement. In certain situations some degree of emotional involvement is expected which is difficult to pretend if the person actually does not feel that emotion. Thus, a mother who punishes her child for wrongdoing might not look sincere enough if she, in fact, was amused by the child's actions; and a person who falsely claims that he is going on a business trip may not show enough interest or enthusiasm when he discusses the business deal he is going to make.[6]

The literature reviews revealed that liars do not seem to show clear signs of nervousness, such as gaze aversion and fidgeting. This is perhaps surprising because, as we will see in the next section, at least in white Western cultures, there is a strong stereotypical belief amongst observers, including professional lie catchers, that liars look away and make grooming gestures (Akehurst et al., 1996; Vrij & Semin, 1996). However, perhaps the absence of signs of nervousness is nothing more than an artifact. Deception research has almost exclusively been conducted in university laboratories where participants (mostly college students) tell the truth or lie for the sake of the experiment. Perhaps in these laboratory studies the stakes (negative consequences of getting caught and positive consequences of getting away with the lie) are not high enough for the liar to elicit clear cues to deception (Miller & Stiff, 1993).

In order to raise the stakes in laboratory experiments, participants have been offered money if their lies are believed by observers (Vrij, 1995). In other studies, participants are told that they will be observed by a peer who will judge their sincerity (DePaulo, Stone, & Lassiter, 1985b). In an attempt to raise the stakes even further, participants in Frank and Ekman's (1997) study were given the opportunity to "steal" US$50. If they could convince the interviewer that they had not taken the money, they could keep all of it. If they took the money and the interviewer judged them as lying, they had to give the US$50 back and also lost their US$10 per hour participation fee. Moreover, some participants faced an additional punishment if they were found to be lying. They were told that they would have to sit on a cold, metal chair inside a cramped, darkened room labeled ominously XXX, where they would have to endure anything from 10 to 40 randomly sequenced 110-decibel starting blasts of white noise over the course of one hour.

A study like this should raise ethical concerns. Yet even despite the ethical issue, one might argue that the stakes in such a study are still not comparable with the stakes in some real life situations, such as during police interviews. Laboratory studies are probably not suitable for examining the responses in high-stake situations as raising the stakes to a comparable extent is not usually possible for ethical reasons. Therefore, examining how liars behave in high-stake real life situations is highly desirable (Riggio, 1994). This has proven to be difficult and, as a result, behavioral examinations of real life high-stake situations are virtually non-existent. Researchers face three problems in particular.

First, it is difficult to obtain appropriate video footage. For example, it is only relatively recently that interviews with suspects have been videotaped in a few constabularies in England and Wales, and even when they are videotaped, researchers are rarely given permission to analyze those videotaped interviews.

Second, it is often difficult in real life cases to establish the so-called *ground truth*, that is, to obtain conclusive evidence that the person is lying or telling the truth. For example, when former U.S. President Bill Clinton testified before the Grand Jury on August 17, 1998, about his alleged sexual affair with Monica Lewinsky, did he lie during that interview? And if so, exactly when during that interview? We simply don't know.

Third, to establish whether someone is lying, a useful method might be to compare the response under investigation with a response the lie detector knows to be truthful. However, the two situations (situation under investigation and responses while telling the truth) should be *comparable*. Take as an example Clinton during his testimony before the Grand Jury in the Monica Lewinsky case. Betty Currie (who was Clinton's personal secretary) had gone to Monica Lewinsky's home to collect the presents she had received from Clinton. During the testimony Clinton was asked several times at different times during the interview whether or not he instructed Betty Currie to do this. When addressing this issue, Clinton displayed a remarkable pattern of behavior that he didn't show in any other part of the interview. For example, his posture became rigid, he sat very still and looked straight into the camera (Vrij, 1998, 2002). Why did he do that? Because he was lying? Or did this particular question trigger a specific behavioral response? This latter explanation cannot be ruled out.

Davis and Hadiks (1995) analyzed the behavior of Iraq's President Saddam Hussein when he was interviewed by the journalist Peter Arnett during the Gulf War (1991). The interview was broadcast on CNN. They found that when discussing Israel, Hussein made specific movements with his left forearm. This behavioral pattern only emerged when he was discussing Israel and Zionism. In other words, specific situations sometimes result in specific behaviors. Researchers (and lie detectors) should be aware of this and should compare situations which are similar to avoid comparing apples with oranges. Unfortunately, during police interviews, apple-orange comparisons are sometimes made (Moston & Engelberg, 1993). In those interviews, suspects' behaviors during smalltalk conversations at the beginning of the interview are compared with their behavior during the actual interrogation. Although police officers are advised to establish comparable truths in this way (Inbau, Reid, & Buckley, 1986; Inbau, Reid, Buckley, & Jayne, 2001), this is an inaccurate comparison. Smalltalk and the actual investigation are different situations. Not surprisingly, both guilty and innocent people tend to show different behaviors during smalltalk and the actual interview (Vrij, 1995). Researchers make the same mistake too. In a rare example of a real life high stake deception study, Hirsch and Wolf (2001) observed 23 nonverbal and verbal cues displayed by Clinton during his Grand Jury Testimony. They examined a 23-minute segment of the videotape and compared this with 11 minutes of the same testimony when he answered basic questions (his name, the attorney's name, etc.). Significant differences were obtained for 19 cues. They also compared the 23-minute segment with 5 minutes of a fund-raising speech to a sympathetic crowd. This time, 20 significant differences emerged. Unfortunately, this study tells us nothing about cues to deception. First, the ground truth in the 23-minute segment has not been established. Second, the comparisons between this 23-fragment and the other fragments are apple-orange comparisons. The problem with comparing the actual interview with basic questions (smalltalk) has already been discussed above. In addition, it is obvious that people show completely different behaviors when they address a crowd in a fund-raising speech than when they are interviewed about an alleged affair. In this respect, it might be more surprising that significant differences were found for only 19 or 20 cues and not for all 23 cues.

Back in 1953, Reid and Arther published a study regarding the behavior of 486 verified guilty and 323 verified innocent people who were suspected of various criminal offences. Their analysis revealed several indicators of deception. However, no details are given about the ground truth in these cases, neither is information provided about the actual interview setting where the observations took place (although the title of their article "Behavior symptoms of lie-detector subjects" gives us some kind of a clue). Horvath (1973) included 100 suspects in his study of which 50 were verified truthful and 50 were verified lying. Suspects' speech content and nonverbal communication were observed during a pre-test interview stage of polygraph examinations. Analyses of their nonverbal behavior revealed several diagnostic cues. Again, no information about the ground truth has been provided.

In a recent study (Mann et al., 2002) we properly addressed these issues. We have examined the behavior displayed by 16 suspects during their police interviews. The suspects were all being interviewed in connection with serious crimes such as murder, rape, and arson. In this study the ground truth was established in all 16 cases and fair comparisons between the suspects' truthful and deceptive behavior were made. Regarding the ground truth, clips of video footage were selected where other sources (reliable witness statements and forensic evidence) provided evidence that the suspect lied or told the truth. In addition, for each suspect, truths and lies were chosen which were as comparable as possible in nature, for example, a suspect who gave a detailed description about how he had assisted in killing a person (truth), later denied any involvement in the crime (lie). Forensic evidence indisputably supported his original version. (See Mann et al., 2002, for further details regarding these ground truth and comparable truth issues.) Table 4.1 shows the results of the study for the total sample ($N = 16$) and for male suspects only ($N = 13$).

As can be seen in Table 4.1, results revealed that the suspects in these high-stake situations did not show clear stereotypical nervous behaviors such as gaze aversion, increased speech disturbances, or increased movements. In fact, they exhibited an increase in pauses and male suspects showed a decrease in hand and arm movements. This is more in agreement with the content complexity and attempted control approaches than with the emotional approach. The strongest evidence that content complexity affected suspects' behavior more than nervousness was the finding regarding eye blinks. Suspects made fewer eye blinks when they lied. Research has shown that nervousness results in an increase in eye blinking (Harrigan & O'Connell, 1996; Tecce, 1992), whereas increased cognitive load results in a decrease in eye blinking (Wallbott & Scherer, 1991).

The apparent predominance of cognitive load processes compared to emotional processes in suspect interviews is perhaps not surprising. Many suspects have had previous regular contact with the police. Therefore, they are probably familiar with police interviews which might decrease their nervousness during that situation. However, suspects in police interviews are often less intelligent than the average person (Gudjonsson, 1992). There is evidence that less intelligent people will have particular difficulty in inventing plausible and convincing stories (Ekman & Frank, 1993).

Table 4.1
Differences Between Truthful and Deceptive Behaviors (Mann, Vrij, & Bull, 2002)

	Total sample (N = 16)	Males only (N = 13)
Gaze aversion	–	–
Eye blinks	<	<
Head movements	–	–
Hand/arm movements	–	<
Pauses	>	>
Speech disturbances[a]	–	–

Notes: < decrease during deception
       > increase during deception
       – no difference
      [a] speech fillers and speech errors combined

How do Police Officers Think Liars Behave?

Which behavioral and auditory cues do people think are associated with deception? In general terms, people find those behaviors that deviate from a normal or expected pattern suspicious (Basket & Freedle, 1974; Bond, Omar, Pitre, Lashley, Skaggs, & Kirk, 1992; Burgoon, Buller, Ebesu, White, & Rockwell, 1996). Thus, eye contact which is either lacking or lasting too long, or pauses which are either too short or too long, etc. all make a suspicious impression. In several studies people were explicitly asked to indicate how they think liars behave (see Vrij, 2000a, for a review of such studies). In some of these studies, conducted in various Western countries such as Sweden, the Netherlands, and the United Kingdom, the same questions have been asked to both laypersons and professional lie catchers such as police officers (Akehurst et al., 1996; Strömwall & Granhag, 2003; Taylor & Vrij, 2000; Vrij & Semin, 1996; Vrij & Taylor, 2003). The answers given by these different groups of respondents were remarkably similar. It appears that there is common belief, at least among Western white people, about how liars behave. Results showed that observers associate deception with a high-pitched voice, many speech hesitations and speech errors, a slow speech rate, a long latency period (period of silence between question and answer), many pauses, gaze aversion, a lot of smiling, and an increase in movements. Many of these behaviors are indicators of nervousness. Apparently, the stereotypical belief is that liars are nervous and will behave accordingly. The surveys have indicated that people, both laypersons and police officers, particularly associate gaze aversion and fidgeting with deception. For example, around 75% of police officers believe that liars look away[7] (Mann, Vrij, & Bull, in press; Vrij & Semin, 1996) and that they make grooming gestures (Vrij & Semin, 1996). As we saw earlier, most of these behaviors are not related to deception (such as gaze aversion) or are related to deception in a different way (for example, illustrators and hand/finger movements tend to decrease during deception rather than increase).

One of the reasons why such incorrect views on deception exist is that people, including police officers, are taught these wrong cues (Gordon, Fleisher, & Weinberg, 2002; Hess, 1997; Inbau et al., 1986; Yeschke, 1997; Zulawski & Wicklander, 1993). Inbau et al. (2001) recently published a new edition of their manual *Criminal interrogation and confessions* which is an update of their 1986 version (Inbau et al., 1986). This manual is highly influential and, as Inbau et al. (2001) point out in their preface, thousands of investigators have been trained to use the techniques contained within their book. Unfortunately, the views described in their book about deceptive indicators of deception are wrong. They describe in detail how, in their view, liars behave. This includes behaviors such as showing gaze aversion, displaying unnatural posture changes, fidgeting and placing a hand over the mouth or eyes when speaking. They based their view on their extensive experience with interviewing suspects. However, none of these behaviors are found to be reliably related to deception in deception research. Neither do Inbau and his colleagues provide any empirical evidence for their claims. Kassin and Fong (1999), however, trained their participants to look at the cues Inbau and colleagues claim to be related to deception, and compared the performance of this group of participants on a subsequent lie detection task with a group of naive observers who received no information at all. The trained participants performed significantly worse compared to the naive observers, which is not surprising given the poor level of training these participants had received. More academics have expressed their concern about police training regarding lie detection (Ekman, 1985; Moston, 1992; Granhag & Strömwall, 1999).

Having incorrect views about cues to deception may have serious consequences for some groups of people, namely those whose natural behavior fits the Western white stereotype of deceptive behavior. Some individuals' nonverbal behavior gives the impression that they are telling the truth (honest demeanor bias), whereas others' natural behavior leaves the impression that they are lying (dishonest demeanor bias) (Riggio, Tucker, & Throckmorton, 1988; Riggio, Tucker, & Widaman, 1987; Vrij, 1993; Vrij & Van Wijngaarden, 1994; Vrij & Winkel, 1992b; Zuckerman, DeFrank, Hall, Larrance, & Rosenthal, 1979). This is related to personality traits. *Expressive people*, for example, exude credibility, regardless of the truth of their assertions. It is not that they are particularly skilled at lying, but their spontaneity tends to disarm suspicion, which makes it easier for them to get away with their lies (Riggio, 1986). On the other hand, people with a strong sense of *public self-consciousness* tend to make a less credible impression on others, regardless of whether they are telling the truth. These are individuals who, while lying, are concerned about being scrutinized by others, which changes their behavior in such a way that it appears dishonest. *Introverts* and *socially anxious* people also impress others as being less credible. The social clumsiness of introverts and the impression of tension, nervousness or fear that is natural to socially anxious individuals is interpreted by observers as indicators of deception.

Interestingly, their demeanor seems not to accurately reflect their behavior. For example, introverted people do not lie frequently (Kashy & DePaulo, 1996). Introverts also commit fewer crimes than extraverts (Eysenck, 1984). Furthermore, socially anxious people are less likely to persist in lying as soon as they are challenged (Vrij & Holland, 1998).

People also differ in how they present themselves when discussing emotional experiences. For example, research with rape victims has distinguished two basic styles of self-presentation, an 'expressed' style in which the victim displays distress which is clearly visible to outsiders, and a more controlled 'numbed' style in which cues of distress are not clearly visible (Burgess, 1985; Burgess & Homstrom, 1974). Although the styles represent a personality factor and are not related to deceit (Littman & Szewczyk, 1983), they have a differential impact on the perceived credibility of victims. Emotional victims are more readily believed than victims who report their experience in a more controlled manner (Baldry, Winkel, & Enthoven, 1997; Kaufmann, Drevland, Wessel, Overskeid, & Magnussen, 2003; Vrij & Fisher, 1997; Winkel & Koppelaar, 1991).

Various ethnic minority groups are also in a disadvantageous position due to the behavior they naturally display. Afro-American people display more gaze aversion than white American people (LaFrance & Mayo, 1976), and people from Turkey and Morocco who are living in the Netherlands show more gaze aversion than native Dutch people (Vrij, 2000a; Vrij, Dragt, & Koppelaar, 1992). Such differences are caused by the fact that gaze patterns are influenced by culture, and that looking into the eyes of a conversation partner is regarded as polite in Western cultures but is considered to be rude in several other cultures (Vrij & Winkel, 1991; Vrij, Winkel, & Koppelaar, 1991).

In the Netherlands, we examined the nonverbal behavioral patterns of white native Dutch and black Surinam citizens (citizens originated from Surinam, a former Dutch colony, but now living in the Netherlands) during simulated police interviews (Vrij & Winkel, 1991). Both a Dutch and a Surinamese interviewer were used, but this had no impact on the findings. Surinam people made more speech disturbances (speech fillers such as 'ah', 'um', 'er' and stutters), exhibited more gaze aversion, smiled more often, and made more self manipulations (scratching the head, wrists, and so on) and illustrators (hand and arm movements designed to modify and/or supplement what is being said verbally), regardless of whether they were lying or not. These behaviors show an overlap with the behaviors Western white people believe liars display, suggesting that typical "Surinam" behavior in experiments in Holland correspond with behavior that makes a suspicious impression on Western white observers. This gives rise to possible *cross-cultural nonverbal communication errors* during cross-cultural interactions. That is, nonverbal behavioral patterns that are typical for Surinam people in these settings may be interpreted by Western white observers as revealing attempts to hide the truth. We tested this idea in a series of experiments (Vrij & Winkel, 1992a, 1994; Vrij et al., 1991). Videotapes were made of simulated police interviews in which native Dutch and Surinam actors participated. Different versions were made of each interview. The actors demonstrated typical 'Dutch' behavior in one version of the interviews (for example, showed a limited amount of gaze aversion) and typical "Surinam" nonverbal behavior in another version of the interviews (showed more gaze aversion). Dutch white police officers were exposed to one version of each interview and were asked to indicate to what extent the actor made a suspicious impression. The actors consistently made a more suspicious impression when they demonstrated "typical Surinam behavior" than when they exhibited "typical Dutch behavior." These findings support the assumption that cross-cultural nonverbal communication errors do occur during cross-cultural interactions, and that nonverbal behavioral patterns that are typical for an ethnic group are often interpreted by Western white observers as signs of deception.

POLICE OFFICERS' ABILITY TO DETECT LIES

In scientific studies concerning detection of deception, observers are typically given videotaped or audiotaped statements of a number of people who are either lying or telling the truth. After each statement observers (typically college students) are asked to judge whether the statement is truthful or false. In such tasks, guessing whether someone is lying or not gives a 50% chance of being correct. Vrij (2000a) has reviewed 37 lie detection studies in which the observers were college students. The total accuracy rate, the percentage of correct answers, was 56.6%, which is only just about the level of chance. The review further revealed that people are to some extent capable of detecting truths (i.e., correctly judging that someone is telling the truth: 67% accuracy rate) but particularly poor at detecting lies (i.e., correctly judging that someone is lying: 44% accuracy rate). In fact, 44% is below the level that could be obtained by chance alone. In other words, people would be more accurate in detecting lies if they simply guessed. The superior accuracy rate for truthful messages is caused by the *truth bias*: judges are more likely to consider that messages are truthful rather than deceptive, and as a result, truthful messages are identified with more accuracy than deceptive ones. There are at least four possible explanations for the truth bias. First, in daily life people are more often confronted with truthful than with deceptive statements, so they are therefore more inclined to assume that the behavior they observe is honest (the so-called *availability heuristic*; O'Sullivan, Ekman, & Friesen, 1988). Second, social conversation rules prevent people from displaying suspicion. A person will very quickly become irritated if their conversation partner questions everything that they say. Unfortunately, it is often necessary to challenge what the person is saying and ask for more information in order to detect deceit (Vrij, 2000a). Third, the truth bias is the result of the incorrect stereotypical views people have about how liars behave. For example, most people expect liars to behave nervously (Akehurst et al., 1996; Strömwall & Granhag, 2003; Taylor & Vrij, 2000; Vrij & Semin, 1996; Vrij & Taylor, 2003). Therefore since many liars do not show nervous behaviors, observers who look for cues of nervousness to detect deceit, yet don't find them, will be inclined to judge many messages as truthful. Fourth, people may be unsure as to whether deception is in fact occurring. Given this uncertainty, the safest and most polite strategy may be to believe what is overtly expressed (DePaulo, Jordan, Irvine, & Laser, 1982).

It could be argued that college students are not habitually called upon to detect deception. Perhaps professional lie-catchers, such as police officers or customs officers, would obtain higher accuracy rates than laypersons. It might be that their experience in interviewing people and catching liars has had a positive influence on their skills in detecting deceit. Unfortunately, not many studies have been conducted with professional lie catchers, perhaps due to the fact that professional lie catchers in some countries are reluctant to participate in lie detection studies or do not wish the outcomes to be published. The studies which have been published are reported in Table 4.2.

In a typical experiment (Ekman, O'Sullivan, & Frank, 1999), professional lie catchers watched video clips of twenty people who gave a statement about a number of current controversial issues which either was their true opinion (truth) or an opinion opposite to their true opinion (lie). For each statement, the professional lie catchers were asked to indicate whether it was a truth or a lie. Three findings emerged from these studies. First, most accuracy rates were similar to the accuracy rates found in studies with college students as observers (most were in the 45%—60% range), suggesting that professional lie catchers are no better than laypersons in detecting deceit. DePaulo and Pfeifer (1986), Ekman and O'Sullivan (1991), Meissner and Kassin (2002) and Vrij and Graham (1997) directly tested this idea by including both laypersons and professional lie catchers as observers in their experiments. DePaulo and Pfeifer (1986), Meissner and Kassin (2002) and Vrij and Graham (1997) found that police officers were as (un)successful as university students in detecting deception. Second, some groups seem to be better than others. Ekman and O'Sullivan (1991) found that police officers (56% accuracy) and polygraph examiners

Table 4.2
Accuracy Scores of Professional Lie Catchers

	Accuracy Rates		
	Truth	Lie	Total
DePaulo and Pfeifer (1986) (federal law enforcement)	64%[a]	42%[a]	53%
Ekman & O'Sullivan (1991) (Secret Service)		64%	
Ekman & O'Sullivan (1991) (federal polygraphers)		56%	
Ekman & O'Sullivan (1991) (police officers)		56%	
Ekman, O'Sullivan, & Frank (1999) (CIA)	66%	80%	73%
Ekman, O'Sullivan, & Frank (1999) (sheriffs)	56%	78%	67%
Ekman, O'Sullivan, Frank (1999) (law enforcement)	54%	48%	51%
Köhnken (1987) (police officers)	58%	31%	45%
Meissner & Kassin (2002) (law enforcement)		50%	
Porter, Woodworth, & Birt (2000) (parole officers)	20%	60%	40%
Vrij (1993) (police detectives)	51%	46%	49%
Vrij & Graham (1997) (police officers)		54%	
Vrij & Mann (2001a) (police officers)	70%	57%	64%
Vrij & Mann (2001b) (police officers)		51%	

Notes :[a]Experienced and inexperienced officers together.
Police officers also took part in Garrido and Masip's (2001) lie detection task. However, no accuracy rates were reported.
In Horvath, Jayne and Buckley's (1994) study, four persons 'trained and experienced in Behavior Analysis Interviewing' participated, reaching 78% truth accuracy and 66% lie accuracy rates. However, the professional background of these four lie detectors were not reported.

(56% accuracy) obtained similar accuracy rates to university students (53% accuracy), whereas members of the Secret Service were better at detecting lies than university students (64% accuracy). Ekman et al. (1999) found that U.S. Federal officers (police officers with a special interest and experience in deception and demeanor) and sheriffs (police officers identified by their department as outstanding interrogators) were considerably better at detecting lies (73% and 67% accuracy respectively) than 'mixed' law-enforcement officers (officers who had not been chosen because of their reputation as interrogators, 51% accuracy). Third, the truth bias, consistently found in studies with students as observers, is much less profound or perhaps even lacking in studies with professional lie catchers. It might be that their jobs and daily experiences make professional lie catchers more cynical and suspicious.

Finally, DePaulo and Pfeifer (1986) and Meissner and Kassin (2002) investigated how confident observers were in the decisions they had made. They found that police officers were more confident than students, which suggests that being a professional lie catcher may increase confidence in the ability to detect deceit, but not accuracy. Allwood and Granhag (1997) pointed out that the tendency to be overconfident is not unique to police officers, but common among many different groups of professional lie catchers.

However, as we pointed out earlier, the poor ability to detect deceit that emerged from detection of deception studies might be the result of an artifact. Deception research has almost exclusively been conducted in university laboratories where participants (mostly college students) tell the truth or lie for the sake of the experiment. Perhaps in these laboratory studies the stakes are not high enough for the liar to elicit clear cues to deception, which makes the task for the lie detector difficult (Miller & Stiff, 1993). Indeed, in a series of experiments in which the stakes were manipulated (although the stakes were never really high), it has been found that high-stake lies were easier to detect than low-stake lies (DePaulo, Kirkendol, Tang, & O'Brien, 1988; DePaulo, Lanier, & Davis, 1983; DePaulo, LeMay, & Epstein, 1991; DePaulo et al., 1985b; Lane & DePaulo, 1999; Vrij, 2000b; Vrij, Harden, Terry, Edward, & Bull, 2001).

Given the low stake settings in these deception detection studies, one could argue that they do not accurately measure police officers' ability to detect deceit. One could argue that the only valid way to investigate police officers' true ability to detect deceit, is to examine their skills when they detect lies and truths told in real life criminal investigation settings. Vrij and Mann (2001a, b) were the first researchers to examine police officers' skills in such situations. Vrij and Mann (2001a) exposed police officers to fragments of a videotaped police interview with a man suspected of murder. However, that study had two limitations. First, fragments of only one suspect were shown, and he could have been displaying untypical behavior. That is, he could have been a particularly good or a particularly poor liar. Second, the police officers could not understand the suspect as he spoke in a foreign language (suspect and police officers were of different nationalities). Vrij and Mann (2001b) exposed judges to videotaped press conferences of people who were asking the general public for help either in finding their missing relatives or the murderers of their relatives. They all lied during these press conferences and they were all subsequently found guilty of having killed the "missing person" themselves. This study had limitations as well. Most importantly, the judges were only subjected to lies. This is problematic as it does not investigate people's ability to detect truths. A good lie detector is good at distinguishing between truths and lies, that is, good at detecting lies *and* good at detecting truths. For example, a police officer who judges every clip he sees as a lie will have a perfect (100%) accuracy rate for detecting lies but a particularly low

(0%) accuracy rate for detecting truths. Thus, overall this is a poor lie detector. However, in a study where judges are only exposed to lies, such a suspicious lie detector will achieve a very high accuracy score.

In our most recent study (Mann et al., 2003) we overcame these limitations. We showed 99 police officers a total of 54 video clips of suspects who told truths and lies during their police interviews. These video clips were the clips we have already discussed in Table 4.1 (Mann et al., 2002). After each clip the police officers were requested to indicate whether the suspect was truthful or not. None of the sample of police officers belonged to one of the specific groups which have been identified by Ekman and his colleagues as being superior lie detectors. The study revealed accuracy rates which were higher than generally found in previous studies. The total accuracy rate was 65%, with a 64% truth accuracy rate and a 66% lie accuracy rate. All these accuracy rates were significantly higher than the 50% level of chance, and both the total accuracy rate and the lie accuracy rates were higher than the accuracy rates which have been found in most previous studies (see Vrij, 2000a, for a review).[8] The accuracy rates were among the highest ever found with ordinary police officers. In other words, this study suggests that ordinary police officers are better at detecting truths and lies than previous research has suggested.

Moreover, there were individual differences, and accuracy rates for individual officers varied from a low 30% to a very high 90% (achieved by three officers, Mann, 2001). How could we explain these individual differences? First, accuracy was not related to confidence. In other words, officers who expressed confidence about the accuracy of their judgments were not better than those who were more uncertain. Not obtaining a significant relationship between accuracy and confidence is by no means uncommon in deception research. Also, in previous deception studies a significant relationship between accuracy and confidence was typically not found (see DePaulo, Charlton, Cooper, Lindsay, & Muhlenbruck, 1997, for a meta-analysis). However, neither did the police officers in our study show overconfidence in their ability. On the contrary, they underestimated their own performance. This finding is uncommon as overconfidence was found in several previous studies (see above). This exception might well be to do with how we measured confidence, as it was assessed somewhat differently from how it was investigated in previous studies (see Mann et al., 2003, for further details).

Second, findings showed a positive relationship between having experience in interviewing suspects and the ability to detect truths and lies, suggesting that experience does make police officers better able to distinguish between truths and lies. This finding has not been obtained in previous deception studies with professionals as observers (DePaulo & Pfeifer, 1986; Ekman & O'Sullivan, 1991; Porter et al., 2000). We believe that this finding was affected by the way we measured experience. Other researchers, for example Ekman and

O'Sullivan (1991), used "years of job experience" as a measurement for experience. Unfortunately, they did not further define "job experience." It might well be that this measurement has been too vague as it does not specifically focus on the officers' actual experience in situations where they will attempt to detect deceit such as during interviews with suspects. There is little reason to suggest that a police officer who had worked for many years in a managerial or administrative position within the police force would be a better lie detector than someone with a similar position outside the police force. Therefore perhaps unsurprisingly, we also did not find a significant correlation between general job experience (i.e., "years of service") and accuracy. In other words, experience might benefit truth and lie detection if only the relevant experience is taken into account. Perhaps a weakness of the way we measured experience is that it was a self-report measure ("How experienced do you consider yourself to be in interviewing suspects?") and not an objective measure. It would be interesting to see whether an objective measure of experience in interviewing suspects (for example, the number of suspect interviews a police officer has conducted) would correlate with accuracy as well. This would strengthen our argument. Unfortunately, the police do not record objective measures of experience with interviewing suspects.

Third, in our study, police officers were asked which cues they looked at when attempting to detect deceit. Several relationships occurred between cues mentioned by the officers as useful to detect deceit and their accuracy in truth and lie detection. First, good lie detectors mentioned story cues (vague reply, contradictions in story, etc.) more often than poor lie detectors. Second, the more body cues (gaze aversion, posture, movements, etc.) participants mentioned, the lower their accuracy became. Particularly police officers who mentioned that liars look away and fidget were poor lie detectors. As mentioned earlier, Inbau and his colleagues (1986/2001) suggested that liars show a variety of body cues, including showing gaze aversion, displaying unnatural posture changes, exhibiting self manipulations, and placing the hand over the mouth or eyes when speaking. We measured the effectiveness of using Inbau's views in our study by examining how good police officers who endorse these views were in our lie detection task. Interestingly, our findings showed that the more the police officers endorsed Inbau's views the worse they became at distinguishing between truths and lies. In other words, looking at Inbau et al.'s (1986/2001) cues is counterproductive.

In other studies the relationship between the cues people claim to pay attention to when attempting to detect deceit and their ability to distinguish between truths and lies were also examined. In one of our own studies (Vrij & Mann, 2001a) we obtained exactly the same outcome as in our recent Mann et al. (2003) study: Those participants who mentioned gaze aversion and fidgeting as cues to deceit achieved the lowest accuracy scores. When other researchers examined such relationships different relationships emerged. For example, Ekman and O'Sullivan (1991) found that those participants who mentioned both speech cues and nonverbal cues obtained the highest accuracy, higher than those who just mentioned speech cues or nonverbal cues, whereas we found that those who just mentioned speech cues were the best lie detectors. Anderson, DePaulo, Mansfield, Tickle, and Greens (1999) and Feeley and Young (2000) found that the more vocal cues (speech errors, speech fillers, pauses, voice) participants mentioned, the higher accuracy they obtained. Porter, Woodworth and Birt (2000) found that the more body cues the participants reported, the better their ability to distinguish between truths and lies became. Frank and Ekman (1997) reported that good lie detectors were better at spotting brief facial expressions of emotions than poor lie detectors. Such micro expressions have not been investigated in any of the other studies discussed here.

In summary, different studies reveal different outcomes, and as a result of this, a clear picture of what distinguishes a good from a poor lie detector is yet to emerge. There are at least four explanations for the lack of consistency in the findings of different studies. One explanation is that the relationships between cues mentioned and accuracy are generally weak. Indeed, the significant correlations which are typically reported are low, usually falling into the $r = .20$ to $r = .30$ range. Another explanation is that in different studies participants faced completely different lie detection situations, and therefore, comparisons are difficult to make. For example, in most studies participants were requested to detect truths and lies in low-stake situations, whereas in some studies participants were exposed to high-stake situations. Interestingly, in both our experiments (Mann et al., 2003; Vrij & Mann, 2001a) participants were requested to detect the truths and lies told during police interviews and both studies obtained similar findings. A third explanation is that perhaps lie detectors simply do not know where they look for deceit, and so lie detection could just be an intuitive skill. We (Mann et al., 2003) obtained some support for this assumption, as good lie detectors reported relying significantly more often on "gut feeling" than poor lie detectors. Finally, weak relationships between cues mentioned and ability to detect deceit and conflicting findings between different studies may be caused by a flaw in the experimental designs used in lie detection studies. In almost all lie detection studies published to date, people's skills to detect deceit were only tested once. The fact that they were good or bad at that particular task might have been a matter of luck, and there is certainly no guarantee that those lie detectors would show the same performance if they were tested a second time. A better way of examining people's ability to detect deceit and the strategies good lie detectors use is to test the same people at various occasions, and to examine which detectors show a consistent performance. Particular attention can then be paid to the cues mentioned by those who are consistently good. To our knowledge, only Frank and Ekman (1997) exposed lie detectors to multiple lie detection tasks and they reported some kind of consistency between the lie detectors' performances on the different tasks.

DIRECTIONS OF FURTHER RESEARCH IN LIE DETECTION

On the basis of the information provided in this article we propose two directions for further research. First, as mentioned in the paragraph above, judges should be exposed to *multiple* lie detection tasks instead of *single* lie detection tasks, as multiple tests probably will give more insight into someone's true ability to detect truths and lies than single lie detection tests. Only those judges with a consistently good performance in such tests should be considered good lie detectors. Then the next step would be to unravel the strategies these good lie detectors use. And perhaps the step after this would be to teach other lie detectors these successful strategies. Although this research might sound straightforward, it is, in fact, hazardous. First, it is unknown how many people will be consistently good at such lie detection tests, but probably not many. Therefore, many people need to be tested to obtain a reasonable sample of good lie detectors. Second, unraveling the strategies these good lie detectors use would not be easy either. Although researchers could directly ask good lie detectors which strategies they use, they probably would find this question difficult to answer, and perhaps do not even know which strategy they use. Rather than asking good lie detectors which strategies they use directly, this could be asked in an indirect way. For example, good lie detectors could be shown videotaped clips of liars and truth tellers and could be asked to indicate which fragments of these clips they consider relevant to their decision making. Researchers could then carefully examine these fragments selected by good lie detectors, particularly those fragments which were selected by *many* good lie detectors. However, it is not certain whether there will be consistency amongst good lie detectors in the fragments they select. Neither is it certain that such analyses will provide any meaningful (interpretable) information. Finally, these direct or indirect ways of unraveling lie detection strategies will not work if good lie detection is primarily an intuitive skill (which cannot be ruled out, as argued above). Obviously, if good lie detection is primarily based upon intuition, teaching others to become better lie detectors would become problematic.

Second, rather than examining the strategies good lie detectors use, the extent to which certain interview techniques might facilitate lie detection could be investigated. The issue of how interview styles might benefit lie detection has been virtually ignored by academics to date, but this approach has potential in our view. For example, as we have discussed above, one reason why cues to deceit emerge is because liars experience more cognitive load than truth tellers. We have argued that this cognitive load aspect might be particularly important in police suspects. Police interviewers could use this by employing interview techniques which increase the cognitive demand in suspects. This should have a greater effect on liars than on truth tellers, thus facilitating discrimination between them.

There are several ways in which cognitive demand could be increased. First, by asking suspects to elaborate on issues they have previously mentioned. This might be more difficult for liars than for truth tellers, especially if they didn't expect to be asked for such elaboration and, subsequently, haven't prepared responses to such questions prior to the interview. In that case, liars need to invent answers which sound plausible and convincing, and which do not contradict evidence. They also need to invent those spontaneous answers rather quickly; otherwise an usually long delay before answering the questions might give the lie away. They also need to remember their inventions in case the interviewer asks them to repeat what they have just said. Second, one valid speech content related cue frequently found in deception research is that truth tellers tend to tell their stories in a more *un*structured way than liars (Vrij, 2000). That is, liars tend to tell their stories in a more fixed chronological order (this happened first, and then this, and then that, and so on) than truth tellers. It has been suggested that it is very difficult for liars to tell a fabrication in a non-chronological order (Steller, 1989; Köhnken, 1999; Zaparniuk, Yuille, & Taylor, 1995). Lie detectors could exploit this difficulty by asking interviewees to tell their stories in a non-chronological order, for example in reverse order. Asking people to tell their stories in reverse order is a technique currently employed in police interviews as part of the Cognitive Interview (Fisher, Brennan, & McCauley, 2002; Fisher & Geiselman, 1992; Fisher, Geiselman, & Amador, 1989; Milne & Bull, 1999), however, it is used as a memory enhancing technique while interviewing witnesses which results in interviewees recalling more information about an event they have witnessed, rather than used as a technique to detect lies in suspects. It is worthwhile to investigate whether lie detection is facilitated by telling stories in reverse order. We expect this to be the case, as it will increase the cognitive demand more for liars than for truth tellers. One factor that might be relevant is rehearsal.

From our informal conversations with the police, we understand that police detectives have the impression that liars, more than truth tellers, rehearse their stories prior to police interviews. Liars may believe that good preparation of the made-up event is essential for them in order to make a credible impression during the police interviews, whereas truth tellers do not feel the same need to be prepared as they can simply explain what they have witnessed. Rehearsal could affect the liars' performance in two ways. It might actually be even more difficult for liars to tell a story in reverse order when they have prepared their false story in advance than when they are unprepared for fabricating. If liars prepare themselves for an interview about an event they probably will rehearse the event in forward order, because that is the natural way for events to unfold in time. If they are in fact then asked to describe the event in reverse order, they are forced to recall a story in a manner that goes against their own preparation. No rehearsal implies less commitment to a forward-order rendition, which should make it easier to reverse the ordering. Alternatively, lying in reverse order after rehearsal could be easier than being unprepared. This means that when the story is rehearsed a liar has easier access to the prepared details of the made-up event.

EPILOGUE

Police officers use nonverbal cues when they attempt to detect deceit. This is a hazardous exercise. Clear cut cues to deceit, the equivalent of Pinocchio's growing nose, do not exist so there is nothing lie detectors can really rely upon. Also, police officers have some incorrect beliefs about how liars behave, partly because they are misguided by police manuals which teach them the wrong cues. Relying on incorrect cues to deception has negative consequences for those whose natural behavior embodies these incorrect beliefs, such as introverted and socially anxious people, and members of several ethnic minority groups. Despite this, some people appear to be better at distinguishing between truths and lies than others, though a clear picture of what distinguishes a good from a poor lie detector has yet to emerge. Given the fact that detecting lies is an important aspect of several professions, for example police work, more insight into the strategies and techniques that could improve lie detection are welcome. We have given two suggestions for research: attempting to unravel the strategies used by good lie detectors, and employing interview techniques which could facilitate distinguishing between liars and truth tellers. We consider the second line of research particularly fruitful.

REFERENCES

Akehurst, L., Köhnken, G., Vrij, A., & Bull, R. (1996). Lay persons' and police officers' beliefs regarding deceptive behaviour. *Applied Cognitive Psychology, 10*, 461–473.

Allwood, C. M., & Granhag, P. A. (1997). Feelings of confidence and the realism of confidence judgments in everyday life. In P. Juslin & H. Montgomery (Eds.), *Judgment and decision making: Neo-Brunswikian and process-tracing approaches* (pp. 123–146). Mahwah NJ: Lawrence Erlbaum Associates.

Anderson, D. E., DePaulo, B. M., Mansfield, M. E., Tickle, J. J., & Green, E. (1999). Beliefs about cues to deception: Mindless stereotypes or untapped wisdom? *Journal of Nonverbal Behavior, 23*, 67–89.

Baldry, A. C., Winkel, F. W., & Enthoven, D. S. (1997). Paralinguistic and nonverbal triggers of biased credibility assessments of rape victims in Dutch police officers: An experimental study of 'Nonevidentiary' bias. In S.

Redondo, V. Garrido, J. Perze, & R. Barbaret (Eds.), *Advances in psychology and law* (pp. 163–174). Berlin: Walter de Gruyter.

Baskett, G. D., & Freedle, R. O. (1974). Aspects of language pragmatics and the social perception of lying. *Journal of Psycholinguistic Research, 3,* 117–131.

Bond, C. F., Omar, A., Pitre, U., Lashley, B. R., Skaggs, L. M., & Kirk, C. T. (1992). Fishy-looking liars: Deception judgment from expectancy violation. *Journal of Personality and Social Psychology, 63,* 969–977.

Brown, R. (1995). *Prejudice: Its social psychology.* Cambridge, MA: Blackwell Publishers.

Bull, R., & Rumsey, N. (1988). *The social psychology of facial appearance.* New York: Springer Verlag.

Buller, D. B., & Burgoon, J. K. (1996). Interpersonal deception theory. *Communication Theory, 6,* 203–242.

Buller, D. B., Strzyzewski, K. D., & Hunsaker, F. G. (1991). Interpersonal deception II: The inferiority of conversational participants as deception detectors. *Communication Monographs, 58,* 25–40.

Burgess, A. W. (1985). *Rape and sexual assault: A research book.* London: Garland.

Burgess, A. W., & Homstrom, L. L. (1974). *Rape: Victims of crisis.* Bowie: Brady.

Burgoon, J. K., Buller, D. B., Ebesu, A. S., White, C. H., & Rockwell, P. A. (1996). Testing interpersonal deception theory: Effects of suspicion on communication behaviors and perception. *Communication Theory, 6,* 243–267.

Davis, M., & Hadiks, D. (1995). Demeanor and credibility. *Semiotica, 106,* 5–54.

DePaulo, B. M., Charlton, K., Cooper, H., Lindsay, J. L., & Muhlenbruck, L. (1997). *Personality and Social Psychology Review, 1,* 346–357.

DePaulo, B. M., & Friedman, H. S. (1998). Nonverbal communication. In D. T. Gilbert, S. T. Fiske, & G. Lindzey (Eds.), *The handbook of social psychology* (pp. 3–40). Boston, MA: McGraw-Hill.

DePaulo, B. M., Jordan, A., Irvine, A., & Laser, P. S. (1982). Age changes in the detection of deception. *Child Development, 53,* 701–709.

DePaulo, B. M., & Kirkendol, S. E. (1989). The motivational impairment effect in the communication of deception. In J. C. Yuille (Ed.), *Credibility assessment* (pp. 51–70). Dordrecht, the Netherlands: Kluwer.

DePaulo, B. M., Kirkendol, S. E., Tang, J., & O'Brien, T. P. (1988). The motivational impairment effect in the communication of deception: Replications and extensions. *Journal of Nonverbal Behavior, 12,* 177–201.

DePaulo, B. M., Lanier, K., & Davis, T. (1983). Detecting the deceit of the motivated liar. *Journal of Personality and Social Psychology, 45,* 1096–1103.

DePaulo, B. M., LeMay, C. S., & Epstein, J. A. (1991). Effects of importance of success and expectations for success on effectiveness at deceiving. *Personality and Social Psychology Bulletin, 17,* 14–24.

DePaulo, B. M., Lindsay, J. L., Malone, B. E., Muhlenbruck, L., Charlton, K., & Cooper, H. (2003). Cues to deception. *Psychological Bulletin, 129,* 74–118.

DePaulo, B. M., & Pfeifer, R. L. (1986). On-the-job experience and skill at detecting deception. *Journal of Applied Social Psychology, 16,* 249–267.

DePaulo, B. M., Stone, J. L., & Lassiter, G. D. (1985a). Deceiving and detecting deceit. In B. R. Schenkler (Ed.), *The self and social life* (pp. 323–370). New York: McGraw-Hill.

DePaulo, B. M., Stone, J. I., & Lassiter, G. D. (1985b). Telling ingratiating lies: Effects of target sex and target attractiveness on verbal and nonverbal deceptive success. *Journal of Personality and Social Psychology, 48,* 1191–1203.

Ekman, P. (1985). *Telling lies: Clues to deceit in the marketplace, politics and marriage.* New York: W. W. Norton & Company. (Reprinted in 1992 and 2001).

Ekman, P., & Frank, M. G. (1993). Lies that fail. In M. Lewis & C. Saarni (Eds.), *Lying and deception in everyday life* (pp. 184–201). New York: Guilford Press.

Ekman, P., & Friesen, W. V. (1969). Nonverbal leakage and clues to deception. *Psychiatry, 32,* 88–106.

Ekman, P., & Friesen, W. V. (1972). Hand movements. *Journal of Communication, 22,* 353–374.

Ekman, P., Friesen, W. V., & Scherer, K. R. (1976). Body movement and voice pitch in deceptive interaction. *Semiotica, 16,* 23–27.

Ekman, P., & O'Sullivan, M. (1991). Who can catch a liar? *American Psychologist, 46,* 913–920.

Ekman, P., O'Sullivan, M., & Frank, M. G. (1999). A few can catch a liar. *Psychological Science, 10,* 263–266.

Eysenck, H. J. (1984). Crime and personality. In D. J. Muller, D. E. Blackman, & A. J. Chapman (Eds.), *Psychology and Law* (pp. 85–100). New York: John Wiley & Sons.

Feeley, T. H., & deTurck, M. A. (1997). *Perceptions of communication as seen by the actor and as seen by the observer: The case of lie detection.* Paper presented at the International Communication Association Annual Conference. Montreal, Canada.

Feeley, T. H., & Young, M. J. (2000). The effects of cognitive capacity on beliefs about deceptive communication. *Communication Quarterly, 48,* 101–119.

Fisher, R. P., Brennan, K. H., & McCauley, M. R. (2002). The cognitive interview method to enhance eyewitness recall. In M. L. Eisen, J. A. Quas, & G. S. Goodman (Eds.), Memory and suggestibility in the forensic interview (pp. 265–286). Mahwah, NJ: Lawrence Erlbaum Associates.

Fisher, R. P., & Geiselman, R. E. (1992). *Memory-enhancing techniques for investigative interviewing: The cognitive interview.* Springfield, IL: Charles Thomas.

Fisher, R. P., Geiselman, R. E., & Amador, M. (1989). Field test of the cognitive interview: Enhancing the recollection of actual victims and witnesses of crime. *Journal of Applied Psychology, 74,* 722–727.

Frank, M. G. & Ekman, P. (1997). The ability to detect deceit generalizes across different types of high-stake lies. *Journal of Personality and Social Psychology, 72,* 1429–1439.

Frank, M. G., & Gilovich, T. (1988). The dark side of self- and social perception: Black uniforms and aggression in professional sports. *Journal of Personality and Social Psychology, 54,* 74–85.

Garrido, E., & Masip, J. (2001). Previous exposure to the sender's behavior and accuracy at judging credibility. In R. Roesch, R. R. Corrado, & R. Dempster (Eds.), *Psychology in the courts: International advances in knowledge* (pp. 271–287). London: Routledge.

Giles, H., & Johnson, P. (1986). Perceived threat, ethnic commitment and interethnic language behavior. In Y. Y. Kim (Ed.), *Interethnic communication: Current research.* Beverly Hills, CA: Sage.

Giles, H., & Powesland, P. F. (1975). *Speech style and social evaluation.* London: Academic Press.

Gordon, N. J., Fleisher, W. L., & Weinberg, C. D. (2002). *Effective interviewing and interrogation techniques.* San Diego, CA: Academic Press.

Granhag, P. A., & Strömwall, L. A. (1999). Repeated interrogations: Stretching the deception detection paradigm. *Expert Evidence: The International Journal of Behavioural Sciences in Legal Contexts, 7,* 163–174.

Granhag, P. A., & Stromwall, L. A. (2000). Effects of preconceptions on deception detection and new answers to why lie catchers often fail. *Psychology, Crime, & Law, 6,* 197–218.

Granhag, P. A., & Strömwall, L. A. (2001a). Deception detection: Examining the consistency heuristic. In C. M. Breur, M. M. Kommer, J. F. Nijboer, & J. M. Reijntjes (Eds.), *New trends in criminal investigation and evidence* (Vol. 2, pp. 309–321). Antwerpen: Intresentia.

Granhag, P. A., & Strömwall, L. A. (2001b). Deception detection: Interrogators' and observers' decoding of consecutive statements. *The Journal of Psychology, 135,* 603–620.

Granhag, P. A., Strömwall, L. A., & Reiman, A. C. (2002). *Partners in crime: How liars in collusion betray themselves.* Manuscript submitted for publication.

Greuel, L. (1992). Police officers' beliefs about cues associated with deception in rape cases. In F. Lösel, D. Bender, & T. Bliesener (Eds.), *Psychology and Law: International perspectives* (pp. 234–239). Berlin, Germany: Walter de Gruyter.

Gudjonsson, G. H. (1992). *The psychology of interrogations, confessions and testimony.* Chichester, England: Wiley & Sons.

Hall, J. A., & Carter, J. D. (1999). Gender-stereotype accuracy as an individual difference. *Journal of Personality and Social Psychology, 77,* 350–359.

Hargie, O., & Tourish, D. (1999). The psychology of interpersonal skill. In A. Memon & R. Bull (Eds.), *Handbook of the psychology of interviewing* (pp. 71–88). Chichester: Wiley.

Harrigan, J. A., & O'Connell, D. M. (1996). Facial movements during anxiety states. *Personality and Individual Differences, 21,* 205–212.

Hess, J. E. (1997). *Interviewing and interrogation for law enforcement.* Reading, United Kingdom: Anderson Publishing Co.

Hirsch, A. R., & Wolf, C. J. (2001). Practical methods for detecting mendacity: A case study. *The Journal of the American Academy of Psychiatry and the Law, 29,* 438–444.

Horvath, F. (1973). Verbal and nonverbal cues to truth and deception during polygraph examinations. *Journal of Police Science and Administration, 1,* 138–152.

Horvath, F., Jayne, B., & Buckley, J. (1994). Differentiation of truthful and deceptive criminal suspects in behavioral analysis interviews. *Journal of Forensic Sciences, 39,* 793–807.

Hummert, M. L. (1999). A social cognitive perspective on age stereotypes. In T. M. Hess & F. Blanchard-Fields (Eds.), *Social cognition and aging* (pp. 175–196). San Diego, CA: Academic Press.

Inbau, F. E., Reid, J. E., & Buckley, J. P. (1986). *Criminal interrogation and confessions, third edition.* Baltimore, MD: Williams & Wilkins.

Inbau, F. E., Reid, J. E., Buckley, J. P., & Jayne, B. C. (2001). *Criminal interrogation and confessions, fourth edition.* Gaithersburg, Maryland: Aspen Publishers.

Kassin, S. M., & Fong, C. T. (1999). 'I'm innocent!': Effects of training on judgments of truth and deception in the interrogation room. *Law and Human Behavior, 23,* 499–516.

Kaufmann, G., Drevland, G. C., Wessel, E., Overskeid, G., & Magnussen, S. (in press). The importance of being earnest: Displayed emotions and witness credibility. *Applied Cognitive Psychology*.

Köhnken, G. (1987). Training police officers to detect deceptive eyewitness statements. Does it work? *Social Behaviour, 2*, 1–17.

Köhnken, G. (1999, July). *Statement Validity Assessment*. Paper presented at the pre-conference program of applied courses 'Assessing credibility' organized by the European Association of Psychology and Law, Dublin, Ireland.

Krauss, R. M., & Chiu, C. Y. (1998). Language and behavior. In D. T. Gilbert, S. T. Fiske, & G. Lindzey (Eds.), *The handbook of social psychology* (pp. 41–88). Boston, MA: McGraw-Hill.

LaFrance, M., & Mayo, C. (1976). Racial differences in gaze behavior during conversations: Two systematic observational studies. *Journal of Personality and Social Psychology, 33*, 547–552.

Lane, J. D., & DePaulo, B. M. (1999). Completing Coyne's cycle: Dysphorics' ability to detect deception. *Journal of Research in Personality, 33*, 311–329.

Mann, S. (2001). *Suspects, lies and videotape: An investigation into telling and detecting lies in police/suspect interviews*. Unpublished PhD thesis. University of Portsmouth, Department of Psychology.

Mann, S., Vrij, A., & Bull, R. (2002). Suspects, lies and videotape: An analysis of authentic high-stakes liars. *Law and Human Behavior, 26*, 365–376

Mann, S., Vrij, A., & Bull, R. (in press). Detecting true lies: Police officers' ability to detect suspects' lies. *Journal of Applied Psychology*.

Meissner, C. A., & Kassin, S. M. (2002). "He's guilty!": Investigator bias in judgments of truth and deception. *Law and Human Behavior, 26*, 469–480.

Mehrabian, A. (1972). *Nonverbal communication*. Chicago: Aldine-Atherton.

Mehrabian, A., & Ferris, S. R. (1967). Inference of attitudes from nonverbal communication in two channels. *Journal of Consulting and Clinical Psychology, 31*, 248–252.

Mehrabian, A., & Wiener, M. (1967). Decoding of inconsistent communication. *Journal of Personality and Social Psychology, 6*, 109–114.

Millar, M. G., & Millar, K. U. (1997). The effects of cognitive capacity and suspicion on truth bias. *Communication Research, 24*, 556–570.

Millar, M. G., & Millar, K. U. (1998). The effects of suspicion on the recall of cues used to make veracity judgments. *Communication Reports, 11*, 57–64.

Miller, G. R., & Stiff, J. B. (1993). *Deceptive Communication*. Newbury Park, CA: Sage.

Milne, R., & Bull, R. (1999). *Investigative interviewing: Psychology and practice*. Chichester: John Wiley & Sons.

Moston, S. (1992). Truth or lies: Are police officers able to distinguish truthful from deceptive statements? *Policing*, November 8.

Moston, S., & Engelberg, T. (1993). Police questioning techniques in tape recorded interviews with criminal suspects. *Policing and Society, 3*, 223–237.

Ofshe, R. (1989). Coerced confessions: The logic of seemingly irrational action. *Cultic Studies Journal, 6*, 1–15.

O'Sullivan, M., Ekman, P., & Friesen, W. V. (1988). The effect of comparisons on detecting deceit. *Journal of Nonverbal Behavior, 12*, 203–216.

Porter, S., Woodworth, M., & Birt, A. R. (2000). Truth, lies, and videotape: An investigation of the ability of federal parole officers to detect deception. *Law and Human Behavior, 24*, 643–658.

Porter, S., & Yuille, J. C. (1995). Credibility assessment of criminal suspects through statement analysis. *Psychology, Crime, & Law, 1*, 319–331.

Porter, S., & Yuille, J. C. (1996). The language of deceit: An investigation of the verbal clues to deception in the interrogation context. *Law and Human Behavior, 20*, 443–459.

Porter, S., Yuille, J. C., & Birt, A. R. (2001). The discrimination of deceptive, mistaken, and truthful witness testimony. In R. Roesch, R. R. Corrado, & R. Dempster (Eds.), *Psychology in the courts: International advances in knowledge.* London: Routledge.

Porter, S., Yuille, J. C., & Lehman, D. R. (1999). The nature of real, implanted and fabricated memories for emotional childhood events: Implications for the recovered memory debate. *Law and Human Behavior, 23*, 517–537.

Reid, J. E., & Arther, R. O. (1953). Behavior symptoms of lie-detector subjects. *Journal of Criminal Law, Criminology and Police Science, 44*, 104–108.

Riggio, R. E. (1986). Assessment of basic social skills. *Journal of Personality and Social Psychology, 51*, 649–660.

Riggio, R. E. (1994). Epilogue: Where are we going, and how do we get there? *Journal of Language and Social Psychology, 13*, 514–518.

Riggio, R. E., Tucker, J., & Throckmorton, B. (1988). Social skills and deception ability. *Personality and Social Psychology Bulletin, 13*, 568–577.

Riggio, R. E., Tucker, J., & Widaman, K. F. (1987). Verbal and nonverbal cues as mediators of deception ability. *Journal of Nonverbal Behavior, 11*, 126–145.

Rozelle, R. M., & Baxter, J. C. (1975). Impression formation and danger recognition in experienced police officers. *The Journal of Social Psychology, 96*, 53–63.

Ruby, C. L., & Brigham, J. C. (1996). A criminal schema: The role of chronicity, race, and socioeconomic status in law enforcement officials' perceptions of others. *Journal of Applied Social Psychology, 26*, 95–112.

Stangor, C., Lynch, L., Changming, D., & Glass, B. (1992). Categorization of individuals on the basis of multiple social features. *Journal of Personality and Social Psychology, 72*, 207–218.

Steller, M. (1989). Recent developments in statement analysis. In J. C. Yuille (1989), *Credibility Assessment* (pp. 135–154). Deventer, the Netherlands: Kluwer.

Steller, M., & Köhnken, G. (1989). Criteria-Based Content Analysis. In D. C. Raskin (Ed.), *Psychological methods in criminal investigation and evidence* (pp. 217–245). New York: Springer-Verlag.

Street, R. L., & Hopper, R. (1982). A model of speech style evaluation. In E. B. Ryan & H. Giles (Eds.), *Attitudes toward language variation: Social and applied contexts* (pp. 175–188). London: Edward Arnold.

Strömwall, L. A., & Granhag, P. A. (2003). Hoe to detect deception? Arresting the beliefs of police officers, prosecutors and judges. *Psychology, Crime, & Law, 9*, 19–36.

Strömwall, L. A., Granhag, P. A., & Jonsson, A. C. (2003). Deception among pairs: 'Let's say we had lunch together and hope they will swallow it'. *Psychology, Crime, & Law, 9*, 109–124.

Taylor, R., & Vrij, A. (2000). The effects of varying stake and cognitive complexity on beliefs about the cues to deception. *International Journal of Police Science and Management, 3*, 111–124.

Tecce, J. J. (1992). *Psychology, physiology and experimental*. In McGraw-Hill yearbook of science and technology (pp. 375–377). New York: McGraw-Hill.

Vrij, A. (1993). Credibility judgments of detectives: The impact of nonverbal behaviour, social skills and physical characteristics on impression formation. *Journal of Social Psychology, 133,* 601–611.

Vrij, A. (1995). Behavioral correlates of deception in a simulated police interview. *Journal of Psychology, 129,* 15–28.

Vrij, A. (1997). Wearing black clothes: The impact of offenders' and suspects' clothing on impression formation. *Applied Cognitive Psychology, 11,* 47–53.

Vrij, A. (1998). To lie or not to lie. *Psychologie, 17,* 12, 22–25.

Vrij, A. (2000a). *Detecting lies and deceit: The psychology of lying and its implications for professional practice.* Chichester: John Wiley and Sons.

Vrij, A. (2000b). Telling and detecting lies as a function of raising the stakes. In C. M. Breur, M. M. Kommer, J. F. Nijboer, & J. M. Reintjes (Eds.), *New trends in criminal investigation and evidence II* (pp. 699–709). Antwerpen, Belgium: Intersentia.

Vrij, A. (2002). Telling and detecting lies. In N. Brace & H. L. Westcott (Eds.), *Applying Psychology* (pp. 179–241). Milton Keynes, Open University.

Vrij, A. (2003). *Criteria-Based Content Analysis: A qualitative review of the first 37 studies.* Manuscript submitted for publication.

Vrij, A., Akehurst, L., Soukara, R., & Bull, R. (in press). Detecting deceit via analyses of verbal and nonverbal behavior in adults and children. *Human Communication Research.*

Vrij, A., Dragt, A. W., & Koppelaar, L. (1992). Interviews with ethnic interviewees: Nonverbal communication errors in impression formation. *Journal of Community and Applied Social Psychology, 2,* 199–209.

Vrij, A., Edward, K., & Bull, R. (2001b). Stereotypical verbal and nonverbal responses while deceiving others. *Personality and Social Psychology Bulletin, 27,* 899–909.

Vrij, A., Edward, K., Roberts, K. P., & Bull, R. (2000). Detecting deceit via analysis of verbal and nonverbal behavior. *Journal of Nonverbal Behavior, 24,* 239–263.

Vrij, A., & Fisher, A. (1997). The role of displays of emotions and ethnicity in judgements of rape victims. *International Review of Victimology, 4,* 255–265.

Vrij, A., Foppes, J. H., Volger, D. M., & Winkel, F. W. (1992). Moeilijk te bepalen wie de waarheid spreekt: Non-verbaal gedrag belangrijkste indicator. *Algemeen Politie Blad, 141,* 13–15.

Vrij, A., & Graham, S. (1997). Individual differences between liars and the ability to detect lies. *Expert evidence: The international digest of human behaviour science and law, 5,* 144–148.

Vrij, A., Harden, F., Terry, J., Edward, K., & Bull, R. (2001d). The influence of personal characteristics, stakes and lie complexity on the accuracy and confidence to detect deceit. In R. Roesch, R. R. Corrado, & R. J. Dempster (Eds.), *Psychology in the courts: International advances in knowledge* (pp. 289–304). London: Routledge.

Vrij, A., & Heaven, S. (1999). Vocal and verbal indicators of deception as a function of lie complexity. *Psychology, Crime, & Law, 4,* 401–413.

Vrij, A., & Holland, M. (1998). Individual differences in persistence in lying and experiences while deceiving. *Communication Research Reports, 15,* 299–308.

Vrij, A., & Lochun, S. Neuro-linguistic programming and the police: Worthwhile or not? *Journal of Police and Criminal Psychology, 12,* 25–31.

Vrij, A., & Mann, S. (2001a). Telling and detecting lies in a high-stake situation: The case of a convicted murderer. *Applied Cognitive Psychology, 15,* 187–203.

Vrij, A., & Mann, S. (2001b). Who killed my relative? Police officers' ability to detect real-life high-stake lies. *Psychology, Crime, & Law, 7,* 119–132.

Vrij, A., & Mann, S. (in press). Detecting deception: The benefit of looking at a combination of behavioral, auditory and speech content related cues in a systematic manner. *Group Discussion and Negotiation.*

Vrij, A., & Semin, G. R. (1996). Lie experts' beliefs about nonverbal indicators of deception. *Journal of Nonverbal Behavior, 20,* 65–80.

Vrij, A., Semin, G. R., & Bull, R. (1996). Insight in behaviour displayed during deception. *Human Communication Research, 22,* 544–562.

Vrij, A., & Taylor, R. (2003). Police officers' and students' beliefs about telling and detecting little and serious lies. *International Journal of Police Science and Management, 5,* 1–9.

Vrij, A., & Van Wijngaarden, J. J. (1994). Will truth come out? Two studies about the detection of false statements expressed by children. *Expert evidence: The international digest of human behaviour, science and law, 3,* 78–84.

Vrij, A., & Winkel, F. W. (1991). Cultural patterns in Dutch and Surinam nonverbal behaviour: An analysis of simulated police/citizen encounters. *Journal of Nonverbal Behavior, 15,* 169–184.

Vrij, A., & Winkel, F. W. (1992a). Cross-cultural police-citizen interactions: The influence of race, beliefs and nonverbal communication on impression formation. *Journal of Applied Social Psychology, 22,* 1546–1559.

Vrij, A., & Winkel, F. W. (1992b). Social skills, distorted perception and being suspect: Studies in impression formation and the ability to deceive. *Journal of Police and Criminal Psychology, 8,* 2–6.

Vrij, A., & Winkel, F. W. (1994). Perceptual distortions in cross-cultural interrogations: The impact of skin color, accent, speech style and spoken fluency on impression formation. *Journal of Cross-Cultural Psychology, 25,* 284–296.

Vrij, A., Winkel, F. W., & Koppelaar, L. (1991). Interactive tussen politiefunctionarissen en allochtone burgers: Twee studies naar de frequentie en het effect van aan-en wegkijken op de impressieformatie. *Nederlands Tijdschrift voor de Psychologie, 46,* 8–20.

Walkley, J. (1985). Reading the suspect. *Police Review,* 15 February.

Wallbott, H. G., & Scherer, K. R. (1991). Stress specifics: Differential effects of coping style, gender, and type of stressor on automatic arousal, facial expression, and subjective feeling. *Journal of Personality and Social Psychology, 61,* 147–156.

Waltman, J. L. (1983). Nonverbal communication in interrogation: Some applications. *Journal of Police and Science Administration, 11,* 166–169.

Winkel, F. W., & Koppelaar, L. (1991). Rape victims' style of self-presentation and secondary victimization by the environment. *Journal of Interpersonal Violence, 6,* 29–40.

Yeschke, C. L. (1997). *The art of investigative interviewing: A human approach to testimonial evidence.*

Zaparniuk, J., Yuille, J. C., & Taylor, S. (1995). Assessing the credibility of true and false statements. *International Journal of Law and Psychiatry, 18,* 343–352.

Zuckerman, M., DeFrank, R. S., Hall, J. A., Larrance, D. T., & Rosenthal, R. (1979). Facial and vocal cues of deception and honesty. *Journal of Experimental Social Pychology, 5*, 378–396.

Zuckerman, M., DePaulo, B. M., & Rosenthal, R. (1981). Verbal and nonverbal communication of deception. In L. Berkowitz (Ed.), *Advances in experimental social psychology, volume 14* (1–57). New York: Academic Press.

Zulawski, D. E., & Wicklander, D. E. (1993). *Practical aspects of interview and interrogation.*

ENDNOTES

1. Whether the lie detector is an actual interviewer or a passive observer might be another variable that influences whether people pay more attention to speech content or to nonverbal communication, although the findings are inconsistent. Buller, Strzyzewski and Hunsaker (1991) and Feeley and deTurck (1997) found that active interviewers pay most attention to nonverbal communication, whereas observers mostly look at speech content. Granhag and Strömwall (2001b), however, found the opposite effect.
   In addition, being suspicious may also have an effect on paying attention to speech content or nonverbal communication while attempting to detect deceit (Millar & Millar, 1997, 1998). Again, the findings are not clear.
2. Somewhat different from speech content is speech style. Speech style addresses the issue whether certain words or phrases indicate deception. Researchers have examined several speech style aspects, including verbal immediacy (the present tense is more immediate than the past tense, and phrases such as "Here's Johnny" is more immediate than "There's Johnny"), generalizing terms (everyone, no one, all, every, etc.), self-references (I, me, mine, myself), group references (we, us, ours), other references (he, she, they, them), tentative constructions (may, might, could, etc.), ritualized speech (you know, well, really), and negative statements (including complaints). DePaulo, Lindsay, Malone, Muhlenebruck, Charlton, and Cooper (2003) reviewed studies examining these aspects and found that liars speak in less immediate terms and include more negative statements into their accounts than truth tellers.
3. Zuckerman, DePaulo, & Rosenthal (1981), who introduced these three factors, also included a fourth factor in their theoretical model, labelled 'arousal'. We left this factor out as, in our view, it shows an overlap with the emotion factor. Zuckerman et al. (1981, p. 9) themselves already suggested this by finishing their arousal factor paragraph with the following statement: "It is possible, however, that the general autonomic responsivity to deception reflects specific emotions. If so, cues to deception may be accounted for by the particular affects that are involved rather than by general arousal."
4. The three processes are hypothetical and are typically introduced post hoc to explain nonverbal and verbal differences between liars and truth tellers. Apart from this 'three factor model', other theoretical models for explaining nonverbal cues to deception are given as well in the deception literature (Buller & Burgoon, 1996; DePaulo et al., 2003; Ekman, 1985; Ekman & Friesen, 1969). See DePaulo et al. (2003) for a description of each of these theoretical models. By discussing only the 'three factor model' we do not suggest that this theoretical model is superior to the other theoretical mod-

els. However, there is evidence that liars actually experience the three processes described in the three factor model when they lie, whereas similar studies have not been carried out regarding the other theoretical models. In one of our own experiments (Vrij, Semin, & Bull, 1996), participants were asked either to lie or to tell the truth. Afterwards they were asked to what extent they had experienced the three processes. Results showed that liars experienced all three processes significantly more than truth tellers. In another experiment (Vrij, Edward, & Bull, 2001) we found individual differences in experiencing these processes. For example, a negative correlation was found between being good at acting and having to think hard while lying. Although these studies were correlational studies, the relationship between the three processes and lying is more likely to be causal: They are the consequence of being engaged in lying.

5. Commercial companies have exploited this idea and brought several voice analyzers on the market which, they say, can be used to detect deceit. However, these analyzers are not as accurate as many companies claim them to be. See Vrij (2000a) for problems lie detectors face when using equipment which measures physiological responses.

6. Ekman's work (1985) has revealed that observing *emotional micro-expressions* in the face might reveal valuable information about deception. Strongly felt emotions almost automatically activate muscle actions in the face. Anger, for example, results in a narrowing of the lips and lowering of the eyebrows, and eyebrows which are raised and pulled together and a raised upper eyelid and tensed lower eyelid typically denote fear. If a person denies an emotional state which is actually being felt, this person will have to suppress these facial expressions. Thus, if a scared person claims not to be afraid, that person has to suppress the facial micro-expressions which typically indicate fear. This is difficult, especially because these emotions can arise unexpectedly. For instance, people do not usually deliberately choose to become frightened, this happens automatically as a result of a particular event that took place, or as the result of a particular thought. The moment fright occurs, a fearful facial expression may be shown which may give the lie away. People are usually able to suppress these expressions within 0.5 of a second after they begin to appear (Ekman, 1985).

The opposite can occur as well. Someone can pretend to experience a particular emotion, whereas in fact this emotion is not felt. Someone can pretend to be angry, whereas in reality the person is not angry at all. In order to be convincing, the liar should produce an angry facial expression, that is, the liar should try to narrow the lips. However, this muscle action is very difficult for most people to make voluntarily (Ekman, 1985).

It is also difficult to fake an emotion other than the one which is actually felt.

For example, a potential hijacker may become scared during a conversation with security personnel when he realizes that they might find out what his plans are, but can decide to mask this emotional state by pretending to be angry with the security personnel because they are checking on him so thoroughly and apparently do not trust him. In order to be convincing, he therefore has to suppress his fearful facial expression and replace it with an angry facial expression. This is difficult, because he has to lower his eyebrows (sign of anger) whereas his eyebrows tend to raise (sign of fear) (Ekman, 1985). Ekman's observations could well be of value. For example, in one of our studies (Vrij & Mann, 2001a) we included a person who held a televised press conference to ask for information about his missing girl-friend. Later it turned out that he himself had killed his girlfriend. A detailed analysis of the videoclip revealed that he showed a micro-expression of a (suppressed) smile during that press conference. His smile was in the given context interesting. Why did the man smile? And why did he attempt to suppress that smile? Although his smiling at a press conference cannot be interpreted as a definite indication of deceit, at least, it made the man suspicious. Unfortunately, no empirical test of the frequency of occurrence of emotional micro-expressions during lying and telling the truth yet appears to have been published in peer reviewed journals, which is also the reason why these micro-expressions did not emerge as cues to deception in recent literature reviews.

7. Sometimes professional lie catchers tell us that they believe that eye movements are associated with deception. They then typically refer to the neurolinguistic programming (NLP) model. However, not a single scientific study has demonstrated that eye movements are related to deception in the way described in the NLP model (Vrij & Lochun, 1997). NLP teachers who claim the opposite therefore are engaged in deceiving their pupils.

8. Although the total and lie accuracy rates were significantly higher than the total and lie accuracy scores obtained by laypersons (mostly college students) in previous research, it cannot be concluded that police officers are actually better lie detectors than laypersons. Laypersons were not included in Mann et al.'s (2003) study, and perhaps they would have achieved similar accuracy rates as police officers if they had participated.

❧ 5 ☙

Nonverbal Behavior and Political Leadership

George R. Goethals
Williams College

Historian Shelby Foote describes the way a military leader's nonverbal behavior, in a particular instance, was misconstrued. During the Civil War, a Union general checked into the Willard Hotel in Washington, D.C. He struck an observer as having "no gait, no station, no manner." Rather, his aspect of "rough, light-brown whiskers, a blue eye, and rather scrubby look withal ... as if he was out of office and on half pay" suggested someone who need not be taken seriously. The desk clerk assumed a superior air. When the general wrote his name in the register, "U.S. Grant ... Galena, Illinois," things changed fast. The clerk rang the bell loudly, and the observer took a new look. On second glance, he "perceived that there was more to him than had been apparent before .... The 'blue eye' became a 'clear blue eye,' and the once stolid-seeming face took on 'a look of resolution, as if he could not be trifled with.' " (Foote, 1963, pp. 3–4).

People's impressions of Ulysses S. Grant during the Civil War, or any leader at any time, are based on several kinds of information, including appearance, nonverbal behavior, and context. Leaders most often speak or write, but their words are often qualified by their nonverbal behavior, and their verbal and nonverbal behavior together are interpreted quite differently depending on contextual information. This chapter considers the role of nonverbal behavior in political leadership. Obviously, nonverbal behavior does not exist in a vacuum. It combines with words to help create an overall impression or reaction. These impressions and reactions are key elements in leading and following.

We will review briefly some basic theoretical formulations about the role of nonverbal behavior in communicating information about relationships, examine anecdotally the role of nonverbal behavior in influ-

95

encing viewer impressions of candidates in political debates, and discuss several studies my colleagues and I have conducted at Williams College on nonverbal behavior and perceptions of leadership.

NONVERBAL BEHAVIOR AND THE DIMENSIONS OF RELATIONSHIP

Timothy Leary's (1957) classic volume, *Interpersonal Diagnosis of Personality*, argued from extensive data bases that interpersonal behavior could be usefully catalogued along two dimensions (cf. Carson, 1969). First, interpersonal behaviors vary along an affective dimension, that is, in how much positive vs. negative feeling they express. Second, they vary along a status dimension, that is, in how much dominance vs. submission they express. Thus, interpersonal behaviors can be categorized as expressing love or friendliness on the one hand versus hate or hostility on the other. Or, they can be categorized as revealing neither distinctly positive nor negative affect. Also, those behaviors can be categorized as expressing dominance, submissiveness, or neither. Since a behavior can express one pole or the other of each dimension, or neither pole, the result, very roughly, is 8 different kinds of interpersonal behavior: behavior that is simply dominant, behavior that is friendly and dominant, behavior that is simply friendly, and so forth. In theory there is a ninth kind of interpersonal behavior, one that expresses neither positive nor negative affect, nor dominance vs. submissiveness.

One of Leary's key contentions was that each type of interpersonal behavior invites or elicits a complementary type. Specifically, on the affective dimension, both friendly and unfriendly behaviors invite similarly friendly or unfriendly behavior in return. In converse, on the status dimension, behaviors invite their opposite or counterpart. Thus while friendly behavior invites friendly behavior in return, dominating behavior invites submission in return. So, for example, friendly-dominant behavior from one person invites friendly-submissive behavior from another. Furthermore, while every interpersonal behavior invites its complement, people often but not always behave in the way they are invited to (Markey, Funder, & Ozer, 2003). For example, friendly-dominant behavior might produce friendly-dominant behavior in return, rather than friendly-submissive behavior. The second individual is happy to have a friendly interaction, but he or she does not want to be submissive.

One can see interpersonal behavior in flux along these lines in one of President John F. Kennedy's exchanges with reporters. Kennedy had a good relationship with the press, and he enjoyed having the upper hand in that relationship. His behavior was friendly-dominant. Luckily for him, most reporters were willing to be essentially submissive in their exchanges with him, complementing and therefore reinforcing his interpersonal behavior. On one occasion during the 1960 campaign a reporter repeatedly pressed the assertion, which Kennedy denied, that he had advocated reducing the federal debt early in his presidential term. Kennedy responded very firmly, but with a smile on his face: "No, never. No ..." The reporter accepted Kennedy's denial, responding in a friendly-submissive way, complementing Kennedy's behavior, after a little urging. The complementary behavior from the reporter avoided a spiraling exchange of dominant behavior from both parties, and it cut off the possibility that behavior in the exchange might become hostile. Leaders frequently employ dominant interpersonal behavior, inviting submissive behavior in return.

Leary argued that although people's actions vary with the situation, each individual's actions are marked by certain preferred categories of interpersonal behavior. These preferred categories reflect "security operations." People behave in ways that are comfortable for them, in large part because they are secure or comfortable when others behave in the complementary fashion that is elicited by their own behavior. The person who characteristically behaves in a friendly-submissive manner does so because he is comfortable performing that kind of behavior and equally comfortable with others behaving in a complementary friendly-dominant fashion.

Roger Brown (1965) proposed an analysis of interpersonal relationships that highlighted the same two dimensions identified by Leary. Brown called them the dimensions of status and solidarity. Just as an interpersonal behavior, or a set of interpersonal behaviors in an interaction, or across interactions, can be classified as friendly vs. unfriendly and dominant vs. submissive, so a relationship can be classified as being friendly or hostile, or neither one particularly, and also as one in which the two parties to the relationship have equal or differential status. The pair might have the same status level, as in the case of two corporals in an infantry unit, or one might have higher status, as in the case of a supervisor and a subordinate.

In this light, one person's interpersonal behavior not only elicits a particular kind of interpersonal behavior from another, it also expresses a definition of their relationship. John Kennedy's friendly-dominant behavior with reporters not only elicited friendly-submissive behavior from them, it signaled his definition of the relationship as one that was warm and cordial, but also one where he had a higher status. In expressing a definition of the relationship, especially along the status dimension, people express their view of themselves and others. Erving Goffman's (1955) essay on face-work makes this point very clear. In social encounters, Goffman argues, a person performs "a pattern of verbal and nonverbal acts by which he expresses his view of the situation and through this his evaluation of the participants, especially himself. Regardless of whether a person intends to [do this], he will find that he has done so in effect" (p. 213).

The idea that interpersonal behavior expresses a definition of the relationship is developed in Watzlawick, Beavin, and Jackson's (1967)

Pragmatics of Human Communication. They argued that every behavior is a communication and that communication takes place on two levels simultaneously. First, at the content level behavior communicates about external tasks, problems to be solved, recreational activities, the stock market, the National Football League, appropriate dress for a party, etc. However, at the relationship level behavior communicates each person's view that the relationship has high solidarity, that it is cordial or even affectionate and close, or that the relationship has low solidarity. In addition it communicates each person's view of the relative status of the two parties in the relationship—they are equal or one is superior.

In sum, the works of Leary, Brown, Goffman, and Watzlawick et al. suggest that both interpersonal behavior and interpersonal relationships can be classified according to dimensions of friendliness and dominance or status, and that one's interpersonal behavior communicates one's view of oneself, the other, and their relationship, and also invites the other to complement the behavior and thereby signal acceptance of that definition of the relationship. In our example above, John Kennedy's firm but smiling, "No, never. No," defined his relationship with the reporter as friendly but unequal, with Kennedy being dominant, or having higher status. The reporter accepted the definition.

Watzlawick et al., and to some extent Roger Brown, in his 1986 *Social Psychology, the Second Edition*, argues that nonverbal behavior plays a critical role in communicating at the relationship level. That is, while words and nonverbal behavior are completely intertwined (Henley, 1977), one can look at their separate contributions to communication. Watzlawick et al. holds that most communication about relationships is done nonverbally for two reasons. First, there are constraints on the candid expression of interpersonal feelings. Second, our verbal vocabulary for describing our feelings about others, especially along lines of solidarity and status, is quite limited. Brown believes that words can express feelings in addition to views about external matters, but that nonverbal behavior is important in communicating about relationships because deceiving people with nonverbal behavior is more difficult than simply telling lies. Our feelings about others sometimes leak, whether we like it or not, through nonverbal channels, especially voice quality. Nonverbal communication that is consistent with words underscores the credibility of what is said. In sum, our views of relationship are expressed implicitly but credibly through various nonverbal expressions: gestures, tone of voice, proxemics, facial expressions, etc.

NONVERBAL BEHAVIOR AND LEADERSHIP ENACTMENTS

People express their view of themselves and their relationship to others largely through nonverbal behavior. In the case of leaders, interpersonal nonverbal behavior will typically be assertive and express superiority in the relationship. In Watzlawick's terms, it will be "one-up" behavior. Others are invited to be "one-down," essentially followers. As many leadership theorists have argued (e.g., Burns, 1978; Hollander, 1993), if leadership is to exist, others must accept the invitation to follow. Burns emphasizes that leadership is a relationship. Hollander begins with the assumption that followers "accord and withdraw support to leaders" (p. 29). Thus leadership is negotiated and followers accord support to individual leaders depending on their own motives. But how precisely do leaders use nonverbal behavior to appeal to others to accord them support?

First, while our focus is on nonverbal behavior, as noted above nonverbal and verbal behavior are distinguishable but inseparable. They combine in a Gestalt. Roger Brown (1986) wrote: "Certainly, good actors can contribute something to the emotional impact of *Romeo and Juliet*, but it is generally supposed that Shakespeare's exclusively verbal contribution (the written transcript) is not negligible." (p. 497). Both verbal and nonverbal elements are important. Also, recall that Erving Goffman's quote above refers to the "pattern of verbal and nonverbal acts" that expresses a person's view of himself, others, and the situation. Finally, Howard Gardner's (1995) *Leading Minds* contends that leadership is primarily about the "stories" leaders tell. In most cases the stories are told or "related" with words. But in addition to telling stories, leaders embody their stories to varying degrees. Their behavior other than words, that is, their nonverbal behavior, may illustrate the story, or may contradict it. Ronald Reagan's story of the importance of a strong American military was somewhat undermined by the fact that he spent World War II in Culver City making movies rather than fighting in Europe or the Pacific. On the other hand, Pope John XXIII preached a message of humility and openness, and embodied it in his nonverbal behavior. He smiled, bowed, and listened. His well-illustrated story provoked a strong negative reaction, a counterstory, from the church hierarchy. But Pope John had the advantage of telling and embodying a story that was resonant with the teachings and life of Jesus. His story was compelling, and many followers accorded him support (Gardner, 1995).

One exploration of leadership that makes plain the interaction of words and nonverbal expression is John Keegan's (1987) *Mask of Command*, a study of military leadership:

> [Leaders] are both shown to and hidden from the mass of humankind, revealed by artifice, presented by theatre. The theatrical impulse will be strong in the successful politician, teacher, entrepreneur, athlete, or divine, and will be both expected and reinforced by the audiences to which they perform …. What they should know of him must be what they hope and require. What they should not know of him must be concealed at all costs. The leader of men in warfare can show himself to his followers only through a mask, a mask that he must make for himself, but a mask

made in such form as will mark him to men of his time and place as the
leader they want and need. (p. 11)

Keegan illustrates this perspective exceptionally well in his treatment of Alexander the Great. Usefully, he comments both on the theat-
rical (largely nonverbal) and oratorical (largely verbal) aspects of
Alexander's leadership. "Theatricality was at the very heart of Alexander's style of leadership ... His appearances in the field of battle [were]
dramatic stage entries, tellingly timed and significantly costumed" (pp.
47–48). As for oratory, Alexander combined verbal and nonverbal elements in leading effectively. He had a "forceful and collected style" and
used the rhetorical devices of a prebattle speech, urging his soldiers to
follow him, and to achieve victory once again as they had in the past.

Richard Brookhiser's (1996) biography of George Washington explains the role of nonverbal behavior in our first president's leadership. He reports that an English visitor wrote during Washington's first
presidential term "Washington has something uncommonly majestic
and commanding in his walk, his address, his figure, and counte-
nance" (p. 52). Brookhiser writes that he "had physical authority in its
simplest form, and though he enhanced it with exercise and adorn-
ment, they functioned as supplements, not substitutes" (p. 56). His facial expression often showed a towering temper, but usually under
firm control. Washington was not an orator, but when he spoke the
nonverbal supports increased his impact and capacity to lead.

A final example is Ronald Reagan. As David Gergen (2000) writes in
Eyewitness to Power, Reagan himself attributed his reputation as "the
great communicator" to what he said: "It was the content. I wasn't a
great communicator, but I communicated great things" (p. 216). Reagan, of course, was kidding. He had honed his speaking skills over
many years, first as an actor and then as a pitchman for General Elec-
tric, and later for Barry Goldwater. There are many mannerisms and
nonverbal attributes that made Reagan effective. Just as one example,
for the moment, many have commented on his "honeyed voice."
Gergen wrote that "He spoke in warm, velvety tones that enveloped listeners and made them feel good—about themselves *and* about him ...
he talked softly, even gently at times" (pp. 218–219). But importantly
as well, the voice and manner matched the words, and gave them additional credibility and impact. Reagan could also speak in a stern, forceful manner, as when he challenged the Russians to historic change in
Berlin: "Mr. Gorbachev, tear down this wall."

There is one fascinating study of the impact of Reagan's manner and
the way his nonverbal behavior drew people in (McHugo, Lanzetta,
Sullivan, Masters, & Englis, 1985). Undergraduates at Dartmouth
College watched videotaped excerpts from Reagan press conferences.
They were asked to report their reactions to what they saw and heard,
and their emotional reactions were also assessed via facial electromyo-
graphy, skin resistance, and heart rate. The students' prior attitudes

toward Reagan influenced their self-reports of their emotional reaction to the videotaped excerpts. They reported more positive reactions if they liked Reagan and agreed with his policies. However, their autonomic and facial muscle responses were independent of their prior attitudes. The results suggest that even those who disagreed with Reagan couldn't help but like him, and weren't fully aware of how positively they were responding to him.

In sum, leaders' appeal to followers or potential followers is based on some combination of their words and their nonverbal behavior. In politics today, much of our information about candidates for office comes through watching them on television. We hear them, but we also see them. The importance of television in conveying potentially influential information about nonverbal behavior is underlined by the McHugo et al. (1985) study noted above. They conclude their discussion of students' reactions to Ronald Reagan stating "the present results indicate that expressive displays ... can cause emotional reactions that are independent of prior attitudes when emitted by a powerful political leader and presented on television. To the extent that there is a trend toward candidate style variables and away from political party and issue positions in determining vote choice, the role of nonverbal behavior in electoral politics is increasingly important." Nonverbal behavior "may play an important role in forming and modifying impressions of political leaders who gain extensive exposure to voters through television" (p. 1528).

One of the ways that political candidates get access to voters is through televised debates. Televised debates between John F. Kennedy and Richard M. Nixon were important in the 1960 election and they have been a staple of presidential elections every four years starting with the 1976 debates between Jimmy Carter and Gerald Ford. We will describe the role of televised debates throughout their history on the American political landscape, and then discuss some of our own research on the role of nonverbal cues in debates.

NONVERBAL BEHAVIOR IN PRESIDENTIAL DEBATES

It has been widely believed since the publication of Marshall McLuhan's (1964) *Understanding Media* that televised debates were critical to John F. Kennedy's slim victory over Richard Nixon in the election of 1960. McLuhan argued that voters who watched the debate on television tended to perceive Kennedy as the winner while those who listed on the radio thought that Nixon won. There are data showing that Kennedy, but not Nixon, was helped by his appearance in the first of four joint debates. Tannenbaum, Greenberg, and Silverman (1962) found that Kennedy was perceived as much more "experienced" after the first debate. This change undermined Nixon's campaign slogan, "Experience Counts," implying that he, Nixon, had more relevant experience for executive leadership than Kennedy. Also, the changes in

voters' perceptions of Kennedy were all in the direction of what people
had specified as their image of the "ideal President." (Weiss, 1968).
Changes in voters' impressions of Nixon were unsystematic. Can we
begin to specify some of the elements that made Kennedy more appealing on television?

One possibility is that Kennedy was simply better looking than
Nixon. We have some data that suggest that good looks are a part of the
story, but only a part. In an experiment, Williams College students
were shown excerpts from the first 1960 Kennedy/Nixon debate in
three conditions. In an Audio Only condition, participants simply listened to an audio recording of debate excerpts. In the Audiovisual condition, the excerpts were ordinary televised versions. In an Audio Still
condition, an audio track was accompanied by a video tape that
showed still or nonmoving pictures taken from the video tape, each
still segment lasting about 20 seconds. The relative ratings of Kennedy
and Nixon were least favorable to Kennedy in the Audio Only condition
and most favorable to Kennedy in the Audiovisual condition, with the
Audio Still condition falling between the other two. Although extremely
preliminary, these results suggest there was more going on than people
simply judging that Kennedy was better looking.

A close look at a videotape of the debate suggests some of the visual
factors that might have made a difference. The camera shows the debate moderator, Howard K. Smith, seated behind a small table. On either side of him is a chair. Kennedy sits on the left of the screen, Smith
is in the middle, and Nixon is on the right. Farther to the left and right
are podiums behind which the candidates are to speak. The procedure
that is followed is that each man rises from his chair next to Smith's table, and walks to his respective podium to speak. In this setting, there
are several telling differences in the candidates' appearance and nonverbal behavior. First, when Howard K. Smith introduces the two candidates, Kennedy nods in a relaxed self-assured manner, while Nixon
fidgets, moving his arms awkwardly, and nods in a jerky manner. Second, at several times during the candidates' eight-minute opening
statements, first by Kennedy, then Nixon, the other candidate is
shown, Nixon while Kennedy is speaking and Kennedy while Nixon is
speaking. Kennedy is shown taking notes while Nixon speaks, writing
in a very rapid, focused and confident manner. Nixon sometimes
seems drawn and haggard, watching Kennedy when Kennedy speaks.
The fact that Kennedy appears more in command of himself and the
occasion when Nixon speaks rather than vice-versa led some observers to joke "The cameraman was a Democrat." Third, at the end of each
of their opening statements, the camera follows the candidates back to
their chairs. Kennedy walks back deliberately, sits down, folds his
hands, crosses his legs, and looks self-satisfied. In contrast, Nixon
moves in one direction and then the other, seemingly unsure of where
he should be going, and then sits down, looking somewhat awkward
and confused.

Finally, there is a fascinating sequence after the opening statements. The first question is directed to Kennedy. He begins answering the question from his chair, right next to Smith. Kennedy is violating the rules for the debate, which specify that when speaking, the candidates should rise from their chairs and walk to their podiums. Nixon looks agitated and gets Smith's attention, and gestures that Kennedy should go to his podium. Perhaps the rules are very much on Nixon's mind, since he was unsure of where he should go the minute before, when he concluded his opening statement. Smith also seems unsure of what action to take. He begins to bang his gavel, his only prop at the table, but then stops, whispers to Kennedy, and points to the podium. With almost no interruption in his response, Kennedy gets up and walks to the podium and continues answering the question. There is a large difference between the ways this moment plays out on television vs. the radio. On the radio, there would be a very brief, but perhaps noticeable, pause in Kennedy's reply. This might be taken to signal that Kennedy is unsure of how to respond. On television, an interesting nonverbal mini-drama plays out. Two men, Nixon and Smith, look slightly perplexed and agitated. One, Kennedy, responds to the flow of events calmly and gracefully. To be sure, the account above is simply this author's guess of how the moment might have come across to radio vs. television audiences. However, we do know that something beyond the candidates' appearances as captured in still frames affected people's reactions. This moment is a strong candidate for one of the somethings that was important.

Following the 1960 election, there were no presidential debates for sixteen years. Lyndon Johnson wanted no part of televised debates when he ran against Barry Goldwater in 1964, and Richard Nixon, once burned, did not choose to debate Hubert Humphrey in 1968 or George McGovern in 1972. However, a series of debates did take place between the presidential and vice-presidential candidates in 1976. Jimmy Carter and Gerald Ford had three debates, and Walter Mondale and Bob Dole participated in the first vice-presidential debate.

Again, a fascinating combination of visual and verbal information was important in shaping people's perceptions, and among the visual elements, a large part was played by candidates' nonverbal behavior. One immediate impression from the outset of the first Carter-Ford debate was that Ford was favored by the stage setting. The candidates stood behind large wooden podiums, unlike the simple orchestra director-style podiums used by Nixon and Kennedy. Gerald Ford, a large former football player at the University of Michigan, leaned over his podium, and seemed to dominate it. Carter, a smaller man, stood behind his podium, and looked more like a choirboy than an athlete. The initial visual impression favored Ford. He appeared more commanding than Carter. A more decisive moment took place in the vice-presidential debate that year between Dole and Mondale. Dole began talking about the number of soldiers who had been killed or wounded during

"Democrat wars" of the 20th century. Viewers and commentators were shocked that Dole would refer to the two world wars, the Korean conflict, and the war in Viet Nam as "Democrat wars." Moreover, as he spoke, Dole leaned on his elbow against the podium, looking very much like a gunslinger in a saloon in an old west cowboy movie. Dole's dark hair and eyes and dry manner of speaking contributed to a very negative image. Mondale calmly criticized the idea that any reasonable person would think that the war against Nazi Germany, and other wars, were partisan. Many years later Mondale (1999) said that he was prepared for Dole's comment, because he had been making it on the campaign trail. However, Mondale had told his advisers that they were "nuts" to think that Dole would say such a thing in a nationally televised debate: "He wouldn't be that stupid." Many political commentators believed that Dole's performance in his debate with Mondale seriously hurt the Ford campaign.

The next two elections, in 1980 and 1984, turned out to be landslide victories for Ronald Reagan, first over Jimmy Carter and then over Walter Mondale. In the single Carter-Reagan debate in 1980, Reagan's slow, calm, and gentle manner of speaking convinced uncertain voters that he was not too bellicose and that he could be entrusted with the power to make war or peace. Reagan's paralinguistic abilities served him extremely well. When he stated at the outset that "our first priority must be world peace," his voice sounded sincere, calm, and most of all, reassuring. James David Barber's (1992) discussion of varying "climates of expectation" implies that the electorate wanted reassurance in 1980, and Reagan delivered it. Reagan's "velvety tones" and "honeyed voice," described by David Gergen (2000), were on full display.

In 1984 Reagan's acting abilities saved him from the embarrassment of losing two debates to Walter Mondale, and paved the way for a forty-nine state landslide. Reagan performed very poorly in his first debate with Mondale, so poorly, in fact, that political pundits began to ask whether Reagan, then 73 years old, was still mentally and physically up to the job of being president. It was perhaps inevitable that during the second debate someone would ask Reagan about his rocky performance and his age. As is well-known, Henry Trewhitt of The Baltimore Sun asked Ronald Reagan: "Mr. President, I want to raise an issue that I think has been lurking out there for two or three weeks, and cast it specifically in national security terms. You already are the oldest President in history, and some of your staff say you were tired after your most recent encounter with Mr. Mondale. I recall yet that President Kennedy had to go for days on end with very little sleep during the Cuba missile crisis. Is there any doubt in your mind that you would be able to function in such circumstances?" The words of Reagan's response have been reported often. They worked very well for the President: "Not at all, Mr. Trewhitt. And I want you to know that also I will not make age an issue in this campaign. I am not going to exploit, for political purposes, my opponent's youth and inexperience." But the impact of what Reagan said, and the entire moment, were greatly affected by the way he said it. As in the Kennedy-Nixon case described above, there unfolded a nonverbal mini-drama, or at least a nonverbal episode.

It plays out as follows. First, when Reagan realizes that the question will be about age, he moves his body and nods in a very serious and confident-looking way. He appears ready for the question. Clearly, he had anticipated the question and planned a response. Second, he speaks in what can be described as a mock-serious manner. That is, he looks and sounds serious, and firm, but the words are not serious, so it becomes clear that the manner is not serious either. Third, the immediate reaction, which Reagan would have anticipated to some degree, works wonderfully in his favor. The audience laughs, Trewhitt laughs, and Walter Mondale laughs. Mondale (1999) said he knew that Reagan was scoring big points, but that he could only do the natural thing, which was to laugh at a very clever and funny remark. Fourth, in the melee, Reagan immediately reaches for a glass of water, calmly and confidently sipping from it, thereby prolonging the moment of laughter, and triumph. He has a confident and self-satisfied look on his face. Fifth, Reagan displays suppressed laughter as Trewhitt tries to stop laughing.

After the laughter subsides, Reagan continues. Looking as if he were reaching back into long-term memory from Eureka College, he adds "If I still have time, I might add, Mr. Trewhitt, I might add, that it was Seneca or it was Cicero, I don't know which, that said, if it was not for the elders correcting the mistakes of the young there would be no state." Trewhitt then ratifies Reagan's knockout punch by stating "Mr. President, I'd like to head for the fence and try to catch that one before it goes over but I'll go on to another question."

We have data showing clearly that more than the words of Reagan's age comment carries the moment (Fein, Goethals, & Kassin, 1999). In two experiments Williams College students were presented with three different televised versions of the second Reagan-Mondale debate discussed above. In the Intact version the complete exchange between Reagan and Trewhitt described above was included. Also included was another memorable Reagan one-liner. In discussing national defense Reagan says that Mondale "has a commercial out where he's appearing on the deck of the Nimitz and watching the F-14s take off and that's an image of strength, except that if he had had his way when the Nimitz was being planned, he would have been deep in the water out there, because there wouldn't have been any Nimitz to stand on. He was against it." Reagan's comment was followed by hoots and laughter. In a Soundbites Deleted condition the Nimitz exchange and the age exchange were both edited out. In a Reaction Deleted condition the initial comments were included, but the audience reactions immediately after the remarks ("he was against it"; "my opponents youth and inexperience") were deleted.

In the case of the age exchange Reagan's drinking water and suppressing laughter were among the elements specifically deleted.

In an initial experiment participants viewed tapes that were about 40 minutes long. Thus slightly less than half of the entire 90-minute debate was shown. Participants then answered a questionnaire beginning with ratings of each candidate's performance on 0–100 point scales. The most telling way to look at the data is to consider the difference between Reagan's ratings and Mondale's. In the Intact condition, Reagan's ratings were 7.50 points higher, 66.25 to 58.75. In the Soundbite Deleted condition Reagan's ratings were 9 points lower (64.17 to 73.03), and in the Reaction Deleted condition Reagan's ratings were nearly 24 points lower (49.29 to 72.86). Consistent with these data, participants were asked at end of a questionnaire Who Won? Reagan, Mondale, or Neither? In the Intact condition, many more participants chose Reagan as the winner over Mondale, 60% to 17%. In the Soundbite Deleted condition, the perceived winner was reversed—Mondale was named the winner more frequently, 43% to 18%. However, in the Reaction Deleted condition, Reagan was completely swamped. Seventy-six percent named Mondale the winner and only six percent named Reagan.

These data suggest a number of things. First, Reagan's one-liners made an immense difference in the debate. It changed him from being perceived as a loser to being perceived as a winner. But, even more important, it is not the words themselves that are important. It is dynamic of the whole situation. When Reagan makes a witty remark, it invites a response. When that response is not heard, the comment itself seems out of place. Although we cannot be sure from these data, Reagan's follow through on the age question seems particularly powerful. Not only did he deliver a witty remark, he anticipated the reaction and then managed, with body movements, physical action, and facial expressions, to extend the moment and to bring it to a successful conclusion with his remark about elders correcting the mistakes of the young. What is impressive is the total orchestration of the moment, using both words and nonverbal behavior to move the audience to his side. No wonder Reagan once commented that he couldn't imagine being a successful president without having been an actor.

A second study was conducted to replicate and extend the study described above. This time the entire 90-minute debate was used, with segments described above deleted in the Soundbite Deleted and Reaction Deleted conditions. In this study, both candidates are given performance ratings of about 60 in the Intact condition. In the Soundbite Deleted and Reaction Deleted Conditions, Mondale's ratings are about 12 points higher. Clearly the soundbites are important, but they only work when the unfolding dynamic of the total situation is seen by viewers. Consistent with our findings, suggesting that what people see is important, a study by Patterson, Churchill, Burger, and Powell (1992) considered the impact of recorded segments from the same 1984 Reagan/Mondale debate. There were four segments showing each candidate, averaging 44 seconds each. Participants were exposed to the candidate's statements in four modalities: audio only, visual only, audiovisual and text. Reagan was rated more favorably in all four variations, but the greatest difference was in the visual only condition. Relative to Mondale, Reagan appealed most to voters who simply watched him. Similarly, studies by Masters and his colleagues of facial displays by Reagan and Mondale in the 1984 campaign suggest that Mondale's facial expressions failed to communicate warmth and reassurance (Masters, Sullivan, Feola, & McHugo, 1987; Sullivan & Masters, 1988).

The story continues to unfold in later debates. In 1988 George Bush had a great height advantage over Michael Dukakis. When they shook hands after their first debate, the difference was striking. During their first debate Bush suggested, without specifically pointing to Dukakis that Dukakis was the "iceman who never makes a mistake." This framing attempted to convert Dukakis' considerable advantage in articulation over Bush into a liability—Bush was imperfect but warm; Dukakis was a cold, Northern intellectual. Dukakis' manner in the second debate between the two candidates seemed to give proof to the Republican's implication. When the first question asked whether he would favor an irrevocable death penalty for the killer who raped and murdered his wife, Dukakis looked unfazed by the image of his dead wife, and said, no, and then changed the subject. The image of Dukakis as the iceman was frozen. In 1992 Clinton's "I feel your pain" voice and direct physical approach to citizens asking questions in the town meeting format helped him look caring and engaged, especially in contrast to George Bush, who was looking at his watch.

Overall, several studies as well as anecdotal accounts of presidential debates suggest that more than words are important. Both visual information and paralingual cues play a role in perceptions of political candidates. We would like to report some preliminary findings from a study that looked at the role of several different kinds of candidate information in a mayoralty election in Seattle in 1997. We find some tantalizing evidence that candidate and voter ethnicity interact with verbal vs. nonverbal behavior to influence people's reactions.

ETHNICITY, NONVERBAL BEHAVIOR, AND PERCEPTIONS OF LEADERSHIP

Past studies have identified several different kinds of nonverbal information that might be relevant to voters' perceptions of leaders, particularly leaders who appear in televised debates. In a study of viewers' reactions to Bob Dole and Walter Mondale in their 1976 vice-presidential debate, Krauss, Apple, Morency, Wenzel, and Winton (1981) identify several kinds of paralinguistic cues that might be relevant once semantic content has been removed from speech, including "pitch, amplitude, rate, voice quality, contour, etc." (Krauss et al., 1981, p.312). They also note the different kinds of information that is conveyed visually through posture, gestures, movement, facial expression, and looks. A particularly interesting study by Warnecke, Masters, and Kempter (1992) found that American adults who were shown silent videotaped images of American and European (French and German) leaders "feel more negatively when seeing the foreigners and judge them more negatively" than American leaders (p. 267). This effect disappeared when sound was included so that nationality was made known. Warnecke et al. suggested that the negative emotions and judgments of foreigners are based on the "preconscious monitoring of nonverbal cues" (p. 267). Perhaps people feel comfortable when they observe someone who moves in familiar ways, and have a more positive reaction to those individuals. The impact of these differences in comfort level and judgment is lessened when information in addition to information about the way individuals move is presented, perhaps due to a dilution effect (Nisbett, Zukier, & Lemley, 1981). Warnecke specifically suggests that "dynamic nonverbal cues," quite possibly head movements, account for their data. They conclude: "bottom line, our responses to leaders—and to others more generally—are often governed more by feelings or 'gut reactions' than by conscious verbal judgments" (p. 280). These feeling or reactions, in turn, are based on responses to nonverbal cues.

Pursuing the issues raised by Warnecke et al. we conducted a study whose major focus was the extent to which ingroup favoritism in judging two candidates in a political debate would vary depending on what verbal and nonverbal information participants had about the two candidates (Farmer, 1998). It considered especially the role of movement cues. Do people respond to the motions of others differently depending on whether those others are similar or different in their ethnicity? Warnecke et al. suggest people respond differently to the motions of others depending on their nationality. What about responding differently to the motions of leaders from different ethnic groups within a nation, specifically, the United States?

Let us begin by identifying four different kinds of information that are conveyed in televised debates. These are words, voice quality, looks, and movement. It is possible to look at the impact of each of these sources of information on perceivers separately. Words can be presented in a written transcript or can be read in a bland voice, thereby neutralizing any effect of differences in candidates' voice quality. Voice quality can be isolated by presenting audio tapes of candidates' content-filtered speech (cf. Krauss et al, 1981). Looks can be presented with still shots from photographs or videotapes. And movement can be presented with silent videotapes. Furthermore, much information about looks can be removed from silent recordings by blurring the face, as is often done to hide the identity of persons speaking on a videotape. Just as each of the four kinds of information can be presented separately, so too can any two kinds of information be presented together. For example, a standard audio tape presents both words and voice quality, but not looks and movement, and a silent video tape shows both looks and movement. Similarly, any three kinds of information can be presented, omitting the fourth. For example, a videotape with content-filtered speech takes out the words but leaves all other information, while blurred head shots take away appearance or looks information but leaves the rest. Similarly, videotapes with dubbed-in neutral voices remove voice quality and audiotapes with still photos remove movement. In principle, there are 15 different combinations of one to four kinds of information that can be presented (see Table 5.1).

Our study employed a debate that took place during the 1997 Seattle mayoral election between Charley Chong, an Asian-American, and Paul Schell, a white male. Information was presented to participants in six different variations. There were five different audio-visual combinations: audio only (Audio Only), still pictures only (Still Only), video with no sound (Video Only), audio with still pictures (Audio Still), and full channel audiovisual (Audiovisual). Also, we included a second audio only variation (Audio Ethnicity) in which we told the participants the names and ethnicities of the two candidates. In addition to the four

Table 5.1
Possible Combinations of Information to be Presented About Candidates in Debates

Presentation	Information			
	Words	Voice	Looks	Motion
A Transcript (Tr)	Yes	No	No	No
B Content filtered speech (CF)	No	Yes	No	No
C Stills only (St)	No	No	Yes	No
D Blurred video (BV)	No	No	No	Yes
AB Audio only (Au)	Yes	Yes	No	No
AC Tr + St	Yes	No	Yes	No
AD Tr + BV	Yes	No	No	Yes
BC CF + St	No	Yes	Yes	No
BD CF + BV	No	Yes	No	Yes
CD Video only (V)	No	No	Yes	Yes
ABC Au + St	Yes	Yes	Yes	No
ABD Au + BV	Yes	Yes	No	Yes
ACD Tr + V	Yes	No	Yes	Yes
BCD V + CF	No	Yes	Yes	Yes
ABCD Au + V (full channel videotape)	Yes	Yes	Yes	Yes

kinds of information discussed above—looks, movement, words, and voice quality—information about race is included in all the conditions except Audio Only. In the Audio Ethnicity condition this information is provided by the experimenter's instructions. In the Still Only, Video Only, Audio Still, and Audiovisual conditions that information is provided by the candidate's appearance and by their names, which were shown from time to time on the videotaped broadcast. Table 5.2 shows the kinds of information that are presented in each of these variations.

We were interested in how white and non-white students would react to the candidates in the different audio-visual variations. First, we felt that Charley Chong would do better with more visual information and less auditory information. Charley moves and gestures more than Paul. We felt that he would be perceived as more active and dominant in a video only variation. On the other hand, Paul speaks more smoothly and has a more soothing voice than Charley, though pretesting showed that neither man's voice suggested his ethnicity. Second, we expected that there would be some in-group bias such that overall nonwhite students would have a more favorable reaction to Charley, the Asian-American candidate, relative to Paul, the white candidate, in comparison to the relative ratings that white students gave to the two candidates.

Again, however, the major focus was on the way ingroup favoritism varied according to whether or not participants saw the candidates move. There are two pairs of conditions in which the only difference is that one variation shows the candidates move while the other variation does not. First, the Video Only variation shows the candidates move while the Still Only variation simply shows still pictures. There is no sound in either one. The only difference is the presence or absence of motion. Similarly, the Audiovisual condition shows the candidates move while the Audio Still condition does not. There is sound in both variations, but the difference is motion. We predicted that ingroup preferences, as revealed in white vs. nonwhite students' preferences for Paul vs. Charlie would be stronger in the Video Only variation than in the Still Only variation, and stronger in the Audiovisual variation than in the Au-

Table 5.2

Information Presented in Seattle Mayoralty Race Study

Variation	Information presented				
	Words	Voice	Ethnicity	Looks	Motion
Audio Only	Yes	Yes	No	No	No
Audio Ethnicity	Yes	Yes	Yes	No	No
Still Only	No	No	Yes	Yes	No
Video Only	No	No	Yes	Yes	Yes
Audio Still	Yes	Yes	Yes	Yes	No
Audiovisual	Yes	Yes	Yes	Yes	Yes

dio Still variation. Furthermore, in line with Warnecke et al. findings, we predicted that the greatest ingroup favoritism would occur in the Video Only condition. Favoritism in that condition would be stronger than in the Audiovisual condition because there would be no audio information to dilute the effect of the nonverbal motion information.

Participants arrived for the study and were told that it was investigating the way different media presentations affect people's perceptions of candidates in political debates, and that different groups of participants were watching different presentations of the debate (a rare instance of truth-telling, or partial truth-telling, in the social psychology lab). They were told, again truthfully, that they would see or hear brief portions of a debate between Paul and Charlie who were candidates for mayor of Seattle. Then each candidate was described in two bland sentences (e.g., Paul "has always wanted to make a difference"). In the Audio Ethnicity variation the experimenter added that Paul is Caucasian-American and that Charlie is Asian-American. The tapes participants saw or heard all 3 minutes and 11 seconds. They contained ten different segments, each lasting about 19 seconds. The candidate's remarks dealt with local transportation and economic development issues, so as to avoid national political issues. In the still variations, a representative still shot during the segment was shown for the entire 19 seconds.

The participants were 132 Williams College students who received either cash or course credit. The nonwhite students were African-American, Asian-American, and/or Latino. Ideally, we would have used only white and Asian-American students, but it would not have been possible to recruit as many Asian-American students as we needed. The results showed that the reactions of the three nonwhite groups to the two candidates were similar.

After watching or listening to the tape, participants rated each candidate's overall performance in the debate on a nine-point scale. Participants also indicated their perceptions of the two candidates on several bipolar nine-point scales including likeable-unlikeable, leader-not a leader, active-passive, confident-unsure, etc. The orthogonal solution to a factor analysis revealed two factors. Four measures correlated with the first factor but not the second: dominant-submissive, leader-not a leader, shy-outgoing, and active-passive. These four measures were combined to create an Overall Leadership measure. Five other measures correlated highly with the second factor but not the first: calm-nervous, appealing-not appealing, rough-smooth, likeable-unlikeable, attractive-unattractive. These five measures were combined to create an Overall Likeability measure. All analyses employed a three-factor ANOVA with two between-subject factors (Medium and Participant Ethnicity) and one within-subjects factor (Candidate).

The results showed two significant effects on the overall performance measure. First, there was a Medium by Candidate interaction showing, as predicted, that Paul was perceived as the better performer in the four variations with sound (Audio Only, Audio Ethnicity, Audio Still, and Audiovisual) while Charlie was perceived as the better performer in the two variations without sound (Still Only, Video Only; $p <$ .02). These results are shown in Table 3. Second, while there was no predicted Candidate by Participant Ethnicity interaction, showing overall ingroup preference, there was a three-way interaction showing, as predicted, that there were varying degrees of ingroup preference in the different media variations ($p < .05$).

The degree of ingroup preference in each media variation can be illustrated by adding the white participants' rating of Paul and the nonwhite participants' rating of Charlie and subtracting from that sum the white participants' rating of Charlie plus the nonwhite participants rating of Paul. The figures for this measure are also shown in Table 5.3. In descending order ingroup preference was strongest in the Video Only variation (1.44), as predicted, and decreased in the remaining variations as follows: Audiovisual (1.10), Audio Ethnicity (1.00), Still Only (0.95), Audio Still (–0.52), and Audio Only (–1.16). In line with specific predictions, ingroup preference was stronger in the Video Only variation than the Still Only variation (1.44 vs. 0.95, $p < .02$) and stronger in the Audiovisual variation than the Audio Still variation (1.10 vs. –0.52, $p < .01$).

In addition to the confirmed predictions, there are a number of other results of interest. First, the participants strongly preferred Paul in the Audio Only condition. This is especially true for nonwhite students. The basis for the nonwhite students' preference for Paul in this condition is not at all clear. It is the only condition in which participants do not know the candidates' ethnicity, and therefore the only condition in which issues of ingroup favoritism would not arise. Comparing the Audio Only and Audio Ethnicity conditions, both white students and nonwhite students evaluate Charlie more favorably in the Audio Ethnicity variation, where they know that he is Asian-American. This effect is much larger for nonwhite students. Nonwhite students

Table 5.3
Overall Performance Ratings

Variation	White students		Non-white students		In-group preference
	Paul	Charlie	Paul	Charlie	
Audio Only	6.63	5.36	7.45	5.02	–1.16
Audio Ethnicity	6.55	5.76	6.14	6.35	1.00
Still Only	5.71	5.98	5.22	6.44	0.95
Video Only	5.69	6.19	5.07	7.01	1.44
Audio Still	6.52	6.28	6.02	5.26	–0.52
Audiovisual	6.38	5.28	6.65	6.65	1.10

evaluate Paul less favorably in the Audio Ethnicity condition, whereas white students evaluate him about the same. Thus nonwhite students give very different evaluations of the two candidates in the two variations, suggesting that their ingroup preferences are strongly shaping their evaluations in the Audio Ethnicity variation, where ethnicity is known. The white students change their evaluations less. They do become more positive about Charlie, perhaps reflecting a tendency to be politically correct, but their changes are less than those of the nonwhite students. Second the Medium by Candidate interaction is interesting in its own right. Both white and nonwhite students respond more positively to Paul when heard and Charlie when seen. Those reactions are shared across the two groups of participants.

One interesting and perhaps reassuring finding is that participants' evaluations of the candidate's performance is not simply a matter of which one they like better. We noted above that a factor analysis yielded an Overall Leadership measure and an Overall Likeability measure. The results on the five-item Overall Leadership measure were very similar to the single overall performance measure discussed above, which was our main measure. The same significant three-way interaction of the Medium, Candidate and Participant Ethnicity variables obtained, with greater ingroup preference in the Video Only (0.90) and Audiovisual (0.95) variations than in the Still Only (0.28) and Audio Still (0.83) variations. In contrast, the Overall Likeability measure simply showed a main effect for Candidate, with both groups of participants liking Paul more than Charlie in all the Medium variations. Thus while participants consistently liked Paul more, they did not always consider him the best leader. The latter judgments were apparently influenced by ingroup favoritism, while the former were not.

The study reported above is an initial attempt to consider the interaction of verbal and nonverbal information in influencing people's reactions to political candidates. We considered whether white students would show some degree of preference for a white candidate and nonwhite students a preference for a nonwhite candidate, and found that it depended on the kind of nonverbal information that was presented about the two candidates. Although the results could be stronger and need to be replicated, they do suggest that people show in-group preferences more when they see political candidates from different groups moving rather than simply seeing their still pictures. The results also suggest that the response to motion is stronger when the motion is not accompanied by sound. Candidates' words seem to take some attention away from the candidates' movements and weaken whatever appeal may arise from positive reactions to the nonverbal behavior of candidates who are ethnically more similar. This may essentially be a dilution effect (Nisbett, Zukier, & Lemley, 1981).

It is not entirely clear how to account for the finding that observing the motion of two potential leaders increases in-group favoritism. The effect may be automatic, whereby the candidates' similarities or differences to the perceiver become clearer as more of their nonverbal behavior is observed. Perhaps there is a certain comfort level with people from one's group, or discomfort level with people from other groups, especially groups that are perceived in opposition or in competition in some way. Warnecke et al. (1992) suggest that their results reflect "preconscious monitoring of nonverbal cues" and such a process may account for our results. A somewhat different explanation emphasizes information processing, but again a nonconscious variety. Possibly confirmation biases are operating, whereby subjects have the hypothesis that the ingroup candidate is the better candidate and movement information is interpreted in a biased way so as to support and strengthen the original bias (Snyder, 1984). Additional research is needed to explore these issues further.

CONCLUSION

Clearly, our perceptions of political leaders are affected by their nonverbal behavior. Both words and music, if we may think of nonverbal behavior as music, are important. The nonverbal information may reinforce, qualify, or contradict the words. Highly skilled political actors, such as Ronald Reagan, have a masterful command of nonverbal behavior and know how to use it to enhance their appeal and influence. David Gergen (2000) suggests that nonverbal behavior reveals whether political leaders are comfortable with themselves and their audience. Listeners reciprocate leaders' comfort and relax when the leader is relaxed. Thus nonverbal behavior affects the relationship between aspiring leaders and potential followers, and affects both the meaning and the credibility of the leader's message. We have a long way to go to understand the subtleties of the way the nonverbal behavior of leaders influence the reactions and perceptions of various followers, or nonfollowers. But we already understand the enduring importance of nonverbal behavior in affecting the dynamic between leaders and followers.

REFERENCES

Barber, J. D. (1992). *The presidential character: Predicting performance in the white house*. Englewood Cliffs, NJ: Prentice Hall.
Brookhiser, R. (1996). A man on horseback. *Atlantic Monthly, 227*, 50–64.
Brown, R. (1965). *Social psychology*. New York: Free Press.
Brown, R. (1986). *Social psychology, The second edition*. New York: Free Press.
Burns, J. M. (1978). *Leadership*. New York: Harper & Row.
Carson, R. C. (1969). *Interaction concepts of personality*. Chicago: Aldine.
Farmer, G. W. (1998). The effects of nonverbal cues and ethnicity in triggering ingroup leader preference. Unpublished Honors Thesis, Williams College.
Fein, S. Goethals, G. R., & Kassin, S. M. (1999). Group influence on political judgments: The case of presidential debates. Unpublished manuscript, Williams College.
Foote, S. (1963). *The civil war: A narrative*. New York: Random House.

Gardner, H. (1995). *Leading minds: An anatomy of leadership*. New York: Basic Books.

Gergen, D. (2000). *Eyewitness to power: The essence of leadership, Nixon to Clinton*. New York: Simon and Schuster.

Goffman, E. (1955). On face-work: An analysis of ritual elements in social interaction. *Psychiatry: Journal for the Study of Interpersonal Processes, 18*, 213–231.

Henley, N. (1977). *Body politics: Power, sex, and nonverbal communication*. Englewood Cliffs, NJ: Prentice Hall.

Hollander, E. P. (1993). Legitimacy, power, and influence: A perspective on relational features of leadership. In M. M. Chemers & R. Ayman (Eds.), *Leadership Theory and Research* (pp. 29–48). San Diego, CA: Academic Press.

Keegan, J. (1986). *The mask of command*. New York: Viking Penguin.

Krauss, R. M., Apple, W., Morency, N., Wenzel, C., & Winton, W. (1981). Verbal, vocal, and visible factors in judgments of another's affect. *Journal of Personality and Social Psychology, 40*, 312–320.

Leary, T. (1957). *The interpersonal diagnosis of personality*. New York: Ronald.

Markey, P. M., Funder, D. C., & Ozer, D. J. (2003). Complementarity of interpersonal behaviors in dyadic interactions. *Personality and Social Psychology Bulletin, 29*, 1082–1090.

Masters, R. D., Sullivan, D. G., Feola, A., & McHugo, G. J. (1987). Television coverage of candidates' display of behavior during the 1984 primaries in the United States. *International Political Science Review, 8*, 121–130.

McHugo, G. J., Lanzetta, J. T., Sullivan, D. G., Masters, R. D., & Englis, B. (1985). Emotional reactions to expressive displays of a political leader. *Journal of Personality and Social Psychology, 49*, 1513–1529.

McLuhan, M. (1964). *Understanding media*. New York: McGraw-Hill.

Mondale, W. F. (1999). Personal Communication. October 21, 1999.

Nisbett, R. E., Zukier, H., & Lemley, R. E. (1981). The dilution effect: Nondiagnostic information weakens the implications of diagnostic information. *Cognitive Psychology, 13*, 248–277.

Patterson, M. L., Churchill, M. E., Burger, G. K., & Powell, J. L. (1992). Verbal and nonverbal modality effects on impressions of political candidates: analysis from the 1984 presidential debates. *Communication Monographs, 59*, 231–242.

Snyder, M. (1984). When belief creates reality. In L. Berkowitz (Ed.), *Advances in Experimental Social Psychology, 18*, 248–306. New York: Academic Press.

Sullivan, D. G., & Masters, R. D. (1988). "Happy warriors": Leaders' facial displays, viewers' emotions, and political support. *American Journal of Political Science, 32*, 345–368.

Tannenbaum, P. H., Greenberg, B. S., & Silverman, F. R. (1962). Candidate images. In S. Kraus (Ed.), *The Great Debates* (pp. 271–288). Bloomington: Indiana University Press.

Warnecke, A. M., Masters, R. D., & Kempter, G. (1992). The roots of nationalism: Nonverbal behavior and xenophobia. *Ethology and Sociobiology, 13*, 267–282.

Watzlawick, P., Beavin, J., & Jackson, D. D. (1967). *Pragmatics of human communication*. New York: Norton.

Weiss, W. (1968). Effects of the mass media of communication. In G. Lindzey & E. Aronson (Eds.), *The handbook of social psychology* (Vol. 5, pp. 77–195). Reading, MA: Addison-Wesley.

❧ III ❧

Applications to Business and Education

❧ 6 ❧

Business Applications of Nonverbal Communication

Ronald E. Riggio
Kravis Leadership Institute
Claremont McKenna College

A number of popular books proclaim the importance of nonverbal communication in businesses and organizations. For instance, the cover of the book, *Body Language in the Workplace*, by Julius Fast (1991), claims "to show us how to understand not just the obvious in the workplace but how to go beyond that to the real meanings and hidden agendas of our co-workers ... [the book] can be used to benefit business dealings of all kinds." In addition, nearly every management textbook mentions the important role that nonverbal communication plays in organizational behavior. Yet, there has been surprisingly little research directly examining nonverbal communication processes in business and organizational settings.

There are several reasons for this paucity of research. First, communication in work settings is quite complex and occurs nonstop. Estimates by Mintzberg (1973), for example, suggest that managers spend 80 percent of their workday engaged in communication. Yet very few of these workplace interactions lend themselves easily to study by nonverbal communication researchers. Second, relatively few nonverbal communication researchers from Psychology, Communication, and other social sciences, are interested in studying organizational behavior. Finally, business organizations typically view research as a nuisance and rarely cooperate with research focusing on basic processes, such as nonverbal communication, that do not seem to have direct ties to organizational productivity and profits. In addition, concerns about privacy issues and rising employment litigation deter researchers from obtaining the videotaped samples of employees' behavior necessary for nonverbal cues analysis. Still, there is great interest in the role

119

that nonverbal communication plays in the workplace, and this interest is growing in a world of work that is increasingly focused on the quality of communication and of the interpersonal relationships among workers.

There are several important trends affecting the world of work (Riggio, 2003, Chapter 1): First, is an increased emphasis on human resources in organizations. Work organizations have come to realize that among their most valuable assets are the quality of their workers, the knowledge and skills that they bring to their jobs, and the ability of these workers to perform well together. Thus, organizations today regularly talk about their "human" or "social capital." A second, related trend is the increased use of teamwork to get the job done. Workers typically work in highly interdependent teams that require a great deal of coordination and social interaction to perform their collective tasks. Both of these trends suggest that the performance of working individuals and work teams are dependent on the quality of communication that takes place on the job. As we know from research on social relationships (see Noller, chap. 9, this volume), nonverbal communication is critically important to the development of good interpersonal relationships, both at home and at work. Finally, two other important trends are the increasing cultural diversity of the workforce, and the increased use of virtual work groups that communicate electronically. Both of these trends have important implications for nonverbal communication in the workplace, related to potential communication "breakdowns." Cultural differences in nonverbal communication (see chap. 11) can lead to miscommunication, and a major concern of scholars studying electronic communication media, such as e-mail, is the impact that the absence of nonverbal cues has on the effective flow of electronic communication (see Kiesler, Siegel, & McGuire, 1984). So, it can be argued that nonverbal communication plays an increasingly important role in the workplace of today and of the future.

This chapter will focus on reviewing research on nonverbal communication in work organizations, focusing mainly on the areas that have received the most research attention, outlining what we have learned from research on nonverbal communication at work, and suggesting what the limitations are for applying this research in business and organizations. Specifically, we will review the role that nonverbal communication plays in person perception in work organizations, with a specific focus on evaluating potential employees (i.e., hiring interviews) and current employees (i.e., performance appraisals). A major portion of the chapter will focus on the role of nonverbal communication in managing relationships with employees— focusing on the role of nonverbal communication in organizational leadership and in teamwork. Also examined will be the role that nonverbal communication processes play in business transactions, including how nonverbal communication impacts sales effectiveness and customer service. Finally, we will briefly review research on nonverbal communication (or the lack thereof) in electronic communications and in the virtual work group.

NONVERBAL COMMUNICATION
IN THE EVALUATION OF PERSONNEL

Much of personnel work involves the evaluation of workers. Personnel professionals attempt to gather information about the suitability of potential employees via resumes, job applications, and employment tests, but especially through evaluations made in hiring interviews (Eder & Harris, 1999). Nonverbal communication plays an important part in the hiring interview from both the applicant's and the interviewer's perspectives (see Posthuma, Morgeson, & Campion, 2002). First, the savvy applicant engages in careful impression management, thoughtfully monitoring verbal responses to emphasize job-related strengths and hide potential weaknesses (Fletcher, 1989; Gilmore, Stevens, Harrell-Cook, & Ferris, 1999). In addition, the applicant strives to display a positive, interested demeanor. Research on the role of nonverbal cues in the hiring interview suggests that applicants displaying more expressive visual nonverbal behaviors, and cues of nonverbal immediacy, such as greater incidence of eye contact and smiling, more interviewer-focused, outward gestures, and a more direct body orientation (e.g., forward lean), receive more favorable evaluations than non-expressive interviewees (Gifford, Ng, & Wilkinson, 1985; Imada & Hakel, 1977; McGovern & Tinsley, 1978; Wexley, Fugita, & Malone, 1975). In addition, paralinguistic cues, such as speech rate and fluency, the absence of speech errors/disturbances, and pitch variability are also positively correlated with evaluations of applicants in interviews (DeGroot & Motowidlo, 1999). Interestingly, static nonverbal cues of physical attractiveness, appropriate business attire, and good grooming also have a positive effect on evaluations of interviewees—typically outweighing the influence of expressive cues (Cann, Siegfried, & Pearce, 1981; Heilman & Saruwatari, 1979; Riggio & Throckmorton, 1988; see also Andersen & Bowman, 1999).

Despite the impact of nonverbal cues on evaluations of interviewees, it is clear that greater attention is paid to what the applicant is saying, with certain verbal misstatements having a huge impact on whether an interviewee is viewed as "hirable" (Riggio & Throckmorton, 1987, 1988). Because one goal of the interview is to uncover the "truth" about an applicant's suitability for a job, research on deception is applicable to interview settings. Some of the deception research and research on channel inconsistencies in affect suggests that if there is perceived inconsistency in what the individual is saying and the nonverbal behavior accompanying the statement, then the nonverbal channel may be given greater weight than the applicant's words in forming an overall impression of the applicant (DePaulo & Rosenthal, 1979; Mehrabian, 1972; Mehrabian & Wiener, 1967; Vrij, 2000; see also Vrij & Mann, chap. 4, this volume). Generalizing to the interview setting, this would be consistent with interviewers who report that although the interviewee gave appropriate answers in the interview, "something did not seem right," causing them to doubt the veracity of the interviewee and to give him or her an overall negative evaluation (see Harris & Eder, 1999).

The increased use of electronic communication technology has led to greater use of videoconferencing to conduct hiring interviews. In a very interesting recent study, Chapman and Rowe (2001) found that interviewers tended to make more positive overall evaluations of applicants in videoconference versus face-to-face interviews. In attempting to interpret this difference, the authors concluded that face-to-face interviews give interviewers access to additional nonverbal cues, most likely cues that reveal the interviewees' anxiety and discomfort, which then leads to more negative evaluations of the more "nervous-looking," live interviewees.

Typically, the impact of nonverbal cues in evaluations made in hiring interviews can be seen as a potential source of bias, particularly such seemingly "irrelevant" cues as physical attractiveness and smiling (Arvey, 1979). Yet, the key question is whether an applicant's nonverbal style in the hiring interview can actually predict future job performance. An interesting study by DeGroot and Motowidlo (1999) had existing managers in a news publishing company participate in a simulated interview where they acted as if they were applying for their current jobs. Content analyses were conducted of both interviewees' visual (e.g., smiling, eye contact) and vocal/paralinguistic cues (e.g., speech rate, pauses, pitch, amplitude). Results indicated that vocal nonverbal cues, but not visual cues, significantly predicted both evaluations of the interviewees (i.e., ratings of "credibility" and "trust") and later performance evaluations conducted by the interviewees' supervisors. The authors concluded that nonverbal vocal style in the interview may predict success in interpersonal relationships at work which was a very important component of these managers' job performance.

It is also important to note that in today's competitive job market, hiring interviews serve as a "marketing tool" for attracting good employees. In other words, it can be as likely that the applicant is "sizing up" the prospective company, as it is that the interviewer is evaluating the suitability of the applicant. Prospective employees may use the hiring interview as a "test" of what the company's culture is like, affecting their decisions to accept certain positions. For example, interviewers who show interest in the applicant and enthusiasm for the vacant position will likely be more influential in encouraging an applicant to accept a job offer (Connerley & Rynes, 1997). The interviewer's nonverbal behavior can also play an important part in influencing the applicant's behavior during the interview. In an interesting study (Liden, Martin, & Parsons, 1993), interviewers behaved in either a "cold" or "warm" manner (little versus more eye contact and smiling and a more or less direct and forward orientation toward the applicant—all cues that signal immediacy). Judges evaluating only the applicants' behavior rated applicants interviewed by the nonverbally warm interviewer as performing better than applicants in the cold interview condition. Clearly, nonverbal behavior of both applicant and interviewer can play a critical role in the success of interviews as a selection tool (Parsons, Liden, & Bauer, 2001).

From the interviewer's perspective, the hiring interview requires skill in decoding nonverbal cues. Similar to a deception situation, the interviewer is processing the verbal content of the interview, but also scrutinizing the interviewee's nonverbal behavior in an attempt to check the veracity of the verbal statements, as well as attempting to discern actual underlying attitudes and temperament that may suggest that the employee is both a good worker and a good "fit" for the job and the organization (see Riggio, 2001).

Do interviewers vary in their ability to successfully decode nonverbal cues? Although there is no direct evidence, we do know that certain interviewers are better than others at selecting successful applicants (e.g., Graves, 1993; Graves & Karren, 1999; Heneman, Schwab, Huett, & Ford, 1975; Zedeck, Tziner, & Middlestadt, 1983), and it has been determined that interviewers can improve their accuracy via training and experience (Pulakos, Schmitt, Whitney, & Smith, 1996), at least partly attributable to presumed improvements in interviewers' interpersonal skills (Connerley, 1997).

Another personnel setting where nonverbal communication plays an important role is during a formal performance appraisal or "coaching" session. In these sessions, a supervisor provides an employee with an evaluation of the employee's recent performance and furnishes constructive feedback to maintain or improve performance. Although there has been no research directly examining nonverbal communication in performance feedback sessions, this, like the hiring interview, represents a significant setting in the workplace where a supervisor's nonverbal encoding and decoding skills are particularly important (see Riggio, 2001). The performance appraisal is also an opportunity for supervisors to energize and motivate workers for future performance, and it is likely in this setting that the importance of the supervisor's positive expectations, and conveying those positive expectations to the worker, is highlighted.

Perhaps the most impactful line of research has examined the role of self-fulfilling prophecies, or the Pygmalion Effect, in the workplace (Rosenthal, 2003; Rosenthal & Jacobson, 1968; see also Harris & Rosenthal, chap. 8, this volume). The Pygmalion effect involves the subtle, often nonverbal, communication of expectations to another individual that influences his or her behavior. In the case of work performance, the Pygmalion effect would most often occur when the expectations of a supervisor are conveyed to the supervising worker, affecting his or her work performance.

Research by Dov Eden and his colleagues (Eden, 1990, 1993; Eden & Shani, 1982), and others, has demonstrated that supervisors can have a significant impact on boosting worker productivity by holding positive expectations about worker performance and conveying these positive expectations via both verbal and nonverbal channels. Conversely, supervisors are cautioned to avoid conveying negative expectations, termed the "Golem effect," to low performing supervisees (Davidson & Eden, 2000).

Two recent meta-analyses of studies examining the Pygmalion effect in the workplace have demonstrated that it has consistent positive effects on worker performance, but that Pygmalion effects seem to be stronger in military rather than business organizations, tend to more consistently affect male rather than female employees, and have greater influence on initially low-performing workers than on already high-performing employees (Kierein & Gold, 2000; McNatt, 2000). Because of these positive research results, and because of its popularity in management circles, there are a number of programs that train supervisors/leaders to communicate positive expectations, both verbally and nonverbally, to their workers. However, recent evaluations of these training programs have been disappointing, suggesting that it is not easy to train managers to hold positive expectations for subordinates, and for them to then be able to successfully communicate these in order to positively influence workers' behavior (Eden, et al., 2000; White & Locke, 2000). More likely, ability to communicate effectively, particularly communicating nonverbally, is a complex skill—one that leaders develop over time (or one that helps these skilled individuals attain positions of leadership).

NONVERBAL COMMUNICATION IN MANAGEMENT AND LEADERSHIP

As mentioned, effective communication and good interpersonal skills have always been considered critical for workplace managers and leaders (Bass, 1990). In particular, leaders who are sensitive to and responsive to followers' needs (presumably much of this skill involves nonverbal decoding) consistently outperform leaders who lack sensitivity (Bass 1960, 1990). Kenny and Zaccaro (1983) suggest that more than 50% of the variance in leadership concerns "the ability to perceive the needs and goals of a constituency and to adjust one's personal approach to group action accordingly " (p. 678).

A number of popular leadership theories emphasize the importance of interpersonal skills in developing high quality leader-follower relationships. For example, according to Leader-Member Exchange (LMX) theory, effective leadership is a function of the quality of the relationship between the leader and particular group members (Dansereau, Graen, & Haga, 1975; Graen & Uhl-Bien, 1995). In high quality leader-member relationships, the leader provides emotional support and motivating encouragement to the follower. These high quality relationships are also characterized by mutual trust, respect, and the leader's sensitivity to the follower's needs (Dienesch & Liden, 1986). The leader's ability to decode follower's feelings and attitudes, presumably emitted substantially through nonverbal channels, and the leader's provision of emotional support and motivation, presumably implicating nonverbal expressive behavior, are critical to leader success. Most recently, Uhl-Bien (2003) suggests that the leader's nonverbal communication skills are some of the key "ingredients" of building effective leader-member relationships.

In addition to the ability to manage relationships, effective leadership depends on the ability of leaders to manage impressions (see also Goethals, Chapter 5, this volume). Indeed, "image management," along with "relationship development" and the leader's ability to utilize the resources at his or her disposal, is one of the three core aspects of leadership according to Chemers' (1997) integrative theory of leadership. Research has found that leaders' self-monitoring—ability to monitor and control one's social behavior, including nonverbal behavior (Snyder, 1974)—is predictive of who emerges as a leader (Dobbins, Long, Dedrick, & Clemons, 1990; Ellis, 1998). In addition, the nonverbal display of dominance and power conveyed through such nonverbal cues as eye contact and posture (e.g., Mehrabian, 1969), amount of speaking time (e.g., Mast, 2002; Mullen, Salas, & Driskell, 1989), and even choice of seating place (e.g., Bass, 1990; Heckel, 1973), can be used to both emerge as a group leader and to help maintain an image of leadership (also see Andersen & Bowman, 1989). Yet, the relationship between displays of power and person perception may be more complex. For instance, it has been found that a more relaxed facial expression and direct eye contact were associated with greater perception of power and credibility in males (Aguinis, Simonson, & Pierce, 1998), but not for females (Aguinis & Henle, 2000).

The role of nonverbal communication in leadership, particularly the communication of emotions, is most clear in theories of charismatic, inspirational, and transformational leaders. Both inspirational and charismatic leaders are characterized by their abilities to arouse and inspire followers and to spur them to action. It is a general consensus that emotional expressiveness underlies much of the charismatic leaders' success in this regard (Bass, 1990; Conger & Kanungo, 1998; Riggio, 1987, 1998; Shamir, House, & Arthur, 1993). Indeed, studies that experimentally manipulated speakers' nonverbal delivery via "strong" and "weak" expressive behavior (i.e., less or more: eye contact, gesturing, facial expressiveness, and variations in pitch) found that a more expressive nonverbal speaking delivery was associated with ratings of speakers' charisma (Awamleh & Gardner, 1999; Holladay & Coombs, 1993, 1994; Howell & Frost, 1989). Using actual workplace leaders and a self-report measure of emotional expressiveness (the Emotional Expressivity Scale from the Social Skills Inventory; Riggio, 1989), Groves (2003) found that more emotionally expressive leaders were rated as more charismatic by their followers than leaders scoring low on expressiveness. However, it is clear that while nonverbal expressive skill contributes to the charismatic leader's dynamic persona, successful charismatic leaders are also exceptional decoders of followers' nonverbal cues—being able to "read" the desires and needs of followers and be responsive to them. It is easy to conjure up the image of the prototypical charismatic leader using forceful and expressive emotional cues to arouse and inspire the crowd, with the leader "feeding off" of the crowd's emotional reactions to bring them to higher and higher levels of collective emotion.

In the related theory of transformational leadership (Bass, 1998), leaders use their nonverbal skills to not only inspire followers, but the transformational leader is a careful impression manager, using herself or himself to model appropriate behavior for followers. Furthermore, the transformational leader establishes good interpersonal relationships with individual followers in an effort to "transform" followers into leaders—stimulating them to be creative problem solvers, and developing followers' communication and relational skills. Effective transformational leaders likely possess both good nonverbal encoding and decoding skills (see Ashkanasy & Tse, 2000; George, 2000).

With the recent surge of interest in the construct of emotional intelligence, best-selling books such as *Primal Leadership* (Goleman, Boyatzis, & McKee, 2002), suggest that ability to communicate emotionally—involving both skill in encoding and decoding nonverbal cues of emotion, along with the ability to regulate emotions (see Caruso, Mayer, & Salovey, 2002; Humphrey, 2002; Riggio, 1987)—are the keys to leadership success. Leadership researchers often refer to the importance of a leader's "empathy" as a critical determinant of the leader's ability to be responsive to followers. This "empathy" can refer both to nonverbal decoding skill, but also ability to take the followers' perspectives (e.g., Kellet, Humphrey, & Sleeth, 2002; Wolff, Pescosolido, & Druskat, 2002; see also Elfenbein & Ambady, 2002).

Although it is clear that there is a connection between charismatic leaders and nonverbal expressiveness, how do charismatic leaders use nonverbal cues to affect followers? One way is through the emotional contagion process (see Hatfield, Cacioppo, & Rapson, 1994). In an early study that captured the emotional contagion process, Friedman and Riggio (1981) had emotionally expressive and non-expressive individuals sitting face-to-face in a waiting room while their moods were measured at the beginning and ending of the silent waiting period. The results showed that the moods of the non-expressive persons were affected by the mood of the expressive person in the 3-member groups—with their moods "converging" on the mood of the highly emotionally expressive, silent "emotional leader" of the group. An interesting series of studies by Cherulnik and his associates (Cherulnik, Donley, Wiewel, & Miller, 2001), found that followers did indeed imitate the nonverbal cues of affect (e.g., smiles) emitted by charismatic speakers, but not the cues of non-charismatic speakers. This pattern was replicated by showing viewers excerpts from the Clinton-Bush debates, with viewers imitating only the nonverbal affect cues of the more charismatic Clinton. In addition to individuals varying in their emotional expressiveness, there is evidence that people also vary in their susceptibility to emotional contagion processes (see Doherty, 1997).

While most research on the expression of emotion in managers and leaders has focused on positive, "motivating" emotions, there is also evidence that some charismatic leaders can be emotionally manipulative and emotionally demanding and exploitative, sometimes creating unhealthy emotional dependency relationships with followers (Conger, 1990).

NONVERBAL COMMUNICATION AND MANAGING EMOTIONS IN THE WORKPLACE

Commensurate with the explosive interest in research on emotions has been increased attention to the role that emotions play in the workplace (e.g., Ashkanasy, Hartel, & Zerbe, 2000; Lord, Klimoski, & Kanfer, 2002). In brief, emotion management in the workplace has to deal with limiting and controlling the expression of negative, undesirable emotions (e.g., anger, jealousy, anxiety) and the encouragement of positive, desirable emotions (e.g., pleasantness, enthusiasm, enjoyment, appreciation). Nonverbal communication is implicated in making employees, particularly managers/leaders, more sensitive to the display of negative emotions in others (e.g., realizing that the behavioral display of anger can be an indicator of a worker's frustration, or may be a precursor to workplace violence; decoding cues of worry or rejection in a supervisee; see Fitness, 2000), and helping employees to express desirable emotions (e.g., encouraging workers to provide service with a smile; providing motivating words and cues of encouragement). It has been suggested that individuals may emerge as leaders of work groups because they are good "managers" of the group's emotion—inspiring them when necessary, displaying positive affect and optimism, and setting or maintaining the group's positive emotional climate (Pescosolido, 2002).

It is interesting to note that although there is a great deal of interest in the expression, decoding, and regulation of emotions in the workplace, the "practice" is getting ahead of the research attempting to understand these processes. For example, a recent article in the practitioner-oriented *Academy of Management Executive* proposes "strategies for developing an emotionally healthy organization," suggesting management take steps to "assess the emotional impact of jobs", create a positive emotional climate, and select and train employees for emotional skills (Ashkanasy & Daus, 2002). The problem is that it is unclear that research has progressed to the point that we can accurately assess and identify an organization's "emotional climate" or the appropriate emotional skills in prospective and current employees.

NONVERBAL COMMUNICATION
IN SALES AND CUSTOMER SERVICE

Ask anyone who has encountered a surly retail salesclerk, or a cheerful and attentive waiter, and it is clear that nonverbal behavior plays an important part in the quality of customer service. However, research actually examining nonverbal behavior and customer service has not progressed much past the "service with a smile" notion. Specifically, there is some evidence that "positive" and more "immediate" nonverbal behaviors by sales and service workers (e.g., smiling, eye contact) are associated with a more positive experience by customers, even to the extent of leading to larger tips for smiling as opposed to unsmiling waitresses (Tidd & Lockard, 1979)—with the effect carrying over to smiling faces drawn by the waitperson on the check (Rind & Bordia, 1996). An interesting study by Davis et al. (1998) suggested that it may indeed be cues of immediacy that are important, as waitpersons who crouched down to the customers' table level received higher tips than upright standing waitpersons. This is consistent with the finding that waitpersons who lightly touch customers also receive higher tips (Crusco & Wetzel, 1984; Stephen & Zweigenhaft, 1986). However, work conditions may also play a part. Sutton and Rafaeli (1988) found that as retail stores became busier, salespersons' positive affect declined in comparison to non-busy stores, but of course sales were better in the busier stores despite the lack of salespersons' positive affect.

In spite of the limited research evidence that suggests a friendly, positive nonverbal style will lead to better quality customer service, and subsequently greater profits, there is a strong belief in the business world that it does indeed matter (e.g., Bonoma & Felder, 1977; Sundaram & Webster, 2000). Training programs in friendly, expressive customer service abound, and there is some evidence that service workers can be trained to be "friendlier"—engaging in more positive and immediate nonverbal behavior (Brown, & Sulzer-Azaroff, 1994; Komaki, Blood, & Holder, 1980).

An area of personal sales that has received a great deal of attention draws on research on interactional synchrony or nonverbal rapport (see Tickle-Degnen & Rosenthal, 1987, 1990, for overviews of research on nonverbal behavior and rapport). The basic idea is that as greater levels of rapport is achieved, interactants begin to mimic each other's nonverbal cues and synchronize them (mirroring posture, gestures, voice tone and inflections, etc.). This mimicry is associated with more positive evaluations of and liking for interactional partners (e.g., Bernieri, 1988; Chartrand & Bargh, 1999; LaFrance, 1982).

The application of nonverbal rapport and mimicry began in psychiatry and clinical psychology as a means of facilitating the therapeutic process by Scheflen (Scheflen, 1964, 1965). This was later applied to the development of an entire "program" of personal selling, called neurolinguistic programming (NLP). In NLP, salespersons are taught to pay attention to potential buyers nonverbal behavior and to mirror their style. Although the claims for the effectiveness of NLP are extensive and enthusiastic (usually from practitioners who have received training in the technique), there has been little in the way of direct, sound empirical investigations of the efficacy of NLP. This is a classic example of putting the "practitioner cart" before the research "horse," as researchers are just beginning to understand how mimicry actually affects people in social interaction (e.g., Lakin & Chartrand, 2003; Lakin, Jefferis, Cheng, & Chartrand, 2003). For example, it is a far cry from research demonstrating that nonconscious mimicry is correlated with a sense of rapport and liking to determining whether it plays a direct part in persuasive selling when a seller intentionally mimics a potential buyer's behavior. Indeed, it has been suggested that NLP may be effective, not because of any direct influence of mimicry, but because by studying buyers' nonverbal behavior in an effort to mimic them, salespersons are actually becoming more interpersonally sensitive (DePaulo, 1992). In addition, there is evidence that overdoing the intentional mimicry of potential customers can backfire (DePaulo, 1992).

Finally, there has been considerable interest in mass marketing and advertising on the role of nonverbal cues in influencing the buying public. This includes the use of nonverbal cues in both print and television advertisements (e.g., use of music, sound effects, concern for the appearance cues of individuals in ads, voice tone and inflections of product spokespersons, etc.; see DePaulo, 1992 and Hecker and Stewart, 1988, for overviews). Most recently, research in marketing has been looking at emotional contagion effects on purchasing (e.g., Howard & Gengler, 2001)—an issue that is a main theme of the best-selling book, *The Tipping Point* (Gladwell, 2000).

NONVERBAL COMMUNICATION AND THE VIRTUAL WORK ORGANIZATION

As workers and work teams rely more and more on electronic communication—including the use of virtual work teams who rarely, if ever, have face-to-face meetings—there is a great deal of concern over what is lost in the electronic modalities. For the most part, the main difference is the significant loss of nonverbal cues in electronic communication (Kiesler, et al., 1984). Many nonverbal cues of immediacy, visual turn taking cues, and cues of status and affect are missing from all forms of electronic communication except for live videoconferencing, and both visual and auditory nonverbal cues are missing from e-mail and text messaging. In a recent study, it was found that evaluative feedback was more positive and more accurate in face-to-face as opposed to e-mail interactions presumably because of the presence of nonverbal cues (Hebert & Vorauer, 2003). This has important implications for conducting performance appraisals in a computer-mediated format.

Moreover, without visual and vocal feedback cues, e-mail users may engage in harsh and insensitive criticism of others (termed "flaming"), which could seriously damage personal and work relationships (Sproul & Kiesler, 1991). This has led to a concern about how to develop and maintain high quality interpersonal relationships among members of virtual work teams (e.g., Lipnack & Stamps, 1997).

Interestingly, people in virtual groups have devised a number of creative strategies to compensate for the missing nonverbal cues in electronic communication. Most notable is the use of "emoticons"—the various smiley-faced characters used to express emotions in e-mail communications (Walther & D'Addario, 2001). In addition, it has been suggested that users of text-based electronic communication may become more precise in their language use to more clearly communicate feelings and emotions, and avoid having the tone of a written message misunderstood by the receiver (Newlands, Anderson, & Mullin, 2003). This even goes so far as to clarify the communication of silence. In face-to-face communication, certain forms of silence can communicate approval, or can indicate confusion or a lack of understanding. Graham and Misanchuk (2004) suggest clarifying episodes of silence verbally in computer-mediated communication (e.g., typing agreement or disagreement; giving reasons for a pause—"I'm thinking it over").

Although much attention has been given to what is lost in computer-mediated electronic communication, there may also be some gains due to the absence of nonverbal cues. For example, the lack of feedback cues may reduce social interaction anxiety and induce people to be more open and willing to disclose personal information (Sproul & Kiesler, 1991). In addition, research on electronic as opposed to face-to-face "brainstorming" (a group strategy intended to stimulate the generation of creative ideas), suggests that electronic groups may be more productive, partly due to the decreased arousal and evaluation anxiety (not to mention the inability to show nonverbal displeasure) in computer mediated brainstorming groups (Paulus & Dzindolet, 1993).

This is obviously an important area, one that deserves the attention of researchers interested in how the ever-present and ever-increasing use of electronic communication affects the communication process, the development of relationships, and the effectiveness and quality of interactions among work team members (see Riva, 2002).

FUTURE DIRECTIONS AND RESEARCH

Clearly there is great interest in the business world in understanding how nonverbal communication affects the behavior of workers and work groups. Yet, it is likely that most business decision-makers do not view the area of nonverbal communication—whether it be improving the nonverbal communication skills of organizational members, or improving the process of nonverbal communication to improve work group interactions and relationships—as a high-priority topic. So, the challenges are twofold: First, for practice purposes, how to emphasize the importance of understanding and applying nonverbal communication research to improve the functioning of organizations and their members? Second, for researchers, where are the areas of opportunity for studying nonverbal communication in the business world?

Conducting research on nonverbal communication in the workplace requires observation of samples of behavioral interactions among workers. The use of videotaped hiring interviews, for example, has led to greater understanding of how nonverbal communication impacts hiring decisions. Another emerging opportunity to videotape workers occurs in assessment centers used either to select or train workplace managers (Thornton, 1992). In assessment centers, participants engage in simulated work exercises, such as group discussions, in a performance appraisal coaching session with a subordinate (actually an actor), or while making a formal presentation. This allows for detailed observation of workers' performance in these simulated work settings. The use of videotaped exercises has been hailed as a cost-effective alternative to live observer assessments (e.g., Riggio et al., 1997), and also offers nonverbal communication scholars research opportunities.

Additional opportunities to both apply nonverbal communication research to the work setting and gather research data may be afforded through certain employee training and selection programs. Specifically, there are a variety of training workshops offered to employees to improve communication skills, including nonverbal skill training. Often, these programs use videotaped segments of trainees practicing communication skills, and engaging in various role-playing exercises with other trainees. These could be used as research data.

As employers realize the value of employees' and managers' communication skills as key elements in performing their jobs, greater attention will be given to systematic assessment of communication skills in employee screening and selection. This offers another opportunity for nonverbal communication scholars to be involved in both developing the means for assessing nonverbal communication skills (as a significant piece of the broader repertoire of communication skills), as well as affording research opportunities. There has been some limited research using communication skill assessment in employee evaluations (see, e.g., Riggio & Taylor, 2000, see also Riggio, 2001), although this research has looked at general skill in communication, or in specific, work-related skills such as interpersonal sensitivity. Yet, one could imagine that certain elements of nonverbal communication skills, such as skill in self-presentation, decoding others' emotional and nonverbal cues, via instruments such as the Profile of Nonverbal Sensitivity; (PONS, Rosenthal et al., 1979) or the Diagnostic Analysis of Nonverbal Accuracy (DANVA; Nowicki & Duke, 1994, 2001), could be used as part of a selection battery for positions in management, sales, public relations, or even in customer service jobs.

As can be seen, the potential for applying nonverbal communication research to the work setting is great. Yet, research in this area is rather scarce. It is hoped that the interest shown by those in business in the potential applications of nonverbal communication theories and research to the work setting, along with renewed interest in "hot" research areas such as emotions, emotional intelligence, and interpersonal communication will help spur additional research.

REFERENCES

Aguinis, H., & Henle, C. A. (2001). Effects of nonverbal behavior on perceptions of a female employee's power bases. *Journal of Social Psychology, 141*(4), 537–549.

Aguinis, H., Simonsen, M. M., & Pierce, C. A. (1998). Effects of nonverbal behavior on perceptions of power bases. *Journal of Social Psychology, 138,* 455–469.

Andersen, P. A., & Bowman, L. L. (1999) Power, persuasion, and deception. Position of power: Nonverbal influence in organizational communication. In L. K. Guerrero & J. A. DeVito et al. (Eds.), *The nonverbal communication reader: Classic and contemporary readings* (2nd ed., pp. 317–376). Long Grove, IL: Waveland Press.

Arvey, R. D. (1979). *Fairness in selecting employees.* Reading, MA: Addison-Wesley.

Ashkanasy, N. M., & Daus, C. S. (2002). Emotion in the workplace: The new challenge for managers. *Academy of Management Executive, 16,* 76–86.

Ashkanasy, N. M., Hartel, C. E. J., & Zerbe, W. J. (Eds.). (2000). *Emotions in the workplace: Research, theory, and practice.* Westport, CT: Quorum.

Ashkanasy, N. M., & Tse, B. (2000). Transformational leadership as management of emotion: A conceptual review. In N. M. Ashkanasy, C. E. J. Hartel, & W. J. Zerbe (Eds.), *Emotions in the workplace: Research, theory, and practice* (pp. 221–235). Westport, CT: Quorum.

Awamleh, R., & Gardner, W. L. (1999). Perceptions of leader charisma and effectiveness: The effects of vision content, delivery, and organizational performance. *Leadership Quarterly, 10,* 345–373.

Bass, B. M. (1960). *Leadership, psychology, and organizational behavior.* New York: Harper.

Bass, B. M. (1990). *Bass & Stogdill's handbook of leadership* (3rd ed.), New York: Free Press.

Bass, B. M. (1998). *Transformational leadership: Industrial, military, and educational impact.* Mahwah, NJ: Lawrence Erlbaum Associates.

Bernieri, F. J. (1988). Coordinated movement and rapport in teacher-student interactions. *Journal of Nonverbal Behavior, 121,* 120–138.

Bonoma, T. V., & Felder, L. C. (1977). Nonverbal communication in marketing: Toward a communicational analysis. *Journal of Marketing Research, 14,* 169–180.

Brown, C. S., & Sulzer-Azaroff, B. (1994). An assessment of the relationships between customer satisfaction and service friendliness. *Journal of Organizational Behavior Management, 14*, 55–75.

Cann, E., Siegfried, W. D., & Pearce, L. (1981). Forced attention to specific applicant qualifications: Impact on physical attractiveness and sex of applicant biases. *Personnel Psychology, 34*, 65–76.

Caruso, D. R., Mayer, J. D., & Salovey, P. (2002). Emotional intelligence and emotional leadership. In R. E. Riggio, S. E. Murphy, & F. J. Pirozzolo (Eds.), *Multiple intelligences and leadership* (pp. 55–74). Mahwah, NJ: Lawrence Erlbaum Associates.

Chapman, D. S., & Rowe, P. M. (2001). The impact of videoconference technology, interview structure, and interviewer gender on interviewer evaluations in the employment interview: A field experiment. *Journal of Occupational and Organizational Psychology, 74*, 279–298.

Chartrand, T. L., & Bargh, J. A. (1999). The chameleon effect: The perception-behavior link and social interaction. *Journal of Personality and Social Psychology, 71*, 893–910.

Chemers, M. M. (1997). *An integrative theory of leadership.* Mahwah, NJ: Lawrence Erlbaum Associates.

Cherulnik, P. D., Donley, K. A., Wiewel, T. S. R., & Miller, S. R. (2001). Charisma is contagious: The effect of leaders' charisma on observers' affect. *Journal of Applied Social Psychology, 31*, 2149–2159.

Conger, J. A. (1990). The dark side of leadership. *Organizational Dynamics, 19*, 44–55.

Conger, J. A., & Kanungo, R. N. (1998). *Charismatic leadership in organizations.* Thousand Oaks, CA: Sage.

Connerley, M. L. (1997). The influence of training on perceptions of recruiters' interpersonal skills and effectiveness. *Journal of Occupational and Organizational Psychology, 70*, 259–272.

Connerley, M. L., & Rynes, S. L. (1997). The influence of recruiter characteristics and organizational recruitment support on perceived recruiter effectiveness: Views from applicants and recruiters. *Human Relations, 50*, 1563–1586.

Crusco, A. H., & Wetzel, C. G. (1984). The Midas Touch: The effects of interpersonal touch on restaurant tipping. *Personality and Social Psychology Bulletin, 10*, 512–517.

Dansereau, F., Graen, G., & Haga, B. (1975). A vertical dyad linkage approach to leadership within formal organizations: A longitudinal investigation of the role making process. *Organizational Behavior and Human Performance, 13*, 46–78.

Davidson, O. B., & Eden, D. (2000). Remedial self-fulfilling prophecy: Two field experiments to prevent Golem effects among disadvantaged women. *Journal of Applied Psychology, 85*, 386–398.

Davis, S. F., Schrader, B., Richardson, T. R., Kring, J. P., & Kieffer, J. C. (1998). Restaurant servers influence tipping behavior. *Psychological Reports, 83*, 223–226.

DeGroot, T., & Motowidlo, S. J. (1999). Why visual and vocal interview cues can affect interviewers' judgments and predict job performance. *Journal of Applied Psychology, 84*, 986–993.

DePaulo, B. M., & Rosenthal, R. (1979). Ambivalence, discrepancy, and deception in nonverbal communication. In R. Rosenthal (Ed.), *Skill in nonverbal communication: Individual differences* (pp. 204–248). Cambridge, MA: Oelgeschlager, Gunn & Hain.

DePaulo, P. J. (1992). Applications of nonverbal behavior research in marketing and management. In R. S. Feldman (Ed.), *Applications of nonverbal behavioral theories and research* (pp. 63–87). Hillsdale, NJ: Lawrence Erlbaum Associates.

Dienesch, R. M., & Liden, R. C. (1986). Leader-member exchange model of leadership: A critique and further development. *Academy of Management Review, 11*, 618–634.

Dobbins, G. H., Long, W. S., Dedrick, E. J., & Clemons, T. C. (1990). The role of self-monitoring and gender on leader emergence: A laboratory and field study. *Journal of Management, 16*, 609–618.

Doherty, R. W. (1997). The Emotional Contagion Scale: A measure of individual differences. *Journal of Nonverbal Behavior, 21*, 131–154.

Eden, D. (1990). *Pygmalion in management: Productivity as a self-fulfilling prophecy.* Lexington, MA: Lexington.

Eden, D. (1993). Interpersonal expectations in organizations. In P.D. Blanck (Ed.), *Interpersonal expectations: Theory, research, and applications* (pp. 154–178). Cambridge, UK: Cambridge University Press.

Eden, D., Geller, D., Gewirtz, A., Gordon-Terner, R., Inbar, I., Liberman, M., Pass, Y., Salomon-Segev, I., & Shalit, M. (2000). Implanting Pygmalion leadership style through workshop training: Seven field experiments. *Leadership Quarterly, 11*, 171–210.

Eden, D., & Shani, A. B. (1982). Pygmalion goes to boot camp: Expectancy, leadership, and trainee performance. *Journal of Applied Psychology, 67*, 194–199.

Eder, R. W., & Harris, M. M. (Eds.). (1999). *The employment interview handbook.* Thousand Oaks, CA: Sage.

Elfenbein, H. A., & Ambady, N. (2002). Predicting workplace outcomes from the ability to eavesdrop on feelings. *Journal of Applied Psychology, 87*(5), 963–971.

Ellis, R. J. (1988). Self-monitoring and leadership emergence in groups. *Personality and Social Psychology Bulletin, 14*, 681–693.

Fast, J. (1991). *Body language in the workplace.* New York: Penguin.

Fitness, J. (2000). Anger in the workplace: An emotion script approach to anger episodes between workers and their superiors, co-workers, and subordinates. *Journal of Organizational Behavior, 21*, 147–162.

Fletcher, C. (1989). Impression management in the selection interview. In R. A. Giacalone & P. Rosenfeld (Eds.), *Impression management in the organization* (pp. 269–281). Hillsdale, NJ: Lawrence Erlbaum Associates.

Friedman, H. S., & Riggio, R. E. (1981). Effect of individual differences in nonverbal expressiveness on transmission of emotions. *Journal of Nonverbal Behavior, 6*, 96–104.

George, J. M. (2000). Emotions and leadership: The role of emotional intelligence. *Human Relations, 53*, 1027–1055.

Gifford, R., Ng, C. F., & Wilkinson, M. (1985). Nonverbal cues in the employment interview: Links between applicant qualities and interviewer judgments. *Journal of Applied Psychology, 70*, 729–736.

Gilmore, D. C., Stevens, C. K., Harrell-Cook, G., & Ferris, G. R. (1999). Impression management tactics. In R. W. Eder & M. M. Harris (Eds.), *The employment interview handbook* (pp. 321–336). Thousand Oaks, CA: Sage.

Gladwell, M. (2000). *The tipping point: How little things can make a big difference.* New York: Little, Brown & Co.

Goleman, D., Boyatzis, R., & McKee, A. (2002). *Primal leadership: Realizing the power of emotional intelligence.* Boston: Harvard Business School Press.

Graen, G. B., & Uhl-Bien, M. (1995). Relationship-based approach to leadership: Development of leader-member exchange (LMX) theory of leadership over 25 years. *Leadership Quarterly, 6,* 219–247.

Graham, C. R., & Misanchuk, M. (2004). Computer-mediated teamwork: Benefits and challenges of using teamwork in online learning environments. In T. S. Roberts (Ed.), *Online collaborative learning: Theory and practice* (pp. 181–202): Hershey, PA: Idea Group, Inc.

Graves, L. M. (1993). Sources of individual differences in interviewer effectiveness: A model and implications for future research. *Journal of Organizational Behavior, 14,* 349–370.

Graves, L. M., & Karren, R. J. (1999). Are some interviewers better than others? In R. W. Eder & M. M. Harris (Eds.), *The employment interview handbook* (pp. 243–258). Thousand Oaks, CA: Sage.

Groves, K. S. (2003). Follower openness to organizational change and leader communication skills as key components of charismatic leadership. Manuscript submitted for publication.

Harris, M. M., & Eder, R. W. (1999). The state of employment interview practice: Commentary and extension. In R. W. Eder & M. M. Harris (Eds.), *The employment interview handbook* (pp. 369–398). Thousand Oaks, CA: Sage.

Hatfield, E., Cacioppo, J. T., & Rapson, R. L. (1994). *Emotional contagion.* Cambridge, UK: Cambridge University Press.

Hebert, B. G., & Vorauer, J. D. (2003). Seeing through the screen: Is evaluative feedback communicated more effectively in face-to-face or computer-mediated exchanges? *Computers in Human Behavior, 19,* 25–38.

Heckel, R. V. (1973). Leadership and voluntary seating choice. *Psychological Reports, 32,* 141–142.

Hecker, S., & Stewart, D. W. (1988). *Nonverbal communication in advertising.* Lexington, MA: Lexington Books.

Heilman, M. E., & Saruwatari, L. R. (1979). When beauty is beastly: The effects of appearance and sex on evaluations of job applicants for managerial and nonmanagerial jobs. *Organizational Behavior and Human Performance, 23,* 360–372.

Heneman, H. G., Schwab, D. P., Huett, D. L., & Ford, J. J. (1975). Interviewer validity as a function of interview structure, biological data, and interviewee order. *Journal of Applied Psychology, 60,* 748–753.

Holladay, S. J., & Coombs, W. T. (1993). Communicating visions: An exploration of the role of delivery in the creation of leader charisma. *Management Communication Quarterly, 6,* 405–427.

Holladay, S. J., & Coombs, W. T. (1994). Speaking of visions and visions being spoken: An exploration of the effects of content and delivery on perceptions of leader charisma. *Management Communication Quarterly, 8,* 165–189.

Howard, D. J., & Gengler, C. (2001). Emotional contagion effects on product attitudes. *Journal of Consumer Research, 28,* 189–201.

Howell, J. M., & Frost, P. J. (1989). A laboratory study of charismatic leadership. *Organizational Behavior and Human Decision Processes, 43,* 243–269.

Humphrey, R. H. (2002). The many faces of emotional leadership. *Leadership Quarterly, 13*, 493–504.

Imada, A. S., & Hakel, M. D. (1977). Influence of nonverbal communication and rater proximity on impressions and decisions in simulated employment interviews. *Journal of Applied Psychology, 62*, 295–300.

Kellett, J. B., Humphrey, R. H., & Sleeth, R. G. (2002). Empathy and complex task performance: Two routes to leadership. *Leadership Quarterly, 13*, 523–544.

Kenny, D. A., & Zaccaro, S. J. (1983). An estimate of variance due to traits in leadership. *Journal of Applied Psychology, 68*, 678–685.

Kierein, N. M., & Gold, M. A. (2000). Pygmalion in work organizations: A meta-analysis. *Journal of Organizational Behavior, 21*, 913–928.

Kiesler, S., Siegal, J., & McGuire, T. W. (1984). Social psychological aspects of computer-mediated communication. *American Psychologist, 39*, 1123–1134.

Komaki, J., Blood, M. R., & Holder, D. (1980). Fostering friendliness in a fast food franchise. *Journal of Organizational Behavior Management, 2*, 151–164.

LaFrance, M. (1982). Posture mirroring and rapport. In M. Davis (Ed.), *Interaction rhythms: Periodicity in communicative behavior* (pp. 279–298). New York: Human Sciences Press.

Lakin, J. L., & Chartrand, T. L. (2003). Using nonconscious behavioral mimicry to create affiliation and rapport. *Psychological Science, 14*, 334–339.

Lakin, J. L., Jefferis, V. E., Cheng, C. M., & Chartrand, T. L. (in press). The chameleon effect as a social glue: Evidence for the evolutionary significance of nonconscious mimicry. *Journal of Nonverbal Behavior.*

Liden, R. C., Martin, C. L., & Parsons, C. K. Interviewer and applicant behaviors in employment interviews. *Academy of Management Journal, 36*, 372–386.

Lipnack, J., & Stamps, J. (1997). *Virtual teams: Reaching across space, time, and organizations with technology.* New York: John Wiley & Sons.

Lord, R. G., Klimoski, R. J., & Kanfer, R. (Eds.). (2002). *Emotions in the workplace: Understanding the structure and role of emotions in organizational behavior.* San Francisco: Jossey-Bass.

Mast, M. S. (2002). Dominance as expressed and inferred through speaking time: A meta-analysis. *Human Communication Research, 28*, 420–450.

McGovern, T. V., & Tinsley, H. E. A. (1978). Interviewer evaluations of interviewee nonverbal behavior. *Journal of Vocational Behavior, 13*, 163–171.

McNatt, D. B. (2000). Ancient Pygmalion joins contemporary management: A meta-analysis of the result. *Journal of Applied Psychology, 85*, 314–322.

Mehrabian, A. (1969). Significance of posture and position in the communication of attitude and status relationships, *Psychological Bulletin, 71*, 359–372.

Mehrabian, A. (1972). *Nonverbal communication.* Chicago, IL: Aldine-Atherton.

Mehrabian, A., & Wiener, M. (1967). Decoding of inconsistent communications. *Journal of Personality and Social Psychology, 6*, 109–114.

Mintzberg, H. (1973). *The nature of managerial work.* New York: Harper & Row.

Mullen, B., Salas, E., & Driskell, J. E. (1989). Salience, motivation, and artifact as contributions to the relation between participation rate and leadership. *Journal of Experimental Social Psychology, 25*, 545–559.

Newlands, A., Anderson, A. H., & Mullin, J. (2003). Adapting communicative strategies to computer-mediated communication: An analysis of task performance and dialogue structure. *Applied Cognitive Psychology, 17*, 325–348.

Nowicki, S., Jr., & Duke, M. P. (2001). Nonverbal receptivity: The Diagnostic Analysis of Nonverbal Accuracy (DANVA). In J. A. Hall & F. J. Bernieri (Eds.), *Interpersonal sensitivity: Theory and measurement* (pp. 183–198). Mahwah, NJ: Lawrence Erlbaum Associates.

Nowicki, S., Jr., & Duke, M. P. (1994). Individual differences in the nonverbal communication of affect: The Diagnostic Analysis of Nonverbal Accuracy scale. *Journal of Nonverbal Behavior, 18*, 9–35.

Parsons, C. K., Liden, R. C., & Bauer, T. N. (2001). Person perception in employment interviews. In M. London (Ed.), *How people evaluate others in organizations* (pp. 67–90). Mahwah, NJ: Lawrence Erlbaum Associates.

Pescosolido, A. T. (2002). Emergent leaders as managers of group emotion. *Leadership Quarterly, 13*, 583–599.

Paulus, P. B., & Dzindolet, M. T. (1993). Social influence processes in group brainstorming. *Journal of Personality and Social Psychology, 64*, 575–586.

Posthuma, R. A., Morgeson, F. P., & Campion, M. A. (2002). Beyond employment interview validity: A comprehensive narrative review of recent research and trends over time. *Personnel Psychology, 55*, 1–81.

Pulakos, E. D., Schmitt, N., Whitney, D., & Smith, M. (1996). Individual differences in interviewer ratings: The impact of standardization, consensus discussion, and sampling error on the validity of a structured interview. *Personnel Psychology, 49*, 85–102.

Riggio, R. E. (1987). *The charisma quotient*. New York: Dodd, Mead.

Riggio, R. E. (1998). Charisma. In H. S. Friedman (Ed.), *Encyclopedia of mental health* (pp. 387–396). San Diego, CA: Academic Press.

Riggio, R. E. (2001). Interpersonal sensitivity research and organizational psychology: Theoretical and methodological applications. In J. A. Hall & F. J. Bernieri (Eds.), *Interpersonal sensitivity: Theory and measurement* (pp. 305–317). Mahwah, NJ: Lawrence Erlbaum Associates.

Riggio, R. E. (1989). *Manual for the social skills inventory: Research edition.* Palo Alto, CA: Consulting Psychologists Press.

Riggio, R. E., Aguirre, M., Mayes, B. T., Belloli, C., & Kubiak, C. (1997). The use of assessment centers for student outcome assessment. *Journal of Social Behavior and Personality, 12*, 273–288.

Riggio, R. E., & Taylor, S. J. (2000). Personality and communication skills as predictors of hospice nurse performance. *Journal of Business and Psychology, 15*, 347–355.

Riggio, R. E., & Throckmorton, B. (1987). Effects of prior training and verbal errors on student performance in job interviews. *Journal of Employment Counseling, 24*, 10–16.

Riggio, R. E., & Throckmorton, B. (1988). The relative effects of verbal and nonverbal behavior, appearance, and social skills on evaluations made in hiring interviews. *Journal of Applied Social Psychology, 18*, 331–348.

Rind, B., & Bordia, P. (1996). Effect of restaurant tipping of male and female servers drawing a happy, smiling face on the backs of customers' checks. *Journal of Applied Social Psychology, 26*, 218–225.

Riva, G. (2002). The sociocognitive psychology of computer-mediated communication: The present and future of technology-based interactions. *CyberPsychology & Behavior, 5*, 581–597.

Rosenthal, R. (2003). Covert communication in laboratories, classrooms, and the truly real world. *Current Directions in Psychological Science, 5*, 151–154.

Rosenthal, R., Hall, J. A., Archer, D., DiMatteo, M. R., & Rogers, P. L. (1979). *The PONS test manual: Profile of Nonverbal Sensitivity.* New York: Irvington.

Rosenthal, R., & Jacobson, L. (1968). *Pygmalion in the classroom: Teacher expectations and pupils' intellectual development.* New York: Holt, Rinehart, & Winston.

Scheflen, A. E. (1964). The significance of posture in communication systems. *Psychiatry, 27,* 316–331.

Scheflen, A. E. (1965). Quasi-courtship behavior in psychotherapy. *Psychiatry, 28,* 245–257.

Snyder, M. (1974). Self-monitoring of expressive behavior. *Journal of Personality and Social Psychology, 30,* 526–537.

Sproul, L., & Kiesler, S. (1991). *Connections: New ways of working in the networked organization.* Cambridge, MA: MIT Press.

Stephen, R., & Zweigenhaft, R. L. (1986). The effect on tipping of a waitress touching male and female customers. *Journal of Social Psychology, 126,* 141–142.

Sundaram, D. S., & Webster, C. (2000). The role of nonverbal communication in service encounters. *Journal of Services Marketing, 14,* 378–391.

Sutton, R. I., & Rafaeli, A. (1988). Untangling the relationship between displayed emotions and organizational sales: The case of convenience stores. *Academy of Management Journal, 31,* 461–487.

Thornton, G. C., III. (1992). *Assessment centers in human resource management.* Reading, MA: Addison-Wesley.

Tickle-Degnen, L., & Rosenthal, R. (1987). Group rapport and nonverbal behavior. *Review of Personality and Social Psychology, 9,* 113–136.

Tickle-Degnen, L., & Rosenthal, R. (1990). The nature of rapport and its nonverbal correlates. *Psychological Inquiry, 1,* 285–293.

Tidd, K. L., & Lockard, J. S. (1978). Monetary significance of the affiliative smile: A case for reciprocal altruism. *Bulletin of the Psychonomic Society, 11,* 44–346.

Uhl-Bien, M. (2004). Relationship development as a key ingredient for leadership development. In S. E. Murphy & R. E. Riggio (Eds.), *The future of leadership development* (pp. 129–147). Mahwah, NJ: Lawrence Erlbaum Associates.

Walther, J. B., & D'Addario, K. P. (2001). The impact of emoticons on message interpretation in computer-mediated communication. *Social Science Computer Review, 19,* 324–347.

Wexley, K. N., Fugita, S., & Malone, M. P. (1975). An applicant's nonverbal behavior and student-evaluators' judgments in a structured interview setting. *Psychological Reports, 36,* 391–394.

White, S. S., & Locke, E. A. (2000). Problems with the Pygmalion effect and some proposed solutions. *Leadership Quarterly, 11,* 389–415.

Wolff, S. B., Pescosolido, A. T., & Druskat, V. U. (2002). Emotional intelligence as the basis of leadership emergence in self-managing teams. *Leadership Quarterly, 13,* 505–522.

Zedeck, S., Tziner, A., & Middlestadt, S. (1983). Interview validity and reliability: An individual analysis approach. *Personnel Psychology, 36,* 355–370.

❧ 7 ❧

Working on a Smile: Responding to Sexual Provocation in the Workplace

Julie A. Woodzicka
Washington and Lee University

Marianne LaFrance
Yale University

Scan any social situation involving both sexes and you will likely see differences in how women and men communicate both verbally and nonverbally. One nonverbal behavior concerns the fact that women tend to smile more than men. Indeed, numerous studies done over several years provide strong support for the finding that women smile more than men irrespective of whether the measure is frequency, duration, or even the size or kind of smile (Hall, 1984; Hecht & LaFrance, 1998; Henley, 1977; LaFrance, Hecht, & Paluck, 2003).

A recent meta-analysis showed, however, that the size of the sex difference in smiling is contingent on several factors (LaFrance, Hecht, & Paluck, 2003). In other words, women do not always smile more than men do. For example, women and men smile in comparable amounts when both sexes believe they are *not* being observed but women smile more than men when everyone is conscious of being evaluated. The sexes also smile in comparable amounts when they are in the same situation, role, or occupation. Both these contexts suggest that there are social expectations for women to smile and for men not to (LaFrance & Hecht, 1999). In fact, smiling women are evaluated more positively than those who do not smile (Deutsch, Le Baron & Fryer, 1987). Women smile more than men when the emotional climate is tense or negative than when the emotional milieu is comfortable and positive. That women smile more when the context is strained may spring from feeling greater obligation to try and do something to set it right.

While such findings suggest when greater smiling by women is to be expected, they do not tell us much about how people perceive a smiling woman. Can people accurately differentiate smiles that indicate pleasure or amusement from those that do not? Do observers consider the possibility that women sometimes smile because they are expected to do so? Do they entertain the hypothesis that a woman may be smiling not because she is feeling pleased but precisely because she is feeling tense and uncomfortable?

The present chapter describes a series of studies aimed at determining whether observers are able to tell the difference between smiles by women that spring from honestly felt pleasurable feelings from smiles that indicate displeasure. We also explore whether women and men are equally able to detect differences in types of smiles. Might it be the case that men are more inclined to take smiles by women on face value? Some early data indicate that men may misinterpret friendly behavior by women. Specifically, Abbey (1982) found that male observers were significantly more likely than female observers to interpret friendly behavior by women in sexual terms. We also wanted to explore the possibility that there are individual differences among men in the inclination to misinterpret a women's smile, to overlook cues indicating that the smile reflects not pleasure but pain. In other words, are some men in some situations more inclined to misinterpret women's smiles?

In order to address this question it is necessary to show that smiles associated with positive emotion can be reliably distinguished from smiles that are not related to enjoyment or pleasure. Research has shown this to be the case: there are several kinds of smiles, only one of which actually reflects positive emotion (Ekman & Friesen, 1982). Specifically, Ekman and Friesen (1982) noted that variants of human smiles could be distinguished on the basis of a number of behavioral markers (i.e., morphology, intensity, timing, location, and laterality). Felt (or Duchenne) smiles have been distinguished from "false" (or non-Duchenne) smiles on the basis of the presence of orbicularis oculi activation, as marked by crow's feet wrinkles at the outer eye corners (Ekman & Friesen, 1982). Several studies have obtained evidence that Duchenne smiles occur more often than other types of smiling when adult participants watched pleasant films or when they self-reported amusement during both solitary and social situations (Ekman & Friesen, 1982; Frank, Ekman, & Friesen, 1993). Non-Duchenne smile types on the other hand appear to be a kind of social lubricant, adopted when social context calls for signs of accommodation or cooperativeness.

We began the investigation by asking how women respond when they are asked sexually provocative questions by a male interviewer during the course of a job interview. In particular, we were interested in knowing how women look when they are on the receiving end of inappropriate queries. On the one hand, by virtue of applying for a job, female applicants need to come across in the best possible light. On the other hand, by virtue of being the recipient of sexually loaded questions, they may need to find some way to convey disinterest in that particular line of questioning. It seemed possible that they might smile but that it would not be a smile of delight. We found that to be the case.

Next, we examined whether men and women are equally able to differentiate false or social smiles from pleasurable ones. Then, we looked more closely at individual differences among male observers. Specifically, we explored differences among men in how they interpret smiling by women in two different contexts. Before describing the specific studies, we first take a look at the larger issue of why women might smile at all when the context is unpleasant.

SEX, POWER, AND NONVERBAL BEHAVIOR

A quarter of a century ago, several communication researchers proposed a set of ideas linking gender, expressiveness, and power. Nancy Henley (1977) argued that men and women display different nonverbal behaviors. Women were described as smiling more, engaging in more eye contact, and displaying greater sensitivity cues from others than men. Robin Lakoff (1973) similarly observed that women used language differently than men, exhibiting more verbal hedges, tag questions, and super polite linguistic forms. Many studies confirmed the existence of sex differences in several verbal and nonverbal modalities (Baird, 1976; Burgoon, Buller, & Woodall, 1989; Frieze, Parsons, Johnson, Ruble, & Zellman 1978; Hall, 1978; Haviland, 1977; LaFrance, Hecht, & Paluck, 2003). There is debate however about how these differences are to be explained. Henley (1977) argued that they are due to the fact that women typically have less power and status than do men. Women were said to be more expressive because they have less power just as subordinates are more expressive because they have less power than their superiors. Subordinates need to demonstrate that they know their place and nonverbal cues are a particularly effective way of conveying this (Ellyson & Dovidio, 1985). For example, it pays for subordinates to signal deference as well as being especially attentive to cues coming from a superior. Lakoff (1973) too characterized women's speech as powerless and argued that women use powerless linguistic forms such as verbal hedges to signal their place and to avoid giving offense. The shared contention is that survival may very well depend on to the ability of people with low power to respond in nonverbally sensitive and deferential ways (Bugental, Shennum, Frank, & Ekman, 2001). In short, sex and power are viewed as inextricably linked and communication is viewed as an important mechanism that keeps the link in working order.

A power explanation for sex differences in nonverbal behavior has received some, but not unanimous, support. For example, Bugental and her colleagues (2001) noted that physically abused children appear to be especially sensitive to nonverbal cues presumably because they need to be able to predict their abuser's moods and actions. With respect to smiling behavior, both Denmark (1977) and Deutsch (1990) found that having lower power was associated with showing more smiling. But other researchers have been unable to replicate a direct relationship between having less power and showing a greater tendency to smile. Some have found no relationship (Dovidio, Brown, Heltman, Ellyson, & Keating, 1988; Hall & Payne, 1995) while others report that high-power people sometimes actually smile more than low-power people (Halberstadt, Dovidio & Davidson, 1988).

Some recent findings provide a possible resolution to the inconsistent findings. Specifically, Hecht & LaFrance (1998) manipulated power in same-sex dyads and measured how much participants smiled. A number of potential mediators were also measured. Specifically, participants rated how positive they felt and how much they felt the need to please the other person during the interaction. Although we found no overall differences in how much low and high power people smiled, we did find that these two groups smiled for very different reasons. For those with low power, how much they smiled was positively associated with how much they experienced the need to please the person with more power. In contrast, for those with more power, their smiling was significantly correlated with how positively they felt. In sum, when those with more power smiled it was related to their feeling good, but those with less power smiled because they felt the obligation to please. Moreover, women felt more obligated to please than did men regardless of their level of assigned power. Even when women had more power, the degree to which they smiled was positively correlated with needing to please. This association was not found among high-power men (Hecht & LaFrance, 1998). That women experience the obligation to smile more because of the diffuse lower status assigned to women is compatible with expectations states theory (Ridgeway & Smith-Lovin, 1999). Communicative behaviors may thus serve as one mechanism by which power inequities between the sexes are reflected and maintained.

SEX, POWER, AND THE WORK ENVIRONMENT

Employment contexts represent fertile ground for observing the management of power via nonverbal behavior. To begin with, evaluation of work performance is strongly affected by how people comport themselves nonverbally (Imada & Hakel, 1977; Spangler, 1995; Washburn & Hakel, 1973). In addition, relationships between workers and superiors are frequently established, negotiated, and maintained via the action of nonverbal behaviors. Subordinates signal their deference and superiors signal their authority and command. However, sometimes these relationships are disrupted when the power of the superior is used for inappropriate purposes.

One distressing misuse of power in a work context is harassment targeted at female workers. According to one estimate, between 42% and 90% of women have experienced sexual harassment (Baker, Terpstra, & Larntz, 1990) and the consensus among investigators is that approximately 50% of women have experienced sexual harassment of one type or another (e.g., Fitzgerald & Ormerod, 1993; Schneider, Swan, & Fitzgerald, 1997). Researchers have characterized sexual harassment along several dimensions including type, severity, and frequency. Legal scholars have taken these dimensions into account in defining two major types of harassment specifically *quid pro quo* and *hostile environment harassment*. The former is based on sexual coercion, namely on demands for sexual favors in return for job-related benefits or escape from retaliation and may be based on a single incident (EEOC, 1980). In contrast, hostile environment harassment characterizes ongoing contexts where workers are subject to intimidating, hostile, or offensive work environments because of their sex (*Meritor Savings Bank v. Vinson*, 1986). Hostile environment harassment usually occurs over a period of time and incorporates behaviors such as sexist jokes and remarks, offensive language and graffiti, requests for sexual favors or dates, nude pinups, and sexual e-mails (Conte, 1997).

Some cases of sexual harassment are so egregious that that there is little doubt that women have been subjected to sexual coercion or longstanding gender-based hostility (Fitzgerald & Ormerod, 1993). In both cases, sexual harassment results in negative consequences for both the individual and the organization. Individuals report that their emotional lives have been negatively impacted (Gutek & Koss, 1993; U.S. Merit Systems Protection Board, 1981). In fact, heightened arousal and intrusive flashbacks observed in the aftermath of severe harassment are similar to symptoms associated with post-traumatic stress disorder (Dansky & Kilpatrick, 1997; Gutek & Koss, 1993). Besides psychological repercussions, severe harassment produces decreased job satisfaction (Fitzgerald, Drasgow, Hulin, Gefland, & Magley, 1997; Gutek & Koss, 1993; Piotrkowski, 1998) and reduced job performance (Crull, 1982; Stockdale, 1998).

Although milder forms of harassment may be insufficiently serious to warrant legal sanctions, it is likely that they can still produce significant emotional and work repercussions. But very little is known about reactions to and effects of harassment that falls below the legal radar screen. While most research on serious sexual harassment has focused on its prevalence and its long-term effects (e.g., Livingston, 1982; Stockdale, 1998), researchers have largely ignored the immediate emotional and job-related effects of milder forms of sexual provocation. In the next section, we describe a study aimed at determining how women manage this kind of untoward behavior by superiors in an employment context.

SMILING IN RESPONSE TO SEXUALLY PROVOCATIVE QUESTIONS

Women sometimes smile when their affect is not especially positive and when their need to please is high. This can happen in both work and home environments. On the job, women are more likely than men to find themselves in a predicament where they are treated as underlings and as objects of heterosexual attention. Like male underlings they are dependent on supervisors and bosses for rewards and resources. Also like males in low power positions they are expected to show a modicum of respect and deference to their superiors. But unlike men they are assumed to be less competent and commanding (Ridgeway & Smith-Lovin, 1999). Also unlike men, women in less powerful positions have the additional task of not giving the "wrong message" to male bosses who may express more than workday interest in them. How do women respond to the double bind that these situations present (Rudman & Glick, 2001)? Specifically, we examined how female job applicants respond to a male who asks them sexually provocative questions during the course of the job interview.

We decided that in order to study immediate reactions to subtle harassment, we would need to create an experimental situation in which research participants would be exposed to realistic harassment and contrast it with an otherwise identical but not sexually provocative situation. To make the situation as realistic as possible, we needed to create a work context in which participants would not be aware that they were in a study. See Woodzicka and LaFrance (2001) for a discussion of the need for this since role-played or imagined reactions to harassment differ substantially from real reactions.

To create a realistic but controlled context, we devised a job interview in which female job applicants were assigned to either an experimental interview or a controlled interview. In the former, participants were asked a few sexually provocative questions interspersed with more typical interview questions. In the control condition, participants were asked a matched set of surprising but not sexually-provocative questions. Interviewees were recruited by campus posters and by advertisements placed in campus and local newspapers. Fifty women (ages 18–39) signed up to participate in the interview that was described as determining eligibility for a job as a research assistant. Participants were told that if they performed well in the interview, they would be placed on a list made available for faculty seeking to hire research assistants. In reality, all participants, regardless of their performance, were placed on the list.

A male interviewer asked female job applicants three experimental or control questions interspersed with other interview questions. In the experimental condition, the questions were marked with sexual innuendo; in the control condition there was a set of matched questions minus the sexual allusion. The experimental and control questions were pre-tested to be comparable with respect to their "surprise" quotient. All questions, whether in the "harassment" condition or in the matched control condition, were rather surprising queries to hear in the context of a job interview. The only difference between conditions was in the amount of sexual content they contained. Specifically, during the course of a sixteen question interview, participants were asked three sexually provocative questions (such as "Do you have a boyfriend?") or matched non-sexual questions (such as "Do you have a best friend?"). Besides the experimental and control questions, the job interviews were handled identically. All participants were unobtrusively videotaped during the interview.

After the interview, a female research assistant escorted participants to another room where they completed a self-report affect scale and several questions designed to elicit reactions to the interview and interviewer. Participants were then fully debriefed, given an opportunity to withdraw their self-report and video data from the study, and paid for their time. One participant in the experimental condition asked that her videotaped interview be erased. This was done immediately. Each participant was also given the names and phone numbers of the psychology department and human-subjects committee chairpersons in the event that she wanted to discuss the study further. Neither of the chairpersons was contacted.

From the videotapes, we coded facial expressions using the Facial Action Coding System (FACS; Ekman & Friesen, 1978). The FACS is a comprehensive system that describes all possible visible facial muscle movement. We coded frequency, duration, onset, and offset for all Action Units (AUs) for a total of 6 seconds, beginning one second prior to the end of each "experimental" target question. This period was chosen to capture most facial expression associated with a particular question.

We were particularly interested in determining whether interviewees smiled during the interviews. If so, we wanted to know how much of it was Duchenne and non-Duchenne smiling. Duchenne or felt smiles involve two specific facial action units. One action entails the lip corners, which are pulled up and back; the second facial action in felt smiles is observed by the cheeks being raised causing wrinkles to form at the outer corners of the eyes. Non-Duchenne smiles, on the other hand, only involve mouth movement and show no reliable relationship to positive feelings (Ekman, Friesen, & Ancoli, 1980).

We found that participants in the sexually provocative condition smiled more than those in the non-sexualized interview. But the type of smile clearly indicated that enjoyment was not the underlying emotion. In response to the sexually provocative questions, nearly all (96%) of the female job interviewees displayed social, that is non-Duchenne, smiling. And in a specific comparison of the experimental and control groups, women asked the provocative questions showed significantly more non-Duchenne than did women asked non-provocative questions, $t(45) = 2.02, p < .05$.

The results clearly showed that the distinction between Duchenne and non-Duchenne smiles was a meaningful one—these two smile types were negatively correlated with each other ($r = -.35$). In other words, as felt smiling decreased, false or social smiling increased. Moreover, there is clear evidence that smiling in response to sexual provocation is not to be taken as evidence that the women were pleased to be asked these provocative questions. We found that amount of non-Duchenne smiling was positively correlated with the degree to which participants reported feeling angry, upset, disgusted, and irritable and *negatively* correlated with feeling strong. In addition, non-Duchenne smiling was positively correlated with perceiving the interviewer as sexist and perceiving the interview as having been sexually harassing. Table 7.1 shows these correlations. In short, the interviewees in the harassment condition noted that the interviewer was behaving inappropriately and they were not happy about it.

These findings indicate then that female interviewees recognized their predicament. They needed to appear pleasant and competent even while having to contend with a harassing interviewer. As applicants, the women had little power because the interviewer was the gateway to a desired job. As recipients of sexually provocative questions, the job applicants had little recourse but to "grin and bear it" which is an apt way to characterize a non-Duchenne smile. Such smiling indicates not equanimity at the unwelcome questions but an attempt to get through an untenable situation.

Had the non-Duchenne smiling been effective at warding off further unwelcome advances or in establishing oneself as particularly compe-

Table 7.1
Correlations Between Non-Duchenne Smiling and Self-Report Measures
for Interviewees Asked Provocative Questions

Interviewee Self-Report	Non-Duchenne Smiling by Interviewee
Affect	
Angry	.19
Upset	.18
Disgusted	.17
Irritable	.15
Strong	−.21
Perceptions of Interview/Interviewer	
Interview is sexually harassing	.33
Interviewer is sexist	.35

tent or professional then it might have been a useful strategy. It did not work that way. We found that non-Duchenne smiling in this context was actually counterproductive. From videotapes of the interviews, an independent group of 50 male and female undergraduates rated the interviewees on several dimensions including how competent and smart they appeared and how likely they would be to hire them. Judges viewed a set of brief, five-second, silent visual clips taken of the interviewees. The more interviewees displayed non-Duchenne smiling the more negatively they were evaluated on competence ($r = -.47$) and intelligence ($r = -.53$). As non-Duchenne smiling increased, ratings of her competence and intelligence decreased.

Moreover, verbal performance in the interview was negatively impacted. Women who were asked sexually provocative questions were less fluent in their answers than those who were asked equally surprising but not sexual, questions, $t(46) = 2.35, p < .05$. In another evaluation of the interviewees, judges from Yale's School of Management rated the answers by harassed women to be of poorer quality than answers given by non-harassed interviewees, $t(46) = 1.99, p < .055$. In sum, sexual harassment reduced job performance as evidenced by both nonverbal behavior and verbal facility.

Faced with sexually loaded questions, the female applicants smiled but it was not the smile of enjoyment. The interviewees clearly perceived that these questions were out-of-line and their non-felt smiling reflected this. Such smiles appear to have been a way to deal with the unwelcome intrusion rather than a sign of assent. But how do men interpret such smiling? There is the possibility that false smiles, displayed in an attempt to appease, may be misinterpreted as indication of interest and enjoyment. Next, we describe two studies that directly address this issue.

INTERPRETING WOMEN'S SMILES

How do men interpret the smiling shown by women in response to inappropriate sexual questions in a job interview? Is it accurately perceived as a social smile or is it instead misinterpreted as a sign that they find the questions pleasing and the attention welcome? We first examined whether men are less likely than women to correctly identify Duchenne and non-Duchenne smiles. Then, we looked at whether there are individual differences in how men perceive women who show non-Duchenne smiles.

Sex Differences in Identifying Duchenne and Non-Duchenne Smiles

Research strongly supports women's superior nonverbal sensitivity (Hall, 1978; Lieberman, Rigo, & Campain, 1988; Rotter & Rotter, 1988; Zuckerman, Hall, DeFrank, & Rosenthal, 1976). Across a range of emotional displays, women are more accurate decoders of facial expressions than are men (Hall, 1984). Consequently we might expect women to be more accurate in distinguishing felt from social smiles.

Thirty male and 30 female participants viewed 32 silent video clips taken of the female participants from the job interview study described above. The clips (presented in two orders) varied from one to three seconds in duration and consisted of eight Duchenne smiles and 24 non-Duchenne smiles. After viewing each clip, participants were asked to indicate whether the smile was genuine/real or fake/false.

Results showed that men were significantly less accurate in decoding non-Duchenne smiles than were women. Specifically, men were less likely than women to correctly label false smiles $t(58) = 2.03, p < .05$. Male participants underestimated the number of non-Duchenne smiles and overestimated the occurrence of Duchenne or felt smiles. In sum, men were less accurate decoders of different smile types shown by women and the errors were in the direction of seeing any smile by a woman as indicating genuine positive feeling. This finding corroborates previous research that found that men mistakenly interpret women's friendliness as indication of sexual interest (Abbey 1982; Abbey & Melby, 1986).

Likelihood to Sexually Harass and Ratings of Smiling and Non-smiling Women

In our final study, we examined whether individual differences among men might affect how they interpret a woman's smile. On the face of it, it seems likely that men who are inclined to take advantage of work situations for sexual purposes will be more likely to misread apparently positive nonverbal behavior from women. Indeed, research has found that certain men are more likely to engage in forms of harassment than are others (Pryor, 1987).

To capture this individual difference, Pryor (1987) developed an instrument, the Likelihood to Sexually Harass Scale (LSH) to measure men's propensity to use power to elicit sex from women by threatening punishment or promising rewards. In the LSH scale, male respondents are given ten hypothetical scenarios that depict a male who has the power to control an important reward or punishment for a female target. They are asked to imagine themselves in the role of the male in each scenario and to indicate the likelihood that they would behave in a sexually exploitative way if there would be no negative consequences to them as a result of their actions.

In one validation study, Pryor (1987) observed the behavior of men who scored either high or low on the LSH. Specifically, males who were pre-tested on the LSH were randomly assigned to train a female confederate how to putt a golf ball or how to play poker. The confederate rated the frequency and nature of the participants' touching behavior toward her during the training session. Results revealed that high LSH males touched the confederate more and behaved in more sexual fashion toward her than low LSH males when the training condition provided acceptable opportunities to do so (i.e., in the golf but not in the poker training condition).

Since the LSH scale has also been found to predict sexualized behavior during an interview (Rudman & Borgida, 1995), it seemed likely that high scorers on the LSH would also be more likely to misread a non-Duchenne smile, especially in a work context. We predicted that men scoring high on LSH would perceive women as happier and more flirtatious than men scoring low on the scale when she displayed non-Duchenne smiling. This was predicted to be especially the case when the smiling is described as occurring during a job interview rather than a casual conversation.

Sixty male participants viewed twelve silent videoclips from the interview study, six of which showed a woman with a neutral facial expression and six showed a woman displaying a non-Duchenne smile. Because physical attractiveness might have affected participant ratings, the smiling and non-smiling women were matched on attractiveness. In addition, we examined the effect of context on participants' ratings. Participants were told that the women they would observe were either "talking to someone" or "interviewing for a job." Participants rated each of the twelve women on a number of state and trait words (e.g., happy, flirtatious, apprehensive).

Male participants were strongly affected by whether the female targets showed a social smile versus not smiling at all. Regardless of likelihood to sexually harass and context, males saw women with a false smile as significantly more happy, amused, friendly, and surprised than women who did not smile. They also rated them as more flirtatious, fake, and less apprehensive than non-smiling women.

It is interesting to note that men's ratings were affected by what they believed she was doing. When they thought she was a job applicant, they rated her as more afraid and uncomfortable if she was smiling than if she was not smiling. However, if they believed they were watching her in conversation, they saw her as less afraid and uncomfortable than non-smiling women. Thus, male raters as a group "know" that smiling in a job interview does not necessarily mean that a person is happy. The critical issue was whether this would be also true of men who show a greater propensity to engage in sexual harassment.

As scores on LSH increased, so did the ratings of the smiling target as flirtatious ($r = .28$) and desirable ($r = .45$). Further, we found a significant interaction between LSH and context on ratings of smiling targets, $F(1,49) = 4.83$, $p < .05$. When told that the female target was interviewing for a job, men with higher scores on LSH rated her as more flirtatious and desirable than did high LSH men who were told the women were just talking to someone. In contrast, men scoring lower on LSH rated the women as more flirtatious when they believed she was just conversing. When the targets did not smile, scores on LSH were positively correlated with ratings of them as vulnerable ($r = .28$), afraid ($r = .31$), and confused ($r = .31$).

In sum, men scoring high in LSH saw smiling women as more flirtatious and desirable and non-smiling women as more vulnerable and confused. Smiling as an attempt to get through an uncomfortable situation was seen by these high scorers on LSH as flirtatious and perhaps as a "green light" to move forward. But it also doesn't work not to smile. Those failing to smile run the risk of being judged as afraid, vulnerable, and confused, not exactly desirable characteristics in a potential employee.

IMPLICATIONS AND FUTURE DIRECTIONS

Social power, sex, and smiling are connected in a complex set of relationships. Low power people do not necessarily smile more than those with more power. Rather, in a relationship characterized by asymmetric power, people with little power appear to be obligated to display some level of smiling regardless of how positively they feel. The more powerful person, on the other hand, appears to have the option to smile, in the sense of only smiling when he or she feels positively inclined. In other words, it is not necessarily the case that people with low status or power smile more than those with greater power. But when they do smile it springs from the feeling of needing to please the other. Women feel this need even more acutely than men even when they are in positions of greater power.

In a job interview, the need to please an interviewer is clearly important. But women in this situation have an even more complex and difficult interpersonal task if the interviewer seems interested in them as sexual objects rather than merely as job candidates. What our investigations showed was that women who are subtly harassed in a work setting showed more social or fake smiling than those who are not harassed. Social smiling makes sense given the double bind they are in. Unfortunately, it doesn't work. Those who show social smiles are rated more negatively as job applicants. Furthermore, some men, namely those who are inclined to sexually harass women, tend to see sexual potential in the smile. They see smiling, especially during a job interview, as indicating flirtatiousness—perhaps a sign that the woman welcomes the advances. Her agenda is of another order altogether. The social smile is employed as a kind of defense against harm either to her well-being or her chances for employment.

Nonverbal cues like smiling appear to be a significant component of interpersonal relationships marked by differences in power. In many situations, they act as efficient yet unspoken confirmation that everyone knows their place. But as the studies described above demonstrate, nonverbal behavior in such contexts can be conveniently misinterpreted. Superiors can read the cues at the most superficial level and protest if anyone were to question them saying that they were merely responding to what they saw.

That women sometimes smile when they are uncomfortable and that such smiling is sometimes misinterpreted can combine to create an insidious self-fulfilling prophecy. For example, Word, Zanna, and Cooper (1974) found that self-fulfilling prophecies were mediated by nonverbal behavior in interracial interactions. We found a similar process in these job interviews. It appears that male interviewers who use their power to harass job applicants can produce interviewee behavior that reinforces sex stereotypes that portray women as less competent and more flirtatious. However, this is just one piece of a larger picture. Sexual harassment is more likely to occur in environments that reinforce gender-based power discrepancies and overlook inappropriate sexual behavior (Pryor, Giedd, & Williams, 1995).

Some men, namely those high in likelihood to sexually harass, are inclined to take advantage of their power, particularly when the workplace overlooks mild sexual harassment. Even high LSH men know that there are serious consequences of *quid pro quo* harassment. But they may engage in subtle sexual provocation of women that they have some power over. Subtle provocation may be the harassment of choice because it can be denied or deemed non-serious in the unlikely event that the target reports it. Our findings suggest that women on the receiving end of the subtle harassment display the non-Duchenne smile which unfortunately is not recognized as a false or appeasement smile. Instead, it is interpreted in two equally harmful ways. It may be taken as a sign of incompetence or as a signal that the target welcomes the harassment. Either way the resulting behavior is attributed to undesirable applicant attributes rather than to the untenable situation interviewers themselves put the applicants in. The attributions diminish women's chances of being hired or promoted and might explain why women tend to receive lower evaluations than men during job interviews (Olian, Schwab, & Haberfeld, 1988). Such attributions could also lead to continued sexual harassment.

Perhaps even more pernicious is reinforced views of women as incompetent and coy. Besides individual harm, sex stereotypes maintain the gender status quo. For example, women as a group may be promoted and paid less because they come into an interview assumed to be less competent and serious than men. If workplaces are to become nondiscriminatory, seemingly innocuous behaviors that put women in a double bind must be discouraged.

It might be countered that women mislead others when they display false smiles whether they intend to or not. Apparently women should smile only when they feel happy; otherwise they are responsible for what follows. However, there are some problems with this simple stipulation. In the first place, research findings indicate that people react rather negatively to non-smiling women. Secondly, advising women to change their behavior misses the point. Instead of taking a close look at inappropriate supervisor behavior, women are criticized for engaging in a behavior which is not only understandable given the context, but which would be criticized if it were not displayed. The responsibility falls on the perpetrator, not the victim, to alter his behavior and discontinue the power play.

When it comes to smiling, women are in a double bind, and even more so with men who have a propensity to harass. Men scoring high on LSH view a smiling woman as flirtatious and desirable and an unsmiling woman as afraid and vulnerable. None of these characteristics are desirable in the workplace. Even those not likely to harass have expectations regarding women's nonverbal behavior. Women are expected to smile and those who do not are judged harshly (Deutsch, LeBaron, & Fryer, 1987). When a woman displays non-Duchenne smiling, she signals that she is non-threatening and ready to please. Though appealing in many interpersonal situations, our results suggest that these displays make women look incompetent in a job interview. It falls to future work to continue to map out the interactions of varying situations, individual differences, and perceptions of women who do and don't smile.

A popular adage over the past years has been "don't sweat the small stuff." In the arena of sex-based harassment and employment, the opposite is probably more advisable. Employers should be encouraged to carefully attend to instances of harassment no matter how trivial they may seem. In other words, they should sweat the small stuff, namely subtle harassment that falls under the legal radar screen. Our research demonstrates that even seemingly harmless sexual provocation has pernicious effects.

If the "sexual provocation-smiling-misinterpretation cycle" is to be interrupted, training programs must be developed and implemented that go beyond merely being in compliance with the law. First and foremost, managers should be taught that subtle harassment is not just offensive but may lead to performance deficits and decreased productivity. Further, severe harassment may grow out of an environment that condones seemingly innocuous sexual behaviors (e.g., sexual jokes, remarks, and questions). Research suggests that women are more likely to experience sex-based harassment in workplaces where men perceive the social norms as permitting such behavior (Pryor, Giedd, & Williams, 1995). Thus, management should be urged to create and support work environments that do not tolerate sexual power plays of any type. Second, training programs should help managers and employees to understand typical and gendered nonverbal responses to displays of power. Specifically, employees should be taught that smiling doesn't always indicate happiness or pleasure. On the contrary, smiling, especially by low-powered individuals, frequently signals unease or discomfort. Management can be taught to use available contextual cues and target characteristics to understand the meaning of and respond appropriately to women's smiling.

ACKNOWLEDGMENTS

We gratefully acknowledge Michelle Moore, Betsy Paluck, Hal Ersner-Hershfield, and Kelly Ganley for their help with these studies. Correspondence concerning this article should be addressed to Julie A. Woodzicka, Department of Psychology, Washington and Lee University, Lexington, VA, 24450, e-mail: woodzickaj@wlu.edu or to Marianne LaFrance, Department of Psychology, Yale University, P.O. Box 208205, New Haven, CT, 06520-8205, e-mail: marianne.lafrance@yale.edu.

REFERENCES

Abbey, A. (1982). Sex differences in attributions for friendly behavior: Do males misperceive female's friendliness? *Journal of Personality and Social Psychology, 42*, 830–838.

Abbey, A., & Melby, C. (1986). The effects of nonverbal cues on gender differences in perceptions of sexual intent. *Sex Roles, 15*, 283–298.

Baird, J. E., Jr. (1976). Sex differences in group communication: A review of relevant research. *Quarterly Journal of Speech, 62*, 179–192.

Baker, D. D., Terpstra, D. E., & Larntz, K. (1990). The influence of individual characteristics and severity of harassing behavior on reactions to sexual harassment. *Sex Roles, 22*, 305–325.

Bugental, D. B., Shennum, W., Frank, M., & Ekman, P. (2001). "True lies": Children's abuse history and power attributions as influences in deception detection. In V. Manusov & J. H. Harvey (Eds.), *Attribution, communication behavior, and close relationships. Advances in personal relations* (pp. 248–265). Cambridge, U.K.: Cambridge University Press.

Burgoon, J. K., Buller, D. B., & Woodall, W. G. (1989). *Nonverbal communication: The unspoken dialogue.* New York: Harper-Collins.

Conte, A. (1997). Legal theories of sexual harassment. In W. O'Donohue (Ed.), *Sexual harassment: Theory, research, and treatment* (pp. 50–83). Boston: Allyn & Bacon.

Crull, P. (1982). Stress effects of sexual harassment on the job: Implications for counseling. *American Journal of Orthopsychiatry, 52*, 539–544.

Dansky, B. S., & Kilpatrick, D. G. (1997). Effects of sexual harassment. In W. O'Donohue (Ed.), *Sexual harassment: Theory, research, and treatment* (pp. 152–174). Boston: Allyn & Bacon.

Denmark, F. L. (1977). Styles of leadership. *Psychology of Women Quarterly, 2*, 99–113.

Deutsch, F. M. (1990). Status, sex, and smiling: The effect of role on smiling in men and women. *Personality and Social Psychology Bulletin, 16*, 531–540.

Deutsch, F. M., LeBaron, D., & Fryer, M. M. (1987). What is in a smile? *Psychology of Women Quarterly, 11*, 341–351.

Dovidio, J. F., Brown, C. E., Heltman, K., Ellyson, S. L., & Keating, C. F. (1988). Power displays between women and men in discussions of gender-linked tasks: A multichannel study. *Journal of Personality and Social Psychology, 55*, 580–587.

EEOC. (1980). "Title 29-Labor, Chapter XIV-Part 1604-Guidelines on Discrimination Because of Sex under Title VII of the Civil Rights Act, as

Amended Adoption of Interim Interpretive Guideline," Washington, DC: U.S. Government Printing Office.

Ekman, P., & Friesen, W. V. (1978). *Facial Action Coding System Manual*. Palo Alto, CA: Consulting Psychologists Press.

Ekman, P., & Friesen, W. V. (1982). Felt, false, and miserable smiles. *Journal of Nonverbal Behavior, 6*, 238–252.

Ekman, P., Friesen, W. V., & Ancoli, _. (1980). Facial signs of emotional experience. *Journal of Personality and Social Psychology, 39*, 1125–1134.

Ellyson, S. L., & Dovidio, J. F. (1985). Power, dominance, and nonverbal behavior: Basic concepts and issues. In S. L. Ellyson & J. F. Dovidio (Eds.), *Power, dominance, and nonverbal behavior* (pp. 1–27). New York: Springer.

Fitzgerald, L. F., Drasgow, F., Hulin, C. L., Gefland, M. J., & Magley, V. J. (1997). Antecedents and consequences of sexual harassment in organizations: A test of an integrated model. *Journal of Applied Psychology, 82*(4), 578–589.

Fitzgerald, L. F., & Ormerod, A. J. (1993). Breaking silence: The sexual harassment of women in academia and the workplace. In F. Denmark & M. Paludi (Eds.), *Psychology of women: A handbook of issues and theories* (pp. 553–582). Westport, CT: Greenwood Press.

Frank, M. G., Ekman, P., & Friesen, W. V. (1993). Behavioral markers and recognizability of the smile of enjoyment. *Journal of Personality and Social Psychology, 64*, 83–93

Frieze, I. H., Parsons, J. E., Johnson, P.B., Ruble, D. N., & Zellman, G. L. (1978). *Women and sex roles: A social psychological perspective*. New York: W. W. Norton.

Gutek, B. A., & Koss, M. P. (1993). Changed women and changed organizations: Consequences of and coping with sexual harassment. *Journal of Vocational Behavior, 42*, 28–48.

Halberstadt, A. G., Dovidio, J. F., & Davidson, L. A. (1988, October). Power, *gender, and smiling*. Paper presented at the annual meeting of the Society for Experimental Social Psychology, Madison, WI.

Hall, J. A. (1978). Gender effects in decoding nonverbal cues. *Psychological Bulletin, 85*, 845–857.

Hall, J. A. (1984). *Nonverbal sex differences*. Baltimore: John Hopkins University Press.

Hall, J. A., & Payne, R. M. (1995). *Smiling in relation to trait and manipulated dominance/status*. Unpublished manuscript, Northeastern University, Boston.

Haviland, J. M. (1977). Sex-related pragmatics in infants' nonverbal communication. *Journal of Communication, 27*, 80–84.

Hecht, M. A., & LaFrance, M. (1998). License or obligation to smile: The effect of power and sex on amount and type of smiling. *Personality and Social Psychology Bulletin, 24*, 1223–1342.

Henley, N. M. (1977). *Body politics: Power, sex, and nonverbal communication*. Englewood Cliffs, NJ: Prentice Hall.

Imada, A. S., & Hakel, M. D. (1977). Influence of nonverbal communication and rater proximity on impressions and decisions in simulated employment interviews. *Journal of Applied Psychology, 62*, 295–300.

LaFrance, M., & Hecht, M. A. (1999). Obliged to smile: The effect of power and gender n facial expression. In P. Philippot, R. S. Feldman, & E. J. Coats (Eds.), *The social context of nonverbal behavior* (pp. 45–70). Cambridge, U.K.: Cambridge University Press.

LaFrance, M., Hecht, M. A., & Paluck, E. L. (2003). The contingent smile: A meta-analysis of sex differences in smiling. *Psychological Bulletin, 129*, 305–334.

Lakoff, R. (1973). Language and woman's place. *Language in Society, 1*(2), 45–80.

Lieberman, D. A., Rigo, T. G., & Campain, R. F. (1988). Age-related differences in nonverbal decoding ability. *Communications Quarterly, 36*(4), 290–297.

Livingston, J. A. (1982). Responses to sexual harassment on the job: Legal, organizational, and individual actions. *Journal of Social Issues, 38*(4), 5–22.

Meritor Savings Bank v. Vinson. (1986). 477 U.S. 57, 40 FEP Case 1822.

Olian, J. D., Schwab, D. P., & Haberfeld, Y. (1988). The impact of applicant gender compared to qualifications on hiring recommendations: A meta-analysis of experimental studies. *Organizational Behavior and Human Decision Process, 41*(2), 180–195.

Piotrkowski, C. S. (1998). Gender harassment, job satisfaction, and distress among employed white and minority women. *Journal of Occupational Health Psychology, 3*, 33–43.

Pryor, J. B. (1987). Sexual harassment proclivities in men. *Sex Roles, 17*, 269–290.

Pryor, J. B., Giedd, J. L., & Williams, K. B. (1995). A social psychological model for predicting sexual harassment. *Journal of Social Issues, 51*, 69–84.

Ridgeway, C. L., & Smith-Lovin, L. (1999). The gender system and interaction. *Annual Review of Sociology, 25*, 191–216.

Rotter, N. G., & Rotter, G. S. (1988). Sex differences in the encoding and decoding of negative facial emotions. *Journal of Nonverbal Behavior, 12*(2), 139–148.

Rudman, L. A., & Borgida, E. (1995). The afterglow of construct accessibility: The behavioral consequences of priming men to view women as sexual objects. *Journal of Experimental Social Psychology, 31*, 493–517.

Rudman, L. A., & Glick, P. (2001). Prescriptive gender stereotypes and backlash toward agentic women. *Journal of Social Issues, 57*, 743–762.

Schneider, K. T., Swan, S., & Fitzgerald, L. F. (1997). Job-related and psychological effects of sexual harassment in the workplace: Empirical evidence from two organizations. *Journal of Applied Psychology, 82*, 401–415.

Spangler, L. (1995). Gender-specific nonverbal communication: Impact for speaker effectiveness. *Human Resource Development Quarterly, 6*, 409–419.

Stockdale, M. S. (1998). The direct and moderating influences of sexual harassment pervasiveness, coping strategies, and gender on work-related outcomes. *Psychology of Women Quarterly, 22*, 521–535.

U.S. Merit Systems Protection Board. (1981). *Sexual harassment of federal workers: Is it a problem?* Washington, DC: U.S. Government Printing Office.

Washburn, P. V., & Hakel, M. D. (1973). Visual cues and verbal content as influence on impressions formed after simulated employment interviews. *Journal of Applied Psychology, 5*(8), 137–141.

Woodzicka, J. A., & LaFrance, M. (2001). Real versus imagined gender harassment. *Journal of Social Issues, 57*, 15–30.

Word, C. O., Zanna, M. P., & Cooper, J. (1974). The nonverbal mediation of self-fulfilling prophecies in interracial interaction. *Journal of Experimental Social Psychology, 10*(2), 109–120.

Zuckerman, M., Hall, J. A., DeFrank, R. S., & Rosenthal, R. (1976). Encoding and decoding of spontaneous and posed facial expression. *Journal of Personality and Social Psychology, 34*, 966–977.

ᷙ 8 ᷚ

No More Teachers' Dirty Looks: Effects of Teacher Nonverbal Behavior on Student Outcomes

Monica J. Harris
University of Kentucky

Robert Rosenthal
University of California, Riverside

Teachers change lives. As the popular bumper sticker attests, the power of teachers to influence the course of a child's life is enormous, rivaling in some cases even that of the child's parents. This influence can be positive or, regrettably, negative. Common lore and our own memories tell us that our images of good and bad teachers are heavily influenced by their nonverbal behaviors. We can all remember our favorite teacher from grade school whose warm smile and kind voice made us feel special. If we were unlucky enough, we might also remember a hated teacher whose sarcasm and obvious hostility undermined our liking for school.

Anecdotally, then, few people would argue against the idea that nonverbal behavior is a critical aspect of teaching effectiveness. Much educational literature makes a similar assertion (Doyle, 1977; Galloway, 1971a, 1971b, 1984; Grant & Hennings, 1971; Grubaugh, 1989; Philippot, Feldman, & McGhee, 1992; Woolfolk & Brooks, 1985; Woolfolk & Galloway, 1984). However, the issue of the impact of teachers' nonverbal behavior on student outcomes is ultimately an empirical one, and thus a logical question is what is the actual *empirical* evidence regarding the effects of teacher nonverbal communication? The purpose of the current chapter is to begin to address this question by reviewing the available empirical literature on the relations between teacher nonverbal behavior and student outcomes.

APPROACH AND SCOPE OF THE CURRENT CHAPTER

In order to identify as comprehensively as possible the available literature on teachers' nonverbal behavior, we conducted a series of literature searches of the PsycINFO and ERIC databases. We began with more global searches that used the keywords "nonverbal behavior" and "nonverbal communication" crossed by "teacher*." After the global searches had identified the major categories or themes of the relevant research, we refined our database searches by using more specific keywords, for example, "teacher nonverbal immediacy." Finally, we adopted the ancestry approach of examining the articles we obtained for references that might have been omitted in our computerized searches.

Our literature searches yielded a pool of over 150 articles tapping into some aspect of teachers' nonverbal behavior. A sizable portion of these articles were nonempirical in nature, that is, mostly theoretical pieces in which the author(s) assert that teachers' nonverbal behavior is important and then speculate on why that might be so, without offering data to support their claims. Those articles will not be reviewed in the current chapter. The remainder of the articles could be classified into one of five major categories, the first four of which will comprise the scope of this chapter: (a) studies examining the relation between perceptions of teachers' global nonverbal immediacy and student outcomes; (b) studies that related one or two specific nonverbal cues, or combinations of cues, to student outcomes; (c) studies on the mediation of teacher expectancy effects; (d) studies that investigated differential teacher behavior displayed toward students varying in race, gender, or ethnicity; and (e) miscellaneous studies that did not fall into any of these four categories, such as qualitative, in-depth analyses of individual teachers' use of nonverbal behavior (e.g., Allen, 2000; Galloway, 1971b; Hendrix, 1997).

For each of the four substantive areas of research on teacher nonverbal behavior, we will offer a succinct review and critical evaluation of the available literature. Our primary goals are twofold: to provide researchers in nonverbal communication with a call to action by describing both what is known in this area and directions for future research, and to offer teachers and other education professionals an empirically-grounded understanding of the role of teacher nonverbal behavior as well as potentially practical guidelines for incorporating nonverbal cues in actual practice. We conclude the chapter with an overall assessment of the strengths and limitations of the literature on teacher nonverbal behavior.

MAKING A CASE FOR THE SPECIAL RELEVANCE
OF NONVERBAL BEHAVIOR IN TEACHING

Before embarking on our review of the literature, one could reasonably ask why researchers in nonverbal communication need to treat education as a special case. Why can we not simply apply the already very large literature on nonverbal behavior in general to the classroom? Are there any reasons to suspect that basic principles of nonverbal communication will differ in teacher-student interactions?

We will argue that there are indeed several aspects of the classroom context that render it a unique setting where the traditional rules governing communication, both verbal and nonverbal, do not always apply and thus demands special research scrutiny. Take, as only one example, the well-established body of research on turn-taking mechanisms, that is, the cues that govern the back and forth nature of conversation. We know a great deal about how dyads negotiate talking turns in everyday interaction, with researchers identifying four basic categories of turn-taking cues: turn-requesting, turn-denying, turn-maintaining, and turn-yielding (Duncan, 1972; Wiemann & Knapp, 1975).

Yet it is not at all obvious that the same processes and cues would hold in the classroom. First, and obviously, the classroom typically does not involve dyadic conversations but rather groups of varying size, interacting across greater distances than are the norm in dyadic interactions. Thus, some of the more subtle turn-taking cues that are highly effective in dyadic conversations (e.g., the barely audible intake of breath that precedes a speaking turn) would generally not be noticeable in the classroom. A second difference is that, unlike everyday group conversations where each participant has a more-or-less equal chance at speaking up, in the classroom the teacher calls the conversational shots. Students speak primarily at the mercy of the teacher and indeed in many classrooms must explicitly request permission to speak by raising their hands, a turn-taking mechanism that does not appear on the standard lists of cues (Wiemann & Knapp, 1975).

Turn-taking thus highlights one of the structural features of the classroom context that has important ramifications for researchers in nonverbal communication, namely that it generally consists of a highly unequal power structure. The typical classroom has one teacher, usually older, who possesses considerable power over a group of students. As Susan Fiske has documented, people in positions of lower power are especially attentive to the behavior of high-power individuals (Fiske, 1993). Thus, because the teacher tends to do the greater share of the talking, and because students will be especially motivated to attend to the teacher, it is likely that students will notice their teacher's nonverbal behavior to a greater extent and such behavior may be more influential than in ordinary conversation.[1]

In short, the stereotypical classroom has a higher-power teacher standing (and therefore highly visible) in front of an audience of lower-power and generally attentive students. The teacher controls the conversational flow and must use nonverbal behavior effectively to do so, for example, by directing his or her gaze and nodding at one particular child in a sea of waving arms to designate who is supposed to answer a question, or by flashing a warning look at a disruptive student without interrupting the delivery of lesson material. Even when teachers are not intentionally controlling their nonverbal behavior to convey a given message, the situational demands of the classroom create hypersensitivity among students to all behaviors, verbal and nonverbal, given off by teachers. To the student, a teacher's smile in response to a suggested answer could be a validation of his or her sense of intellectual achievement and thus affect the student's self-esteem much more strongly than perhaps the teacher could ever suspect. Regrettably, the converse is also true, and a cold or hostile glance (whether intended or not, or even caused by any action of the student or not) can evoke in the student a sense of shame or despair.

Given the great prominence that teachers' nonverbal behavior can have in an academic context, and given the unique features of the classroom that make it difficult to apply directly traditional theories of nonverbal communication (Doyle, 1977), the need for nonverbal research that takes place in the classroom is great. In the sections that follow, we review what is known about the possible effects of teachers' nonverbal behavior in the four areas identified earlier.

Teacher Nonverbal Immediacy and Student Outcomes

The nonverbal research question attracting perhaps the greatest attention in the education literature has been the relation between teachers' nonverbal immediacy and various student outcomes. *Nonverbal immediacy* is a global construct, originally introduced to the nonverbal literature by Mehrabian (1966) and defined as the degree of perceived physical or psychological closeness between people. From the beginning, immediacy was conceptualized as being inextricably linked with positive affect and liking toward another person, with Mehrabian (1971) declaring that immediacy and liking are "two sides of the same coin. That is, liking encourages greater immediacy, and immediacy produces more liking" (p. 77).

Meta-Analysis of the Teacher Nonverbal Immediacy Literature

The nonverbal immediacy construct was first applied in the educational literature in a highly influential dissertation and subsequent journal publication by Janis Andersen (1978, 1979). This study sparked a rush of other studies investigating the relation between teacher nonverbal immediacy and student outcomes. Because these studies share a similar hypothesis (as immediacy increases, so does the positivity of student outcomes), and because they demonstrate a remarkable homogeneity of methodological and analytic approaches, even to the extent of often using identical measures, this body of literature is ideally suited for a meta-analytic review. In this section, then, we present the results of a meta-analysis of the teacher nonverbal immediacy literature.[2]

Our literature search identified a total of 37 independent studies looking at the relation between teacher nonverbal immediacy and student outcomes. From each study, we coded: (a) the size and nature of the sample (undergraduate, secondary, or primary school students); (b) whether nonverbal immediacy was experimentally manipulated or measured as a naturally occurring variable; (c) the type of student outcome measured; and (d) the effect size, as indexed by the Pearson r, for the immediacy-outcome relation for each of the dependent measures reported. The vast majority of teacher immediacy studies adopt an affective, behavioral, and cognitive learning distinction, and our meta-analysis thus preserves this distinction by computing and reporting results separately by category. "Affective learning" refers to students' evaluative reactions toward either the course or the teacher. "Behavioral learning" is somewhat of a misnomer; although it can refer in principle to the mastery of performance tasks (cf., Comstock, Rowell, & Bowers, 1995), in an overwhelming number of the studies used in the current meta-analysis, behavioral learning instead refers to behavioral intention variables, for example, asking students how likely they would be to take another class with the same teacher or on the same topic. To avoid confusion and represent the spirit of those results more accurately, we will refer instead to this category as "behavioral intentions."

"Cognitive learning" refers to more traditional conceptions of student academic performance. In the teacher immediacy literature, cognitive learning is generally measured in one of two ways: scores on actual performance measures, such as a recall test of material presented in a lecture or course grades, or students' self-reports of how much they had learned in class. Most of the studies using the latter type of cognitive learning variable relied on Richmond, Gorham, and McCroskey's (1987) *learning loss* measure, which asks students, first, how much they learned in the class with the current instructor and, second, how much they think they *could* have learned in the class if they had an ideal instructor. The learning loss score is created by subtracting responses to the first question from responses to the second question. Because we suspected that students' self-reports might yield different results than actual performance measures, we analyzed effect sizes for the two subcategories of cognitive learning measures separately.

The prototypical study in this literature consisted of recruiting large classes of undergraduates to rate their teachers on nonverbal immediacy, and those ratings were then correlated with student self-reports of affective, behavioral, and cognitive learning. The nonverbal immediacy scales used in these studies were all highly similar, varying only slightly with respect to a few items and changes in the anchors of the items. Table 8.1 lists the fourteen immediacy items introduced by Richmond et al. (1987); most studies used either this scale or a ten-item version that deleted items with (a) low base-rates, such as the item asking about touching behavior, or (b) low item-total correlations. One of the admirable methodological features of this literature is that most of the studies included in the meta-analysis followed a procedure whereby students were not asked to rate the teacher of the class they were currently sitting in but rather the teacher of the class they had immediately preceding or following. This resulted in greater variability of course content, immediacy ratings, and student outcomes. It also ensured a wider range of teaching effectiveness to be addressed, as presumably very poor teachers would be less likely to allow researchers in their classroom for a study on teaching effectiveness.

Table 8.2 shows the meta analytic results for the four categories of dependent measures. When studies reported more than one result for each category (as would be the case, for example, if a study reported correlations for both attitudes toward the teacher and attitudes toward the course), we first computed the mean effect size across measures for each category of dependent measures, thus preserving the independence of effect sizes within category. Because correlation coefficients are not normally distributed, all Pearson rs were transformed

Table 8.1
Immediacy Behavior Items (Richmond et al., 1987)

1. Sits behind desk when teaching. (R)
2. Gestures when talking to the class.
3. Uses monotone/dull voice when talking to the class. (R)
4. Looks at the class when talking.
5. Smiles at the class as a whole, not just individual students.
6. Has a very tense body position when talking to the class. (R)
7. Touches students in the class.
8. Moves around the classroom when teaching.
9. Sits on a desk or in a chair when teaching. (R)
10. Looks at board or notes when talking to the class. (R)
11. Stands behind podium or desk when talking to the class. (R)
12. Has a very relaxed body position when talking to the class.
13. Smiles at individual students in the class.
14. Uses a variety of vocal expressions when talking to the class.

Note: (R) denotes reversed item.

Table 8.2
Meta-Analysis of the Teacher Nonverbal Immediacy Literature

	Affective Learning	Behavioral Intentions	Cognitive Learning	Cognitive Performance
Mean *r* (unweighted)	.43	.32	.36	.14
Number of studies (*k*)	33	19	21	6
Mean *r* (weighted by *N*)	.48	.35	.42	.11
Range of effect sizes	.09 – .62	.00 – .54	–.12 – .70	.00 – .45
95% confidence interval	.38 – .48	.23 – .40	.26 – .45	–.06 – .33

Note: Positive effect sizes mean greater immediacy is related to more positive outcomes. "Cognitive Learning" refers to self–report measures of learning, and "Cognitive Performance" refers to measures of actual performance.

via the Fisher *r*-to-*z* transformation (Rosenthal, 1991) prior to any computations. For ease of interpretation, however, mean effect sizes were transformed back and are reported in terms of Pearson *r*s in presenting the results.

Looking first at the results for the affective learning measures, which was far and above the most common type of dependent measure reported in this literature, we identified 33 independent effect sizes. The mean effect size for the 33 samples was an *r* of .43, which using Cohen's (1969) criteria could be considered a medium-to-large effect. Thus, as teachers' nonverbal immediacy increased, so did students' positive evaluations of the course and teacher. Put another way, using the Binomial Effect Size Display (BESD; Rosenthal & Rubin, 1982), this effect size can be interpreted as meaning that having a teacher high in nonverbal immediacy is associated with an increase in students' positive evaluations from 28.5% to 71.5%.

With respect to behavioral intentions, the mean effect size for the 19 independent samples investigating this category of dependent variable was an *r* of .32. Students of teachers high in nonverbal immediacy were more likely to report that they would be interested in taking another course from this teacher or on a similar topic. In terms of the BESD, this effect can be interpreted as meaning that having a high-immediate teacher is associated with an increase in favorable behavioral intentions from 34 to 66%.

As noted earlier, we analyzed results for the cognitive learning dependent variables separately according to whether the measure was a self-report of perceived learning or a measure of actual cognitive performance on a task. Far more studies incorporated the former type of measure than the latter. With respect to self-reports of cognitive learning, 21 independent effect sizes were located. The mean effect size for these samples was comparable to that found for the behavioral intentions variables, corresponding to an r of .36, indicating that teachers' nonverbal immediacy was positively related to students' self-reported learning. In BESD terms, this means that having a teacher high in nonverbal immediacy was associated with an increase in self-reported learning from 32% to 68%.

As we will discuss in more detail later, the use of self-reported cognitive learning measures raises obvious validity concerns. Thus, an important question for this literature is whether the same relation between teacher nonverbal immediacy and learning would hold for measures of actual cognitive performance. Alas, very few of the studies in this area collected data that would enable us to answer this question. We were able to locate only six independent effect sizes based on cognitive performance measures such as recall tests or course grades. The mean effect size for these six samples was an r of only .14, substantially lower than that obtained for self-reported learning. In BESD terms, this means that having a teacher high in nonverbal immediacy was associated with an increase in test performance from 43% to 57%.

In short, the results of the meta-analysis reveal that teacher nonverbal immediacy is strongly related to many positive student outcomes: liking for the course and teacher, willingness to take more classes with the teacher, and students' perceptions that they have learned a lot in the class. What is not yet clear is the degree to which these positive outcomes may be translated into gains in actual student achievement. Although this meta-analysis found a small effect for the cognitive performance studies, the estimate was based on a very small number of studies and thus should be interpreted only cautiously.

As researchers, we must always be wary of committing the correlational fallacy. While it may be tempting to conclude that the causal pathway of the teacher immediacy-student outcome finding flows from the teacher to the student, the reality is that a meta-analytic result based on both correlational and experimental studies does not permit such a conclusion. The causal pathway could potentially run in the opposite direction. Certainly, any teacher can tell you that a friendly, receptive audience helps to elicit expressive teaching behavior—and that an unfriendly audience can dim the enthusiasm of even the best teachers. In order to draw a firm causal conclusion that teacher immediacy leads to positive student outcomes, one needs to review studies that experimentally manipulated teacher nonverbal immediacy and randomly assigned participants to condition. Only five studies in the current data set met those criteria by including such an experimental manipulation, which was usually in the form of preparing two videotaped versions of the same lecture—one delivered by the instructor in a highly immediate style (vocal variety, gaze at camera/students, expressive gestures and movement, etc.) and one delivered in a non-immediate manner (speaking in a monotone, looking steadily at notes, etc.). The mean effect size for the five experimental studies was an r of .34, not appreciably different from the mean effect size of .39 for the correlational studies. Moreover, a one-sample t test of the five effect sizes yielded a $t(4) = 2.94$, $p = .02$, one-tailed, with 95% confidence intervals of .02 to .59. Thus, even though there were only five studies, we can generalize both to other studies of this ilk (experimental manipulations involving one lecturer providing both treatments) as well as to the four dependent variable domains (affective learning, behavioral intentions, cognitive learning, and cognitive performance), as the mean effect sizes obtained for those domains fall within the confidence interval for the experimental studies.

Implications for Research on Teacher Nonverbal Immediacy: Where Do We Go From Here?

Our meta-analysis demonstrates convincingly that there is a strong, positive relation between perceptions of teachers' nonverbal immediacy and students' evaluations of the teacher, class, and self-reported learning. Although only a small number of these studies involved experimental manipulations, the effect sizes obtained from the experimental studies were consistent enough with the overall effect sizes to allow us to conclude that teacher nonverbal immediacy is very likely to be a causal factor in affecting student outcomes. The consistency and overall magnitude of the mean effect sizes obtained in this literature thus provide empirical support for McCroskey and Richmond's (1992) claim that "teaching immediacy may be one of the most critical variables in determining teaching effectiveness" (p. 119). We explore now the implications of these results and offer directions for future research on teacher nonverbal immediacy.

First, it seems obvious that there is little left to be learned from studies asking undergraduates to rate their teachers' nonverbal immediacy and provide self-reports of outcome variables. We had hoped to report comparisons between results from studies using undergraduates and those using elementary or secondary school students, because one could offer a fairly compelling argument that variations in nonverbal immediacy should have a greater effect for younger students given the more affectively-tinged environment of elementary classrooms and increased one-on-one interaction between teachers and students in the lower grades. Unfortunately, we were unable to address that question in the current meta-analysis, as only *one* of the 37 studies we located used anything other than an undergraduate sample (and it was a study of secondary school students). Clearly, one of the directions for future research in this area should be to probe the nature of the teacher immediacy-student outcome relation with younger students.

Equally important, more research needs to be done using behavioral outcomes (i.e., actual cognitive performance) rather than relying on self-reports of learning. The cognitive learning self-reports used in this literature have been defended heavily by the researchers employing them, who argue that students have accurate insight regarding how much they have learned and that course grades are confounded by variables such as "attendance, writing skills, participation, student preparation, and perceived motivation and may reflect student compliance as much as learning" (Gorham, 1988, p. 44). Because most of the studies assessing cognitive learning relied solely on self-report, data on the validity of the self-reports are scarce. Chesebro and McCroskey (2000) reported a correlation coefficient of $r = -.50$ between the standard learning loss measure and scores on a quiz covering the material presented in the lecture in question (with a negative correlation indicating greater validity, as a high score on the learning loss variable indicates less learning), but in a similar study, Witt and Wheeless (2001) obtained an r between the two variables of only $-.21$. Thus, the magnitude of the validity coefficients for the self-reported learning loss variable is not appreciably large. Also telling is that a different pattern of results is obtained with the two types of dependent measures, with moderate-to-large effect sizes obtained for self-reports but much smaller effect sizes obtained for actual cognitive performance measures. This suggests one of two things: (a) either shared method variance is contributing to the large effect sizes obtained in the self-report studies, or (b) the two types of measures tap into overlapping but distinct constructs. In either event, it may not be safe to generalize from the self-report studies that immediacy has the same positive effects on actual learning.

For researchers of nonverbal behavior, perhaps the most pressing question stemming from this literature is an analogous concern regarding the validity of the most commonly used paper and pencil measures of immediacy and the specification of what, exactly, comprises nonverbal immediacy. Andersen (1979) originally defined nonverbal immediacy as the nonverbal manifestation of high affect or the behaviors that indicate physical or psychological closeness (p. 545), a definition that is more functional than theoretical in origin. The immediacy scale items shown in Table 8.1 (Richmond et al., 1987) are certainly broad in scope. However, what we do not yet know is the relative contribution of these individual behaviors to producing immediacy. Some researchers have reported results separately for each of the items of the immediacy scale; these studies indicate stronger relations for some items (e.g., vocal variety, eye contact, smiling, and relaxed body position) than for others (e.g., McCroskey, Fayer, Richmond, Sallinen, & Barraclough, 1996; Richmond et al., 1987). However, there are probably halo effects occurring when participants rate an instructor on all 14 items at one time, making it difficult to parse the contributions of individual behaviors.

Moreover, a troubling aspect of this literature is its over-reliance on student report of teacher nonverbal behavior. As was the case with the cognitive learning variables, data on the validity of the paper and pencil measures of nonverbal immediacy are sparse. The first Andersen (1979) study on this topic was actually one of the few studies to collect independent ratings of nonverbal immediacy in an effort to validate the student report measures. This study found that the objective judges' ratings of immediacy correlated highly with the student reports, $r =$ .80 across 13 class sections. Other studies where nonverbal immediacy was experimentally manipulated have similarly shown that students' perceptions of immediacy are significantly and substantially affected by the immediacy manipulation (Booth-Butterfield, Mosher, & Mollish, 1992; Comstock et al., 1995).

While these studies provide reassuring evidence for the validity of the student rating measures, the fact that so few studies of teacher immediacy incorporate direct observational, behavioral measures of teachers' nonverbal behavior remains a limitation of this area. An important thrust of the research agenda for teacher nonverbal immediacy thus should be a more detailed analysis of the precise nature of the nonverbal behaviors that communicate immediacy through detailed coding of videotapes of high- and low-immediacy teachers. Follow-up studies should then systematically manipulate the identified behaviors to determine which are most critical in affecting student outcomes.

OTHER RESEARCH ON THE RELATIONS BETWEEN TEACHER NONVERBAL BEHAVIORS AND STUDENT OUTCOMES

In this section, we review the findings of studies that systematically explored the relations between nonverbal behaviors and student outcomes. Whereas the nonverbal immediacy literature was more molar in perspective, looking at the contribution of general nonverbal behavior, globally defined, studies in this section often took a more molecular approach: How do nonverbal cues relate to teaching effectiveness on an individual basis? Because these studies involve such a diverse range of independent variables, we do not attempt a meta-analytic review but instead conduct a more traditional narrative review of this literature.

We discuss first the subset of studies that address "positive vs. negative" teacher nonverbal behavior or similar constructs such as "high or low affect" toward students or "still vs. active" teaching styles. We did not include these articles in the immediacy section because the authors did not identify their studies as falling in that domain, and their methodology was often fairly different, although the degree of conceptual overlap between immediacy and such things as "positive teacher behavior" is obviously high.

Not surprisingly given the conceptual overlap, the results of these studies are generally consistent with the teacher nonverbal immediacy literature. Several studies looked at the effects of "vivid" or "active" nonverbal behavior on the part of teachers, with three of the studies involving experimental manipulations of teacher behavior (Schiefer, 1986; Seals & Kaufman, 1975; Sims, 1986) and one involving self-reported teacher nonverbal expressiveness (Hamann, Lineburgh, &

Paul, 1998). These studies found consistent positive relations between a more expressive teaching style and students' evaluation of the teacher or class, but no consistent relation with student performance outcomes. For example, undergraduates watching a lecture presented in a vivid manner did not have better recall on a test over the material (Schiefer, 1986); similarly, preschoolers listening to musical selections while the teacher displayed enthusiastic facial expressions did not show greater recognition of the selections than when the teacher exhibited a bored expression (Sims, 1986).[3]

Other studies manipulated the valence of nonverbal cues more so than their intensity. These studies, on the whole, yielded a similar pattern whereby positive teacher nonverbal behavior had positive effects on students' subjective reactions but either nonsignificant or even *negative* effects on students' cognitive performance. For example, Anita Woolfolk and her colleagues have conducted a program of research in which teachers' verbal and nonverbal behavior are manipulated in a factorial design. In one study that was reported in a series of articles, 128 sixth grade students were given a short vocabulary lesson by one of four undergraduate "teachers," who were trained to administer the lesson accompanied by either positive or negative verbal and nonverbal cues, with positive nonverbal behavior operationalized by head nods, positive voice tone, and smiles. Woolfolk and her colleagues found that the students had more positive reactions toward the teachers when they used positive nonverbal behaviors, especially the female teachers (Woolfolk, Woolfolk, & Garlinsky, 1977), and they were equally willing to self-disclose to nonverbally positive and negative teachers (Woolfolk, Garlinsky, & Nicolich, 1977). However, students receiving positive nonverbal behaviors from the teacher actually produced *fewer* sentences using the vocabulary words and, for female students, performed worse on the subsequent spelling test (Woolfolk, 1978). In a separate experiment, Woolfolk and Woolfolk (1975) found that positive teacher nonverbal behavior was associated with an increased willingness to self-disclose. Thus, these studies reveal once again that positive, friendly nonverbal behavior—while perceived favorably by students—does not necessarily result in improved learning, and indeed they raise the possibility suggested by Woolfolk (1978) that "teacher negative nonverbal behavior may be more motivating than teacher positive nonverbal behavior" (p. 93).

A similar study was conducted by Goldberg and colleagues, who had 120 2nd and 6th grade students watch a videotape of a teacher presenting material using either positive, neutral, or negative nonverbal behaviors. A similar pattern of results was obtained. When using positive nonverbal behavior, the teacher was evaluated more positively by the students (Goldberg & Mayerberg, 1973). However, in a second article reporting the student performance data, there was no consistent effect of nonverbal behavior. For one task, students in the neutral condition performed worse, with no difference between students in the negative and positive nonverbal conditions, whereas in a second task, students in the negative nonverbal condition performed worse than students in the neutral and positive conditions, who did not differ (Goldberg & Mayerberg, 1975).

In contrast to the experimental studies just described, Harris, Rosenthal, and Snodgrass (1986) reported an observational study linking teachers' warmth to student cognitive performance. Ten teachers were videotaped while administering a ten-minute lesson, consisting of sentence-completion problems and arithmetic word problems, to students from kindergarten to second grade. Videotapes were coded for a variety of verbal and nonverbal behaviors. Regression analyses indicated that judges' global ratings of teacher warmth significantly predicted students' performance on the lesson, $r = .32$. However, because teacher warmth was not experimentally manipulated, the possibility exists that good student performance elicited more positive teacher behavior rather than vice versa.

Other studies show similarly positive effects of positive teacher nonverbal behavior on non-cognitive student outcomes such as evaluations of the instructor, liking for the class, or attentive behavior (Bettencourt, Gillet, Gall, & Hull, 1983; Chaikin, Gillen, Derlega, Heinen, & Wilson, 1978; Guerrero & Miller, 1998; Harris et al., 1986; Kazdin & Klock, 1973; Keith, Tornatzky, & Pettigrew, 1974; Kleinfeld, 1974; Neill, 1986, 1989a, 1989b; van Tartwijk, Brekelmans, & Wubbels, 1998; Wass, 1973). Clearly, an important riddle for educational and nonverbal researchers to solve is why, exactly, teacher nonverbal behavior appears to affect students' evaluative reactions more so than their cognitive performance. There are several possible explanations. The studies reviewed here that assessed cognitive performance almost always did so in the context of an artificial, short-term teaching encounter, e.g., watching a 10-minute videotape of an unfamiliar teacher and then being tested immediately over the content of that videotape. Perhaps teachers' nonverbal behavior has a greater impact on cognitive performance in the context of a long-term teaching relationship, when there is more opportunity for it to affect important mediators of academic performance such as student motivation. This could explain the seemingly counterintuitive findings of Woolfolk (1978) and other researchers that negative nonverbal behavior resulted in better task performance. Perhaps negative teacher behavior can be effective in the short term, but in the long run it undermines students' liking for school and motivation and thus would be damaging. A second possible explanation for the failure to find strong effects of teacher nonverbal behavior on cognitive performance is that perhaps performance on these tasks is determined so strongly by other factors (student ability, content of the material, nature of the assessment, etc.) that teachers' nonverbal style simply is less relevant.

Studies Looking at Discrete Nonverbal Behaviors.

Most of the studies we identified looking at teachers' nonverbal behavior did so in a holistic manner, operationalizing teacher behavior in global terms such as "immediate," "positive," or "active," or measuring or manipulating several discrete nonverbal cues simultaneously. This strategy has both positive and negative consequences. The positive features of operationalizing nonverbal behavior holistically is that it reflects the reality that nonverbal behaviors do not occur in isolation; teachers emit a broad constellation of behaviors, verbal and nonverbal, and all behaviors take place and are interpreted in the larger context of the other behaviors that are being emitted.

There are drawbacks to operationalizing teacher nonverbal behavior globally, however. The primary limitation, as discussed earlier, is that it becomes impossible to determine which discrete nonverbal cues play a causal role in affecting student outcomes. Yet such a determination is an important consideration when teacher training programs are contemplated. Because we know that immediate, positive teacher nonverbal behavior is perceived positively by students, teacher education programs may want to offer explicit training in behaving in a more nonverbally immediate and positive manner. But if research were to show, for example, that teacher smiles were the primary causal factor in producing positive student outcomes, training could be more efficient, simpler, and ultimately more successful if it focused on increasing the frequency of teacher smiles rather than trying to increase simultaneously all 14 behaviors on the nonverbal immediacy scale shown in Table 8.1.

Unfortunately, the teacher nonverbal behavior literature is not at the stage where such detailed considerations can be made. We located few studies that manipulated or measured discrete nonverbal behaviors and analyzed them in isolation. Some of the studies reviewed earlier come close to doing this, by manipulating or measuring two or three nonverbal cues simultaneously. For example, in Kleinfeld (1974), nonverbal warmth was operationalized by having the guidance counselor sit closer, smile often, and touch the student twice briefly; Kazdin and Klock (1973) similarly manipulated nonverbal approval through smiling and touch, and Sims (1986) manipulated gaze and facial expressions. Manipulating a smaller number of variables as in these studies narrows down the possible causal factors when significant results are obtained, but it still remains impossible to determine which one (or all) of the two or three cues manipulated was the most important.

Guerrero and Miller (1998) attempted to answer that question by asking students to rate instructors on four different nonverbal style variables separately (nonverbal warmth, speaking style, eye contact, and articulation) and then correlated those variables with students' impressions of the teacher. They found that nonverbal warmth was most strongly related to student evaluations, although the other three variables were nonetheless significantly related. However, as in the immediacy literature, because the nonverbal variables were coded subjectively, the possibility remains that they are contaminated by halo effects.

Wass (1973) was one of the few researchers to manipulate discrete behaviors in a factorial manner. Students (307 3rd-6th graders) watched videotaped clips of a teacher providing feedback to a hypothetical student via verbal, voice tone, and facial expression channels, with the valence of the channels manipulated factorially; for example, the verbal statement was either praising or critical, and the facial expression was either smiling or frowning. Students then rated whether the feedback given was good, bad, or neither good nor bad. Results showed that the valence of the verbal channel overwhelmingly influenced students' judgments; for example, over 80% of the students rated the message good if the verbal statement was positive, regardless of the valence of the nonverbal channels. Of course, given that the content of the verbal statement included an explicit evaluation of the hypothetical student's performance, it is not surprising that the verbal content predominated in students' judgments. It would be interesting in future research to determine the relative impact of nonverbal channels using this design with more standard academic verbal content.

Other researchers have similarly studied differences across verbal and nonverbal channels. Schiefer (1986) manipulated verbal and nonverbal "vividness" in a 2 × 2 factorial. Although no significant main effect of nonverbal vividness was obtained, "there was a positive effect of verbal vividness combined with nonverbal vividness" on students' ability to follow the lecture (p. 1106). Schmidt and McCutcheon (1994) had 180 undergraduates provide evaluations of seven lectures under two conditions: audio-only and video-only. Although no significant differences emerged on the composite teacher ratings between conditions, when items were analyzed separately, teachers received more negative ratings in the audio-only condition on hesitant speaking style, being well prepared, and communicating effectively.

We located two studies that entailed a fairly exhaustive coding of a wide range of discrete nonverbal cues. Keith et al. (1974) coded videotapes of 43 preservice teachers (students in teacher training programs) on a total of 38 separate behaviors in such categories as gestures; body movements and orientation; facial expression; head, physical, and visual orientation; and facial attractiveness. They also coded 19 verbal and nonverbal responses of the students (grades K–6). Using a similar methodology, Fox and Poppleton (1983) coded a total of 47 variables while observing physical education teachers interacting with students, of which 11 were nonverbal in nature, such as proximity, touch, general body orientation, body movement, and facial expression. Both of these studies thus collected the data that in principle could allow a determination of the relations between individual nonverbal cues and student outcomes. Somewhat disappointingly, from our perspective at least, in both studies the analyses that were reported were factor or cluster analyses of all variables (teacher and student verbal and nonverbal behaviors) combined together. These analyses provide interesting insight into the patterns of naturally co-occurring teacher and student behaviors; for example, Keith et al. (1974) identified three major clusters of behaviors that they termed (a) positive task-relevant interaction, (b) observation and group interaction, and (c) teacher disapproval and pupil misbehavior. But they do leave unanswered the question of which individual cues best predict student outcomes.

A handful of studies have examined the impact of a single nonverbal behavior on student outcomes. For example, in a study of elementary school children, Otteson and Otteson (1978) found that teachers who read a short story while engaging in eye contact with the students facilitated their recall of the story. Gesture is the nonverbal cue that has received the most rigorous research attention, and studies on gesture—unlike studies of other aspects of teacher nonverbal behavior—have focused primarily on student learning as the outcome variable of interest. (See Roth, 2001, for a recent excellent review of the role of gesture in education.) Several empirical studies have documented that a teacher's gestures can predict student learning, especially when the material covered is complex and/or involves scientific or mathematical concepts (Flevares & Perry, 2001; Goldin-Meadow, Kim, & Singer, 1999; McNeil, Alibali, & Evans, 2000; Roth, 2001; Valenzeno, Alibali, & Klatzky, 2003).

A prototypical example of this research is a study by Goldin-Meadow et al. (1999). In this study, eight teachers were videotaped while presenting a math lesson to 49 3rd and 4th grade students. The videotapes were coded for the problem-solving strategies conveyed both verbally and gesturally by the teachers (e.g., pointing to the addends to be summed), and students' comprehension of the strategies was assessed, as operationalized by their ability to repeat it back to the teacher. Analysis of the videotapes indicated that 60% of the teacher's speaking turns contained both speech and gesture; of these, there was a 2:1 ratio of speaking turns where the verbal and nonverbal strategies were matched vs. mismatched. Looking at how the teachers' gestures related to student comprehension, the researchers found that children were more likely to reiterate the strategy when it was accompanied by gesture than when no gesture accompanied it, and they were less likely to reiterate the strategy when the gesture did not match it than when no gesture accompanied it. Goldin-Meadow et al. (1999) thus concluded, "gesture aided comprehension of teacher speech when it matched that speech, and hurt child comprehension of teacher speech when it mismatched that speech" (p. 726).

Similar results were found by Valenzeno et al. (2003), who showed preschool children one of two videotapes explaining the concept of symmetry. In one version, the teacher did not use any gestures, whereas in the other version, she produced pointing and tracing gestures as she explained symmetry. Children were then administered a posttest wherein they were asked to judge six objects as being either symmetrical or asymmetrical. Those who saw the verbal + gesture videotape scored significantly higher on the posttest than did children who saw the verbal-only videotape.

Summary and Conclusions

What can teachers conclude from this set of studies? Consistent with the immediacy literature, teachers who engage in warm, active nonverbal behavior are evaluated more positively by their students. Also consistent with the immediacy literature, it is not clear, though, that this behavior predicts greater amounts of learning, and at least a couple of studies found better task performance associated with negative teacher nonverbal behavior. Does that mean that the old teachers' adage, "Don't smile until Christmas," is correct? Not necessarily. Again, too few of the studies included learning as a dependent variable to arrive at any firm conclusions. The research on gesture, moreover, indicates definite positive effects of teacher nonverbal behavior on learning. It would also be unwise, perhaps, to discount the strong motivating role of positive student evaluations in facilitating academic performance. Students may initially work harder for a teacher who is strict and stern, but overly negative teacher behavior can lead to the students' intrinsic motivation for schoolwork being undermined. Further research is needed that tracks teachers' nonverbal behavior and its influence on students' evaluative reactions to the teacher and cognitive performance longitudinally.

For researchers in nonverbal communication, this set of studies represents an advance over the nonverbal immediacy literature, as most of these studies involved the objective coding or manipulation of nonverbal behaviors, rather than measuring them subjectively through Likert-type scales that ask for relative judgments of behaviors. Moreover, most of the studies in this section involved experimental manipulations of teachers' nonverbal behavior, thus permitting stronger causal inferences regarding the role of nonverbal behavior. However, there is much more that can be done with this area. As noted earlier, most of the studies manipulated or measured nonverbal cues in combination, making it impossible to untangle the contributions of a teacher's smiles from his or her tone of voice, for example. More studies need to be done that analyze the effects of individual cues, with the recent work on gestures being an excellent example of the kinds of careful, informative studies that can be done in this regard.

MEDIATION OF TEACHER EXPECTANCY EFFECTS

The teacher nonverbal behavior literature reviewed so far has concerned "main effects," as it were, of teacher behavior, that is, the relations between a teacher's behavior toward an entire class and student outcomes. In the remainder of this chapter, we look at the question of differential teacher behavior toward certain subgroups of students. In other words, within a single classroom, do teachers treat some students differently than others, and how does that differential behavior affect those students' outcomes? We begin with a review of the large literature on the mediation of teacher expectancy effects and conclude with a review of the literature on differential teacher behavior toward students varying in race, ethnicity, and gender. Because the teacher expectancy literature has been the topic of extensive reviews in the past (see Babad, 1992; Harris & Rosenthal, 1985), we do not describe individual studies in this section but rather summarize the major conclusions of this literature.

Beginning in the mid-1950s, there has been a growing literature on the phenomenon of "interpersonal expectancy effects." This term refers to the finding that one person's expectation for the behavior of another can come to serve as a self-fulfilling prophecy. Thus, experimenters collecting psychological data have been shown to obtain data consistent with the type of data they had been led to expect. For example, when experimenters were told that the research subjects they were assigned were "success-perceivers," those subjects rated the faces of other people as more successful. When experimenters were told that the research subjects they were assigned were "failure-perceivers," those subjects rated the faces of other people as less successful. In these and many other studies with human subjects, psychological experimenters tended to obtain the data they had been led to expect (Rosenthal, 1963, 1969; Rosenthal & Rubin, 1978).

Subsequent research showed that even when animal subjects were employed, experimenters led to expect better learning of mazes by their rats obtained better learning of mazes than did experimenters led to expect less learning from their rats (Rosenthal & Fode, 1963). Similar findings were obtained when Skinner boxes were employed instead of mazes. Rats expected to learn sequences of responses more readily learned those sequences more readily (Rosenthal & Lawson, 1964).

If rats learned better when expected to, then it seemed not farfetched to think that children might learn better when expected to by their teachers. Indeed, that turned out to be the case. When teachers in an elementary school were led to believe that certain children in their class would show unusual gains in intellectual performance over the course of a school year, those certain children (whose names had been selected by means of a table of random numbers), actually did gain more in intellectual performance than did the children of the control group (Rosenthal & Jacobson, 1992). Meta-analyses of the 19 studies of the effects of teachers' expectations showed not only that there was an overall non-negligible effect of experimentally induced effects of teacher expectations, but that the magnitude of the effect increased linearly with the plausibility of the manipulation (Raudenbush, 1984, 1994; Rosenthal, 2002).

Mediating Variables

As more was learned about the occurrence and generality of interpersonal expectancy effects, more was also learned about the processes of communication that probably served to mediate the effect. If we label the experimentally induced expectancy for the behavior of another person, E, the communicating or mediating variables, M, and the outcome responses of the person for whom the expectations were held, O, we can diagram the mediation process by means of the following three arrows:

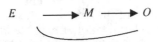

The E-O arrow or link describes the experimental effect of E on O. The E-M arrow or link describes the experimental effect of E on M. The M-O arrow or link describes the relationship between the mediating variable and the outcome variable. We should note that the E-O and E-M arrows are causal links because we have experimentally induced E. The M-O link, however, is not usually a causal link because M has not been experimentally manipulated. We return to this important, but often overlooked, point later.

Four Factors

On the basis of the first 30 or so published studies relevant to mediation, a four-factor "theory" of the mediation of teacher expectancy effects was proposed (Harris & Rosenthal, 1985, 1986; Rosenthal, 1994). The "theory" describes four major groupings of teacher behaviors hypothesized to be involved in mediation. The first factor, *climate*, refers to the warmer socioemotional climate that teachers tend to create for high expectancy students, a warmth that can be communicated both verbally and nonverbally. The *input* factor refers to the tendency for teachers to teach more material to their "special" students. The *output* factor refers to the tendency for teachers to give their "special" students greater opportunities for responding. Finally, the *feedback* factor refers to the tendency for teachers to give more differentiated feedback to their "special," high expectancy students. By differentiated, we mean that the feedback will be contingent on the correctness or incorrectness of the student's response and that the content of the feedback will tend to be directly related to what the student has said.

Meta-analyses conducted by Harris and Rosenthal (1986) were designed to summarize the many studies examining either the *E-M* or *M-O* links (or both) and to come up with a quantitative estimate of the importance of each of the four factors in the mediation of interpersonal expectancy effects. Table 8.3 gives the average magnitude of the role of each factor separately for the *E-M* and *M-O* links. While all four factors received ample support in terms of significance testing, the magnitudes of the effects for the *climate* and *input* factors were especially impressive. Teachers appear to teach more and to teach it more warmly to students for whom they have more favorable expectations.

Mediating Variables and Causal Inference

Teachers' expectations for their pupils' intellectual functioning have been shown to serve as self-fulfilling prophecies. The performance expected came to pass *because* the teacher expected it. We can draw that causal conclusion about the *E-O* link and the *E-M* link because of the randomized experiments that have been conducted, reported, and summarized quantitatively. But there is a causal conclusion we can *not* draw, and it's a big one. Although the relationships between mediating variables and outcome variables are well-established, almost nothing can be said about the *effects* of the mediating variables on the outcome variables because the mediators have rarely been manipulated experimentally. We may find that experimentally manipulated teacher expectations *cause* both greater teacher warmth and better student intellectual performance, and that greater teacher warmth *predicts*

Table 8.3
Meta-Analytically Derived Average Correlations Indexing the Effect Sizes of the Four Factor Theory (After Harris & Rosenthal, 1986)

	Correlations		
	(E-M Link)	(M-O Link)	Geometric Mean of E-M and M-O Links
Primary Factors			
1. Climate (Affect)	.23	.36	.29
2. Input (Effort)	.26	.28	.27
Secondary Factors			
3. Output	.18	.16	.17
4. Feedback	.13	.08	.10

Note: All correlations are significantly greater than zero at $p < .002$. The correlation between the magnitudes of the average E-M and M-O links is .88.

better student intellectual performance. From this it is tempting to conclude that the expectancy-caused warmth caused the improved outcome. Tempting, but quite unjustified. If we want to conclude that warmth is the mediator variable caused by raised teacher expectancy and, in turn, causing improved student performance, we must manipulate teacher warmth directly. Valid causal inferences are not available "on the cheap" no matter how fancy the "causal inferential" software. When randomization is truly impossible (e.g., for ethical reasons) we should use those statistical procedures such as subclassification on propensity scores (Rubin, 1998) ranking highest not only in sophistication about validity, but also in transparency.

Applications and Remaining Questions

We have learned a good deal about some processes of communication in classrooms. But for all we have learned there is more that we do not yet know. For example, now that we know that teachers' behaving more warmly toward their students is associated with better performance on the part of their students, can't we just apply this knowledge and train teachers to treat students more warmly in order to improve student performance? This simple question is really two questions, neither of which we can answer very well. First, we don't know the degree to which teacher warmth can be trained. Although various training programs have been developed for teachers, experimental studies of their effectiveness are few and far between. In a later section of this chapter we describe a few of those programs. Second, we don't know whether teachers trained to be warmer would in fact elicit better performance from their students. It would take specifically designed randomized studies to learn the degree to which we can train teachers to treat their students more warmly, and if these studies showed that we could, it would take additional randomized studies to show that this increased teacher warmth brought about improved student performance. These unanswered questions are not cause for pessimism; they just indicate that our task is not yet completed.

DIFFERENTIAL TEACHER NONVERBAL BEHAVIOR IN OTHER DOMAINS

The research summarized above on the mediation of teacher expectancy effects focused on the question of whether teachers treat high-expectancy students differently than they treat low-expectancy students. In this section, we focus instead on whether teachers display differential nonverbal behavior to students varying on dimensions besides academic expectations. In other words, do teachers act differently toward students varying in race, gender, ethnic group, or other variables? These studies obviously overlap conceptually with the teacher expectancy literature, as teachers' academic expectancies stem in part from their beliefs about ability differences across racial, gender, and other subgroupings of students (Dusek & Joseph, 1985). A primary difference is that these studies typically do not report data to show that teachers' differential behavior culminates in differences in student outcomes.

Do Teachers Demonstrate Different Nonverbal Behaviors Toward Girls and Boys?

One of the most controversial issues in education in the past decade has been the assertion that teachers pay disproportionately greater attention to boys, on both subtle and overt levels, creating a "chilly climate" in the classroom for girls (American Association of University Women, 1992; LaFrance, 1985; Sandler, Silverberg, & Hall, 1996; Sadker & Sadker, 1994). This notion has been argued persuasively and passionately by academic feminists and disseminated so widely in the popular media that many—if not most—educators would agree unblinkingly that there is a chilly climate in today's schools for girls. However, this assertion has not gone unchallenged by critics, who note that chilly climate proponents do not offer convincing empirical evidence for their claims, and they point to a large array of data suggesting instead that boys are at greater risk for poor educational outcomes than are girls (Kleinfeld, 1998; Sommers, 2000).

Most of the chilly climate articles have focused on differential verbal behaviors, such as calling on boys more than girls or discouraging girls from taking math or science courses. For our purposes, we are interested in the narrower question of whether teachers exhibit different nonverbal behavior toward girls and boys. Given the "hotness" of gender issues in psychology today, the paucity of empirical studies on this question (and, as we will see later, the question of differential behavior according to student race) is disheartening.

What have the few empirical studies on this question found? The results of two studies suggest that the sex of the teacher interacts in important ways with the sex of student to determine teachers' nonverbal behavior. Perdue and Connor (1978) analyzed touching patterns between both male and female teachers and their male and female preschool students. The primary result is that there were greater amounts of teacher touch in same-sex teacher-student dyads than in opposite-sex dyads. Instances of touch were also coded as to whether they were friendly, helpful, attentional, or incidental, and there were differences due to student sex with respect to the frequencies of these categories. Most of the touches received by girls were of the helpful category (40%), with only 18% of the touches being deemed "friendly." Boys, on the other hand, received significantly more friendly touches than girls (29%) and fewer helpful touches (23%).

In a study with an undergraduate student population, Hechtman and Rosenthal (1991) videotaped 60 preservice students while teaching two short lessons—one verbal, one mechanical/quantitative—to undergraduates, with the students tested on the content before and after the lesson. Analyses revealed that teachers appeared more nonverbally hostile when teaching sex role counter-stereotypic lessons, that is, when teaching the verbal lesson to the men and the mechanical lesson to the women. There was also a three-way interaction between lesson, student sex, and teacher sex such that men showed this biased teaching behavior more than did the women. This differential behavior was evidently picked up by the students, who in turn were less satisfied with the lesson when male teachers taught counter-stereotypic material.

In an observational study examining both race and gender, Simpson and Erickson (1983) found that boys received more nonverbal criticism than did girls. More specifically, White teachers gave the most nonverbal criticism to Black boys relative to Black girls, White boys, and White girls. In another study examining race and teacher liking for students, Lyon (1977) found that boys who were evaluated negatively by the teacher also received more negative nonverbal behavior from them, in the form of frowns, head shakes, glares, and restraining touches.

Given the extremely limited number of studies directly addressing this issue, conclusions regarding sex bias—or the lack thereof—in teachers' nonverbal behavior would be premature, as the evidence in these studies is mixed with respect to which gender is "favored" nonverbally. Clearly, more descriptive research is needed to document patterns of teachers' nonverbal behavior toward male and female students. Equally important, future studies should collect data that would allow linking differential teacher behavior to student outcomes. Merely establishing that teachers treat boys and girls differently would not be sufficient grounds for alarm; one would want to show that these differences affect one gender unfairly. One would also want to rule out student behavior as a causal eliciting factor prior to making claims of teacher bias. For example, if boys do receive more negative nonverbal criticism as suggested by Simpson and Ericson (1983), it would be important to discover whether this held true even after controlling for, say, student misbehavior or off-task behavior.

Do Teachers Show Different Nonverbal Behavior to Students of Different Races?

As conscious or unconscious racism in the classroom is often suggested as a root cause of the achievement gap between Blacks and Whites, the effects of student race on teachers' nonverbal behavior is a research question of obvious importance. A leading researcher on this topic is Robert Feldman, whose group has conducted several studies examining differential teacher nonverbal behavior as a function of student race (see Feldman, 1985; Feldman & Saletsky, 1986, for reviews of this literature). In the first study in this research program, Feldman and Donohoe (1978) videotaped 36 undergraduates delivering an analogy lesson to Black or White confederates. These videotapes were rated for the extent to which the teacher appeared pleased with the student. Analyses indicated a very large effect of student race, with teachers rated as appearing more pleased when interacting with a White confederate than a Black confederate. Student race also interacted significantly with teacher prejudice level, such that the magnitude of the race difference was greater for high-prejudice teachers than low-prejudice teachers. A second experiment reported in the article replicated the main effect of student race found in the first study. This study also included a sample of Black undergraduates role-playing the teacher, and there were no differences due to student race for Black teacher nonverbal behavior, at least when ratings were made by White raters. When Black raters were used, however, the teachers appeared more pleased with Black students, raising the possibility of same-race favoritism that can only be detected by members of that race.

Feldman and Orchowsky (1979) used a similar methodology and once again obtained a strong effect of student race, with undergraduate role-playing teachers appearing more pleased with White confederates than Black confederates. This particular study also manipulated the task performance of the confederates, and an even larger effect was found for this variable, with teachers appearing more pleased when a student did well than when he or she did poorly.

An observational study of the behavior exhibited by one teacher toward 12 educationally handicapped students, however, failed to demonstrate differences in teacher behavior as a function of student race (Lyon, 1977). Correlations between student race and teacher gaze, smiles, head movements, touch, and proximity were all reported to be nonsignificant, although given the very small sample size, it is not possible to interpret the null results as reflecting a zero population effect size.

In addition to the studies reviewed above, which do not yield a strong consensus in their findings, several studies from the teacher expectancy domain also included race of student as an independent variable and thus are relevant here. Taylor (1979) looked at the joint effects of student race and teacher expectancy, using a sample of preservice teachers asked to administer a lesson to a "student," described as varying in ability and race, who was allegedly on the other side of a one-way mirror. Although no significant main effects of student race were obtained for teachers' nonverbal behavior, a Race x Expectancy interaction was obtained such that teachers displayed the greatest amount of nonverbal warmth to high-ability Blacks and low-ability Whites. Chaikin and Derlega (1978) had undergraduate role-playing teachers administer a lesson to two Black and two White 10-year-old confederates. The White confederates received more smiles and gaze than did the Black confederates. In another role-playing study where Black undergraduates were asked to teach a fire safety lesson to confederates of differing race, Derlega, McAnulty, Strout, and Reavis (1980) found that the teachers maintained greater physical distance with White confederates than they did with Black confederates. Rubovits and Maehr (1973) found that Black junior high schools students were treated more negatively on a range of variables, primarily verbal, but also including ignoring by the teacher.

Taken together, these studies suggest that, when differential behavior occurs, it is more likely to favor White students than Black students, but that there also appears to be a tendency for teachers to behave more positively toward students of the same race as the teacher. Again, the paucity of empirical research on student race effects is discouraging given the obvious applied importance and great social interest in these issues.

Differential Teacher Behavior as a Function of Other Variables

Although race and gender are the individual difference variables attracting the most concern among educators, a handful of studies exists looking at differential teacher behavior as a function of other variables. Some have looked at differences in teacher behavior directed toward other ethnic and cultural groups and differences between socioeconomic groups. For example, Greenbaum (1985) showed that teachers at Indian reservation schools paused longer than did teachers in largely-White schools, although this difference is difficult to interpret given the small number of teachers involved (four) and the confounding of teachers with schools. Davis, Dobson, and Shelton (1973) coded "encouraging" and "restricting" nonverbal behaviors of 20 first grade teachers, 11 of whom taught in schools with primarily low-SES students and 9 of whom taught in schools with largely middle-class students. This study found no differences between SES categories with respect to either total quantity of nonverbal behaviors or encouraging behaviors, and only a small, nonsignificant trend for low-SES classes to receive fewer restrictive behaviors ($r = .22$).

Elisha Babad and his colleagues have also conducted an impressive program of research documenting differential teacher nonverbal behavior (see Babad, 1993, for a review of this literature). In addition to studies showing that teachers' expectations for their students are leaked through nonverbal channels (Babad, Bernieri, & Rosenthal, 1989a, 1989b; Babad & Taylor, 1992), these studies have also found that teachers behave differently according to the type of class being taught (preschool vs. elementary), and whether or not the student is a teacher's pet. For example, Babad, Bernieri, and Rosenthal (1987) had raters judge short (10-sec) clips of preschool, remedial, and elementary school teachers' behavior. Preschool teachers showed the least amount of negative nonverbal affect and teacher dogmatism, whereas elementary school teachers showed the most, with remedial teachers falling between the two groups. Interestingly, there were no significant differences on the more positive composite of "active" teaching behavior. Examination across nonverbal channels indicated that the differences in negative affect were found only for those channels showing the face, whereas the differences in dogmatism were generally obtained across all nonverbal channels.

Because most people can remember either being a teacher's pet themselves or being irritated by somebody else who was a teacher's pet, one of the more intriguing questions for researchers of teachers' nonverbal behavior is whether teachers display favoritism nonverbally and how that affects those students and others in the classroom. We located several studies that investigated differences between teachers as a function of their liking for the students. In a study that involved an experimental manipulation of liking for particular students, Feldman (1976) found that undergraduates role-playing teachers appeared more nonverbally pleased with students they had been led to like. This result was confirmed by an observational study by Lyon (1977), who found teachers displaying more negative nonverbal behaviors (e.g., glares and frowns) to disliked students, but there was no difference in frequencies of positive nonverbal behaviors. With respect to proximity, Brooks and Wilson (1978) found that teachers stood further away from disliked students.

In a survey study of 80 elementary classrooms, Babad (1995) discovered that in many classrooms, students arrived at good consensus regarding which student(s) were teacher's pets, and this consensus was related to perceived differences in teachers' behavior toward students, especially affect-related behaviors. Moreover, perceived differential affect was in turn related negatively to students' morale and satisfaction. Thus, to the extent that students can pick up on favoritism in teachers, such favoritism may have adverse effects on the classroom climate. Given the universal awareness of "teacher's pets," and the negative consequences that can accrue both for those students who are and those who are not favored by the teacher (Tal & Babad, 1990), more research on this critical dimension is clearly needed. For example, observational studies are needed to identify the cues that students use to determine who is regarded as a teacher's pet. A reasonable hypothesis is that these cues are primarily nonverbal in nature, as most teachers are motivated to avoid showing favoritism verbally.

IMPLICATIONS AND SUGGESTIONS
FOR RESEARCHERS AND TEACHERS

What Have We Learned So Far And Where Do We Go From Here?

Taking the four domains of literature on teachers' nonverbal behavior together, one is left with the unmistakable conclusion that progress on these research questions is uneven. We have a very good grasp on the effects of teacher nonverbal immediacy and warmth on students' affective reactions to their educational experience. We also have a good grasp on the general question of how teachers' expectations are communicated nonverbally. In other domains, however, the literature is disquietingly sparse. Moreover, the literature is also disquietingly dated, with most of the studies reviewed here published during the 1970s and 1980s, and much fewer dating from the 1990s or later.

Interest in specific topics waxes and wanes in any research domain, and there are probably several reasons for the recent neglect of teacher's nonverbal behavior as a research endeavor. As any nonverbal researcher can attest, doing nonverbal research is a difficult, labor-intensive, time-consuming process. Coding even a fairly small data set (say, 30 minutes of videotaped classroom interactions from a sample of 30 teachers) can take months. And as any educational researcher can attest, the prevailing ethical requirements for studying schoolchildren have become increasingly stringent and conducting research in the classroom correspondingly more difficult. For example, most IRBs today would require researchers interested in videotaping classroom interactions to obtain the active consent of the families of every student in the class before they could appear on the videotape, a difficult feat. School administrators are also increasingly reluctant to allow researchers in the classroom to administer surveys or other dependent measures, given increasing demands on instructional time. Thus, researchers interested in teachers' nonverbal behavior are faced with a "double whammy" that makes conducting this research extremely difficult.

Given the logistical difficulties in doing such research, it is not surprising that so many researchers turn to role-play analogues of the teaching relationship, using undergraduates, and/or rely on self-report measures of nonverbal behavior. Although such studies can serve to provide encouraging preliminary data and to generate hypotheses to be tested in an actual school context, we feel that such reliance on undergraduate analogues and self-reports limits the external validity of our research. Undergraduates may act entirely differently than teachers, who have acquired hard-earned professional expertise through years in the classroom trenches. Self-reports, while expedient, also raise considerable validity concerns, especially in the domain of nonverbal behavior, given the extent to which nonverbal expression takes place outside the conscious awareness and control of an individual.

As noted earlier, more research is needed that looks at the relation between individual nonverbal cues and student outcomes, especially performance outcomes such as student grades or recall. The recent work on gestures described earlier (Goldin-Meadow et al., 1999; Valenzeno et al., 2003) serves as an excellent model for future research in which nonverbal behaviors are carefully defined, coded, and analyzed within the context of a meaningful theoretical framework. More research is also needed on the intriguing possibility that teachers' nonverbal behaviors may be more important in some contexts than in others. The Wass (1973) study described earlier found that nonverbal behavior had a negligible impact when accompanying verbal feedback; other researchers have similarly found that teachers' words often carry more weight than their nonverbal behaviors (Woolfolk & Woolfolk, 1974). However, a considerable body of literature exists purporting that teachers' nonverbal cues, gestures in particular, may be particularly helpful in the teaching of foreign language, a domain where the verbal channel is not necessarily straightforward (Allen, 2000; Antes, 1996; Barnett, 1983; Beattie, 1977; von Raffler-Engel, 1980; Ward & von Raffler-Engel, 1980).

Training in Nonverbal Behaviors

Within the domain of nonverbal behavior in the classroom, perhaps the topic of greatest interest to educators is the extent to which it is possible to train teachers to use nonverbal behaviors more effectively. Identifying the behaviors that are associated positively with student motivation, affect, and learning is all well and good, but one could make a case that such knowledge is not really helpful unless it can be translated into training programs to help teachers become more effective. Although many teacher education programs address nonverbal behavior in their curricula, few empirically validated nonverbal training programs exist. For example, French (1971) designed an inservice training program that included two "assignments" intended to enhance teachers' use and awareness of nonverbal communication: (a) teaming up with a trusted colleague, observing each other's classes, and exchanging feedback regarding each teacher's use of nonverbal behavior, and (b) devoting two five-minute intervals in the classroom to presenting lesson material exclusively nonverbally as a way of increasing awareness of nonverbal cues and their impact on students. Unfortunately, the article describing this training model did not provide any evaluation data, so its efficacy is unknown. Love and Roderick (1971) developed an awareness unit targeting ten categories of teacher nonverbal behavior. The unit consisted of having teachers (a) read about nonverbal behavior; (b) observe a videotape of another teacher and attend to that teacher's nonverbal behavior in a general way; (c) learn to recognize the ten categories of nonverbal behavior more specifically; (d) practice the behaviors in small role-playing groups; and then (e) practice the behaviors in a real setting. Love and Roderick (1971) state that they pilot tested this awareness unit; unfortunately they do not report details about the pilot study (such as number of teachers sampled or any detailed results), stating merely that teachers used more categories of nonverbal behavior on the posttest compared to the pretest.

Fetter (1983) developed another training program whereby teachers were asked first to fill out a self-report inventory of their own nonverbal behavior and then were asked to observe in private a videotape of themselves teaching while referring to the nonverbal behaviors identified in the self-report instrument. A pilot study comparing 14 teachers who undertook this training to 14 control teachers showed that teachers in the training condition increased gaze and movement toward students and decreased frowns and exasperated looks, although with these modest sample sizes, the differences were not significant.

Finally, Richmond, McCroskey, Plax, and Kearney (1986) found that teachers who had taken a course in nonverbal communication stressing the nonverbal behaviors associated with immediacy were perceived as being more nonverbally immediate by their students than did students of teachers who had not received such training. These findings must be interpreted with caution, although, given the posttest-only nature of the design and the failure to assign teachers randomly to training conditions.

In sum, although several nonverbal training programs have been developed, none of them has been subjected to the type of rigorous randomized, controlled trials and empirical evaluation that most researchers would want to see prior to advocating their widespread use in teacher education programs. These training programs, moreover, are fairly dated and thus do not reflect the advances in research on teachers' nonverbal behavior made in the past couple of decades. A critical direction for future research, therefore, would be the development and empirical evaluation of nonverbal training units that could be incorporated into teacher training programs. In designing these units, we echo the sentiment raised earlier that the selection of nonverbal behaviors to be targeted for training should be done on an empirical basis, based on experimental studies indicating a true causal effect of the targeted behavior. Given the relative lack of solid experimental data on individual teacher behaviors, it could well be that the first step must be to expand the body of basic, experimental research on teachers' behavior where nonverbal cues are experimentally manipulated and their effects on students measured.

Closing Thoughts

That teachers exert a strong effect on students' lives, either in a positive or negative way, is undisputed. The literature reviewed here shows that an important part of teachers' influence is nonverbal in nature. Our review also indicates that, with the few notable exceptions described above, we do not have firm answers to questions regarding the precise nonverbal mechanisms underlying teachers' influence. Charles Galloway's apt comment in 1984 that "the field of nonverbal has demonstrated complexities and variant interpretations beyond anything the pioneers in the field could have imagined" thus holds just as true today (Galloway, 1984, p. 412). The "more research is needed" conclusion is trite, overused, and lame, yet in this case it may be the most honest way to close our chapter. Studying the nonverbal behavior of teachers is fraught with difficulty, but we hope we have convinced readers that it is a challenge worth the effort.

ACKNOWLEDGMENTS

We thank MaryLu Rosenthal for her assistance in searching the literature and data entry. Correspondence concerning this chapter should be addressed to Monica Harris, Department of Psychology, University of Kentucky, Lexington, Kentucky 40506–0044. E-mail: harris@uky.edu

NOTES

1. Although it is beyond the scope of the present chapter, this unequal power structure, combined with the distracting cognitive demands placed on a teacher of formulating and delivering educational material, may well result in students' nonverbal behavior being *less* noticed by teachers and less influential than in ordinary interaction.
2. Space limitations do not permit full description of the meta-analytic procedures and results for this literature; see Harris and Rosenthal (2003) for more detail, including a bibliography of articles included in the meta-analysis.
3. However, neither article provides statistics from which an effect size can be computed, so we are unable to conclude that there is truly no effect (i.e., that r is near 0), only that p is > .05. Such a failure to provide precise statistics is especially common in older studies, and thus this caveat holds true for many of the subsequent articles we summarize where it is stated that results are not significant.

REFERENCES

Allen, L. Q. (2000). Nonverbal accommodations in foreign language teacher talk. *Applied Language Learning, 11,* 155–176.

American Association of University Women. (1992). *How schools shortchange girls: A study of major findings on girls and education.* Washington, DC: AAUW Educational Foundation.

Andersen, J. F. (1978). *The relationship between teacher immediacy and teaching effectiveness.* Unpublished doctoral dissertation, West Virginia University, Morgantown, WV.

Andersen, J. F. (1979). Teacher immediacy as a predictor of teaching effectiveness. In D. Nimmo (Ed.), *Communication Yearbook, 3* (pp. 543–559). New Brunswick, NJ: Transaction Books.

Antes, T. A. (1996). Kinesics: The value of gesture in language and in the language classroom. *Foreign Language Annals, 29,* 439–448.

Babad, E. (1992). Teacher expectancies and nonverbal behavior. In R. S. Feldman (Ed.), *Applications of nonverbal behavioral theories and research* (pp. 167–190). Hillsdale, NJ: Lawrence Erlbaum Associates.

Babad, E. (1993). Teachers' differential behavior. *Educational Psychology Review, 5,* 347–376.

Babad, E. (1995). The "teacher's pet" phenomenon, students' perceptions of teachers' differential behavior, and students' morale. *Journal of Educational Psychology, 87*, 361–374.

Babad, E., Bernieri, F., & Rosenthal, R. (1987). Nonverbal and verbal behavior of preschool, remedial, and elementary school teachers. *American Educational Research Journal, 24*, 405–415.

Babad, E., Bernieri, F., & Rosenthal, R. (1989a). Nonverbal communication and leakage in the behavior of biased and unbiased teachers. *Journal of Personality and Social Psychology, 56*, 89–94.

Babad, E., Bernieri, F., & Rosenthal, R. (1989b). When less information is more informative: Diagnosing teacher expectations from brief samples of behaviour. *British Journal of Educational Psychology, 59*, 281–295.

Babad, E., & Taylor, P. J. (1992). Transparency of teacher expectancies across language, cultural boundaries. *Journal of Educational Research, 86*, 120–125.

Barnett, M. A. (1983). Replacing teacher talk with gestures: Nonverbal communication in the foreign language classroom. *Foreign Language Annals, 16*, 173–176.

Beattie, N. (1977). Nonverbal aspects of the teaching and learning of foreign languages. *Audio-Visual Language Journal, 15*, 175–181.

Bettencourt, E. M., Gillet, M., Gall, M., & Hull, R. E. (1983). Effects of teacher enthusiasm on student on-task behavior and achievement. *American Educational Research Journal, 20*, 435–450.

Booth-Butterfield, S., Mosher, N., & Mollish, D. (1992). Teacher immediacy and student involvement: A dual process analysis. *Communication Research Reports, 9*, 13–21.

Brooks, D. M., & Wilson, B. J. (1978). Teacher verbal and nonverbal behavioral expression toward selected pupils. *Journal of Educational Psychology, 70*, 147–153.

Chaikin, A. L., & Derlega, V. J. (1978). Nonverbal mediators of expectancy effects in Black and White children. *Journal of Applied Social Psychology, 8*, 117–125.

Chaikin, A. L., Gillen, B., Derlega, V., J., Heinen, J. R. K., & Wilson, M. (1978). Students' reactions to teachers' physical attractiveness and nonverbal behavior: Two exploratory studies. *Psychology in the Schools, 15*, 588–595.

Chesebro, J. L., & McCroskey, J. C. (2000). The relationship between students' reports of learning and their actual recall of material: A validity test. *Communication Education, 49*, 297–301.

Cohen, J. (1969). *Statistical power analysis for the behavioral sciences.* New York: Academic Press.

Comstock, J., Rowell, E., & Bowers, J. W. (1995). Food for thought: Teacher nonverbal immediacy, student learning, and curvilinearity. *Communication Education, 44*, 251–266.

Davis, G., Dobson, R., & Shelton, J. (1973). Nonverbal behavior of first grade teachers in different socioeconomic level elementary schools. *Journal of the Student Personnel Association for Teacher Education, 12*, 76–80.

Derlega, V. J., McAnulty, M., Strout, S., Reavis, C. A. (1980). Pygmalion effects among Blacks: When and how expectancies occur. *Journal of Applied Social Psychology, 10*, 260–271.

Doyle, W. (1977). The uses of nonverbal behavior: Toward an ecological model of classrooms. *Merrill-Palmer Quarterly, 23*, 179–192.

Duncan, S. (1972). Some signals and rules for taking speaking turns in conversations. *Journal of Personality and Social Psychology, 23,* 283–292.

Dusek, J. B., & Joseph, G. (1985). The bases of teacher expectancies. In J. B. Dusek (Ed.), *Teacher expectancies* (pp. 229–250). Hillsdale, NJ: Lawrence Erlbaum Associates.

Feldman, R. S. (1976). Nonverbal disclosure of teacher deception and interpersonal affect. *Journal of Educational Psychology, 68,* 807–816.

Feldman, R. S. (1985). Nonverbal behavior, race, and the classroom teacher. *Theory Into Practice, 24,* 45–49.

Feldman, R. S., & Donohoe, L. F. (1978). Nonverbal communication of affect in interracial dyads. *Journal of Educational Psychology, 70,* 979–987.

Feldman, R. S., & Orchowsky, S. (1979). Race and performance of student as determinants of teacher nonverbal behavior. *Contemporary Educational Psychology, 4,* 324–333.

Feldman, R. S., & Saletsky, R. D. (1986). Nonverbal communication in interracial teacher-student interaction. In F. S. Feldman (Ed.), *The social psychology of education: Current research and theory* (pp. 115–131).

Fetter, M. P. (1983). Nonverbal teaching behavior and the health educator. *JOSH, 53,* 431–432.

Fiske, S. T. (1993). Controlling other people: The impact of power on stereotyping. *American Psychologist, 48,* 621–628.

Flevares, L. M., & Perry, M. (2001). How many do you see? The use of nonspoken representations in first-grade mathematics lessons. *Journal of Educational Psychology, 93,* 330–345.

Fox, C., & Poppleton, P. (1983). Verbal and nonverbal communication in teaching: A study of trainee P. E. teachers in the gymnasium. *British Journal of Educational Psychology, 53,* 107–120.

French, R. L. (1971). Analyzing and improving nonverbal communication: A model for inservice education. *Theory Into Practice, 10,* 305–309.

Galloway, C. M. (1971a). Analysis of theories and research in nonverbal communication. *Journal of the Association for the Study in Perception, 6,* 1–21.

Galloway, C. M. (1971b). Nonverbal: The language of sensitivity. *Theory Into Practice, 10,* 227–230.

Galloway, C. M. (1984). Nonverbal and teacher-student relationships: An intercultural perspective. In A. Wolfgang (Ed.), *Nonverbal behavior: Perspectives, applications, and intercultural insights* (pp. 411–430). Kirkland, WA: Hogrefe & Huber Publishers.

Goldberg, G., & Mayerberg, C. K. (1973). Emotional reactions of students to nonverbal teacher behavior. *The Journal of Experimental Education, 42,* 29–32.

Goldberg, G., & Mayerberg, C. K. (1975). Effects of three types of affective teacher behavior on student performance. *Child Study Journal, 5,* 99–105.

Goldin-Meadow, S., Kim, S., & Singer, M. (1999). What the teacher's hands tell the student's mind about math. *Journal of Educational Psychology, 91,* 720–730.

Gorham, J. (1988). The relationship between verbal teacher immediacy behaviors and student learning. *Communication Education, 37,* 40–53.

Grant, B. M., & Hennings, D. G. (1971). *The teacher moves: An analysis of nonverbal activity.* New York: Teachers College Press.

Greenbaum, P. E. (1985). Nonverbal differences in communication style between American Indian and Anglo elementary classrooms. *American Educational Research Journal, 22,* 101–115.

Grubaugh, S. (1989). Non-verbal language techniques for better classroom management and discipline. *High School Journal, 73*, 34–40.

Guerrero, L. K., & Miller, T. A. (1998). Associations between nonverbal behaviors and initial impressions of instructor competence and course content in video-taped distance education courses. *Communication Education, 47, 30–42.*

Hamann, D. L., Lineburgh, N., & Paul, S. (1998). Teaching effectiveness and social skill development. *Journal of Research in Music Education, 46*, 87–101.

Harris, M. J., & Rosenthal, R. (1985). The mediation of interpersonal expectancy effects: 31 meta-analyses. *Psychological Bulletin, 97*, 363–386.

Harris, M. J., & Rosenthal, R. (1986). Four factors in the mediation of teacher expectancy effects. In R. S. Feldman (Ed.), *The social psychology of education* (pp. 91–114). NY: Cambridge University Press.

Harris, M. J., & Rosenthal, R. (2003). *Teacher nonverbal immediacy and student outcomes: A meta-analysis.* Manuscript in preparation.

Harris, M. J., Rosenthal, R., & Snodgrass, S. E. (1986). The effects of teacher expectations, gender, and behavior on pupil academic performance and self-concept. *Journal of Educational Research, 79*, 173–179.

Hechtman, S. B., & Rosenthal, R. (1991). Teacher gender and nonverbal behavior in the teaching of gender-stereotyped materials. *Journal of Applied Social Psychology, 21*, 446–459.

Hendrix, K. G. (1997). Student perceptions of verbal and nonverbal cues leading to images of Black and White professor credibility. *The Howard Journal of Communications, 8*, 251–273.

Kazdin, A. E., & Klock, J. (1973). The effect of nonverbal teacher approval on student attentive behavior. *Journal of Applied Behavior Analysis, 6*, 643–654.

Keith, L. T., Tornatzky, L. G., & Pettigrew, L. E. (1974). An analysis of verbal and nonverbal classroom teaching behaviors. *The Journal of Experimental Education, 42*, 30–38.

Kleinfeld, J. S. (1974). Effects of nonverbal warmth on the learning of Eskimo and White students. *Journal of Social Psychology, 92*, 3–9.

Kleinfeld, J. (1998). *The myth that schools shortchange girls: Social science in the service of deception.* Washington, DC: The Women's Freedom Network.

LaFrance, M. (1985). The school of hard knocks: Nonverbal sexism in the classroom. *Theory into Practice, 24*, 40–44.

Love, A. M., & Roderick, J. A. (1971). Teacher nonverbal communication: The development and field testing of an awareness unit. *Theory Into Practice, 10*, 295–299.

Lyon, S. (1977). Teacher nonverbal behavior related to perceived pupil social-personal attributes. *Journal of Learning Disabilities, 10*, 52–56.

McCroskey, J. C., Fayer, J. M., Richmond, V. P, Sallinen, A., & Barraclough, R. A. (1996). A multi-cultural examination of the relationships between nonverbal immediacy and affective learning. *Communication Quarterly, 44*, 297–307.

McCroskey, J. C., & Richmond, V. P. (1992). Increasing teacher influence through immediacy. In V. P. Richmond & J. C. McCroskey (Eds.), *Power in the classroom: Communication, control, and concern* (pp.101–119). Hillsdale, NJ: Lawrence Erlbaum Associates.

McNeil, N. M., Alibali, M. W., & Evans, J. L. (2000). The role of gesture in children's comprehension of spoken language: Now they need it, now they don't. *Journal of Nonverbal Behavior, 24*, 131–150.

Mehrabian, A. (1966). Immediacy: An indicator of attitudes in linguistic communication. *Journal of Personality, 34,* 26–34.

Mehrabian, A. (1971). *Silent messages.* Belmont, CA: Wadsworth.

Neill, S. R. St J. (1986). Children's reported responses to teachers' nonverbal signals: A pilot study. *Journal of Education for Teaching, 12,* 53–61.

Neill, S. R. St. J. (1989a). Children's reported responses to teachers' and non-teachers' nonverbal communication. *Educational Research, 31,* 71–74.

Neill, S. R. St. J. (1989b). The effects of facial expression and posture on children's reported responses to teacher nonverbal communication. *British Educational Research Journal, 15,* 195–204.

Otteson, J. P., & Otteson, C. R. (1980). Effects of teacher gaze on children's story recall. *Perceptual and Motor Skills, 50,* 35–42.

Perdue, V. P., & Connor, J. M. (1978). Patterns of touching between preschool children and male and female teachers. *Child Development, 49,* 1258–1262.

Philippot, P., Feldman, R. S., & McGee, G. (1992). Nonverbal behavioral skills in an educational context: Typical and atypical populations. In R. S. Feldman (Ed.), *Applications of nonverbal behavioral theories and research* (pp. 191–213). Hillsdale, NJ: Lawrence Erlbaum Associates.

Raffler-Engel, W. von. (1980). Kinesics and paralinguistics: A neglected factor in second-language research and teaching. *Modern Language Review, 36,* 225–237.

Raudenbush, S. W. (1984). Magnitude of teacher expectancy effects on pupil IQ as a function of the credibility of expectancy induction: A synthesis of findings from 18 experiments. *Journal of Educational Psychology, 76,* 85–97.

Raudenbush, S. W. (1994). Random effects models. In H. Cooper & L. V. Hedges (Eds.), *The handbook of research synthesis* (pp. 301–321). New York: Russell Sage Foundation.

Richmond, V. P., Gorham, J. S., & McCroskey, J. C. (1987). The relationship between selected immediacy behaviors and cognitive learning. *Communication Yearbook, 10,* 574–590.

Richmond, V. P., McCroskey, J. C., Plax, T. G., & Kearney, P. (1986). Teacher nonverbal immediacy training and student affect. *World Communication, 15,* 181–194.

Rosenthal, R. (1963). On the social psychology of the psychological experiment: The experimenter's hypothesis as unintended determinant of experimental results. *American Scientist, 51,* 268–283.

Rosenthal, R. (1969). Interpersonal expectations. In R. Rosenthal and R. L. Rosnow (Eds.), *Artifact in behavioral research* (pp. 181–277). New York: Academic Press.

Rosenthal, R. (1991). *Meta-analytic procedures for social research* (rev. ed.). Newbury Park: Sage.

Rosenthal, R. (1994). Interpersonal expectancy effects: A 30-year perspective. *Current Directions in Psychological Science, 3,* 176–179.

Rosenthal, R. (2002). Covert communication in classrooms, clinics, courtrooms, and cubicles. *American Psychologist, 57,* 839–849.

Rosenthal, R., & Fode, K. L. (1963). The effect of experimenter bias on the performance of the albino rat. *Behavioral Science, 8,* 183–189.

Rosenthal, R., & Jacobson, L. (1992). *Pygmalion in the classroom* (expanded edition). New York: Irvington.

Rosenthal, R., & Lawson, R. (1964). A longitudinal study of the effects of experimenter bias on the operant learning of laboratory rats. *Journal of Psychiatric Research, 2,* 61–72

Rosenthal, R., & Rubin, D. B. (1978). Interpersonal expectancy effects: The first 345 studies. *The Behavioral and Brain Sciences, 3,* 377–386.

Rosenthal, R., & Rubin, D. B. (1982). A simple, general purpose display of magnitude of experimental effect. *Journal of Educational Psychology, 74,* 166–169.

Roth, W. (2001). Gestures: Their role in teaching and learning. *Review of Educational Research, 71,* 365–392.

Rubin, D. B. (1998). Estimation from nonrandomized treatment comparisons using subclassification on propensity scores. *Annals of Internal Medicine, 127(8),* 757–763.

Rubovits, P. C., & Maehr, M. L. (1973). Pygmalion black and white. *Journal of Personality and Social Psychology, 25,* 210–218.

Sadker, M., & Sadker, D. (1994). *Failing at fairness: How America's schools cheat girls.* New York: MacMillan Publishing Co.

Sandler, B. R., Silverberg, L. A., & Hall, R. M. (1996). *The chilly classroom climate: A guide to improve the education of women.* Washington, DC: National Association for Women in Education.

Schiefer, H. J. (1986). Effect of verbal and nonverbal vividness on students' information-processing. *Perceptual and Motor Skills, 63,* 1106.

Schmidt, C. P., & McCutcheon, J. W. (1994). Verbal versus nonverbal cues in evaluations of teaching. *Journal of Research and Development in Education, 27,* 118–125.

Seals, J. M., & Kaufman, P. A. (1975). Effects of nonverbal behavior on student attitudes in the college classroom. *The Humanist Educator, 14,* 51–55.

Simpson, A. W., & Erickson, M. T. (1983). Teachers' verbal and nonverbal communication patterns as a function of teacher race, student gender, and student race. *American Educational Research Journal, 20,* 183–198.

Sims, W. L. (1986). The effect of high versus low teacher affect and passive versus active student activity during music listening on preschool children's attention, piece preference, time spent listening, and piece recognition. *Journal of Research in Music Education, 34,* 173–191.

Sommers, C. H. (2000). The war against boys. *Atlantic Monthly, 285,* 59–74.

Tal, Z., & Babad, E. (1990). The teacher's pet phenomenon: Rate of occurrence, correlates, and psychological costs. *Journal of Educational Psychology, 82,* 637–645.

Taylor, M. C. (1979). Race, sex, and the expression of self-fulfilling prophecies in a laboratory teaching situation. *Journal of Personality and Social Psychology, 37,* 897–912.

Valenzeno, L., Alibali, M. W., & Klatzky, R. (2003). Teachers' gestures facilitate students' learning: A lesson in symmetry. *Contemporary Educational Psychology, 28,* 187–204.

Van Tartwijk, J., Brekelmans, M., & Wubbels, T. (1998). Students' perceptions of teacher interpersonal style: The front of the classroom as the teacher's stage. *Teaching and Teacher Education, 14,* 607–617.

Ward, L., & Raffler-Engel, W. von. (1980). The impact of nonverbal behavior on foreign language teaching. In W. von Raffler-Engel (Ed.), *Aspects of nonverbal behavior* (pp. 287–311). Lisse: Swets & Zeitlinger.

Wass, H. (1973). Pupil evaluations of teacher messages in three channels of communication. *Florida Journal of Educational Research, 15,* 46–52.

Wiemann, J. M., & Knapp, M. L. (1975). Turn-taking in conversations. *Journal of Communication, 25,* 75–92.

Witt, P. L., & Wheeless, L. R. (2001). An experimental study of teachers' verbal and nonverbal immediacy and students' affective and cognitive learning. *Communication Education, 50*, 327–342.

Woolfolk, A. E. (1978). Student learning and performance under varying conditions of teacher verbal and nonverbal evaluative communication. *Journal of Educational Psychology, 70*, 87–94.

Woolfolk, A. E., & Brooks, D. M. (1985). The influence of teachers' nonverbal behaviors on students' perceptions and performance. *The Elementary School Journal, 85*, 513–528.

Woolfolk, A. E., & Galloway, C. M. (1985). Nonverbal communication and the study of teaching. *Theory Into Practice, 24*, 77–84.

Woolfolk, A. E., Garlinsky, K. S., & Nicolich, M. J. (1977). The impact of teacher behavior, teacher sex, and student sex upon student self-disclosure. *Contemporary Educational Psychology, 2*, 124–132.

Woolfolk, A. E., & Woolfolk, R. L. (1975). Student self-disclosure in response to teacher verbal and nonverbal behavior. *Journal of Experimental Education, 44*, 36–40.

Woolfolk, R. L., & Woolfolk, A. E. (1974). Effects of teacher verbal and nonverbal behavior on student perceptions and attitudes. *American Educational Research Journal, 11*, 297–303.

Woolfolk, R. L., Woolfolk, A. E., & Garlinsky, K. S. (1977). Nonverbal behavior of teachers: Some empirical findings. *Environmental Psychology and Nonverbal Behavior, 2*, 45–61.

❧ IV ❧

Social and Cultural Issues

❧9❧

Nonverbal Behavior in Couple Relationships: Exploring the Causes and Consequences of Withdrawal

Patricia Noller
Judith A. Feeney
Nigel Roberts
University of Queensland

Andrew Christensen
University of California, Los Angeles

The importance of communication in close relationships is highlighted by Wood's assertion that "communication is not only a central, generative process of intimacy, but is actually what we experience as relationships" (1995, p.125). Although communication usually consists of both verbal and nonverbal channels, there is evidence that the nonverbal channels may be particularly crucial to relationship processes and outcomes (Gottman, Markman, & Notarius, 1977; Noller, 1984). Burgoon and Dillman (1995) suggest that "nonverbal relational messages signal how participants regard each other, their relationship and themselves in the relationship." Similarly, Watzlawick and his colleagues (Watzlawick, Beavin & Jackson, 1967) suggest that communication involves two levels of meaning: the content and relationship levels. The content level involves the literal meaning of the words that are spoken. In contrast, the relationship level conveys important information about how the partners are feeling about each other. This relational information is generally conveyed nonverbally, and can modify the meaning of the words. Our goals in this chapter are to review the literature on the interrelated topics of nonverbal behavior in close personal relationships and withdrawal in couple interactions, and to report on three of our empirical studies in this area.

NONVERBAL COMMUNICATION, POWER, INTIMACY, AND RELATIONSHIP SATISFACTION

Patterson (1983) has argued that nonverbal communication has five important functions: providing information, regulating interaction, expressing intimacy, exercising social control, and facilitating task or service goals. Of these five functions, the present chapter focuses particularly on expressing intimacy and exercising social control. We see these two functions as central to close personal relationships. Burgoon and Dillman (1995) have argued that knowing who wields power, and how that power is expressed through nonverbal behavior, is central to understanding any given relationship. Nonverbal communication is a rich source of power-related messages, as expressed through such behaviors as physical appearance (e.g., 'power dressing', height), touch, gaze, body movements and spacing (Guerrero, Andersen, & Afifi, 2001). Similarly, these authors have proposed that feelings of intimacy, including love, passion and interpersonal warmth, lie at the heart of intimate relationships. A study by Gonzaga, Keltner, Londahl and Smith (2001) provides evidence for nonverbal displays of love, including head nods, forward lean, and Duchenne (candid as opposed to contrived) smiles.

Given that expressions of power and intimacy are fundamental to personal relationships, nonverbal behaviors that create psychological closeness or distance between partners are of special interest to researchers and clinicians. Such behaviors, termed immediacy or involvement cues, have been described by Andersen (1985) as actions that signal warmth, communicate availability, decrease psychological and/or physical distance, and promote involvement in interactions. Immediacy behaviors include gaze, close distance, lean, body orientation, touch and smiling. Conversely, a lack of these behaviors is likely to indicate distance or coolness in the relationship.

Despite the key relational roles played by nonverbal expressions of power and intimacy, it is important to recognize that nonverbal communication is a relatively unreliable system. That is, there is no dictionary that neatly and unambiguously defines the meaning of a given nonverbal behavior. In fact, Manusov (2002, p. 15) has noted that "one of the most intriguing aspects of nonverbal communication is its ability to be interpreted in myriad ways." There are several reasons for the ambiguity of nonverbal behavior. First, relational messages tend to involve multiple rather than isolated cues. For this reason, any given cue needs to be understood in the context of other nonverbal cues that may be present (Burgoon & Dillman, 1995).

Second, variables such as relationship satisfaction appear to influence both the specific perceived function of a partner's nonverbal communication and the response to it. For example, couples who are happier with their relationships tend to make more relationship-enhancing attributions for their partner's nonverbal behavior (Manusov, 1990). Similarly, happy couples are more likely to notice positive partner behaviors, and to interpret these behaviors in a positive way (Manusov, Floyd, & Kerssen-Griep, 1997).

Third, another contextual factor that impacts on the understanding of nonverbal behavior is gender. There is considerable evidence that men and women differ on many aspects of their nonverbal displays. For example, women tend to use immediacy cues such as eye contact to express affiliation more than do men. There is also evidence that nonverbal behavior is likely to be interpreted differently, depending on whether it was enacted by a male or female. Burgoon, Coker, and Coker (1986) found that when a male engaged in high levels of eye contact, this behavior was interpreted as dominance, but when a female behaved similarly, the behavior was seen as submissive. This finding suggests that the interpretation of nonverbal behavior is affected by gender stereotypes.

Finally, attachment security is also likely to affect expressions of intimacy and power in close relationships. This proposition is supported by the work of Tucker and Anders (1998), who observed dating couples while they discussed positive aspects of their relationships. These researchers found that secure attachment was associated with more emotional expressivity; that is, higher levels of gaze, touch, smiling, and laughing. Conversely, preoccupied attachment was associated with lower levels of touch and smiling, and avoidant attachment was associated with lower levels of gaze, touch, and smiling. In another study of the interactions of dating couples, Simpson and his colleagues observed partners interacting while the female member of the dyad believed that she was about to take part in a stressful experiment (Simpson, Rholes, & Nelligan, 1992). In this situation, women's nonverbal responses to their partner's touch varied depending on their attachment security. Specifically, secure women responded by engaging in touching and kissing, whereas avoidant women tended to resist physical contact. These links between attachment security and nonverbal behavior are likely to reflect the relational goals of the different attachment styles, especially with regard to intimacy and affection.

Despite the ambiguity of much nonverbal behavior, there is clear evidence that particular patterns of nonverbal behavior are linked to relationship satisfaction. That is, relationship satisfaction is likely to be influenced by nonverbal behavior (although, as already noted, relationship satisfaction also affects perceptions of nonverbal behavior). In particular, unhappy couples display more negative nonverbal behaviors than happy couples. They display less positive emotion, and tend to exchange many more negative nonverbal cues than do those who are more satisfied with their relationships (Burgoon, Buller, & Woodall, 1996). More specifically, Gottman (1996) has argued that happy couples tend to display five positive behaviors for each negative behavior, whereas unhappy couples have a much lower positive-to-negative ratio. Researchers have also shown that unhappy couples are more likely to reciprocate negative behaviors than are happy couples (Gottman et al., 1977; Pike & Sillars, 1985). These findings highlight the importance of promoting positive nonverbal behaviors between intimate partners.

NONVERBAL BEHAVIORS RELATED TO WITHDRAWAL, POWER AND INTIMACY

In this chapter, we have chosen to illustrate issues of nonverbal behavior, power and intimacy, through studies of withdrawal in couple interactions. Withdrawal in couple interactions may reflect a lack of intimacy, or attempts to control and manipulate the partner. In either case, withdrawal, by its very nature, tends to involve an absence of nonverbal immediacy or involvement cues (as already noted, the lack of such cues creates psychological distance or lack of closeness between partners).

Withdrawal in marital interaction, particularly in response to conflict, has long been a topic of interest to researchers and to clinicians who work with distressed couples (Christensen, 1988; Fogarty, 1976; Napier, 1978; Wile, 1981). Withdrawal may be subtle (as in becoming silent, looking away, changing the topic or diverting attention), or more blatant (as in storming out of the room, or refusing to talk). Because of its consequences, withdrawing during conflict is generally seen as a negative behavior (Fruzzetti, 1996); specifically, issues are not resolved and may cause further conflict, and the person who tries to raise the issue may become resentful and angry. This anger and resentment may eventually lead to coldness and distance between the partners, and a reduced level of intimacy. Withdrawal may also lead to ongoing power struggles; as Holtzworth-Munroe, Smutzler and Stuart (1998) have noted, "a pattern of coercive efforts can gradually develop, creating a rigid pattern of negative, polarized interaction" (p. 732). Similarly, in Blake and Mouton's (1964) model of interpersonal communication, withdrawal is seen as reflecting low concern for self (an unwillingness or inability to clearly express one's own needs and issues) and low concern for the relationship (an unwillingness to work at resolving conflict for the sake of the relationship). On the other hand, some researchers have argued that withdrawal from conflict is not necessarily negative, if partners are not introspective, and if they share a strong bond of mutual affection (Raush, Barry, Hertel, & Swain, 1974).

In many couples, a more common pattern than mutual withdrawal is what has become known as demand/withdraw, where one member of the couple wants to talk about the issue and becomes demanding, and the partner withdraws and is unwilling to discuss the issue. According to Schaap and his colleagues (Schaap et al., 1988), the more demanding one partner becomes, the more the other partner is likely to withdraw.

There is evidence for a gender linkage to this interaction pattern, with females being more likely to be the demanders and males more likely to be the withdrawers (Christensen, 1988; Christensen & Heavey, 1990). Gottman and Levenson (1988) have argued that males are more likely to withdraw in the context of intense conflict, because of the high level of physiological arousal they experience in such situations. Although both husbands and wives are more likely to demand on issues where they want change and more likely to withdraw on issues where the partner wants change, males are more likely to withdraw overall, and particularly likely to withdraw when the female's issue is being discussed (Christensen & Heavey, 1990). In this situation, males' withdrawal may be a power play: Refusal to discuss the issue inhibits its resolution and maintains the status quo. As Klinetob and Smith (1996) have noted "Because of their different motivations, women demand in order to bring about change, whereas men withdraw in order to avoid change" (p. 946).

A follow-up study (Heavey, Layne & Christensen, 1993) replicated the finding that it is particularly when wives' issues are being discussed that wives demand and husbands withdraw. These researchers also found that wife-demand/husband-withdraw interaction predicted a decline in wives' marital satisfaction over a one-year period, whereas husband-demand/wife-withdraw predicted an *increase* in wives' marital satisfaction over the same period. In a further study, Heavey, Christensen, and Malamuth (1995) replicated this finding with a different sample followed over a period of 2.5 years.

These studies by Christensen and his colleagues were designed to test the social structure perspective, which proposes that gender differences in conflict patterns are a function of men's and women's place in the social structure (rather than individual differences). Although they were able to show the predicted pattern for discussion of wives' issues, the pattern for discussion of husbands' issues was less clear (see above). Klinetob and Smith (1996) criticized Christensen and Heavey's (1990) study, arguing that limiting the discussion topics to parenting behavior (generally considered the purview of women) could have promoted more of the traditional wife-demand/husband-withdraw pattern than would have occurred if a wider range of topics were allowed. These researchers, using both self-report and observational methodologies, were able to obtain a full reversal of behavior patterns across topics. In other words, there was more wife-demand/husband-withdraw when the wife's issue was being discussed, and more husband-demand/wife-withdraw when the husband's issue was being discussed.

Christensen and Shenk (1991) tested the possibility that the demand-withdraw pattern is related to partners being discrepant in their desires for intimacy and independence; that is, the demander seeks greater intimacy and the withdrawer seeks greater independence. As predicted, these researchers found significant correlations between discrepancies in desired independence and reports of wife-demand/husband-withdraw communication.

In another analysis of the factors linked to destructive conflict patterns, Newton, Kiecolt-Glaser, Glaser and Malarkey (1995) tested the links between hostility, defensiveness and spouses' communication behavior. They found that high levels of hostility and low levels of defensiveness predicted destructive conflict engagement for husbands (criticism, disagreement, interrupting partner), whereas for wives, these same variables predicted withdrawal. The researchers speculated that hostility may be expressed in a 'hot' way (expressive and arousing) by husbands, but in a 'cold' way (distant and aloof) by wives. Wives' withdrawal could then be seen not as a way of avoiding issues, but as a different way of expressing hostility.

Roberts (2000) has discussed three different types of withdrawal. Angry withdrawal is seen as an expression of negative affect, whereas conflict avoidance involves "withdrawal from the conflict without rejection of the partner" (p. 696). The third type of withdrawal, which Roberts labels intimacy avoidance, involves withdrawal following a partner's intimate disclosure. In a questionnaire study, all three types of withdrawal were related to concurrent marital distress for both husbands and wives.

We now report on three studies from our own work on interaction patterns involving withdrawal. In the first study, we explore the nonverbal concomitants of withdrawal in couple interactions. In the second study, we explore the associations between attachment security and withdrawal in the context of relationship-centered anxiety. In the third study, we use time-series analysis to compare couples in violent and nonviolent relationships in terms of their withdrawal.

STUDY I: THE NONVERBAL CONCOMITANTS OF WITHDRAWAL

The first study reported here follows on from the work of Christensen and his colleagues on the demand-withdraw pattern of conflict interaction, and was carried out by Noller and Christensen (unpublished, 1991). The goal of this study was to explore the nonverbal concomitants of the demand-withdraw pattern, although this chapter focuses specifically on the nonverbal behaviors that accompany withdrawal. We expected that withdrawal would be related to low levels of nonverbal behaviors that reflect involvement and immediacy, such as expressiveness and gaze, and to use of avoidance behaviors such as head down and head turn (Patterson, 1983).

The married couples involved in the study engaged in two conflict discussions, one involving an issue of dissatisfaction reported by the wife, and the other involving an issue of dissatisfaction reported by the husband. Undergraduate research assistants coded the videotaped discussions for the presence or absence of 18 nonverbal behaviors using 15-second time intervals. The behaviors coded included a wide range of nonverbal behaviors (e.g., gaze; open and closed smiles; open, neutral and closed gestures; eyebrow and head movements). A different group of undergraduate assistants made global ratings of demanding and withdrawing for each member of each couple, after watching the entire interaction. The Conflict Rating System (Heavey, Layne, & Christensen, 1993) was used for these ratings. These global ratings were then correlated with the total frequencies of the relevant nonverbal behaviors for each spouse.

The top section of Table 9.1 presents the significant correlations of spouses' nonverbal behaviors with global ratings of withdrawal for wives' issues, and the lower section presents the correlations for husbands' issues. As can be seen from the table, the clearest pattern of nonverbal behavior was for husbands withdrawing during discussion of their wives' issues. This pattern was characterized by a lack of

Table 9.1

Correlations Between Nonverbal Behaviors and Ratings of Withdrawal For Husbands' and Wives' on Wives' and Husbands' Issues

Nonverbal behavior	Husband withdraw	Wife withdraw
Wives' issue		
Husbands' open smile	.08	.08
Husbands' closed smile	−.004	−.03
Husbands' closed gestures	.26	.45*
Husbands' open gestures	−.38*	.11
Husbands' gaze	−.52**	−.13
Husbands' head down	.68**	−.05
Husbands' head turn	.43*	−.16
Wives' open gestures	−.16	−.38*
Husbands' issue		
Husbands' open gestures	−.15	.47*
Husbands' head down	.44*	.11
Wives' neutral gestures	−.22	−.36*
Wives' head down	.52**	.37*
Wives' head shake	.49**	.003

Note: Only correlations significant for at least one partner are included in this table.
$p < .05^*$; $p < .01^{**}$

open gestures and gaze, and by head down and head turn. Wives were rated as withdrawing on their own issue when they used few open gestures, and withdrawing on their husband's issue when they used few neutral gestures and engaged in head down. Husbands were rated as withdrawing on their own issue when they engaged in head down. Hence the single behavior most characteristic of ratings of withdrawal was head down. It is also interesting to note that when we correlated husbands' and wives' withdrawal on their own issue with their withdrawal on their partner's issue, there was a strong correlation for husbands, $r = .70$. In other words, husbands' withdrawal was quite consistent, irrespective of whose issue was being discussed. In contrast, there was no such consistency for wives.

There was also evidence, particularly when couples discussed husbands' issues, that partners' nonverbal behaviors were linked to each other's withdrawal (see Table 9.1). Husbands' open gestures were associated with wife withdrawal, and wives' head down and head shake were associated with husband withdrawal. Of course, without time-series analysis, we can not be sure about the sequential order involved in these effects.

Analyses of variance with sex, issue and marital satisfaction as the independent variables showed that the frequencies of the nonverbal behaviors were affected by all three of these variables. Wives used more head shake than husbands. There was more gaze on wives' issues than husbands' issues, and wives used more head down on their own issues than on husbands' issues. In addition, open gestures were used more by high satisfaction spouses on husbands' issues than on wives' issues, and wives used more open gestures on their own issues than on husbands' issues. High satisfaction spouses used less head down than low satisfaction spouses. These findings are consistent with highly satisfied spouses being more open and less withdrawn in their discussions.

STUDY 2: ATTACHMENT SECURITY AND WITHDRAWAL DURING CONFLICT

In recent years, several studies have explored the association between dimensions of attachment security (comfort with closeness and anxiety over abandonment) and withdrawal during conflict. Withdrawal is more common in relationships where the wife is insecure, than in relationships involving two secure partners (Feeney, Noller, & Callan, 1994; Senchak & Leonard, 1992). Links between wives' anxiety over abandonment and the demand/withdraw pattern of interaction have been found both concurrently and longitudinally (Feeney et al., 1994; Fitzpatrick, Fey, Segrin, & Schiff, 1993). In addition, wives high in anxiety over abandonment have been shown to use avoidance strategies in response to marital conflict (Feeney et al., 1994). Links between discomfort with closeness and withdrawal/avoidance have been less consistent, with some researchers finding no links (Feeney et al., 1994; Levy & Davis, 1988; Pistole, 1989) and others finding significant links (Fitzpatrick et al., 1993).

Roberts and Noller (1998) found evidence that communication patterns mediate the association between attachment and couple violence. In other words, attachment insecurity seems to affect violence through couples' destructive communication patterns. These researchers found that demand/withdraw communication mediated the association between anxiety over abandonment and violence for both males and·females. These authors note:

> These results are consistent with a situation in which one partner's fear of being abandoned leads to the development of destructive patterns of communication within a relationship, such as one partner making demands while the other withdraws, which, in turn, fosters an environment in which couple violence is more likely to occur. (p. 337)

Our second study follows on from the work of Raush and his colleagues (1974), and was designed to assess the link between attachment security and withdrawal in the context of relationship-centered anxiety. Relationship-centered anxiety (that is, anxiety about the nature and viability of the couple relationship) is likely to be particularly problematic for insecure individuals; paradoxically, these individuals may react in hostile or avoidant ways, which may threaten their relationships and hence exacerbate their insecurities.

The study employed an observational methodology. Couples who had been dating for at least 12 months engaged in three interactions: one in which the male partner was asked to act cold and distant (show low levels of immediacy behaviors) and the female partner was asked to try to reconcile; one involving a reversal of those roles; and one involving an issue-based interaction about leisure activities (Feeney, 1998). Our report here focuses on the "partner-distant" interaction, which was expected to create relationship-centered anxiety for the individuals involved.

Emotional reactions were rated using 7-point scales assessing five emotions: anger, anxiety, sadness, disgust and happiness. Nonverbal behaviors were coded using a scheme based on the one used by Simpson and his colleagues (Simpson et al., 1992). Behaviors coded included hugging, holding hands, turning head or body toward or away from partner, and resisting contact. Factor analysis was used for each construct, to reduce the number of variables. Two attachment factors were obtained from questionnaire items: Comfort with closeness and Anxiety over abandonment; these are the two factors most commonly found in measures of romantic attachment. Two negative affect factors were found: Worry and hostility, and there were also two factors of nonverbal behavior: Touch (e.g., hugging, holding hands) and avoidance (turning head or body away from partner, resisting contact).

Analyses revealed several significant correlations among attach-ment scales, affect and nonverbal behavior, although these were gener-ally modest in size. For females, comfort with closeness was inversely related to the measures of negative affect ($r = -.23, p < .05$ for hostile affect and $r = -.30, p < .01$ for worried affect), and anxiety over aban-donment was related to nonverbal behaviors, with anxious females en-gaging in high levels of avoidance ($r = .38, p < .01$) and low levels of touch ($r = .23, p < .05$).

For males, comfort with closeness was related to high levels of touch ($r = .23, p < .05$) and low levels of avoidance ($r = -.30, p < .05$), but at-tachment dimensions were unrelated to ratings of affect. Interestingly, other measures and analyses (beyond the scope of this chapter) indi-cated that males' anxiety over abandonment was related to their de-structive verbal behavior (such as coercion) in response to partner's distancing.

For both genders, satisfaction with the relationship was negatively correlated with avoidance in the female-distant scene in response to partners' primed distancing behaviors, $r = -.23, p < .05$ for males and $r = -.29, p < .05$ for females. Thus, those in more satisfying relation-ships were less likely to respond with avoidance behaviors when the partner acted cold and distant.

These findings illustrate the roles of both attachment security and relationship satisfaction in predicting low levels of withdrawal/avoid-ance. Consistent with a number of other studies (e.g., Kirkpatrick & Davis, 1994), the relevance of partner attachment dimensions de-pended on gender. Males who were uncomfortable with closeness, and females who feared abandonment, responded to partners' distancing behaviors by withdrawing physically from the partner. Further, fe-males who were uncomfortable with closeness were rated as display-ing both worry and hostility in the face of partners' distancing. Interestingly, the results suggest that insecure and distressed partners are likely to act in ways that increase the distance between them, rather than create a climate in which reconciliation can occur.

STUDY 3: WITHDRAWAL IN THE INTERACTIONS
OF VIOLENT COUPLES

Little is known about the use of withdrawal by violent couples, al-though Murphy and O'Farrell (1997) found that behaviors related to withdrawal and avoidance discriminated between couples in which the husband was alcoholic and violent and those in which the husband was alcoholic but not violent. Specifically, more withdrawal occurred where the husband was violent.

Holtzworth-Munroe, Smutzler, and Stuart (1998) reported two studies assessing the links among marital distress, violence, and de-manding and withdrawing during conflict. Study 1 relied on hus-bands' self-reports, and found that distressed groups reported significantly higher levels of wife-demand/husband-withdraw than did the nonviolent nondistressed group. In addition, violent groups reported more husband-demand/wife-withdraw communication than did nonviolent groups. The second study compared the demand and withdraw interactions of violent and nonviolent couples, based on the coding of videotaped interactions. The violent distressed group tended to engage in the most withdrawal, and the nonviolent nondistressed group in the least withdrawal.

Roberts and Krokoff (1990) used time-series analysis to examine withdrawal in couple interactions. They explored sequence and patterning in the interactions of distressed and nondistressed couples, focusing on three variables: withdrawal/involvement, hostility/friendliness and displeasure/pleasure. The strongest finding was that in dissatisfied marriages, the husband's withdrawal predicted the wife's hostility, suggesting that the destructive process seems to be initiated by the husband's withdrawal (rather than by the wife's demanding). In this study, there were no differences between satisfied and dissatisfied couples in terms of their overall use of withdrawal.

Klinetob and Smith (1996) also used time-series analysis of observational data, and found that demand and withdraw behaviors were temporally associated across spouses during the course of a discussion. These researchers also explored the direction of influence, but found that the results were more complex than suggested by Roberts and Krokoff's (1990) findings: Patterns of dependency between one partner's demanding and the other partner's withdrawal varied depending on whose issue was being discussed.

In our third study, we compared four groups of couples in terms of their use of withdrawing behaviors: a satisfied nonviolent group, a distressed nonviolent group, a distressed violent group, and a satisfied violent group (Noller & Roberts, 2002). Couples engaged in four interactions: Discussion of a serious issue proposed by the wife, a serious issue proposed by the husband, a trivial issue, and the sharing of a recent disappointment or sadness. Only discussions of the serious conflicts will be reported in this chapter. These videotaped interactions were coded by trained coders for expressions of affect and communication behaviors.

We found men used more withdrawal overall than women, especially if they were in unhappy relationships. In addition, when the female's issue was being discussed, men in unhappy relationships withdrew more than women in unhappy relationships. We also found that withdrawal was used more during the female's than the male's issue by couples in violent distressed relationships.

In this study, time-series analysis was also used. Two physiological measures were included: Inter-beat interval and galvanic skin response. Participants also reported on their level of experienced anxiety. Using these data, Noller and Roberts were able to explore the links between anxiety/arousal and withdrawal. Bivariate time-series analysis was used to quantify, in the form of a Z-score, the extent to which one time-series (e.g., heart-rate) accounted for a second time-series (e.g., withdrawal), controlling for the second time-series own past. The number of lags was limited to three (i.e., 30 seconds). Anxiety/arousal in this study involved the average of three measures of the extent to which one variable (e.g., female-anxiety/arousal) could be predicted by another variable (e.g., withdrawal). The Z-scores were then used as the dependent variables in ANOVAs exploring the variables affecting these associations. Measures of behavior such as withdrawal and hostility were averaged across the two discussions (his and her issues).

The anxiety/arousal of men in violent relationships was linked to their later withdrawal (within 30 seconds), supporting Gottman and Levenson's (1988) contention that high levels of arousal are causally related to male withdrawal, although their claim was not specific to violent relationships. The withdrawal of males in violent relationships was also linked to the later anxiety of their female partners, as well as to their female partner's later withdrawal. Thus male withdrawal during serious conflict is affected by his own anxiety, and in turn, affects the anxiety of his partner, as well as her own withdrawal. In addition, hostility of the male partner was associated with the later withdrawal of his partner.

One problem with this method of data analysis is that, although it can show us the associations between different behaviors, and even tell us the order in which particular behaviors occur, it cannot specify whether the later behavior increases or decreases as a result of the prior behavior. In other words, although this Gottman-Ringland procedure (Williams & Gottman, 1981) has the advantage of controlling for auto-correlation effects, the statistics provide a measure of the strength of the association between two variables, but not the direction of the effect. In the discussion section, we will discuss the most plausible interpretations of these findings, based on theory and previous research.

GENERAL DISCUSSION

Our initial study showed that there are distinctive patterns of nonverbal withdrawal, and that these behaviors are used particularly by men in distressed relationships while discussing issues raised by their wives. Behaviors such as head down, head turn, lack of gaze and lack of open gestures were particularly characteristic of husbands withdrawing during discussion of their wives' issues. In short, as expected, husbands responded to their wives' pressures for change by engaging in low levels of involvement behaviors. The pattern was not nearly so clear for wives' withdrawal, or for either spouse's withdrawal when husbands' issues were being discussed.

Husbands' withdrawal on their own issues was related to their use of head down, but also to nonverbal behaviors of their wives, particularly head shake and head down. These results suggest that husbands may withdraw in response to these signals that their wives are not accepting their arguments or suggestions. Overall, these findings are suggestive of a power struggle, in which husbands respond to their wives' disagreement by refusing to discuss the issue further. There was also some evidence that husbands and wives were involved in mutual withdrawal, both with their heads down, while discussing husbands' issues.

The findings for sex, issue, and marital satisfaction indicate that all three of these variables affect nonverbal behavior, with sex and issue often having interactive effects. Wives seem to be both more open and more withdrawn on their own issues; perhaps they are more open in expressing their feelings but more withdrawn in response to husbands' counter-arguments. High satisfaction spouses were generally more open and less withdrawn than dissatisfied spouses, suggesting an emotional climate of openness and intimacy, in which issues are more likely to be aired and resolved.

The second study showed links between withdrawal behavior and both relationship satisfaction and attachment security. Consistent with the first study, partners in more satisfying relationships were less likely to respond to conflict with nonverbal behaviors reflecting avoidance. In line with the findings of Tucker and Anders (1998), females who were anxious about abandonment tended to engage in high levels of avoidance and low levels of touch. Further, for males, comfort with closeness was associated with high levels of touch and low levels of avoidance. Hence, in the context of a partner acting cold and distant, insecure and distressed individuals seem to act to create more distance, rather than working towards achieving intimacy, understanding, or reconciliation.

The finding that both attachment dimensions were related to withdrawal (avoidance) differs from the findings of Simpson et al. (1992), who reported no relations between attachment anxiety and responses to partner distancing. However, it is important to note that Simpson et al.'s study focused on support processes, rather than conflict. The current findings demonstrate the salience of conflict, especially for those who are anxious about their relationships, and particularly when the conflict centers on the core issues of closeness and distance.

It is important to note that the two attachment dimensions were differentially related to responses to relationship stress for males and females (Feeney, 1998). For females, negative affect was linked to discomfort with closeness, and nonverbal behavior indicative of distancing was linked to anxiety over abandonment. In contrast, males' nonverbal behavior was affected by their comfort with closeness, with those low in comfort reporting higher levels of avoidance and lower levels of touch. Anxiety over abandonment was unrelated to males' affect, but predicted more negative verbal behaviors, such as coercion and aggression. Together, these results suggest that in the face of a part-

ner's distancing, anxiety over abandonment predisposes females to reciprocate by avoiding intimacy themselves, and predisposes males to
respond by exerting power through coercive remarks. Here, as in other
studies of romantic attachment (e.g., Feeney et al., 1994), anxious partners tend to engage in behaviors that exacerbate conflict and distance,
and that are likely to bring about the outcomes that they fear most.

In the third study, men were particularly likely to engage in withdrawal during conflict discussions, especially if they were in distressed relationships. Also, withdrawal was used more during
discussion of the females' issues, particularly by those in violent relationships. When we take into account the findings from the time-series
analysis, the sequential pattern becomes clearer. For males in violent
relationships, withdrawal was temporally linked to feeling anxious, as
argued by Gottman and Levenson (1988). Males' withdrawal was also
linked to the later anxiety of the female partner. The most plausible interpretation of this finding is that females' anxiety *increases* when
their partners withdraw. In this situation, females may feel powerless
because the probability of their issues being resolved decreases; they
are also likely to feel distressed at the disruption of intimacy. Roberts
and Krokoff (1990) found that wives tended to become hostile after
husbands withdrew, suggesting that the termination of the discussion
is aversive for wives (however, these researchers had no way of showing whether wives' hostility was linked to their anxiety). The withdrawal of females in violent relationships was also linked to the
partner's hostility. It seems that females are *more likely* to withdraw
when the husband becomes hostile, perhaps as a way of avoiding
conflict, and even violence.

Thus, both males and females in violent relationships tend to be
highly reactive to one another's withdrawal, in the sense that they
change their own behavior in response to partner withdrawal. They
seem to walk a fine line between avoiding violence on the one hand, and
avoiding a build-up of resentment and explosive anger on the other.
Again, issues related to power and intimacy are likely to underlie the
reciprocation of withdrawal behavior in these couples.

In a diary study comparing violent and nonviolent men's reactions
to daily stresses, Umberson, Anderson, Williams, and Chen (2003)
found that unlike nonviolent men, violent men did not seem to experience changes in their emotional experience in response to daily
stresses and relationship conflict. These researchers suggest that relationship stresses that elicit negative emotional reactions in nonviolent
men may result in violent men repressing their emotions in order to reduce their arousal, and subsequently expressing the ensuing build-up
of emotion through violent acts that reassert their masculine identity
and sense of power and control. This finding was also supported by an
interview study in which men reported on their responses to relationship stress (Umberson, Williams, & Anderson, 2002). It is important
to note that the violent men included in this study were recruited

through a violence program, and this sample is likely to include men involved in serious, rather than "common couple" violence.

Further research on withdrawal in violent couples should seek to differentiate between different types of withdrawal, as suggested by Roberts (2000), and to examine more closely the links between masculinity/femininity, withdrawal, and violence in couples as suggested by Umberson and her colleagues (Umberson et al., 2002, 2003). Another important research question centers on Newton et al.'s (1995) suggestion that withdrawal may be different for males and females: Withdrawal for husbands may be 'hot' (that is, expressive and arousing, like stomping out of the room), whereas for wives, it may be 'cold' (distant and aloof, such as epitomized in "the silent treatment"). In both of these contexts, withdrawal was seen as expressing anger, but in very different ways. More research is needed to clarify these issues.

IMPLICATIONS OF THE FINDINGS

The findings of these studies suggest many ways in which therapists may be able to help couples to understand the use and misuse of withdrawal in their conflict interactions. First, discussing models of conflict behavior (e.g., Blake & Mouton, 1964; Rusbult, 1987) may help couples think more seriously about alternative ways of handling conflict, and key issues such as their concern for self and their concern for the relationship. Problem solving can be presented as the most constructive way of dealing with conflict, because it involves concern for both the self and the relationship, and hence promotes both individual and relational adjustment.

Second, couples may need help to understand the possible negative consequences for the relationship brought on by withdrawing during conflict. For example, when withdrawal occurs, conflict issues do not get recognized and aired, and opportunities for achieving greater intimacy are lost. In addition, partners' needs and desires cannot be included in a possible solution unless they are expressed in the context of a problem-solving discussion. Clearly, if only one partner makes their desires known, that partner tends to have more power in relation to problem-solving and decision-making. Couples may need help in expressing their needs and concerns in a nonblaming and nondefensive way (both verbally and nonverbally). Couples also need to be made aware that unresolved problems are likely to recur, creating more conflict and distress for the couple. In addition, unresolved conflict may lead to a build-up of resentment, with one of two possible negative consequences: Either violence as an expression of suppressed rage, or increasing coldness and distance in the relationship.

Third, couples may need assistance to recognize the more subtle signs of withdrawal (such as head down and averted gaze), and begin to talk about their meaning. They may also need to decide what to do when one partner wants to withdraw from discussing an issue. There are legitimate reasons for withdrawing from or postponing a conflict discussion, such as a lack of information to resolve the issue, or spouses being too tired and/or upset to continue a fruitful discussion. In these situations, partners may need to make a definite "appointment" for a time when they can consider the issue further.

Fourth, spouses may need help to become more aware of their own withdrawal, the reasons behind it and its implications for the relationship. In some cases it may be important to focus on attachment or other issues that may be driving the withdrawal. For example, those who are anxious about abandonment may require help to explore and face their fears and perhaps talk to the partner about his or her commitment to the relationship. Clearly, unmet needs for intimacy and security underlie many relationship issues and conflicts.

Let us hasten to add that in focusing on directions for individual and couple therapy, we are not suggesting that teaching people to deal with withdrawal will necessarily solve all problems in their relationships. In fact, some caution should be exercised in relation to the reduction of withdrawal behaviors. For couples who tend to become violent when discussing serious conflict issues, withdrawal may function to defuse tension, at least in the short term. These couples need a focus on constructive skills for resolving conflict, as well as on reducing withdrawal. It is also important to remember that all relationships are different, and any intervention will need to take into account the specific characteristics of each partner.

We also need to bear in mind that most of the violent couples in our third study were involved in "common couple" violence (Johnson & Ferraro, 2000), involving pushing, shoving and throwing things, and that the violence was often mutual. These couples are very different from the "batterers" included in some studies, and may respond positively to couple therapy that helps them deal with their conflicts more constructively. Batterers, in contrast, are generally considered unsuitable for couple therapy, given the risk of provoking violence through raising serious issues in the therapy session.

Generally, however, helping couples to deal with their issues and resolve their problems is likely to be the most constructive path. Of course, not all relationship problems are easily resolved, and not all partner behaviors, no matter how annoying they may be, are easily changed. In some situations, partners may need to accept differences between them if they want a satisfying, supportive relationship (Christensen & Jacobson, 2000). As Christensen notes in the preface to his book:

> We [Christensen & Jacobson] had developed ways in which partners could experience and accept the normal vulnerabilities that we all have and the very natural incompatibilities that crop up between two unique individuals. With this acceptance, something paradoxical often occurred: many of the needs and demands for change evaporated, and

each partner became more amenable to making the changes that were truly important to the other. (p. xiv)

REFERENCES

Andersen, P. A. (1985). Nonverbal immediacy in interpersonal communication. In A. W. Siegman & S. Feldstein (Eds.), *Multichannel integrations of nonverbal behavior* (pp. 1–36). Hillsdale, NJ: Lawrence Erlbaum Associates.

Blake, R. R., & Mouton, J. S. (1964). *The managerial grid.* Houston: Gulf Publishing Company.

Burgoon, J. K., Buller, D. B., & Woodall, W. G. (1996). *Nonverbal communication: The unspoken dialogue* (2nd ed.) New York: McGraw-Hill.

Burgoon, J. K., Coker, D. A., & Coker, R. A. (1986). Communicative effects of gaze behavior: A test of two contrasting explanations. *Human Communication Research, 12,* 495–524.

Burgoon, J. K., & Dillman, L. (1995). Gender, immediacy and nonverbal communication. In P. J. Kalbfleisch & M. J. Cody (Eds.), *Gender, power and communication in human relationships* (pp. 63–81). Hillsdale, NJ: Lawrence Erlbaum Associates.

Christensen, A. (1988). Dysfunctional interaction patterns in couples. In P. Noller & M. A. Fitzpatrick (Eds.), *Perspectives on marital interaction* (pp. 31–52). Clevedon and Philadelphia: Multilingual Matters.

Christensen, A., & Heavey, C. L. (1990). Gender and social structure in the demand/withdraw pattern of marital conflict. *Journal of Personality and Social Psychology, 59,* 73–81.

Christensen, A., & Jacobson, N. J. (2000). *Reconcilable differences.* New York: The Guilford Press.

Christensen, A., & Shenk, J. (1991). Communication, conflict and psychological distance in nondistressed, clinic and divorcing couples. *Journal of Consulting and Clinical Psychology, 59,* 458–463.

Feeney, J. A. (1998). Adult attachment and relationship-centered anxiety: Responses to physical and emotional distancing. In J. A. Simpson & W. S. Rholes (Eds.), *Attachment theory and close relationships* (pp. 189–218). New York: The Guilford Press.

Feeney, J. A., Noller, P., & Callan, V. J. (1994). Attachment style, communication and satisfaction in the early years of marriage. *Advances in Personal Relationships, 5,* 269–308.

Fitzpatrick, M. A., Fey, J., Segrin, C., & Schiff, J. L. (1993). Internal working models of relationships and marital communication. *Journal of Language and Social Psychology, 12,* 103–131.

Fogarty, T. F. (1976). Marital crisis. In P. J. Guerin (Ed.), *Family therapy: Theory and practice* (pp. 325–334). New York: Gardner Press.

Fruzzetti, A. E. (1996). Causes and consequences: Individual distress in the couple interaction. *Journal of Consulting and Clinical Psychology, 64,* 1192–1202.

Gonzaga, G. C., Keltner, D., Londahl, E. A., & Smith, M. D. (2001). Love and the commitment problem in romantic relations and friendship. *Journal of Personality and Social Psychology, 81,* 247–262.

Gottman, J. M., & Levenson, R. L. (1988). The social psychophysiology of marriage. In P. Noller & M. A. Fitzpatrick (Eds.), *Perspectives on marital interaction* (pp. 182–200). Clevedon and Philadelphia: Multilingual Matters.

Gottman, J. M., Markman, H. J., & Notarius, C. I. (1977). The topography of marital conflict: A sequential analysis of verbal and nonverbal behavior. *Journal of Marriage and the Family, 39*, 461–477.

Guerrero, L., Andersen, P., & Afifi, W. (2001). *Close encounters: communicating in relationships.* New York: McGraw-Hill.

Heavey, C. L., Christensen, A., & Malamuth, N. (1995). The longitudinal impact of demand and withdrawal during marital conflict. *Journal of Consulting and Clinical Psychology, 63*, 797–801.

Heavey, C. L., Layne, C., & Christensen, A. (1993). Gender and conflict structure in marital interaction: A replication and extension. *Journal of Consulting and Clinical Psychology, 61*, 16–27.

Holtzworth-Munroe, A., Smutzler, N., & Stuart, G. L. (1998). Demand and withdraw communication among couples experiencing husband violence. *Journal of Consulting and Clinical Psychology, 66*, 731–743.

Johnson, M. P., & Ferraro, K. J., (2000). Research on domestic violence in the 1990s; making distinctions. *Journal of Marriage and the Family, 62*, 948–963.

Kirkpatrick, L. A., & Davis, K. E. (1994). Attachment style, gender and relationship stability: A longitudinal analysis. *Journal of Personality and Social Psychology, 66*, 502–512.

Klinetob, N. A., & Smith, D. A. (1996). Demand-withdraw communication in marital interaction: Tests of interspousal contingency and gender role hypotheses. *Journal of Marriage and the Family, 58*, 945–957.

Levy, M. B., & Davis, K. E. (1988). Lovestyles and attachment styles compared: Their relations to each others and to various relationship characteristics. *Journal of Social and Personal Relationships, 5*, 439–471.

Manusov, V. (2002). Thought and action: connecting attributions to behaviors in married couples' interactions. In P. Noller & J. A. Feeney (Eds.), *Understanding marriage: Developments in the study of couple interaction* (pp. 14–31). New York: Cambridge University Press.

Manusov, V., Floyd, K., & Kerssen-Griep, J. (1997). Yours, mine and ours: Mutual attributions for nonverbal behaviors in couple interactions. *Communication Research, 24*, 234–260.

Murphy, C. M., & O'Farrell, T. J. (1997). Couple communication patterns of maritally aggressive and nonaggressive male alcoholics. *Journal of Studies on Alcohol, 58*, 83–90.

Napier, A. Y. (1978). The rejection-intrusion pattern: A central family dynamic. *Journal of Marriage and Family Counseling, 4*, 5–12.

Newton, T. L., Kiecolt-Glaser, J. K., Glaser, R., & Malarkey, W. (1995). Conflict and withdrawal during marital interaction: The roles of hostility and defensiveness. *Personality and Social Psychology Bulletin, 21*, 512–524.

Noller, P., & Christensen, A. (unpublished). Nonverbal behavior and the demand/withdraw pattern of marital interaction. University of Queensland.

Noller, P., & Roberts, N. D. (2002). The communication of couples in violent and nonviolent relationships: Temporal associations with own and partners' anxiety/arousal and behavior. In P. Noller & J. A. Feeney (Eds.), *Understanding marriage: Developments in the study of couple interaction* (pp. 348–378). New York: Cambridge University Press.

Patterson, M. L. (1983). *Nonverbal behavior: A functional perspective.* New York: Springer-Verlag.

Pike, G. R., & Sillars, A. L. (1985). Reciprocity of marital communication. *Journal of Social and Personal Relationships, 2*, 303–324.

Pistole, M. C. (1989). Attachment and adult romantic relationships: Style of conflict resolution and relationship satisfaction. *Journal of Social and Personal Relationships, 6*, 505–510.

Raush, H. L., Barry, W. A., Hertel, R. K., & Swain, M. E. (1974). *Communication, conflict and marriage*. San Francisco: Jossey-Bass.

Roberts, L. J. (2000). Fire and ice in marital communication: Hostile and distancing behaviors as predictors of marital distress. *Journal of Marriage and the Family, 62*, 693–707.

Roberts, L. J., & Krokoff, L. J. (1990). A time-series analysis of withdrawal, hostility and displeasure in satisfied and dissatisfied marriages. *Journal of Marriage and the Family, 52*, 95–105.

Roberts, N. D., & Noller, P. (1998). The associations between adult attachment and couple violence. In J. A. Simpson & W. S. Rholes (Eds.), *Attachment theory and close relationships* (pp. 317–350). New York: The Guilford Press.

Rusbult, C. E. (1987). Responses to dissatisfaction in close relationships: The exit-voice-loyalty-neglect model. In D. Perlman & S. Duck (Eds.), *Intimate relationships: Development, dynamics and deterioration* (pp. 209–237). Beverly Hills: Sage.

Schaap, C., Buunk, A. P., & Kerkstra, A. (1988). Marital conflict resolution. In P. Noller & M. A. Fitzpatrick (Eds.), *Perspectives on marital interaction* (pp. 203–244). Clevedon and Philadelphia: Multilingual Matters.

Senchak, M., & Leonard, K. E. (1992). Attachment styles and marital adjustment among newlyweds. *Journal of Social and Personal Relationships, 9*, 51–64.

Simpson, J. A., Rholes, W. S., & Nelligan, J. S. (1992). Support-seeking and support-giving within couples in an anxiety-provoking situation: The role of attachment. *Journal of Personality and Social Psychology, 62*, 434–446.

Tucker, J. S., & Anders, S. L. (1998). Adult attachment style and nonverbal closeness in dating couples. *Journal of Nonverbal Behavior, 22*, 109–124.

Umberson, D., Anderson, K. L., Williams, K., & Chen, M. (2003). Relationship dynamics, emotional state and domestic violence: A stress and masculinities perspective. *Journal of Marriage and the Family, 65*, 233–247.

Umberson, D., Williams, K. L., & Anderson, K. (2002). Violent behavior: A measure of emotional upset. *Journal of Health and Social Behavior, 43*, 189–206.

Watzlawick, P., Beavin, J., & Jackson, D. (1967). *Pragmatics of human communication*. New York: Norton & Co.

Wile, D. B. (1981). *Couples therapy: A nontraditional approach*. New York: Wiley.

Williams, E., & Gottman, J. M. (1981). *A user's guide to the Gottman-Williams time-series analysis computer programs for social scientists*. New York: Cambridge University Press.

Wood, J. T. (1995). *Relational communication: Continuity and change in personal relationships*. Belmont, CA: Wadsworth Publishing.

✤ 10 ✤

Emotional Intelligence and Deception Detection: Why Most People Can't "Read" Others, But a Few Can

Maureen O'Sullivan
University of San Francisco

In this chapter we will consider why most people seem impervious to the many nonverbal cues that they could use to understand the thoughts, feelings and intentions of others. Evidence will be offered that there are such cues that can be used to detect deception, as well as some initial findings from a small group of lie detection "wizards" which suggest that at least some people are able to use these cues in understanding others.

Although other research areas (e.g., social cognition, personality assessment) could be surveyed, this review focuses on the relevance of nonverbal cues to detecting deception as a particular example of what is currently called emotional intelligence (Goleman, 1995; Salovey & Mayer, 1990), but which has also been referred to as social intelligence (Thorndike, 1920), empathy (Lipps, 1926; Ickes, 1993; Mehrabian & Epstein, 1972), social insight (Chapin, 1942), behavioral intelligence (O'Sullivan & Guilford, 1975), applied intelligence (Sternberg, 1986) or Intra- and Interpersonal intelligence (Gardner, 1993).

It is well known that nonverbal clues are involved in "reading" people as trade books such as "Reading people" (Dimitrius & Mazzarella, 1999) presume. Books with titles like "Never be lied to again" (Lieberman, 1998) and "Conquering Deception" (Nance, 2000) suggest that understanding nonverbal clues involved in deception is as easy and natural as learning to speak your native language. This chapter will demonstrate that this is not true.

The first part of the chapter will review the evidence, both theoretical and empirical, for the relevance and importance of nonverbal behavior in emotional intelligence and in detecting deception. The middle part of the chapter will review a wide variety of explanations for why most people don't use these cues. It may seem counter-intuitive, in a book about applications of nonverbal communication, to discuss reasons why most people are unable to make such applications. My hope is that pointing out the difficulties involved in using nonverbal cues may suggest techniques for alleviating them. The last part of the chapter will describe an ongoing study with a small group of expert lie detectors who avoid the many difficulties experienced by most people and are able to use nonverbal behavior (and other information) accurately to determine whether a person is truthful or not.

ONE HUNDRED AND THIRTY YEARS OF RESEARCH ON NONVERBAL BEHAVIOR AND EMOTIONAL/SOCIAL INTELLIGENCE: A BRIEF SURVEY

In 1872, Darwin's description of the nonverbal behaviors involved in the emotional communications of humans and animals (1998) was not only one of the earliest, but has been the most influential. Other early psychologists also described nonverbal behavior. In his theory of emotion, for example, James (1884) emphasized the centrality of the body, so it is no surprise that he was an astute observer of what we now refer to as nonverbal communication. "Can one fancy the state of rage and picture no ebullition of it in the chest, no flushing of the face, no dilatation (sic) of the nostrils, no clenching of the teeth, no impulse to vigorous action, but in their stead limp muscles, calm breathing, and a placid face?" (p. 194). Similarly, Wundt (1897) was well aware of "... expressive movements (that) correspond exactly to the psychical elements of emotions and their fundamental attributes: ... intensity, ... quality, ... and ... ideational content" (p. 173).

In the first part of the twentieth century, many eminent psychologists attempted to understand and measure the ability to understand others through the use of nonverbal behavior. Among these was E. L. Thorndike (1920) who wrote that people "had varying amount of different intelligences" (p. 228). He distinguished three of them: Abstract (verbal and symbolic) intelligence, mechanical intelligence and social intelligence, or "the ability to understand others, to manage (other people) ... wisely." His article contained photographs of a woman posing various facial expressions of emotion, though he noted the limitations of such stimuli and underscored the importance of real-life and interactive stimuli in composing tests of social intelligence.

Many leading psychologists of the era attempted to measure the ability to understand the expressive behavior of others. Boring and Titchener (1923) devised a schematic profile that was disappointingly unreliable. Guilford (1929) studied individual differences in the ability to recognize facial expressions of emotions while Frois-Wittmann (1930) produced a series of photographs of himself posing a variety of facial expressions of emotion. But the most ambitious attempt to measure emotional/social intelligence was made by Moss and his colleagues (Moss, 1931; Moss, Hunt, Omwake, & Woodward, 1955) who developed the George Washington University Social Intelligence Tests, some of which are still in use today. A series of factor analyses of the Moss tests (Thorndike & Stein, 1937) demonstrated that the tests showed convergent validity (they were highly inter correlated with one another), but they did not demonstrate discriminant validity (they were also highly correlated with measures of verbal ability).

From the 1930s to the 1960s little work on individual differences in expressive or nonverbal behavior was done. One exception was a 1924 dissertation by Wedeck published in 1947. He devised a series of tests based on the assumption that nonverbal behavior is essential to what he called "psychological ability." He did not pursue this research and so his work never received the attention it merited.

Interest in expressive (nonverbal) behavior never totally died out, however. A few researchers remained interested in the face, the voice and gesture. Efron (1941) studied the transmission of hand gestures across generations in two groups of New York immigrants. His description of emblems, nonverbal gestures that substitute for words, is still used. Engen, Levy, and Schlosberg (1957) studied the Marjorie Lightfoot series of photographs, which was used in many early studies of emotion recognition.

Attempts to measure social/emotional intelligence also continued. Examples of measures from this early period that are still in use are Chapin's Social Insight Test (1942), which describes interpersonal problems and asks the examinee to choose the most accurate or wisest comment about it.

Mehrabian & Epstein (1972) developed a self-report instrument of empathic accuracy that asks examinees how astute they are in responding to nonverbal behaviors. Although termed accuracy, this is a self-report measure and score variations may or may not correlate with scores on tests of empathic ability or aptitude. More contemporary measures of self-reported social skill have been provided by Riggio (1989) and Bar-On (Bar-On, Brown, Kirkcaldy, & Thorne, 2000).

Lipps' (1926) analysis of empathy focused on the internal feelings that one person has in response to another person rather than on their perceiving and responding to another person's nonverbal (external) behavior. Although it is likely that nonverbal behavior is at least a mediator of this process, Lipps' analysis emphasizes the internal processes involved rather than issues of accuracy. His terminology survives in Ickes' (1993) work on empathic accuracy. Ickes and Simpsons (1997) discussion of the processes involved in empathic accuracy is relevant to understanding some of the problems described later in this chapter concerning why most people are inaccurate in detecting deception, a kind of empathic accuracy.

With the increasing availability of photographs and videos, the 1960s and 1970s saw a marked increase in attempts to measure social/emotional intelligence. Guilford (1956) initiated a series of studies based on his Structure of Intellect model. O'Sullivan and Guilford (1975) devised 23 different measures of "cognitive behavioral intelligence" based on Guilford's model of intelligence and the belief that earlier social intelligence tests failed to achieve discriminant validity because they were mostly verbally stated.

They devised tests that were totally nonverbal, except for orally presented instructions. Although the tests defined the hypothesized factors and some of them continue to be used, there has been limited work relating them to real-life criteria.

More successful in this regard is the Profile of Nonverbal Sensitivity (PONS; Rosenthal, Hall, DiMatteo, Rogers, & Archer, 1979), 90 videotaped items showing a young woman posing social situations such as giving directions, comforting a lost child, praying, and getting angry. Research on the PONS was characterized by the creativity with which it demonstrated construct validity. Discriminant validity was evidenced in the lack of correlation with measures of IQ. Convergent validity was supported by predicted correlations with performance as a foreign service officer, being the mother of a pre-verbal child and other, equally intriguing criterion measures. Convergent validity with other measures of nonverbal sensitivity, however, has been limited.

Archer & Akert (1977) designed the Interpersonal Perception Test (IPT) which has a number of salutary features. Chief among them is the undeniable accuracy of its scoring key; the items of the IPT show real-life situations for which the truth is known. One item shows two adults playing with a child. The question is: Which adult is the parent? Another item shows two people talking: Which is the supervisor? In both cases, the correct answer is indisputable. Two of the 15 items of the IPT also show two people lying and telling the truth about events in their lives. The task is to pick the scenario in which each person is lying. The IPT is still available for use (Costanzo & Archer, 1993); however, its strength is also its weakness. It is likely that many different kinds of social/emotional intelligence are measured by this instrument, but each is represented only by a few items. The total score probably reflects a variety of social skills.

Buck (1976) developed the Communication of Affect Receiving Ability Test in which men and women were videotaped watching neutral or emotionally arousing slides. Given the difficulty and ethical restraints of arousing emotion in the laboratory, most of the facial expressions shown were subtle or ambiguous, so the meaning of scores on this measure is unclear.

Ekman and Friesen (1975) developed a Brief Affect Recognition Test (BART), in which photographs of prototypic facial expressions were shown for 1/15th or 1/30th of a second. Almost everyone can accurately identify facial expressions of basic or prototypic emotions (such as happiness, fear, or anger) if they are presented for a second or longer. With briefer exposure times, a nearly normal distribution of accuracy scores results. The technology available when BART was produced meant that in order to simulate micro-momentary facial expressions, the photographs had to be presented tachistoscopically, which presented several difficulties (O'Sullivan, 1982).

More recently, Ekman (2003) has developed two CD's that are combination training tools and micro-facial-expression recognition accuracy measures. The Measuring Emotional Expressions Tool (Ekman, 2003) contains 56 colored photographs in which a neutral face is the background on which a prototypic facial expression of the same person is then flashed at speeds of 1/15th or 1/30th of a second. The Subtle Emotional Expression Tool (Ekman, 2003) contains black and white photographs of one young woman posing subtle variations of many different facial expressions. The tool allows the user to self-test at various speeds.

Ekman has also developed several measures of the ability to detect deception, a more narrow aspect of emotional intelligence, but one which may identify people with emotional intelligence in other areas as well. His first test (Ekman, Friesen, O'Sullivan & Scherer, 1980) shows nurses lying or telling the truth about whether they are watching a pleasant nature film or a gruesome surgical one. Two other deception detection measures (Frank & Ekman, 1997) show young men being interviewed about whether or not they stole $50 or are telling the truth about a controversial opinion. These measures were used to identify the expert lie detectors described at the end of this chapter and will be referred to, respectively, as the emotion, crime and opinion tapes since these are the topics about which the participants lied or told the truth. Behavioral measurements of all three tapes indicate that there are significant nonverbal clues that could be used in accurately assessing truthfulness or deception.

O'Sullivan and Ekman (O'Sullivan, 1983) developed the Affect Blend Test (ABT), in which people of different ages posed facial expressions in which two or more different emotions were combined. The photographs were produced based on criteria developed from the Facial Action Coding System (Ekman & Friesen, 1978). The ABT is of interest because it relates to the work on deception that Ekman and his colleagues have done over the last thirty years, in which leakage of emotion is important. That is, while attempting to portray one emotional state (i.e., pleasant unconcern) the "real" emotion (fear of apprehension, or guilt, or delight at duping the interviewer) will "leak" in fragments of the facial expression that the liar cannot fully control. The ABT simulates this phenomenon by showing complex mixes of emotions in which the constituent parts are readily identifiable.

By the 1980s, as interest in cognitive psychology increased, interest in nonverbal behavior per se waned. Two major theoreticians of human intelligence, Sternberg (1988) and Gardner (1993) described understanding self and others as an aspect of human cognitive ability in which there were marked individual differences. Sternberg emphasized what he called "practical intelligence," the ability to understand what is necessary in a situation, to be able to try different solutions to solve interpersonal problems and then to have the practical wisdom to leave a situation if one's best efforts have failed. Although Sternberg and his students published interesting work related to academic promotion and business success, the measures of practical intelligence were not easily accessible, and the measures of nonverbal behavior (Sternberg, 1986) that were provided did not seem superior to similar ones already available, such as Costanzo and Archer's IPT. Gardner's theory of multiple intelligences includes both an interpersonal and an intrapersonal ability. Although no psychometrically validated scales for these abilities have been published, his ideas have been well-received in educational circles.

The fulcrum for research in emotional/social intelligence, however, was the publication of Goleman's best-selling book (1995) on the topic. Based largely on Salovey and Mayer's (1990) work on emotional intelligence, Goleman's contribution was to link the idea of understanding the emotions of others to the concept of understanding and mastering one's own emotions for pro-social purposes. His popularized presentation of these concepts spurred an explosion of research on emotional intelligence over the next several years.

Although Goleman's book was long on exhortation and description, it was short on measurement methods. So, relatively hoary instruments like the O'Sullivan-Guilford tests, the Chapin Social Insight Test, and the IPT were resurrected. More recently, several new measures have been constructed. Mayer, Salovey and Caruso (2002) developed the MSCEIT, a multifactorial measure of emotional intelligence in which the criterion is determined largely by consensual validation. Cronbach (1955) distinguished differential accuracy (what most earlier measures of emotional intelligence attempted to assess) and stereotypic or consensual accuracy, which is the basis for the MSCEIT. Another unusual aspect of the MSCEIT is that sensitivity to artistic expressions of emotion is measured along with sensitivity to human nonverbal expressions of emotions. Nowicki (Nowicki & Duke, 2001) has produced several measures of emotional intelligence that emphasizes differential accuracy of affect recognition in face and voice. Separate measures are available for adults and children. A number of studies have been conducted using these measures. The DANVA (Diagnostic Analysis of Nonverbal Accuracy) is not highly correlated with general intelligence (discriminant validity) and shows some evidence of convergent validity through prediction of school achievement (not school aptitude) and at least one significant correlation with the PONS.

Although conducted over a 130 year period, these research efforts have at least one commonality. They assume that understanding other people's thoughts, feelings and intentions depends on understanding their expressive, nonverbal behavior. This book presents a number of approaches to understanding nonverbal communication. Let us now consider what is known about nonverbal cues to understanding one aspect of another person—whether she is lying or telling the truth.

NONVERBAL CUES TO DECEPTION

Nonverbal behavior is an integral and distinguishing characteristic of the self-presentation and coherence of each person (DePaulo, 1992). So, each individual varies in the ways in which she behaves when lying, or puzzled, or anxious. Researchers have identified some of the nonverbal behaviors that distinguish lying from truthful communication, but those behaviors don't occur in every case, and they must always be interpreted in the context of the unique individual displaying it.

Although other reviews have been done (Zuckerman & Driver, 1985), the current gold standard in reviews of nonverbal cues to deception is the meta-analysis performed by DePaulo, Lindsay, Malone, Muhlenbruck, Charlton, and Cooper (2003). They identified 158 cues to deception that were studied using 1,300 different estimates from 120 independent samples. Like all meta-analyses, theirs evaluated, by summing over similar cues, whether there were recurring and significant differences in the nonverbal behavior shown by truth-telling and deceiving people.

The meta-analyses done by DePaulo and her colleagues are notable for their clarity, inclusiveness and organization. The effect sizes are presented in an accessible and engaging fashion, with 83 of the 158 cues discussed in the light of DePaulo's self-presentational theory. A drawback of this approach, however, is that some cues (those based on smaller numbers of estimates, or not relevant to the self-presentational theory) were included only in an appendix. Also, the cues are not separated into verbal and nonverbal categories. For the purpose of this chapter, therefore, I have taken the liberty of re-ordering the 158 cues. Rather than discussing the relevance of the cues to a particular theory of deception, they are listed based on whether they are nonverbal cues (in whole or part) or verbal cues.

A complete list of the nonverbal and mixed cues is given in Tables 10.1 and 10.2. The mixed cues are those that involved both verbal and nonverbal elements, such as "verbal and vocal immediacy." The deception research literature, as synthesized by DePaulo and her colleagues, suggests that somewhat more than half of the cues that have been studied as cues to deception are nonverbal or mixed ($n = 87$); the rest are verbal ($n = 71$). In terms of significant effect sizes, about 25% of each of the two domains of cues (nonverbal and verbal) is significant, sug-

TABLE 10.1
Nonverbal and Mixed Cues to Deception With Significant Effect Sizes[a]

Id[b]	Cue Description	d
154	Changes in foot movement	**1.05**
155	Pupillary changes	**0.90**
117	Genuine smile	−0.70
050	Cooperative*	−0.66
090	Indifferent, unconcerned*	**0.59**
025	Verbal and vocal immediacy*	−0.55
065	Pupil dilation	0.39
114	Specific hand and arm movements	−0.36
091	Seems planned, not spontaneous*	0.35
014	Discrepant, ambivalent*	0.34
088	Intensity of facial expression*	−0.32
031	Verbal and vocal uncertainty*	0.30
061	Nervous, tense (overall)*	0.27
062	Vocal tension*	0.26
033	Chin raise	0.25
063	Pitch (frequency)**	0.21
016	Verbal and vocal involvement*	−0.21
105	Direct orientation	−0.20
070	Fidgeting (undifferentiated)	0.16
011	Presses lips	0.16
018	Illustrators (gestures with speech)	−0.14
054	Facial pleasantness*	−0.12

a. Adapted from DePaulo et al., (2003). d's were computed by subtracting the mean for truthful persons from the mean for liars and dividing that value by the average of the standard deviations obtained by the two groups (truthful and deceptive). Positive d's mean that the liars obtained significantly higher scores; negative d's that the truthful persons obtained higher values. Values for d greater than 0.50 (in bold) represent large effect sizes.
b. Id's are the numbers assigned by DePaulo et al.
* Measured using subjective methods such as ratings or overall impressions.
** Vocal tension and pitch were measured by both subjective and objective methods.

gesting that liars and truth tellers can be distinguished on the bases of both nonverbal and verbal behaviors.

Verbal cues included measures such as word and phrase repetitions, plausibility of the statements made, and contextual embedding. The effect size used in the DePaulo meta-analysis was "... d, defined as

TABLE 10.2
Nonverbal Cues to Deception With Non-Significant Effect Sizes[a]

Id[b]	Cue Description	d
157	Facial reaction time	0.49
095	iPtch changes	0.42
118	Feigned smile	0.31
121	Relaxed face*	−0.29
122	Hand, arm, leg relaxation*	−0.26
144	Eye blink latency	−0.21
151	Hands together	0.21
047	Arm movements	−0.17
049	Friendly, pleasant (overall)*	−0.16
149	Tongue out	−0.16
020	Verbal immediacy (temporal)	0.15
152	Hands apart	−0.15
120	Mouth asymmetry	0.14
104	Facial immediacy**	0.13
017	Facial expressiveness*	0.12
067	Object fidgeting	−0.12
094	Pitch variety	0.12
096	Rate change	0.12
119	Head shakes	−0.12
029	Eye shifts	0.11
043	Body animation, activity	0.11
053	Vocal pleasantness	−0.11
158	Neck muscles tightened	−0.10
048	Foot or leg movements	−0.09
147	Eyelids droop	0.09
015	Involved, expressive (overall)*	0.08
069	Facial fidgeting	0.08
115	Competent*	−0.08
132	Lips apart	−0.08
145	Eye flutters	−0.08
148	Lip pucker	−0.08
010	Rate of speaking	0.07
026	Nonverbal immediacy	−0.07

(continued)

223

TABLE 10.2   (continued)

Id[b]	Cue Description	d
066	Blinking	0.07
051	Attractive (overall)*	−0.06
089	Face changes**	−0.06
131	Eyes closed	−0.06
032	Amplitude, loudness	−0.05
044	Posture shifts	0.05
034	Shrugs	0.04
056	Brow lowering	0.04
130	Brow raise	−0.04
028	Gaze aversion	0.03
009	Response latency	0.02
045	Head movements (undifferentiated)	−0.02
057	Sneers	0.02
064	Relaxed posture	−0.02
146	Eyelids tight	−0.02
027	Eye contact	0.01
055	Head nods	0.01
068	Self fidgeting	−0.01
129	Brow raise	0.01
153	Emblems	0.01
060	Eye (AU 6) no positive emotion	−0.00
046	Hand movements	0.00
058	Smiling (undifferentiated)	0.00
059	Lip corner pull (AU 12)	0.00
086	Facial shielding	0.00
093	Serious	0.00
097	Loudness variety	0.00
106	Proximity	0.00
116	Ingratiation	0.00
133	Jaw drop	0.00
150	Duration of facial expression	0.00
156	Biting lips	0.00

a. Adapted from DePaulo et al., (2003).
b. Id's assigned by DePaulo et al.
* Variables measured using subjective methods.
** Measured using both subjective and objective methods.

the mean for the deceptive condition (i.e., the lies) minus the mean for the truthful condition (i.e., the truths), divided by the mean of the standard deviations for the truths and the lies .... Positive ds therefore indicate that the behavior occurred more often during the lies than the truths, whereas negative ds indicate that the behavior occurred less often during lies than truths" (DePaulo et al., 2003, p. 89). Table 10.1 lists the nonverbal cues that had significant effect sizes, ordered according to the size of the effect. The table also gives the identification codes (from 1 to 158) and the value of the effect sizes reported by the DePaulo group. Table 10.2 gives the same information for the nonverbal cues that did not have significant ds. A d of .50 or greater is considered large. By that criterion, although 21 significant effect sizes were found for the nonverbal cues to deception, only six of them qualify as large effects. These are:

1. Liars show more changes in their foot and leg movements. ($d = 1.05$)
2. Liars show more changes in the size of their pupils. ($d = 0.90$)
3. Liars seem indifferent or unconcerned. ($d = 0.59$)
4. Truthful people show more genuine (Duchenne) smiles than liars. ($d = -0.70$)
5. Truthful people seem more cooperative. ($d = -0.66$)
6. Truthful people have more verbal and vocal immediacy. ($d = -0.55$)

The organization of the nonverbal cues presented here was dictated by the focus of this chapter. The estimates of some of the ds are based on more independent samples than others and may, therefore, be more reliable. In general, but not always, cues with lower numbered identification codes (83 or less) are based on more independent samples than cues with codes greater than 84.

THE ISSUE OF DISCREPANCY

Although many deception theorists (e.g., Bugental, Kaswan & Love, 1970) have suggested that discrepancy, either within a channel or among verbal and nonverbal channels is a salient cue to deception, only one such clue (discrepant, ambivalent, $d = 0.34$) is represented among the 158 cues surveyed. This variable, surveyed over several studies, is described as "Speakers' communications seem internally inconsistent or discrepant; information from different sources (e.g., face vs. voice) seems contradictory; speaker seems to be ambivalent ..." (DePaulo et al., 2003, p. 113). Obviously, given the difficulties of measuring nonverbal behaviors, the added difficulty of reliably determining discrepancies among them seems to have limited researcher's enthusiasm for doing so. The fact that the one variable that did assess discrepancy was significantly discriminating of liars and truth tellers is noteworthy.

Individual Differences and Deviations From Baseline

Several writers have urged human lie detectors to ground their observations of others in the baseline behavior of the person being observed. Zuckerman, DeFrank, Hall, Larrance and Rosenthal (1979) described what they called the demeanor bias, a tendency for people to be seen as always honest or always deceptive regardless of their actual veracity. Ekman (2001) cautioned against the idiosyncrasy error—always interpreting a particular nonverbal behavior, such as changes in foot and leg movements, without determining whether this is a recurring aspect of a person's ordinary behavior. On average, liars are significantly more likely to show more changes in their foot and leg movements than truthful people (see Table 10.1), but not everyone does this when lying, and some truthful people may characteristically jiggle their feet. As with discrepancies, although theorists recommend attending to such behavior changes, few of the 158 cues surveyed in the DePaulo meta-analysis measured such changes. Seven of the 158 deception cues reflect change from baseline and of these, two (changes in foot movement and pupillary change) have the highest ds reported: 1.05 and 0.90 respectively.

THE GOLDILOCKS PHENOMENON: TOO BIG, TOO SMALL, AND JUST RIGHT

There Are Smiles and There Are Smiles

Another finding, more noticeable when the data are grouped as they are in Tables 10.1 and 10.2, is the importance of the level of measurement used in describing nonverbal behavior. On the one hand, for discrete behavioral entities, it seems better to assess variables in a highly specific, well-defined manner. For example, genuine or Duchenne smiles had one of the higher effect sizes ($d = -0.70$), suggesting that truth tellers will show more of these kinds of smiles than liars. On the other hand, feigned smiles were more frequent among liars, although the d associated with this difference was insignificant. Obviously, if the two kinds of smiles are summed, they will cancel each other out, and show no overall effect, since one kind of smile is more frequent in truth tellers and the other is more frequent in liars. In fact, that is what happened. Undifferentiated smiles had an insignificant effect size. LaFrance's study (chap. 7, this volume) is another example of the importance of differentiating among different kinds of smiles. She videotaped the nonverbal behavior of applicants who were harassed during their job interview. Applicants who responded to the harassment with non-Duchenne (feigned) smiles were rated by as less competent and less likely to be hired than women who showed felt enjoyment (Duchenne) smiles.

Hand and Feet Movements

Another example of the importance of specificity in measuring nonverbal behavior is the very high effect size ($d = 1.05$) for changes in foot and leg movements ("Changes in the number of foot or leg movements over time (absolute value)," DePaulo et al., 2003, p.117) and specific hand and arm movements ($d = -.0.36$) ("Hand movements that do not include arm movements and finger movements that do not include hand movements." DePaulo et al., 2003, p. 116). Notice, however, that these significant effect sizes go in opposite directions! Liars are significantly more likely to show changes in foot and leg movements and significantly less likely to show the specific hand and arm movements described. Further complicating this issue is Vrij's report (this volume) that some liars show particular hand and arm movements.

Illustrators vs. Emblems

This principle of specifying exactly what behavior is of interest is also demonstrated by the findings with two different hand gestures—illustrators and emblems. Illustrators, hand gestures accompanying speech, were significantly more frequent among truth tellers ($d = -0.14$), but emblems, gestures that can substitute for speech, are not significantly different in liars and truth tellers ($d = 0.01$). It is likely that a generic "hand gestures" category would not have distinguished liars and truthful people whereas illustrators do.

Fidgeting

On the other hand, overall ratings of the amount of fidgeting ("Object fidgeting and/or self-fidgeting and/or facial fidgeting (undifferentiated)" DePaulo et al., 2003, p. 115) are significantly higher for liars than truthful people ($d = 0.16$). The component parts of this variable (object fidgeting, self-fidgeting and facial fidgeting) are not significant in their own right, but are when included in a summary measure. The d associated with overall fidgeting is small, albeit significant. This significance may be due merely to the large number of estimates ($n = 14$) on which it was based.

So, why is the summary measure significant for fidgeting while the components are not? My speculations are as follows: Differences between smiles and between illustrators and emblems are theoretically based (Ekman & Friesen, 1969) and were predicted beforehand to relate differently to truthful and deceptive behavior. A change from one's baseline behavior has also been postulated as a marker of discomfort, or emotional or cognitive shift so the significant finding that changes in foot and leg movements tend to characterize liars and not truth tellers was predicted. (The finding with specific hand and finger movements is not predicted by the baseline thesis, however. See Vrij, chap. 4, this volume.)

Fidgeting is generally interpreted as a sign of nervousness or anxiety, although there are no data relating fidgeting to self-reported anxiety or physiologically-related arousal. There is no theory, however, about what kind of fidget goes with what kind of lie, what kind of emotion or what kind of cognitive activity. So whether the fidget involves an object, the self or the body is irrelevant and probably relates only to idiosyncrasies of the individual rather than the lying per se. What is important is to get a reliable overall estimate of fidgeting and this is best done, it seems, by summing across all fidgeting occurrences. Other sources of information for which a general measurement seems more productive are attributional ratings.

Trait Ratings of Liars and Truth Tellers

Some of the more significant ds were obtained with overall subjective ratings of attributes of the person being judged. As seen in Table 10.1, ratings of cooperative, indifferent or unconcerned, verbal and vocal immediacy, seems planned or not spontaneous, discrepant, or ambivalent and nervous, tense (overall) significantly discriminated liars and truth tellers. Note, however, that all of these descriptions relate to a particular gestalt—of people who are open, concerned, immediate, spontaneous, consistent, and generally relaxed on the one hand (i.e., truth tellers) and uncooperative, indifferent, distant, non spontaneous, ambivalent, and tense or nervous on the other (i.e., liars). Ratings not included in this particular gestalt, such as attractive, competent or friendly did not significantly differentiate liars and truth tellers. More recently, O'Sullivan (2003) reported that there were no differences between liars and truth tellers in how observers rated their likeability, intelligence or attractiveness. Also, one of the more perplexing findings in the field of deception research is that most people cannot accurately identify when others are lying or telling the truth. In other words, ratings of "honest" or "trustworthy" do not significantly differentiate liars and truth tellers. Reasons for this particular rating error are discussed below. At this point, what should be noted is that subjective overall ratings of personal characteristics with relevance to honesty (but not ratings of honesty themselves) significantly distinguish liars and non-liars. Such ratings, by necessity, are general summations of many aspects of a person's behavior. The inability of raters/observers to make the summary conclusion that an individual who they perceive as uncooperative, non-immediate, non-spontaneous, tense, and ambivalent may well be telling a lie is one of the more intriguing puzzles in the field of deception detection.

But why are attributional ratings included in a chapter on nonverbal behavior? Just as emotional intelligence researchers assume that knowledge of another's inner life must be mediated by observable exterior cues, i.e., nonverbal expressions, most interpersonal perception theorists would accept the idea that judgments about other people's attributes must come from observable aspects of them and their behavior. Self-ratings, on the other hand, are probably more dependent on internal processes than one's external nonverbal behaviors of which most of us are unaware.

Although the particular nonverbal behaviors that are being emphasized in this chapter reflect dynamic cognitive, motivational and emotional aspects of people, other nonverbal behaviors are also available for use in detecting deception. As Sherlock Holmes (Doyle, 1892) routinely demonstrated, general appearance provides a great deal of information about people. Visual cues include information about age, which implies information about values, health, interests, experiences and a host of other conclusions, many likely to be accurate. Visual clues also permit conclusions about attractiveness, vanity, ethnicity, concern for fashion, place of residence, health, social status, tidiness, occupation and paternity. Clothing, rings, pins, and other jewelry convey information about recreational activities, marital and sexual orientation, organizational memberships, educational level and religiosity. Vocal cues, in addition to emotional, cognitive and motivational processes, may give information about the country or region of origin, age, energy level, health, education and sexual orientation. Even olfactory cues can be used in judging others. Odor was a diagnostic indicator for physicians entering homes to treat the ill in the early part of this century. Pheromones affect sexual attraction, menstrual cycling and infants suckling. Although we are not consciously aware of these nonverbal indicators of biological processes, our bodies are and that information may guide our judgments more than we know. Thus, it seems appropriate to include those summary judgments that must be based on nonverbal cues with other, more objectively measured nonverbal cues to deception

WHAT KIND OF LIE IS IT?

In early work, Ekman and his colleagues (Ekman, et al., 1980), found no difference between liars and truth tellers in the number of shrugs that each group made. In more recent work (Frank & Ekman, 1997), in which men lied about strongly held opinions, shrugs that were inconsistent with what was being said were more likely to occur when the men were lying. This suggests that the kind of lie told may affect the kind of nonverbal behavior involved in different kinds of deception. A related finding is discussed in the last part of this chapter describing work with expert lie detectors, in which the kind of lie told affected the lie detectors' accuracy.

DePaulo and her colleagues (2003) were also interested in the impact of the kind of lie told on nonverbal behavior. They reported that when the lie was about a transgression, liars had more changes in foot or leg movements, spoke at a faster rate, did more eye blinking and were rated as more nervous and tense.

In Lie Detecting, Ignorance Is Not Bliss

The DePaulo meta-analysis provides evidence that many culturally-held beliefs about what people look like when they lie are often incorrect (Zuckerman & Driver, 1985; O'Sullivan, 2000; Vrij, this volume). In the United States, eye gaze aversion is widely assumed to be a cue to deception. But, overall, eye gaze aversion is not a significant difference between liars and truth tellers. This is an example of misinformation. Missing information is exemplified by nonverbal behaviors that are reliable cues to deception that most people ignore. Examples include pitch (frequency) of voice, the quality of verbal and vocal immediacy, pupillary change and pupil dilation, and specific hand and finger movements. Because many of these behaviors are fleeting (micro-momentary), people either ignore them or do not notice them at all.

What this review of nonverbal cues to deception suggests is that research in this area must specify exactly what kind of nonverbal behavior is of interest. The utility of greater specificity may be seen in Vrij's work on a particular kind of small hand movement in a particular situation (chap. 4, this volume) and LaFrance's distinction between Duchenne and non-Duchenne smiles in hiring (chap. 7, this volume). The theory behind predicting the occurrence of a particular kind of nonverbal behavior should also be made clear, as Ekman, Friesen, and O'Sullivan (1988) did in predicting different kinds of smiles when people are lying or telling the truth. Ekman (2001) and others (Burgoon, Buller, White, Afifi, & Buslig, 1999) have emphasized the importance of the context within which the nonverbal behavior occurs. Ekman emphasizes the baseline demeanor of the individual; Burgoon, the interpersonal relationship within which the deception or truthfulness occurs. O'Sullivan (2003) suggested that the cognitive heuristics involved in understanding other people should also be specified.

WHY MOST PEOPLE CAN'T TELL WHEN OTHERS ARE LYING

Although it is clear that there are significant mean differences between honest and deceptive individuals in terms of the nonverbal behaviors they show, most people are unable or unwilling to use them as a basis of detecting deception (Ekman & O'Sullivan, 1991; Malone & DePaulo, 2001). Many reasons for this difficulty in social cognition have been suggested or can be inferred from the literature. For ease of discussion, they have been organized into six categories: 1) strategic errors, 2) cognitive biases, 3) knowledge deficiencies, 4) characteristics of the liar or truth teller, 5) motivations of the lie catcher, and 6) evolutionary biases.

Strategic Errors

The first strategic error, and the one most relevant to the focus of this book, is most people's inattention to the nonverbal information available to them when attempting to detect deception. The fact that people disregard nonverbal information that could be useful in understanding others was demonstrated in an early study of how observers judge honest and deceptive behavior. Ekman and his colleagues (1980) found that although observers could not accurately identify liars and truth-tellers, they used different strategies in describing them. Verbal and nonverbal channels (facial expressions, hand gestures, body postures and vocal qualities) were used equally often when the behavior being judged was honest. When the behavior was deceptive, however, judges paid more attention to the speech (verbal) channel. Ekman and his colleagues offered three sources of evidence to support their contention that one of the major differences between good and poor lie detectors is the greater utilization of nonverbal clues by good lie detectors. These sources are:

1) Self-reports of accurate lie detectors, who indicate using either nonverbal clues alone, or a combination of verbal and nonverbal clues. This was found in a large group of medical school respondents (Ekman, private communication, June, 2003) as well as in groups of college students and fraud investigators (O'Sullivan, 2000). Less accurate lie detectors reported using mostly verbal clues;

2) A positive correlation between lie detection accuracy and a measure of the ability to recognize micro momentary facial expressions of emotion (Frank & Ekman, 1997) and;

3) Greater accuracy in lie detection by people with left-brain lesions which force them to use nonverbal clues to make judgments of others (Etcoff, Ekman, Magee, & Frank, 2000).

The second strategic error is related to the first. When judging someone who is lying, people tend to pay attention to the content of speech rather than to vocal quality (DePaulo, Rosenthal, Rosenkrantz, & Green, 1982). In a follow-up to the study described above (Ekman et al., 1980), O'Sullivan, Ekman, Friesen, and Scherer (1985) demonstrated that observers paid more attention to the content of speech (what was said) than its vocal or nonverbal quality when they rated deceptive behavior, but not when they rated honest behavior. In the materials used, vocal pitch was significantly higher in the deceptive condition, so ignoring the nonverbal aspects of speech was not a wise strategy. This finding illustrates two paradoxes. The first is that although the judges were not accurate in labeling people as honest or deceptive, they used different impression formation strategies in describing those who were honest and those who were deceptive. Judges used both verbal and nonverbal channels equally in describing honest behavior, but depended principally on the content of speech in describing their impressions of deceptive behavior. The second paradox is that most people can control the content of their speech more easily than they can control their facial expression, voice quality or body language. Yet, in the face of inconsistent information, observers switch from a complex processing mode in which they weigh many information sources, both verbal and nonverbal, to one in which they weigh most heavily the information channel that is most easily controlled.

In addition to the strategic errors of under-utilizing nonverbal clues and over-emphasizing the content of speech, a third strategic error is to believe that a single nonverbal clue always or nearly always indicates the presence of deception. Ekman and Friesen (1969) termed these deception clues. They and other lie detection researchers (DePaulo et al., 2003) now know that a dedicated deception clue, like Pinocchio's nose, is just a fairy tale. There is no behavior, nonverbal or otherwise, that always occurs when someone lies. This does not mean that some individuals won't betray that they are lying with typical and consistent nonverbal behaviors. Champion poker players report being able to spot the "tells" of their opponents. (Tells are behaviors that players show when they are trying to bluff and pretend they hold better cards than they actually do. Poker players might also be pleased or disappointed with the cards they have been dealt and have to hide those reactions as well.)

Champion poker players do not commit the fourth strategic error, the "idiosyncrasy error." Most people fail to allow sufficiently for the many unique and bizarre behaviors most people display as their baseline behavior (Ekman, 2001). Even professional interviewers like Tom Brokaw will say "I don't look at a person's face for signs that he is lying. What I'm after are convoluted answers or sophisticated evasions." (as cited in Ekman, 2001, pp. 90–91). There is ample evidence that many people will not show this behavior when they lie, so depending on an idiosyncrasy of some to detect the deceptiveness of all is a strategic error. Another example of the idiosyncrasy error is what Ekman (2001) termed the Othello error. In Shakespeare's play, Othello believes that his wife, Desdemona has been unfaithful. He interprets her fear as proof that she has lied to him. The truth, however, is that she fears that he will not believe her. He does not and kills her. Desdemona's fear was well-founded. People differ in terms of their reaction to not being believed. Fear of not being believed can lead some innocent people to look guilty, leading as Othello tragically discovered, to the wrong conclusion.

Cognitive Biases

Although psychology has been in the throes of the "cognitive revolution" for more than 40 years, knowledge from that field has not been sufficiently incorporated into our understanding of the processes in lie detection. Another difficulty is that the names given to certain cognitive or motivational errors in deception research are not the same as those widely used by social-cognitive psychologists and so their existence, although well-documented, is not usually included in general theorizing about social cognition.

Truthfulness Bias (and Deception Bias) a.k.a. Availability Heuristic. Zuckerman and his colleagues (1979) were among the first to suggest that most people have a truthfulness bias—they tend to judge others as truthful most of the time. In the ordinary course of events, most people do not expect to be lied to; they presume that most people are honest. Consider the many interactions we have during the course of the day. "What time is it?" "Did you see my keys?" "Listen to what I just read in the newspaper." If people tell two lies a day (DePaulo, Kirkendol, Kashy, Wyer, & Epstein, 1996), this is a trivial percentage of the thousands of interactions that occur each day. With such a high base rate of honesty, it makes sense for people, in the ordinary conduct of their life, to presume that most people are telling the truth. When a significant proportion of individuals are in fact lying, as they are in most deception studies (usually about half of the targets to be judged are deceptive) unless observers switch their base rate assumptions, which is difficult for most people to do (Pronin, Lin, & Ross, 2002), they will be inaccurate in detecting lies, i.e., they will judge others as truthful when they are not.

Ekman (2001) described a related deception bias among some law enforcement personnel who frequently rated others as lying. Since the underlying error involved in the truthfulness bias is that of availability, it makes sense that one group that does not show this bias is police officers. Most police officers interview people who lie to them, either as perpetrators of a crime or as witnesses to it, so the base rate of lying that they are exposed to is much higher than that of most people. (Some businesses and some cultures might also have a higher base rate of lying.) It is adaptive given the availability of information to adjust one's cognitive strategy to that base rate and so we see many police officers showing a deception bias rather than a truthfulness bias.

Anchoring, a.k.a. Representativeness. Zuckerman, Koestner, Colella, and Alton (1984) demonstrated that the baseline or anchor behavior that observers use in judging individuals will significantly affect their judgments of truthfulness. O'Sullivan, Ekman, and Friesen (1988) demonstrated that if the first sample of a person's behavior is honest, and the second sample is deceptive, accuracy in detecting the change from the first sample to the second increased significantly. If, however, the first sample of behavior is deceptive, because of the truthfulness bias, observers seem to assume that the sample shows the person being honest. Therefore, when they are later shown a sample of honest behavior they call it deceptive and their accuracy decreases. Their "anchoring" or assuming that the sample they have been given is representative of that person's ordinary (i.e., honest) behavior misleads them into believing that the change they have observed is from honest to deceptive, when, in fact, the change is in the opposite direction.

The Boy-Who-Cried-Wolf Effect, a.k.a. Fundamental Attribution.   Another cognitive heuristic that distorts the accurate utilization of nonverbal behavior in detecting deception is a variant of the fundamental attribution error (FAE; Ross & Nisbett, 1991). O'Sullivan (2003) has argued: 1) that most people make automatic and almost instantaneous trait judgments about people's credibility (fundamental attribution error); 2) that these judgments, like all fundamental attribution errors, will be difficult to change (Pronin et al., 2002) and, if corrected, will only rebound with greater strength (Yzerbyt, Corneille, Dumont, & Hahn, 2001); and 3) that the confusion between the trait of credibility or trustworthiness and the state judgment of honest or truthful is a particularly pernicious variant of the FAE. I called this version of the FAE the boy-who-cried-wolf effect after Aesop's fable (1793) about the shepherd boy who lied about a wolf stalking his sheep so often that the townspeople no longer believed him. Their attribution of him as a liar (enduring trait characterization) undermined their ability to recognize when he told the truth (temporary, state or situational reality). Once someone has decided that another person is generally credible or generally untrustworthy (i.e., they have attributed enduring characteristics to them related to honesty), it will be extremely difficult for them to see the credible person as deceptive, or like Aesop's shepherd boy, the liar as telling the truth. My data suggest that this error is problematic even for accurate lie detectors. They are able to judge generally trustworthy people as deceptive, but even they are unwilling or unable to believe that someone they think is generally untrustworthy will tell the truth in a specific instance. The implications of this finding will be addressed below in the section on accusatory reluctance.

Inaccurate Clue Paradigms a.k.a. Representativeness.   Another reason for poor accuracy in detecting deception is the inaccurate paradigms most observers have about what lying behavior looks like. The mismatch between subjects' beliefs about deception clues and the actual behavior that occurs in lying is well documented (DePaulo et al., 1982). For example, most Americans believe that liars won't look you in the eye. Since most Americans know about this display rule (Ekman & Friesen, 1969), in laboratory studies of deception (Riggio & Friedman, 1983), when people lie, they sometimes do more eye gaze than when they are telling the truth. There is little research on the reasons that people give for thinking that others are lying or telling the truth (O'Sullivan, 2000; Vrij, this volume) and it is not clear whether these misunderstandings about the appearance of truthful and lying behavior are cognitive heuristics, in which case they will be difficult to change (Yzerbyt et al., 2003), or merely a lack of correct information (discussed below) which can be significantly affected by training and education (Devine, 1989).

Knowledge Deficiencies

Many people do not accurately assess truthful and deceptive behavior because they lack the requisite information. Reasons for this incompetent information base include: 1) lack of feedback about accuracy, 2) inaccurate or incomplete information about the appearance of lying and truthful behavior, 3) limited experience with the different kinds of lies that people can tell, and 4) inadequate social or emotional intelligence.

Ignorance Is Bliss—No Feedback About Accuracy.   Ekman (2001) suggested that low accuracy in detecting deception was due principally to the fact that most of us do not get good feedback about our lie detection hit rate. We will say "I can always tell when my child lies to me." "My friend is a terrible liar. I can always tell when she is trying to put one over on me." But, of course, we only know the lies we have caught. If we have been lied to successfully, we are blissfully ignorant of this fact. As with lie detecting ability, lie-telling ability is probably a continuum, which if not normally distributed, is at least symmetrical, with fewer people at the ends of the distribution than in the middle. Very few people are extremely bad or extremely good liars. The really terrible, always-detected liar is probably the model, the representation, which most of us have in our minds about what a liar looks like. This information serves not only as a short-cut heuristic that will bias our decisions (an inaccurate cue paradigm as discussed earlier), but it is only incorrect information, a knowledge deficiency.

Perceptual Inadequacies.   Lack of feedback is one reason for knowledge or informational errors. Another is misperception or no perception at all. Although there are many cues to deception, as indicated earlier in this chapter, most people seem to be unaware of them. Either they do not know that such cues may indicate cognitive or emotional changes that may be related to deception (Ekman & Friesen, 1974) or the nonverbal cues are so subtle or so brief that they do not see or hear them. Alternately, they may perceive them but not interpret them accurately, for reasons suggested below.

Different Lies May Involve Different Cues.   In one of the earliest studies of honest and deceptive behavior, Hartshorne and May (1928) found that people's tendency to lie did not generalize across different situations. Honesty depended on the kind of lie required, the situation in which the lying or cheating occurred. Detecting deception accurately may also be situation-bound, and most deception detection studies use a rather narrow range of lie types. DePaulo, Stone, and Lassiter (1985), for example, reported findings that illustrate this phenomenon. The attractiveness of the truth teller or liar affected the accuracy with which they were detected. Ekman and Frank (1997) have argued for a general lie detection ability across different kinds of lies. They reported a significant correlation ($r = .37$, $p < .05$) between accuracy scores on two different kinds of lie detection tasks and identified several groups of professional lie catchers who are highly superior in two kinds of lies (Ekman, O'Sullivan, & Frank, 1999). But both lie tasks involved people talking. There may be other kinds of lie detection abilities, e.g., spotting loan defaulters, shop-lifters or husband-stealers, which may depend on other kinds of lie detection abilities.

Although Frank and Ekman (1997) reported a positive correlation in lie detection accuracy across two different kinds of lies, the size of the correlation was moderate, suggesting that different kinds of lies may be involved in different kinds of verbal and nonverbal behaviors. Shrugs, for example, which suggest some negation of what is being said, may be more common when discussing opinions or beliefs than when discussing feelings. Emotional leakage, in the face and in the voice, may be more common in:

- lies about feelings
- serious lies, not polite, "white" lies or false compliments
- unauthorized lies, not those involved in bargaining, gaming or acting
- lies told to people who are loved, admired, respected or feared
- lies told to protect the self as opposed to lies told to protect others
- lies told to be helpful or supportive
- lies about transgressions

This list of lies is suggested by the emotional requirements of the relationship between the liar and the target of the lie. Anderson, DePaulo, and Ansfield (2002) presented data showing that the gender pairings (male to male, male to female, etc.) as well as the sample (college students vs. community adults) will make a difference in the frequency with which people will report telling each of several different kinds of lies.

Ekman (2001) suggested that how the lie is told is one way of classifying lies. He distinguished concealment, falsification and telling the truth falsely. Different strategies in lying should result in different behavioral cues. As noted above, people attend to different cues in judg-ing others. If the cue they are aware of and accurate in detecting is relevant to one kind of lie but not another, they will be differentially accurate in detecting them.

Differences In Social or Emotional Intelligence.   The thesis of this chap-ter is that detecting deception is one manifestation of emotional or so-cial intelligence. Riggio, Tucker, and Throckmorton (1987) did the earliest work on this hypothesis by examining the relationship be-tween emotional/social intelligence as measured by Riggio's Social Skills Inventory (1989) and lie detection accuracy. Costanzo and Ar-cher (1993) by including lie detection items in their Social Interpreta-tion Task also agreed with this premise. It is likely that emotional intelligence is distributed as general intelligence is, i.e., most people are average and only a very few are very emotionally intelligent or very emotionally unintelligent. By extrapolation, this suggests that few peo-ple will be very good at detecting deception. This conclusion is sup-ported by many years of lie detection accuracy research (Ekman & O'Sullivan, 1991; Malone & DePaulo, 2001) as well as the study of ex-pert lie detectors described below.

Characteristics of the Liar or Truth Teller

Even if the lie catcher is socially and emotionally intelligent, has accu-rate information about the dynamic clues to deception, has received feedback about his accuracy in detecting lies, and is not hampered by cognitive heuristics and strategic errors, there are still pitfalls to be avoided in searching for the truth. Some individuals, by virtue of their culture, appearance or personality will be misinterpreted.

Cultural Differences.   Despite obvious differences, there has been surprisingly little work on cross-cultural differences in beliefs about ly-ing, sanctions against lying and the appearance of lying in different cul-tures (Bond, Omar, Mahmoud, & Bonser, 1990). We know that one class of nonverbal behaviors, emblems (hand and facial gestures that are substitutes for words) are markedly different in every culture sampled (Ekman & Friesen, 1969). Although certain facial expressions of emo-tions will be recognized in all cultures (Ekman et al., 1987) there are also subtle variations among these expressions even after people have lived in the United States for many generations (Tsai, personal commu-nication, May, 2003). Since nonverbal decoding is one of the bases for recognizing whether someone is lying or telling the truth, these subtle differences between generations and among cultural groups within a country need to be acknowledged and the behavior of the person being observed evaluated with that standard in mind. It is likely, based on the information presented earlier concerning cognitive heuristics and knowledge deficiencies, which members of out-groups (Devine, 1989) are more likely to be judged as lying than members of in-groups. The research on these questions, however, remains to be done.

Idiosyncrasy Errors.   The idiosyncrasy error has already been discussed as a cognitive heuristic (representativeness). In that discussion it was described as an aspect of the lie catcher's world view that might contribute to his or her inaccuracy. It is included here because some individuals' honesty may consistently be misjudged based on unique aspects of their appearance or behavior. People who are more socially skilled will be judged as more honest, whether they are or not (Riggio, Salinas, & Tucker, 1988). Frank and Ekman (in press) have described a "credibility generalization" related to dynamic aspects of the facial expressions of truth tellers and liars. Zuckerman and his colleagues (1979) reported a similar finding except that they measured a more static overall assessment of "demeanor."

Other researchers have also reported the effect of static appearance cues on judgments about honesty. Zebrowitz, Voinescu, and Collins (1996) demonstrated that "baby-faced" subjects, with high foreheads and widely-spaced eyes were more likely to be judged as honest when compared with non baby-faced peers. Bond, Omar, Pitre, and Lashley (1992) found that if targets were weird-looking, or "fishy-eyed," observers described them as liars when other labels, such as mentally incompetent, were not available. Observers tend to misinterpret deviations from the norm as signs of deception, so people with ordinary non-verbal behavior and "baby faces" who are not fishy-eyed or weird-looking are more likely to be judged as truthful.

Personality.   Riggio and his colleagues (1988) reported that extroverted individuals were more likely to be described as truthful, even when they were lying. Riggio and Friedman (1983) also reported individual differences in personality that corresponded with differences in nonverbal behaviors when people were lying and telling the truth. This suggests that understanding the basic personality of the person whose honesty is being evaluated may be related to accuracy in detecting deception.

Motivations of the Lie Catcher

The motivations of lie catchers may also affect their accuracy. Four different motives can be distinguished: 1) cognitive laziness, 2) socialization practices, 3) accusatory reluctance and 4) collusion and other self-deceptions.

Cognitive Laziness.   The literature on social cognition is replete with examples of the importance of motivation in the processes involved in one person's understanding of another. Fiske (1992) has written about cognitive pragmatism or "satisficing," in which observers settle for "good enough" in making decisions about others. This laissez-faire attitude may be even more prevalent when the judgment concerns honesty or deception. A number of researchers have reported that most people think many kinds of lies are trivial. Feldman, Forrest, and Happ (2002) found that even in a brief, casual conversation, college students reported many instances of exaggeration, misstatements, and omissions. In a study of lies in romantic relationships, O'Sullivan's (1999) subjects reported that they were extremely likely to tell a variety of lies to their romantic partner and that they thought most of these lies were not very serious. If lying is not considered serious, spending cognitive capital to determine whether lying has occurred may not be regarded as a wise investment for most people who seem to husband their cognitive resources (Baumeister, 1993).

Socialization Practices. In order to live together, human beings must subjugate personal desires for the common good (Freud, 1938). Children are taught early to dissemble (Saarni & Weber, 1999) to feign interest in class, delight at an unwanted present, or forgiveness of a mischievous sibling. The lessons are two-fold. Children are overtly instructed in how to manage their behavior, but, covertly, they are also being instructed to accept the deceptions that others offer to them, in the guise of unfelt thanks, unmeant apologies, insincere compliments. Lewis, Stanger, and Sullivan (1989) demonstrated quite sophisticated and successful lie behavior in children as young as three years of age. It is likely that skills learned so early are not highly amenable to conscious control or awareness in adulthood. Although most societies discourage deception, they encourage politeness and other misleading impression-management strategies. Learning to cooperate in this social choreography, by pretending to believe white lies or overlooking the social mistakes of others, may undermine the skills needed to detect deception.

Accusatory Reluctance. Social life seems to provide not only positive reinforcement to those who engage in the semi-lies of courtesy, but also negative reinforcements both to those who lie (or are caught lying) and those who detect lies and let others know that they have done so. Earlier, I described a study (Ekman et al., 1980) in which subjects who were inaccurate in labeling truthful and deceptive behavior with the labels "lying" and "truthful" nonetheless used different sources of verbal and nonverbal information in describing their impressions of other people. The observers seemed reluctant to accuse people of lying, even though, at some level, they were aware of a mismatch in their behavior, since they ignored the nonverbal behavior that occurred during deception, concentrating instead on the content of speech (O'Sullivan et al., 1985). More recently, DePaulo (1998) described a related phenomenon. Observers, who are at chance in labeling people as truthful or lying, achieve significantly better accuracy if they are asked instead to rate how comfortable the people looked.

DePaulo and Rosenthal (1979) questioned whether being too accurate in lie detection might be a liability in modern day social life. There is little cultural consensus about how to behave when lying is observed. And the costs incurred, in embarrassment, if incorrect in one's accusation, anger from the one accused, and damage from the fraying of the social fabric is quite high. One example of the high price of detecting lies is the ubiquitous fate of whistleblowers, those individuals who reveal the dishonest practices of their business colleagues or government officials (Johnson, 2002). Most whistleblowers lose their jobs, thereby incurring substantial economic and social losses. For those who are highly sensitive to lies and deception, knowing too much about other people may make it difficult to have ordinary social interactions with them.

Earlier, the-boy-who-cried-wolf-effect, a variant of the fundamental attribution error was described. Although this heuristic was evident in the judgments about both the liars and the truth tellers, it seemed to be particularly intransigent with respect to judgments in which people were described as generally untrustworthy. Although accurate lie catchers would frequently rate generally trustworthy individuals as having lied in a particular situation, if they had labeled someone as generally untrustworthy, they rarely described that person as truthful, even when he was. The intransigence of the label "liar" (once affixed, never removed) seems to make even astute observers of others loathe to label them as dishonest.

A related aspect of accusatory reluctance is the truthfulness bias described earlier. The difference between them is this: The truthfulness bias is based on a particular world view, and functions like a representativeness heuristic. Accusatory reluctance is a response variable. At some level, subjects observing lying behavior are aware of discomfort and the disjunction between verbal and nonverbal behavior. They are unwilling, however, to label such observed discomfort or such discrepancies as lying.

Collusion and Other Self-Deceptions.   Although no empirical evidence could be found, common sense and everyday observation suggests that people often cooperate in being deluded. Freud (1938) argued that some truths are too painful to know, so we forget them, transform them, project them, sublimate them or distort them into a form we can bear. Examples of this lie detection difficulty range from Chamberlain's believing Hitler's incredible protestations (Ekman, 1988) to spouses' overlooking blatant infidelity (Baumeister, 1993). Although self deception and collusion are distortions of reality, they help people to maintain their sense of themselves and to organize what might otherwise be ambiguous or threatening information.

EVOLUTIONARILY-BASED BIASES

The social cost for identifying liars, whether correctly or incorrectly has been of concern to evolutionary psychologists for some time. Bond and his colleagues (Bond, Kahler, & Paolicelli, 1985; Bond & Robinson, 1988) and other evolutionists have argued that humans have developed acute lie detection abilities. This assertion is inconsistent with the resounding evidence that most people are only at chance in recognizing the truthful and lying behavior of others. On the other hand, Ekman (1996) argued that the cost for detecting lies in our evolutionary history was probably so severe that there was no widespread selection for this ability. Socialization practices and reinforcement schedules related to courtesy training and accusatory reluctance are more consistent with Ekman's speculations than with Bond's.

Clore suggested (personal communication, August, 2002) that what has developed is the ability to detect chronic cheaters who can then be sanctioned. Ekman and Clore's hypotheses are in concert with the many reasons outlined here for why most people do not, can not, or will not label liars. What they offer are evolutionarily based reasons, rather than socially or cognitively based ones. Of course, both approaches could be correct. The social cognitive biases discussed here could have developed as ways of implementing the biologically-based motivation to avoid the high costs of detecting deception.

THE LIE DETECTION WIZARDS

Given the many reasons why most people are inaccurate in detecting deception one might reasonably ask: Can anyone accurately detect deception from verbal and nonverbal clues? Ekman, Frank and I (Ekman & O'Sullivan, 1991; Ekman et al., 1999) have described several different groups, who, as groups, were significantly above chance in their lie detection accuracy. We noticed that within each group there were some individuals who were extraordinarily accurate, scoring 70% or higher on various tests of deception accuracy. As would be expected from the binomial distribution, across all the groups we studied, not just the highly accurate ones, about 10% of people score significantly above chance. All the groups we studied were rather small in size. When we (see O'Sullivan & Ekman, in press, for more details) tested the lie deception accuracy of 1200 therapists, we found that the same level of accuracy characterized the scores of this large group. Relatively few of the therapists obtained very high scores, but, given the large size of the sample, there were enough of them to encourage us to do an idiographic analysis of highly accurate lie catchers.

As we continued to lecture to law enforcement and other professional groups we asked the participants in our workshops to raise their hands if they obtained scores of 90% or higher on a videotaped lie detection measure that showed ten men lying or telling the truth about a strongly held opinion. (For more information about this measure, see Frank & Ekman, 1997.) We then asked these very high scorers if they were willing to participate in a research project on expert lie detection. Those participants who gave us their contact information were then sent two additional lie detection accuracy tests, one of ten men lying or telling the truth about whether they had stolen $50 (the crime video; Frank & Ekman, 1997) and the other of ten women lying or telling the truth about their feelings as they watched either a pleasant nature film or a gruesome surgical film (Ekman et al., 1980). To qualify as "ultimate" experts, participants had to obtain scores of 80% or better on both tests. (See O'Sullivan & Ekman, in press, for more details.) As of August 2003, 14 such experts have been identified. Over the last 15 years, we estimate that we have tested over 12,000 people, most of them adults working in professions for which lie detection is relevant.

An additional 15 experts, having received a score of 90% on the initial screening test (opinion video), received a score of 80% or greater on only one of the two other tests. We noticed that the nine therapists in this group were highly accurate on the test showing lies about feeling, but not on the test in which the lies involved a crime. The opposite pattern was found with six law enforcement personnel. They were highly accurate (scoring 80% or better) when the lie or truth concerned a crime, but not when it concerned feelings. A chi square analysis of these data was highly significant ($\chi^2 = 11.429, p < .00072$). Because this error pattern was linked to professional experience, we included these "penultimate" experts in our sample, as well. As of August 2003, we have identified 15 such penultimate experts, giving us a total "wizard of deception detection" group of 29.

THE PROTOCOL

After the experts are identified, they meet with one or both of the experimenters (O'Sullivan & Ekman) to review their responses to each of the three videos. They are instructed to say aloud anything that occurs to them as they watch the video. They are encouraged, in other words, to "think aloud"(Ericsson & Simon, 1998). This procedure was usually the first activity we did with the experts because we were trying not to influence their recall or their reporting of the process they used in detecting deception. This initial review procedure lasts from one to two hours and is tape-recorded and transcribed.

A semi-standardized interview about personal and life history information was then recorded. Early on, we found that this interview was adequate for gaining factual information and, occasionally, information about career choices, mentors, and the like, but, especially with the police personnel, it did not yield much information. Consequently, when possible, we try to spend time with the experts and their friends and family members as well.

In addition to the think-aloud procedures and the gathering of data about their personal and professional lives, a series of psychological tests will be administered to the experts. These will include the NEO personality inventory, a short measure of verbal comprehension as an indirect measure of IQ, and, perhaps a measure of attributional or cognitive complexity.

THE CONTROL GROUP

One of the dilemmas of this project has been the problem of defining an adequate control group. The members of the control group would have to be non-expert lie detectors, by our criterion, but also be interested to participate in the research project. They would have to be similar to the experts in terms of social class, educational level, geographic location and age. There was no pre-existing group that met these requirements, so we decided to use each expert's spouse or close family member as his or her control. In most cases, the family member is interested in the project, and in their spouses' involvement. In some cases, before we had decided to use spouses as controls, husband or wives of the potential expert took the test, too, out of personal interest. In one case, the wife was the target and did not qualify. Her husband took the test, and did qualify!

At this point we have just started to interview the lie detection experts, so the following observations are merely that—observations based on interview data. The comments will be organized in line with the reasons for detection inaccuracy outlined above.

STRATEGIES

Nonverbal Cues

The deception detection wizards seem more aware of nonverbal behavior and attend to it more closely, base judgments on it more frequently and have more sophisticated and unusual descriptions of nonverbal behavior than other people we have interviewed. Every one of them has spontaneously described nonverbal behavior and discrepancies between verbal and nonverbal behavior. This does not mean that they use nonverbal behavior in every instance. They do not. But nonverbal cues are an important part of their deception detection armamentarium.

The wizards also observe and use types of nonverbal behaviors that have not been studied in the research lab. One law enforcement officer, for example, who had not yet been identified as an expert, was attending a conference at which several already-identified experts were teaching. She called the groups' attention to a subtle, micro momentary lip stretch, occurring at an important point in the interview, that none of the other experts had seen, until she called it to their attention.

Another wizard, comparing two truthful men, noted that they made similar circular head movements, as though saying, with their head, "Well, that about wraps it up." It was a loose, relaxed head movement, in synchrony with the pace and content of their story. This same expert also differentiated the quality of the eye gaze of the truth telling and the deceptive men. She did not depend merely on an eye gaze vs. no-eye gaze distinction, but rather evaluated the quality of the eye gaze, whether the individual was intently watching the interviewer to see whether he was being believed, or merely looking, in the ordinary way of conversational partners.

Verbal Cues

Many of our wizards are lawyers, or professional interrogators, so they pay a great deal of attention to the nuanced use of language. They observe slips of the tongue, rather than making sense of them, or excusing them as the average observer tends to do. They also use language to assess the education and intelligence of the people they are observing, thereby forming an assessment of the person as an individual. This individual assessment then seems to be used as a kind of baseline for assessing the nonverbal behavior that occurs.

No Pinocchio Noses

Other than the over-all category of "nonverbal behavior" and discrepancies within that behavior, there is no single clue that every wizard uses. On the other hand, each of the wizards seems to have a finite number of behaviors to which they attend with great precision and intensity. For one, it might be voice quality; for another (noted above) the combination of head and eye movements. If these preferred behaviors are not shown by the person they are observing, however, they switch to other clues or depend more on their overall assessment of the individual's personality. It is also interesting, that like the rest of us, there are many reliable clues to deception and truthfulness in the videos we reviewed together of which the wizards were blissfully unaware. They seem to have developed a set of tools that works very well for them, but there are other tools that other people use with equally good results. So, even the most accurate lie catcher has something still to learn. Incidentally, although there were a few 100% scores among the 29 wizards, no one got 100% on all three tests.

Cognitive Biases

Obviously, by virtue of their having received very high scores, the expert lie detectors do not have either a truthfulness bias or a deception bias, since that would prevent their obtaining high scores. In fact, an analysis of the errors made by the 29 wizards shows an equal number of incorrect lying and truthful answers. The wizards also did not show evidence of either the anchoring or the boy-who-cried-wolf effect. Many times, even during a one minute interview, they would change their assessment or evaluation of the person they were watching. One expert watched the entire interview, took in all the available information, and only then made her judgment even though she had seen the video before. Also, the wizard's base rate of information (representativeness) seems to be more accurate than that of most observers. As will be noted below, many of them have a wide range of life experiences which seems to have enriched their knowledge about people in general.

Knowledge and Motivation

In his realistic accuracy model of judging personality, Funder (1999) suggests that there are three aspects to accurate appraisal of others: ability, motivation and knowledge. The ability to understand whether someone is truthful or deceptive seems also to reflect these elements. We have already given some examples of the kinds of acute sensitivity to both verbal and nonverbal behaviors that characterize the deception detection wizards. In addition, these highly emotionally intelligent wizards are characterized by both exceptional motivation and unusual knowledge.

In our early studies of groups of experts (Ekman & O'Sullivan, 1991; Ekman et al., 1999), we speculated that superior lie catchers were distinguished by their motivation to do well at the task. We suggested that the very fact of their taking a workshop on the topic of detecting deception when others in their professions did not was evidence of this motivation. This observation is even more apt for the lie detection wizards. They not only attended workshops, or contacted Ekman in response to media coverage of his work, but they agreed to participate in a research project and most of them have continued through every step of the research process. The wizards, like the experts identified earlier, seek out information to validate their impressions and improve their performance. One wizard called me at 10 pm. He had been watching the TV show, American Justice, and was excited because he was sure the person featured on the show was telling the truth, and he wanted to let someone know his opinion before the "truth" was revealed on the program. This man retired from his law enforcement many years ago. Nonetheless, he was highly motivated to test himself, to be measured against an objective reality, to be proven wrong. And if he had been wrong, he wanted to discuss it with someone and learn from it.

As a group, the wizards are concerned about excellent performance, whether it is lie detection, playing hockey, singing in the church choir or riding their Harley. In completing the think-aloud protocol, a few wizards changed some of their responses, giving an incorrect answer. They were quite distressed about this, mentioning it several times, and still referring to it days later, attempting to understand why they had changed their response, why they made the wrong assessment.

Ericsson (1996), in his review of expertise in professions as widely varying as grand master chess champions and concert violists, argued that the characteristic that distinguishes the highly expert from the merely good was an extended period of intensive practice, usually lasting ten years, at the start of their careers. Recently, Brassington (2003) reported similar findings with prima ballerinas and members of the corps de ballet. Prima ballerinas reported more practice, more visualizing about their performance, more planning. Given that only a third of the wizards have been interviewed, at this point it seems that an intense focus and investment in their performance, and concentrated attempts to improve it, are characteristic of most, if not all, of the wizards. They are a highly motivated group.

An aspect of their performance that also fits under the rubric of knowledge is what I have termed the Miss Marple effect. Miss Marple is a character invented by Agatha Christie (1985) who solves crimes through her analysis of the personalities of suspects. She compares suspects to people she has known. She has a broad and accurate "rolodex" of relevant "types" against which to compare the individuals she is trying to assess. Many of the wizards have a similar capacity. One described a truthful man as looking "like a choir boy who has not been assaulted." Another wizard described a different young man this way. "He has trouble with authority, but he is an honest man. He has been well-taken care of." Although some of the wizards will mention stereotypes of various sorts, they do not let such views interfere with their attempts to understand a particular young woman or a particular black man when they are in their professional mode.

In terms of their own personality, most of the wizards seem to be introverts. This is inconsistent with research showing that extroverts are more socially skilled than introverts (Riggio et al., 1987). Lieberman and Rosenthal (2001), however, suggest that introverts do well on social tasks if that is their focus. And the wizards are exceptionally focused individuals. Another aspect of the "introversion" description was amplified by a wizard who said "I am quiet, but I am not shy." As we explore aspects of personality related to emotional intelligence, distinctions like this should be made.

Another surprising finding from this research is the deep, wide and unusual experiences with other people that the wizards have had, usually in connection with their work, but sometimes as a consequence of a family situation. The basis for friendship and marriage is almost always similarity, so most of us spend our lives with people much like ourselves. The wizards, by choice or necessity, seem to have a much wider base of social experience, based on interaction with many different kinds of people. One sheriff, for example, spent his career, first with psychiatric patients in the county jail, then with prostitutes and drug addicts of both genders in one of the most dangerous areas of Los Angeles. But he spends his free time helping his daughter find Daisy Duck collectibles at garage sales. An arbitrator, over the course of his career, has dealt, in significant ways, with mentally retarded blue collar workers, wild-cat coal mine operators in the Appalachians, and CEO's of international companies in the Mid-West. Some of the wizards' breadth of experience comes from challenging childhoods either because of abusive parents or an unusual social situation—being part of an isolated immigrant group or having a working mother at a time when that was uncommon.

Because of their high level of motivation the wizards seek information to correct inaccurate clue paradigms through feedback, reading and participation in relevant workshops and experiences, such as participating in this research. They have knowledge of many kinds of people in many kinds of situations, so are better prepared to identify lies of many sorts.

On the basis of their ability to interpret nonverbal behavior accurately, the wizards are highly emotionally intelligent. Many of them, if not all, are very talented role players as well. When a situation calls for it, these reserved, sensitive people can be as outrageous as necessary. In terms of managing their own emotions, an aspect of emotional intelligence that some theories suggest, the picture is more mixed. All of the wizards seem highly professional in their work lives, but several of them have had difficult love relationships. Some of the wizards seem able to turn off their acute sensitivity in non work situations; others do not, or can not and seem to be scanning the world all the time. Elfenbein and Ambady (2002) have demonstrated the differential effect on supervisors' ratings of sensitivity to different kinds of nonverbal cues. They argued that noticing subtle evidence of negative emotion that co-workers or supervisors were attempting to hide impaired workers' perceived job effectiveness. Based on this perspective, in order to achieve professional success, the lie detection wizards would need to manage their own behavior—to not indicate knowledge of others' emotional states when such knowledge was unwelcome.

In terms of accusatory reluctance, an analysis of the few errors that the experts made in the three lie detection tests showed no truthfulness bias. There were as many errors where they incorrectly labeled the person as deceptive as honest. In terms of collusion with the liar and other forms of self-deception, the wizards do not usually do this when they are focused on the task of detecting lies. In their personal lives, however, they can collude with their loved ones as well as the rest of us, and deceive themselves about relationships, goals, and life outcomes.

CONCLUSION

In sum, the expert lie detectors are extraordinarily emotionally intelligent people. They observe the emotions of others accurately. They are aware of their own emotional reactions to others and can use this information in understanding others, especially with respect to detecting deception. For Olympic athletes, talent is a necessary, but not a sufficient condition for athletic excellence. The development of even the greatest gifts takes practice, feedback and motivation. It is likely that the same is true for the development of the ability to understand others. The lie detection wizards do not use "tricks" that can be taught in a seminar. They do not "do" lie detection; they listen and watch people in order to understand them and then, having understood them, they are able to accurately determine their truthfulness. And they seek to improve their already considerable ability to do this. Through the kinds of careers that most of them have chosen, by their willingness to participate in a research project investigating their rare and precious gifts, they are choosing to use their talents for the welfare of all. God bless them, every one.

REFERENCES

Aesop. (1793). *The fables of Aesop: With a life of the author and embellished with one hundred and twelve plates.* London: John Stockdale.

Anderson, E. D., DePaulo, B. M., & Ansfield, M. E. (2002). The development of deception detection skill: A longitudinal study of same-sex friends. *The Society of Personality and Social Psychology, 28*(4), 536–545.

Archer, D., & Akert, R. M. (1977). Words and everything else: Verbal and nonverbal clues in social interpretation. *Journal of Personality and Social Psychology, 35*, 443–449.

Bar-On, R., Brown, J. M., Kirkcaldy, B. D., & Thome, E. P. (2000) Emotional expression and implications for occupational stress; An application of the Emotional Quotient Inventory (EQ-I). *Personality and Individual Differences, 28*(6), 1107–1118.

Baumeister, R. F. (1993). Lying to yourself: The enigma of self-deception. In M. Lewis & C. Saarni (Eds.), *Deception in everyday life* (pp. 166–183). New York: The Guilford Press.

Bond, C. F., Kahler, K. N., & Paolicelli, L. M. (1985). The miscommunication of deception: An adaptive perspective. *Journal of Experimental Social Psychology, 21*(4), 331–345.

Bond, C. F., Omar, A., Mahmoud, A., & Bonser, R. N. (1990). Lie detection across cultures. *Journal of Nonverbal Behavior, 14*(3), 189–204.

Bond, C. F., Omar, A., Pitre, U., & Lashley, B. R. (1992). Fishy-looking liars: Deception judgment from expectancy violation. *Journal of Personality and Social Psychology, 63*(6), 969–977.

Bond, C. F., & Robinson, M. (1988). The evolution of deception. *Journal of Nonverbal Behavior, 12*(4, Pt. 2), 295–307.

Boring, E. G., & Titchener, E. B. (1923). A model for the demonstration of facial expressions. *American Journal of Psychology, 34*, 471–485.

Brassington, G. (2003, May). *Mental skills distinguish elite soloist ballet dancers form corps dancers*. Paper presented at the annual meeting of the Western Psychological Association Convention, Vancouver, B.C.

Buck, R. (1976). A test of nonverbal receiving ability: Preliminary studies. *Human Communication Research, 2*(2), 162–171.

Bugental, D., Kaswan, J., & Love, L. (1970). Perceptions of contradictory meanings conveyed by verbal and nonverbal channels. *Journal of Personality and Social Psychology, 16*, 647–655.

Burgoon, J. K., Buller, D. B., White, C. H., Afifi, W., & Buslig, A. L. S. (1999). The role of conversational involvement in deceptive interpersonal interactions. *Personality and Social Psychology Bulletin, 25*(6), 669–685.

Chapin, F. S. (1942). Preliminary standardization of a social insight scale. *American Sociological Review, 7*, 214–225.

Christie, A. (1985). *Miss Marple: The complete short stories*. New York: Dodd, Mead.

Costanzo, M., & Archer, D. (1993). *The Interpersonal Perception Task-15* (IPT-15). Berkeley, CA: University of California Center for Media and Independent Learning.

Cronbach, L. J. (1955). Processes affecting scores on "understanding of others" and "assumed similarity." *Psychological Bulletin, 52*, 177–193.

Darwin, C. (1998). *The expression of the emotions in man and animals* (3rd ed.). With an introduction, afterward and commentary by P. Ekman. New York: Oxford University Press.

DePaulo, B. M. (1992). Nonverbal behavior and self-presentation. *Psychological Bulletin, 111*(2), 203–243.

DePaulo, B. M. (1998, May). *eceiving and detecting deceit: Insights and oversights from the first several hundred studies*. Invited address. American Psychological Society, Washington, D.C.

DePaulo, B. M., Kirkendol, S. E., Kashy, D. A., Wyer, M. M., & Epstein, J. A. (1996). Lying in everyday life. *Journal of Personality and Social Psychology, 70*(5), 979–995.

DePaulo, B. M., Lindsay, J. J., Malone, B. E., Muhlenbruck, L., Charlton, K., & Cooper, H. (2003). Cues to deception. *Psychological Bulletin, 129*(1), 74–118.

DePaulo, B. M., & Rosenthal, R. (1979). Telling lies. *Journal of Personality and Social Psychology, 37*(10), 1713–1722.

DePaulo, B. M., Rosenthal, R., Rosenkrantz, J., & Green, C. R. (1982). Actual and perceived cues to deception: A closer look at speech. *Basic and Applied Social Psychology, 3*(4), 291–312.

DePaulo, B. M., Stone, J. I., & Lassiter, D. G. (1985). Telling ingratiating lies: effects of target sex and target attractiveness on verbal and nonverbal deceptive success. *Journal of Personality and Social Psychology, 48*(5), 1191–1203.

Devine, P. G. (1989). Stereotypes and prejudice: their automatic and controlled components. *Journal of Personality and Social Psychology, 56*, 5–18.

Dimitrius, J., & Mazzarella, M. C. (1999). *Reading people*. New York: Ballantine Books.

Doyle, C. A. (1892). *The adventures of Sherlock Holmes*. London: G. Newnes.

Efron, D. (1941). *Gesture and environment*. Oxford, England: King's Crown Press.

Ekman, P. (1988). Self-deception and detection of misinformation. In J. S. Lockard & D. L. Paulhus (Eds.), *Self-deception: An adaptive mechanism?* (pp. 229–257). Englewood, NJ: Prentice-Hall.

Ekman, P. (1996). Why don't we catch liars? *Social Research, 63*(3), 801–817.

Ekman, P. (2001). *Telling lies: Clues to deceit in the marketplace, politics, and marriage* (3rd ed.). New York: W. W. Norton.

Ekman, P. (2003). *The Micro Momentary Expression Recognition Tool.* Available from: http://www.emotionsrevealed.com

Ekman, P. (2003). *The Subtle Expression Recognition Tool.* Available from: http://www.emotionsrevealed.com

Ekman, P., & Friesen, W. V. (1969). Nonverbal leakage and clues to deception. *Psychiatry: Journal for the Study of Interpersonal Processes, 32*(1), 88–106.

Ekman, P., & Friesen, W. V. (1969). The repertoire of nonverbal behavior: Categories, origins, usage, and coding. *Semiotica, 1*, 49–98.

Ekman, P., & Friesen, W. V. (1974). Detecting deception from body or face. *Journal of Personality and Social Psychology, 29*, 288–298.

Ekman, P. & Friesen, W. V. (1975). *Unmasking the face.* Englewood: Prentice Hall.

Ekman, P., & Friesen, W. V. (1978). *Facial action coding system.* Palo Alto, CA: Consulting Psychologists Press.

Ekman, P., Friesen, W. V. & O'Sullivan, M. (1988). Smiles when lying. *Journal of Personality and Social Psychology, 54*, 414–420.

Ekman, P., Friesen, W. V., O'Sullivan, M., & Scherer, K. R. (1980). Relative importance of face, body, and speech in judgments of personality and affect. *Journal of Personality and Social Psychology, 38*(2), 270–277.

Ekman, P., Friesen, W. V., O'Sullivan, M., Chan, A., Diacoyanni-Tarlatzis, I., Heider, K., Krause, R., LeCompte, W. A., Pitcairn, T., Ricci-Bitti, P. E., Scherer, K. R., Tomita, M., & Tzavaras, A. (1987). Universals and cultural differences in the judgments of facial expressions of emotion. *Journal of Personality and Social Psychology, 53*, 712–717.

Ekman, P., & O'Sullivan, M. (1991). Who can catch a liar? *American Psychologist, 46*(9), 913–920.

Ekman, P., O'Sullivan, M., & Frank, M. G. (1999). A few can catch a liar. *Psychological Science, 10*(3), 263–266.

Elfenbein, H. A., & Ambady, N. (2002). Predicting workplace outcomes from the ability to eavesdrop on feelings. *Journal of Applied Psychology, 87*(5), 963–971.

Engen, T., Levy, N., & Schlosberg, H. (1957). A new series of facial expressions. *American Psychologist, 12*, 264–266.

Ericcson, K. A. (1996). The acquisition of expert performance: An introduction to some of the issues. In K. A. Ericsson (Ed.), *The road to excellence: The acquisition of expert performance in the arts and sciences, sports, and game* (pp. 1–50). Hillsdale, NJ: Lawrence Erlbaum Associates.

Ericcson, K. A., & Simon, H. A. (1998). How to study thinking in everyday life: Contrasting think-aloud protocols with descriptions and explanations of thinking. *Mind, Culture and Activity, 5*(3), 178–186.

Etcoff, N. L., Ekman, P., Magee, J. J., & Frank, M. G. (2000). Lie detection and language comprehension. *Nature, 405*(6783), 139.

Feldman, R. S., Forrest, J. A. & Happ, B. R. (2002). Self-presentation and verbal deception: Do self-presenters lie more? *Basic & Applied Social Psychology, 24*(2), 163–170.

Fiske, S. T. (1992). Thinking is for doing: Portraits of social cognition from Daguerreotype to laser photo. *Journal of Personality and Social Psychology, 63*(6), 877–889.

Freud, S. (1938). *The basic writings of Sigmund Freud* (trans. & ed. by A. A. Brill). New York: The Modern Library.

Frank, M. G., & Ekman, P. (1997). The ability to detect deceit generalizes across different types of high-stake lies. *Journal of Personality and Social Psychology, 72*(6), 1429–1439.

Frank, M. G., & Ekman, P. (in press). Appearing truthful generalizes across different deception situations. *Journal of Personality and Social Psychology*.

Frois-Wittmann, J. F. (1930). The judgment of facial expression. *Journal of Experimental Psychology, 13*, 113–151.

Funder, D. (1999). *Personality judgment: A realistic approach to person perception*. San Diego, CA: Academic Press.

Gardner, H. (1993). *Multiple intelligences: The theory in practice*. New York: Basic Books.

Guilford, J. P. (1929). An experiment in learning to read facial expressions. *Journal of Abnormal Social Psychology, 24*, 191–202.

Guilford, J. P. (1956). The structure of intellect. *Psychological Bulletin, 53*, 267–293.

Goleman, D. (1995). *Emotional intelligence*. New York: Bantam Books.

Hartshorne, H., & May, M. A. (1928). *Studies in deceit. Book I. General methods and results. Book II. Statistical methods and results*. New York: MacMillan.

Ickes, W. (1993). Empathic accuracy. *Journal of Personality, 61*, 587–610.

Ickes, W., & Simpson, J. A. (1997). Managing empathic accuracy in close relationships. In W. Ickes (Ed.), *Empathic Accuracy* (pp. 218–250). New York: Guilford Press.

James, W. (1884). What is an Emotion? *Mind, 9*(34), 188–205.

Johnson, R. A. (2002). *Whistleblowing: When it works and when it doesn't*. Boulder, CO: Lynne Rienner Publisher.

Lewis, M., Stanger, C., & Sullivan, M. W. (1989). Deception in 3-year-olds. *Developmental Psychology, 25*(3), 439–443.

Lieberman, D. (1998). *Never be lied to again*. New York: St. Martin's Griffin.

Lieberman, M. D., & Rosenthal, R. (2001). Why introverts can't always tell who likes them: Multi-tasking and nonverbal decoding. *Journal of Personality and Social Psychology, 80*(2), 294–310.

Lipps, T. (1926). *Psychological Studies*. (Trans. by H. C. Sanborn). Oxford, UK: Williams & Wilkins.

Malone, B. E., & DePaulo, B. M. (2001). Measuring sensitivity to deception. In J. A. Hall & F. J. Bernieri (Eds.), *Interpersonal sensitivity: theory and measurement* (pp. 103–124). Mahwah, NJ: Lawrence Erlbaum Associates.

Mayer, J. D., Salovey, P., & Caruso, D. (2002). *Mayer-Salovey-Caruso emotional intelligence test user's manual*. Toronto, Canada: Multi-Health Systems

Mehrabian, A., & Epstein, N. (1972). A measure of emotional empathy. *Journal of Personality, 40*, 525–543.

Moss, F. A. (1931). Preliminary report of a study of social intelligence and executive ability. *Pub. Personnel Studies, 9*, 2–9.

Moss, F. S., Hunt, T., Omwake, K. T., & Woodward, L. G. (1955). *Social Intelligence Test*. Washington, DC: George Washington University.

Nance, J. (2000). *Conquering deception*. Kansas City, KS: Irvin-Benham.

Nowicki, S. J. (2001). Nonverbal receptivity: The Diagnostic Analysis of Nonverbal Accuracy (DANVA). In J. A. Hall & F. J. Bernieri (Eds.), *Interpersonal sensitivity: Theory and measurement* (pp. 183–198). Mahwah, NJ: Lawrence Erlbaum Associates.

O'Sullivan, M. (1982). Measuring the ability to recognize facial expressions of emotion. In P. Ekman (Ed.), *Emotion in the human face* (2nd ed., pp. 281–317). Cambridge, UK: Cambridge University Press.

O'Sullivan, M. (1983). *The Affect Blend Test: A new facial recognition test.* Symposium on Social Intelligence; American Psychological Association Convention, Anaheim, CA.

O'Sullivan, M. (July 2000). *Why I think you're lying.* Paper presented at the International Congress of Psychology, Stockholm, Sweden.

O'Sullivan,, M. (2003). The fundamental attribution error in detecting deception: The boy-who-cried-wolf effect. *Personality and Social Psychology Bulletin, 29*(10), 1316–1327.

O'Sullivan, M., & Ekman, P. (in press). The wizards of deception detection. In P. A. Granhag & L. Stromwell (Eds.), *Detecting deception in forensic context.* Cambridge, UK: Cambridge University Press.

O'Sullivan, M., Ekman, P., Friesen, W., & Scherer, K. R. (1985). What you say and how you say it: The contribution of speech content and voice quality to judgments of others. *Journal of Personality and Social Psychology, 48*(1), 54–62.

O'Sullivan, M., Ekman, P., & Friesen, W. V. (1988). The effect of comparisons on detecting deceit. *Journal of Nonverbal Behavior, 12*(3, Pt. 1), 203–215.

O'Sullivan, M., & Guilford, J. P. (1975). Six factors of behavioral cognition: Understanding other people. *Journal of Educational Measurement, 12*(4), 255–271.

Pronin, E., Lin, D. Y., & Ross, L. (2002). The bias blind spot: Perceptions of bias in self versus others. *Personality and Social Psychology Bulletin, 28*(3), 369–381.

Riggio, R. E. (1989). *Social skills inventory.* Palo Alto, CA: Consulting Psychologists Press.

Riggio, R. E., & Friedman, H. S. (1983). Individual differences and cues to deception. *Journal of Personality and Social Psychology, 45*(4), 899–915.

Riggio, R. E., Salinas, C., & Tucker, J. (1988). Personality and deception ability. *Personality and Individual Differences, 9*(1), 189–191.

Riggio, R. E., Tucker, J., & Throckmorton, B. (1987). Social skills and deception ability. *Personality and Social Psychology Bulletin, 13*(4), 568–577.

Rosenthal, R., Hall, J. A., DiMatteo, M. R., Rogers, P., & Archer, D. (1979). *Sensitivity to nonverbal communication: A profile approach to the measurement of individual differences.* Baltimore: Johns Hopkins University Press.

Ross, L., & Nisbett, R. E. (1991). *The person and the situation: Perspectives of social psychology.* New York: McGraw-Hill.

Saarni, C., & Weber, H. (1999). Emotional displays and dissemblance in childhood: Implications for self-presentation. In P. Philippot (Ed.), *The social context of nonverbal behavior* (pp. 71–105). New York: Cambridge University Press.

Salovey, P., & Mayer, J. D. (1989–1990). Emotional intelligence. *Imagination, Cognition, & Personality, 9*(3), 185–211.

Sternberg, R. J. (1986). *Intelligence applied.* New York: Harcourt Brace Jovanovich.

Sternberg, R. J. (1988). *The triarchic mind: A new theory of human intelligence.* New York: Penguin Books.

Thorndike, E. L. (1920). Intelligence and its uses. *Harper's Magazine, 140,* 227–235.

Thorndike, R. L., & Stein, S. (1937). An evaluation of the attempts to measure social intelligence. *Psychological Bulletin, 34,* 275–285.

Tsai, J. L., & Chentsova-Dutton, Y. (in press). Variation among European Americans in emotional facial expression. *Journal of Cross-Cultural Psychology.*

Wedeck, J. (1947). The relationship between personality and 'psychological ability.' *British Journal of Psychology, 37,* 133–151.

Wundt, W. (1897). *Outlines of psychology* (translated by C. W. Judd). Leipzig: Wilhelm Engelman.

Yzerbyt, V. Y., Corneille, O., Dumont, M., & Hahn, K. (2001). The dispositional inference strikes back: Situational focus and dispositional suppression in causal attribution. *Journal of Personality and Social Psychology, 81*(3), 365–376.

Zebrowitz, L. A., Voinescu, L., & Collins, M. A. (1996). "Wide-eyed" and "crooked-faced": Determinants of perceived and real honesty across the life span. *Personality and Social Psychology Bulletin, 22*(12), 1258–1269.

Zuckerman, M., DeFrank, R. S., Hall, J. A., Larrance, D. T., & Rosenthal, R. (1979). Facial and vocal cues of deception and honesty. *Journal of Experimental Social Psychology, 15,* 378–396.

Zuckerman, M., & Driver, R. E. (1985). Telling lies: Verbal and nonverbal correlates of deception. In W. A. Siegman & S. Feldstein (Eds.), *Multichannel integration of nonverbal behavior* (pp. 129–147). Hillsdale, NJ: Lawrence Erlbaum Associates.

Zuckerman, M., Koestner, R., Colella, M. J., & Alton, A. O. (1984). Anchoring in the detection of deception and leakage. *Journal of Personality and Social Psychology, 47*(2), 301–311.

❧ 11 ❧

Culture and Applied Nonverbal Communication

David Matsumoto
Seung Hee Yoo
San Francisco State University

As this volume has indicated there is now a rich literature examining the nonverbal behaviors in many applied settings. These studies continue to document exactly how important nonverbal behaviors are in real life situations and that they have real life consequences as well.

In addition to this literature there is a large basic research literature examining the influence of culture on nonverbal behaviors. This literature is important because it informs us of the ways in which nonverbal behaviors and communication processes in general can be similar and different across cultures. They provide a platform by which many basic studies of nonverbal behaviors and communication have occurred in the past, and will occur in the future.

The domain of cross-cultural research on applied nonverbal behavior, however, is in its infancy, and to date there have only been a handful of studies that have been published in peer-reviewed journals. The goal of this chapter is to encourage such research to blossom. To do so we first discuss a conceptual understanding and definition of culture, and then how culture influences the encoding and decoding of nonverbal behaviors. We then discuss several methodological issues concerning cross-cultural research that researchers should be aware of. At the end of this chapter we briefly describe an example of an applied study of nonverbal behaviors from our laboratory. We hope that this information becomes some of the nutrients needed for future research to take root and grow.

WHAT IS CULTURE?

Human Nature

In order to understand and define culture it is inevitable to start with some assumptions about human nature. The view of human nature that provides the best platform to account for not only pancultural universals but also culture-specifics is that of evolutionary psychology. This perspective suggests that people have evolved a set of motives and strivings that are ultimately related to reproductive success (Buss, 2001). Reproductive success and other biological functions such as eating and sleeping are biological imperatives if people are to survive.

In the evolutionary psychology perspective survival is related to the degree to which people can adapt to their environments and to the contexts in which they live. Over the history of time people must have had to solve a host of distinct social problems in order to adapt and thus achieve reproductive success. These social problems include negotiating complex status hierarchies, forming successful work and social groups, attracting mates, fighting off potential rivals of food and sexual partners, giving birth and raising children, and battling nature (Buss, 1988, 1989, 1991, 2000, 2001). In fact we need to do these things in our everyday lives today as well. Thus universal biological imperatives have become associated with a universal set of psychological problems that people need to solve in order to survive.

That is, all individuals and groups of individuals have a universal problem of how to adapt to their environments in order to deal with their universal biological needs and functions and the imperative of reproductive success. Thus all individuals and groups of individuals must create ways to deal with these universal problems. These ways can be very specific to each group, because the context in which each group lives—the physical environment, the social factors, and the types and sizes of their families and communities—are different. The ways that each group develops then become each group's culture.

Culture

Culture is created as people have adapted to their environments in order to survive. In our view, culture is the product of the interaction between universal biological needs and functions, universal social problems created to address those needs, and the context in which people live. Culture results from the process of individuals' attempts to adapt to their contexts in addressing the universal social problems and biological needs.

In the past there have been many attempts at defining exactly what those biological and social needs are, and the aspects of culture that address them. For example, Malinowski suggested that all individuals had universal basic needs related to metabolism, reproduction, bodily comforts, safety, movement, growth, and health (Malinowski, 1927, 1961, 1944, 1960). According to Malinowski all cultures must create ways to deal with each of these social motives, producing a cultural "response" that corresponds ultimately to the universal biological functions (Table 11.1).

Similarly social scientists have been interested in culture and how it influences people for well over 100 years. Consequently there have been many different definitions of culture over the years, with similarities as well as differences (Berry, Poortinga, Segall, & Dasen, 1992; Jahoda, 1984; Kroeber & Kluckholn, 1952/1963; Linton, 1936; Rohner, 1984; Triandis, 1972). In our work we define culture simply as *a shared system of socially transmitted behavior that describe, define, and guide people's ways of life.*

The Characteristics of Culture

Culture touches on all aspects of our lives. It involves subjective and objective elements (Triandis, 1972). It explains differences in the types of foods we eat and how we eat them. It explains the clothes we wear and our home life. We use culture to describe our activities, values, attitudes, opinions, and beliefs, and to describe our communities, religion, and even our government. We use culture to explain similarities within and differences between groups of people (Tooby & Cosmides, 1992).

The subjective elements of culture are psychological. Culture influences many psychological processes, such as attitudes, beliefs, norms, opinions, values, and behaviors. Culture in this sense is like a syndrome, a constellation of separate but interrelated psychological components that collectively characterize a condition (Triandis, 1994).

Culture is always changing, even slowly. It is not a static entity, but a living, breathing one. What we commonly know as "the generation gap" is a cultural difference as it refers to different ways of life and being for people who are raised in different periods of time (Pipher, 1998). Many

Table 11.1
Malinowski's Conceptualization of Basic Needs and Cultural Responses

Basic Needs	Cultural Response
Metabolism	Commissariat
Reproduction	Kinship
Bodily comforts	Shelter
Safety	Protection
Movement	Activities
Growth	Training
Health	Hygiene

countries around the world including the U.S. have undergone cultural changes across time and will continue to do so in the future as our ways of life change.

Culture exists on multiple levels. Individuals are part of small groups, and smaller groups are part of larger and even larger groups. Each group can have its own culture and in this way culture can exist on many levels. This is true for different ethnic and community groups that live in a large country like the U.S., as well as among different departments, sections, and work units of large companies.

Culture enhances survival. Cultures provide rules for living, tell people how to interact, and how to work and play with each other. Culture provides a hierarchy for decision-making and sets the standards for group cooperation and divisions of labor. With culture there is some order to life; without culture there is chaos. Even people who think they have no culture have a culture; it is just the culture to believe they have no culture. Culture is often difficult to perceive because we do not recognize alternative possibilities without having experienced them. That's why people learn as much about their own culture as they do about others when they travel to or live in new cultures. Of all the possible things people could do, culture helps to limit what we should do in order to survive in the environment in which we live (Poortinga, 1990).

Culture is communicated across generations. This ensures that many aspects of culture are durable. Beliefs and attitudes that become popular from time to time and that are shared by many people may be what we know of as "popular culture," but the culture we are concerned with here is more stable across time. Many elements of culture are communicated across generations, including the rules we learned when we were children, the holidays and cultural activities we celebrate, and the foods we eat at home.

Culture both enables behavior, allowing it to be created or invented, while at the same time it constrains or restricts behavior (Adamopoulous & Lonner, 2001). On one hand, individualism, for example, fosters uniqueness, independence, autonomy, and creativity. It provides the cultural framework within which behaviors can be invented. Jazz musicians, writers, poets, artists, rock stars and even disciplines like psychology can thrive and flourish in such an environment (Buss, 2001). On the other hand, culture also provides rules for constraining behavior. Laws exist in every country and culture of the world, and these laws define what is right and wrong, acceptable and not, in every land. Cultures also provide for social sanctions against inappropriate behavior. In many cultures, for instance, shame is used as a powerful and important social sanction that limits behavior and keeps everyone in line. In many Asian cultures the concept of "face" is important, and keeping and protecting one's face is as important as invention is in individualistic cultures (Oetzel et al., 2001).

Universal and Culture-Specific Psychological Processes

While cultures can be unique to the groups of individuals that live in them and the contexts in which they live, they all must deal with the same set of biological needs and functions and universal social problems. Thus it is very possible and in many cases very likely that the ways in which they are addressed are the same, even though the cultures may be different. That is, universal biological needs and social problems can lead to similar solutions across cultures, especially over time in our evolutionary history.

For this reason many aspects of our psychology—our mental processes and behaviors—are universal, that is, common to all people of all cultures and backgrounds. For example all humans appear to have some degree of specific fears, such as to snakes, spiders, heights, and darkness because these types of fears have led in our evolutionary history to greater probability of survival (Seligman & Hager, 1972, cited in Buss, 2001). All people have a tendency to perceive their own ingroup as heterogeneous, fully recognizing the individual differences that exist in that group, while they perceive other groups as more homogeneous, assuming less diversity within the group (Linville & Jones, 1980; Triandis, McCusker, & Hui, 1990). People also seem to have a natural proclivity to fears of strangers and outgroup members, which may be a universal basis for ethnocentrism, prejudice, aggression, and even war (Buss, 2001). The differences in how we treat ingroup and outgroup members are likely rooted in our evolutionary history because such distinctions were useful in the past to our reproductive success. Other universal psychological processes, such as incest avoidance, facial expressions of emotion, division of labor by sex, revenge and retaliation, mate selection and sexual jealousy, self-enhancement, and personality can be traced to the core aspect of a universal human nature based on biological imperatives and universal social problems of adaptation and living.

But many psychological processes are also culture specific. Different cultures have developed different ways of dealing with the biological imperatives and universal social problems based on their contexts. Language is a good example of a very culture-specific behavior. Each culture has its own language, with its own set of vocabulary, syntax, grammar, phonology, and pragmatics. The need to have language may be a pancultural universal problem; and having a language may be a universal solution to this problem. But the specific way in which each culture solves this problem—that is develops its own language—is different in every culture.

Culture is a pretty fuzzy construct with a pretty fuzzy definition. There are no hard and fast rules of how to determine what a culture is or who belongs to that culture. But its influence on psychology and nonverbal behavior cannot be denied.

CULTURE AND NONVERBAL BEHAVIORS

Culture has a pervasive and profound influence on verbal and nonverbal encoding and decoding processes, which we discuss in this section.

Cultural Influences on Encoding Nonverbal Behaviors

Culture exerts considerable influence over the verbal languages that we speak, from the syntax of a language to its pragmatics. But just as culture influences our verbal languages, culture also exerts considerable influence over our nonverbal languages. People of all cultures learn to use nonverbal behaviors—facial expressions, gestures, distance, gaze, and postures—as part of their communication repertoire, but people in each culture learn to use them in different ways. All humans are born with the capacity to form all types of sounds; culture dictates how we shape and mold those sounds into particular languages. In the same way, culture shapes and molds nonverbal behaviors into each culture's nonverbal language.

Some kinds of nonverbal behaviors are common to many cultures, such as greeting behaviors (for example, the eyebrow raise), whereas others differ radically (for example, touching behaviors; Keating, 1976). Developmental research has suggested that rules governing nonverbal behavior are as old as verbal languages, and that children learn their cultural rules governing nonverbal behaviors as they learn the rules of vocal expression and acquire verbal language (Von-Raffler Engel, 1981). If this is the case, it is no wonder that the cultural rules of nonverbal behavior are well ingrained in us by the time we are adults, and that we use them without much second thought.

There are many examples in the literature of cultural differences in encoding nonverbal behaviors. For instance, the universality of facial expressions of emotion is no longer debated in psychology; people all around the world, despite differences in culture, have the ability to express anger, contempt, disgust, fear, happiness, sadness, and surprise in the same ways (Ekman, 1999; Matsumoto, 2001). Yet all people learn rules that govern how to manage and modify these universal emotional expressions based on social circumstances. These rules, called cultural display rules (Ekman & Friesen, 1969), are learned early on and are an important part of the socialization and enculturation process (Saarni, 1979). We know that compared to Americans, Japanese, Poles, and Hungarians are likely to express more positive and less negative emotions toward ingroup members, and more negative and less positive emotions to outgroups (Biehl, Matsumoto, & Kasri, in press; Matsumoto, 1990). Also compared to Americans, Germans tend to minimize their expressions of negative emotions by deamplifying or neutralizing them, but not by qualifying them with a smile (Koopmann & Matsumoto, 2003).

Emblems and gestures also differ across cultures (Morris, Collett, Marsh, & O'Shaughnessy, 1980), as when a Japanese person nods his or her "yes" and says "hai" (literally, yes) and does not necessarily mean "yes." There are cultural differences in gaze and visual attention, touching, and interpersonal space as well. Well known is the "diplomatic dance" that occurs when Americans are uncomfortable when they interact with some peoples of middle eastern cultures, who have learned to interact with others at a distance at which they can feel your breath.

Cultural Influences on Decoding Nonverbal Behaviors

Culture affects the decoding process in several ways. Here we summarize three sets of psychological processes related to decoding that are affected by culture.

Cultural Filters, Ethnocentrism, Emotions, and Value Judgments.   As we grow up, we learn cultural rules of appropriate communicative encoding with respect to both verbal and nonverbal behaviors. When we are little, these rules are constantly reinforced by parents, friends, teachers, and other enculturation agents. Many rules are also transmitted and reinforced by organizations and institutions (as in our study of language through the school system). As we get older, we need to be reminded less about these rules, and their use requires less conscious effort. The inevitable result is unique, culture-specific ways in which communication—verbal and nonverbal—occurs.

As we grow, we also learn how to perceive signals and interpret messages; that is, we learn cultural rules of appropriate decoding as well. Because we share a set of encoding and decoding rules with people of our culture, we develop a set of expectations about communication. These rules and expectations form a basis of tacit understanding that need not be spoken each time we, as adult members of the same culture, communicate with one another.

Not only do we have certain expectations about the communication process; we have also learned emotional reactions associated with those expectations. These reactions can range from acceptance and pleasure to outrage, hostility, and frustration. Our emotions, in turn, are intimately tied to value judgments, which we often make without a second thought. These judgments seem only natural because they are rooted in our upbringing; they are the only types of judgments we have learned to make. Emotions and values serve as guidelines in helping us form opinions about others and ourselves.

A recent set of studies in our laboratory highlights these relationships (Matsumoto, Choi, Hirayama, Domae, & Yamaguchi, 2003). Across three studies American and Japanese observers were shown either neutral, low intensity or high intensity emotional expressions and were asked to judge how strong the external display of the expressor was, and how much emotion they really thought the expressor was feeling. These are, in effect, judgments of other's display rules, as observers made judgments of how much emotion was expressed in relation to how much they thought was actually felt. In addition the observers completed measures of their own display rules or emotion regulation processes. In all three studies there were significant culture by rating type interactions. For instance, there was no difference between the two rating types on neutral expressions for Americans while the Japanese rated internal experience higher than external display. In every instance in which a culture by rating type interaction occurred, the difference disappeared when the observers' own display rules or emotion regulation scores were controlled, indicating that the differences occurred entirely because of differences in display rules.

Thus, decoding rules, and their associated emotions and value judgments, form the basis of the "filters" that we use in seeing the world. As we become more enculturated, we add more layers to those filters. These filters are like lenses that allow us to perceive the world in a certain way. By the time we are adults, we share the same filters with others in our cultural group. They become part of our self, inseparable and invisible, and are a normal part of our psychological composition because of the way we have been enculturated.

Culture and Stereotypes.   Stereotypes are generalizations about people, particularly about their underlying psychological characteristics or personality traits. Stereotypes are inevitable products of normal psychological processes, including selective attention, appraisal, concept formation and categorization, attributions, emotion, and memory. Stereotypes are invaluable mental aids, helping us organize information about the world. They are important in helping us interact with others in our world, and are especially important in communication.

Stereotypes prime our expectations. We may selectively attend to events that support our stereotypes, and ignore, albeit unconsciously, events and situations that challenge them. Negative attributions may reinforce negative stereotypes. Even when we perceive events contrary to stereotype, we may convince ourselves that the stereotype is correct. Such dismissals can occur quickly, without much conscious thought or effort, and are resilient to emotion.

These psychological processes—including selective attention, attribution, and emotion—are all part of our self-concept. They reinforce the cultural knowledge we have learned from many years of enculturation, and thereby reinforce our sense of self. As we confirm our stereotypes, therefore, we reinforce our self-concept. Stereotypes are thus an integral part of the package of psychological processes, and are intimately tied to our emotions, values, and core self.

Culture and Social Cognition.   Culture influences how we interpret the actions of others—that is, our attributions regarding others. Americans, for example, tend to draw inferences about other people's internal states or dispositions that supposedly underlie or even cause their behavior. This bias is known as fundamental attribution error (Ross, 1977). Cross-cultural research has shown that this bias may not exist in other cultures. For instance such dispositional explanations were common for Americans but much less so for the Hindus (Miller, 1984); the Hindus provided explanations in terms of the actor's duties, social roles, and other situation-specific characteristics (see also Shweder & Bourne, 1984). Other attributional tendencies, such as self-serving bias and defensive attributions are also manifested differently in different cultures.

In summary, culture plays a large role in decoding signals during communication episodes—first, because of the close relationship between cultural rules governing encoding and decoding, and second, because of cultural influences in the development of ethnocentrism, stereotyping, and social cognition. Cultural decoding rules are intimately associated with emotions and value judgments, which collectively form our self-concepts.

CONDUCTING APPLIED RESEARCH ON NONVERBAL BEHAVIOR ACROSS CULTURES

In this section we consider methodological issues that underlie the conduct of cross-cultural research on nonverbal behaviors. There are many different types of cross-cultural studies and space limitations do not permit a full discussion of many of them; interested readers are referred to Matsumoto (2003) for a fuller discussion of the problems and possible solutions. Here we focus exclusively on cross-cultural comparisons, and only on a few issues within that, namely sampling, measurement, and data equivalence. We begin with a discussion of the concept of equivalence.

Equivalence (and Bias)

In reality, there are only a few issues specific to the conduct of cross-cultural research that set it apart from general experimentation; the same problems and solutions that are typically used to describe issues concerning experimental methodology in general can and should be applied to most, if not all, cross-cultural comparisons. Most of the issues raised in this section, therefore, with the notable exception of language issues, are generally true of "good" experimentation in monocultural studies as well. Cross-cultural research, however, has been useful in highlighting them.

One concept that is of crucial importance in the conduct and evaluation of all aspects of cross-cultural comparison is that of equivalence and its corresponding construct, bias. (Bias is generally viewed as non-equivalence. For this reason, we will generally refer to one.) Equivalence in cross-cultural research can be defined as a state or condition of similarity in conceptual meaning and empirical method between cultures that allows comparisons to be meaningful. In a strict sense, the greater the non-equivalence (thus bias) of any aspect of a cross-cultural study in meaning or method across the cultures being compared, then the less meaningful the comparison. Lack of equivalence in a cross-cultural study creates the proverbial situation of comparing apples and oranges. If and only if, however, the theoretical framework and hypotheses have generally equivalent meaning in the cultures being compared, and the methods of data collection, management, and analysis have equivalent meanings, only then are the results from that comparison meaningful.

Of course, this is true in any between-group comparison study. Still, it is important to remember that the perfectly equivalent cross-cultural study is an impossibility; there will always be some aspect of the comparison that is not perfectly equivalent to each other. Thus, it is probably more accurate to suggest that for cross-cultural comparisons to be valid and meaningful, they have to be "equivalent enough." The difficult part of this concept, however, that frustrates students and researchers alike is that there is no direct method, no mathematical formula, no easy way, to determine what is "equivalent enough." Sometimes a study may have a lot of little non-equivalences, but still be meaningful. Sometimes a study may have one fatal non-equivalence, and thus be meaningless. These issues differ from study to study, and we cannot tell you here what the fatal flaw will always be. As usual, experience and conscientiousness are probably two of the largest teachers.

The issues described here, and in most descriptions of experimentation, therefore, are the ideals. The closer to the ideals the study is, the more valid the comparison (of course, this may also mean that it is farther from reality).

Sampling Equivalence

Sampling Adequacy. Researchers need to insure that the participants in their study are adequate representatives of the cultures that they are supposed to represent. More often than not researchers generally assume that people who happen to fit into the categorical label of culture as operationalized (e.g., by nationality) are "good" representatives of that particular culture. In doing so there is an unacceptable assumption of homogeneity among the participants with regard to culture that can, in its worse sense, only serve to perpetuate stereotypic impressions and interpretations based on the findings. When differences are found, researchers assume that the differences are "cultural" because they assume that the samples are representatives of culture.

While this issue is relatively straightforward and easy to understand, in practice it is extremely difficult to achieve. In its strictest sense, proper addressing of this issue would require the following steps: (a) the researcher would have to be able to theoretically define exactly what the cultures are that are being tested; (b) the researcher would have to be able to access a pool of individuals from the larger population that embodied those characteristics; (c) the researcher would have to randomly sample from that larger population; and (d) the researcher would have to measure those social, cultural, and psychological characteristics in their participants and empirically demonstrate that their culture manipulations occurred as intended.

Unfortunately, this is a tall order that is not, and perhaps cannot, be filled currently because of the limitations to our abilities to theorize about, and subsequently measure, culture on the individual level, and our inability to randomly access all members of any given cultural population. Given that we cannot currently achieve this ideal, the real issue facing researchers concerns the degree to which they understand how far from this ideal they are, and how much they use this information to temper their interpretations. In a practical sense, a sound cross-cultural comparison would entail the collection of data from multiple sites within the same cultural group, either in the same study or across studies, to demonstrate the replicability of a finding across different samples within the same culture.

Non-Cultural, Demographic Equivalence.   Researchers need to insure that the differences they obtain in a study are due to culture and not to any other non-cultural demographic variables on which the samples may differ. That is, researchers need to make sure the samples they compare are equivalent on variables such as gender, age, SES, educational level, religious orientation, geographic area (e.g., rural vs. urban), and such. If they are not equivalent on non-cultural, demographic variables, then those variables on which they are not equivalent may confound the comparison.

The conceptual problem that arises in cross-cultural research, which is not as apparent in mono-cultural studies, is that some non-cultural demographic characteristics are inextricably intertwined with culture such that researchers cannot hold them constant across samples in a comparison. Religion is such an example. There are differences in the meaning and practice of religions across cultures that make them inextricably bound to culture oftentimes. Holding religion constant across cultures does not address the issue, because being Catholic in the U.S. just does not mean the same thing as being Catholic in Japan or Malaysia. Randomly sampling without regard to religion will result in samples that are different not only on culture, but also on religion (to the extent that one can separate the two's influences). Thus, presumed cultural differences often reflect religious differences across samples as well. The same is also true oftentimes for SES, as there are vast differences in SES across cultural samples from around the world.

Measurement Equivalence

Conceptual Equivalence.   Researchers need to insure that the psychological variables being measured in their studies are conceptually equivalent across the cultures being compared. Different cultures may conceptually define a construct differently. Common examples of constructs that have widely divergent meanings across cultures include such topics as intelligence, self-concept, personality, or emotion. Clearly, just because something has the same name in two or more cultures does not mean that it refers to the same thing in those cultures (Wittgenstein, 1953, cited in Poortinga, 1989). If a concept means different things to people of different cultures, then there is a lack of equivalence in the definition of the construct, and comparisons of cultures based on non-equivalent constructs will lack meaning. Researchers wishing to compare cultures on psychological constructs, therefore, have the onus of demonstrating, either empirically or conceptually, that the constructs themselves are equivalent across the cultures being compared.

Empirical Equivalence.   Even if a construct is conceptually equivalent across cultures, reliable and valid measurement of it may take different forms across cultures. Concretely this requires that researchers use measures that have been empirically demonstrated to reliably and validly measure the construct of interest in the cultures being studied. Simply taking an existing test developed in one culture and translating it for use in other cultures is not methodologically adequate, although this has often been the case previously. Cross-cultural validations often require extensive testing in the target cultures in order to establish a reasonable amount of reliability and validity parameters, especially with regard to convergent and predictive validity. Questionnaires that involve multiple scales and items will need to have been tested to establish the cross-cultural equivalence of item and scale meaning, especially concerning equivalence in factor structures and item loadings.

For example, one applied cross-cultural study examined how emotion displays of French and American political leaders on TV affect voters in France and the U.S., respectively (Masters & Sullivan, 1989). They showed videoclips of political leaders of one's own country displaying three types of emotion (happy, anger, fear) to French and American judges, and made ratings of the behavior of the political leaders, self-reports of their own emotional responses, and attitudes toward politics, leaders, and the media. The measures were back-translated (see below), and the French version was pretested to confirm that scales were used in the same way with French participants as it was the American participants, offering some evidence of convergent validity. Self-report of emotional response was factor analyzed separately for each culture and was found to have similar factor structures providing support that measures and procedure in both cultures were equivalent.

Still, factor equivalence is only one step in establishing the empirical equivalence of measures across cultures. These are not easy issues to deal with, and cross-validation is not as easy as it seems. Some writers have suggested that tests of psychological abilities are inherently incomparable across cultures. Greenfield, for example, argues that constructs such as intelligence and cognitive ability are inherently symbolic products of a culture (Greenfield, 1997). As such, the constructs and tests of it presuppose a certain cultural framework in the first place in order to be valid. As these frameworks are not usually universally shared, cross-cultural comparisons of ability and intelligence therefore become meaningless.

Similar questions may exist concerning the equivalence in construct and operation of values. Peng and others, for example, have argued that common methods for assessing values, which include providing participants with a list of values and asking them either to rate them or rank them in order of importance, may not be valid across cultures because of implicit social comparison processes (Peng, Nisbett, & Wong, 1997). They suggested that such methods may be invalid because of cultural differences in the meanings of specific value items, and because of the possibility that some value judgments are based on inherent social comparisons with others instead of making a direct inference about a private, personal value system. In order to investigate this possibility, these researchers examined four different value survey methods, including the traditional ranking, rating, and attitude scaling procedures, as well as a behavioral scenario rating method. The only method that yielded reasonable validity estimates was the behavioral scenario rating method, which is the most unorthodox of all measures tested.

Poortinga has suggested that when a measure has high content validity in all cultures being tested (i.e., it has been shown to mean the same thing in all cultures), and when the construct being measured is in a psychological domain that is similar or identical across cultures (e.g., color schemes, pitch scale for tones), valid comparisons are generally possible (Poortinga, 1989). When unobservable psychological traits and attributes of individuals are being measured, comparison may be possible as long as equivalence in the conceptual meaning of the psychological domain and its measurement in all participating cultures have been established. Other than these two situations, all other research situations, according to Poortinga (1989), preclude valid comparison across cultures.

Linguistic Equivalence.   Researchers need to insure that the research protocols used in their studies are linguistically equivalent across the cultures being compared. While most other methodological issues described in this chapter pertain to all group difference research, mono- or cross-cultural, this issue is one of the few that is specific to cross-cultural research.

Cross-cultural research often cannot be conducted solely in one language, because the samples being tested are frequently comprised of two or more distinct language groups. There are generally two procedures used to establish linguistic equivalence. One is known as back translation (Brislin, 1970), which involves taking the research protocol in one language, translating it to the other language(s), and having someone else translate it back to the original. The second approach is to utilize the committee approach, in which several bilingual informants collectively translate a research protocol into a target language on a consensual basis. Actually, a third approach is also available, which is a combination of the first two approaches.

Regardless of the approach, a major caveat for researchers here is that "closest semantic equivalent" does not mean "the same." Getting protocols that are "the same," in fact, is probably impossible. Even if the words being used in the two languages are the agreed upon translations, there is no guarantee that those words have exactly the same meanings, with the same nuances, across cultures. There is also the additional problem to deal with which concerns the difference between linguistic and cultural equivalence. That is, you can have a protocol that is linguistically equivalent to its original in another language, but that just does not make sense in the target language. In this case, the researcher needs to make a decision concerning whether to go with the literal translation, which may be awkward and difficult to interpret but is the closest semantic equivalent, or to go with the cultural translation, which will make sense but is not linguistically equivalent.

Data Equivalence

Cultural Response Sets.   When analyzing data, researchers need to be aware of the possible existence of cultural response sets, and if they do exist deal with them. Cultural response sets are tendencies for members of a culture to use certain parts of a scale when responding. For example, participants of culture A in a two-culture comparison may tend to use the entire scale, whereas participants of culture B may tend to use only a part of the scale (e.g., the middle). These tendencies may exist for several reasons, including cultural differences in attitudes and values regarding self-expression of personal opinions. There have been numerous suggestions in the past that members of collectivistic cultures hesitate using the extreme end points of a scale in congruence with a cultural hesitation to "stick out," resulting in the use of the middle of a scale. There have also been some studies that have shown tendencies for members of some cultural groups to use the endpoints. Bachman and O'Malley, for example, found such evidence in extreme response styles among African Americans (Bachman & O'Malley, 1984), and Marin and colleagues found similar evidence for Hispanics (Marin, Gamba, & Marin, 1992). If they exist, cultural response sets may confound between-culture differences because it is difficult to know whether differences are occurring because of response sets or because of "meaningful" differences in real scores on the target variables of interest.

Effect Size Analyses.   Cultural differences in mean values on any scale do not readily predict how individuals are different between cultures. Statistical significance does not mean "practical" significance in a realistic or pragmatic sense, especially because statistical significance is so dependent on sample size. One mistake that researchers and consumers of research alike make when interpreting group differences is that they assume that most people of those groups differ in ways corresponding to the mean values. Thus, if a statistically significant difference is found between Americans and Japanese, for instance, on emotional expressivity such that Americans had statistically significantly higher scores than the Japanese, people often conclude that all Americans are more expressive than all Japanese. This, of course, is a mistake in interpretation that is fueled by the field's fascination and single-minded concern with statistical significance and perhaps with cultural myths that are easy to perpetuate.

In reality, there are statistical procedures available that help to determine the degree to which differences in mean values reflect meaningful differences among individuals. The general class of statistics that do this is called effect size statistics, and when used in a cross-cultural setting, Matsumoto and his colleagues called them cultural effect size statistics (Matsumoto, Grissom, & Dinnel, 2001). It is beyond the scope of this chapter to present them in detail; Matsumoto et al. (2001) present four such statistics that they deemed most relevant for cross-cultural analyses, with reanalyses from two previously published studies as examples. Whether cross-cultural researchers use these or others, it is incumbent on them to include some kind of effect size analysis when comparing cultures so that informed readers can determine the degree to which the differences reported reflect meaningful differences among people.

Dealing With Non-Equivalent Data.   Despite the best attempts to establish equivalence in theory, hypothesis, method, and data management, cross-cultural comparisons are often inextricably, inherently, and inevitably non-equivalent. That is, it is impossible to create any cross-cultural study that means exactly the same thing to all participating cultures, both conceptually and empirically. What cross-cultural researchers often end up with are best approximations of the closest equivalents in terms of theory and method in a study.

Thus, researchers are often faced with the question of how to deal with non-equivalent data. Poortinga (1989) outlined four different ways in which the problem of non-equivalence of cross-cultural data can be handled:

Preclude Comparison. The most conservative thing a researcher could do is to not make the comparison in the first place, concluding that such a comparison would be meaningless.

Reduce the Non-Equivalence in the Data. Many researchers engage in empirical steps to identify equivalent and non-equivalent parts of their methods, and then refocus their comparisons solely on the equivalent parts. For example, to compare perceptions of teacher immediacy in U.S. and Japan, Neuliep asked American and Japanese university students to complete the Verbal Immediacy Behaviors Scale, the Nonverbal Immediacy Measure, and various ratings of attitudes toward content of course, attitudes toward teacher, likelihood of using behaviors taught in class, likelihood of taking another class by same teacher, and own perception of how much they learned (Neuliep, 1997). The 20-item Verbal Immediacy Behaviors Scale and the 14-item Nonverbal Immediacy Measure were factor analyzed separately after each item was standardized within each culture to eliminate cultural differences. The factor analysis reduced the Verbal Immediacy Scale to 14 items and Nonverbal Immediacy Measure to 9 items and the scales with reduced items were analyzed in the study.

Interpret the Non-Equivalence. A third strategy is for the researcher to interpret the non-equivalence as an important piece of information concerning cultural differences.

Ignore the Non-Equivalence. While this is what most cross-cultural researchers should not do, this is in fact what many end up doing. Poortinga (1989) suggests that this is because many researchers hold onto beliefs concerning scale invariance across cultures, despite the lack of evidence to support such beliefs.

Obviously, how a researcher handles the interpretation of his or her data, given non-equivalence, is dependent on his or her experience and biases, and on the nature of the data and the findings. Because of the lack of equivalence in much cross-cultural research, researchers are often faced with many gray areas in interpreting findings from their cross-cultural studies. This is, of course, to be expected, because the study of culture is neither black nor white. Culture itself is a complex phenomenon that is replete with gray, and we see that in research every day and in the journals. It is the objective and experienced researcher who can deal with the gray area in creating sound, valid, and reliable interpretations that are justified on the basis of the data. And it is the astute consumer of that research who can sit back and judge those interpretations relative to the data in their own minds and not be swayed by the arguments of the researchers.

The Need for Unpackaging Studies

The field has come to increasingly recognize the limitations of the traditional cross-cultural comparison in which two or more cultures are compared on one or more target dependent variables. The problem with this approach is that "culture" is really only a label that summarizes many concrete and specific aspects of a group's way of life. As such, it is impossible for us to know in a typical cross-cultural comparison exactly what about cultures produced the differences we observed, and why.

To address this issue, researchers have begun to identify specific, concrete, and measurable psychological variables that they believe represent at least some of the contents of culture most pertinent to their variables of interest and to include them in their cross-cultural comparisons. "Culture," then, as a global construct is replaced by these specific, measurable variables, which are called context variables. Analyses are then directed to examine the degree to which these context variables actually account for the cultural differences. In this sense, the context variables are akin to nuisance variables in traditional experimentation, and the approach is exactly that of studies of covariance, as the context (nuisance) variables are treated as covariates in Analyses of Covariance or hierarchical multiple regression schemes. These types of cross-cultural studies are called unpackaging studies.

A number of examples of unpackaging studies can now be found in the literature. Bond and Tedeschi, for example, give an excellent review of cross-cultural studies on aggression both with and without unpackaging (Bond & Tedeschi, 2001). Singelis and his colleagues use the concept of self-construals to unpackage cultural influences on self-esteem and embarassability (Singelis, Bond, Sharkey, & Lai, 1999). Matsumoto and his colleagues have used the concepts of individualism-collectivism and status differentiation to unpackage cultural differences in cultural display rules and judgments of emotion. (Matsumoto et al., 2002; Matsumoto, Takeuchi, Andayani, Kouznetsova, & Krupp, 1998) Most recently, they have also shown that display rules of emotional expression mediate cultural differences in judgments of the emotional regulation of others (Matsumoto et al., 2003).

Unpackaging studies force researchers to think about cultures in ways that they did not in the past, breaking them down to specific, measurable constructs in considering how they influence the target variables of interest. Thus they force theoretical developments in our understanding of culture. They also allow us to examine the specific degree to which the hypothesized context variables actually do account for between culture differences. When they do not account for 100% of the differences, they force us to think about other ways in which culture influences our target constructs, helping us to refine our theoretical understanding of culture. We urge researchers interested in examining cultural effects on nonverbal behaviors to consider the design and conduct of unpackaging studies.

APPLIED RESEARCH IN OUR LABORATORY: DOES THE ABILITY TO RECOGNIZE EMOTIONS PREDICT INTERCULTURAL ADJUSTMENT?

For several years our laboratory has been engaged in exploring the psychological skills that predict successful intercultural adjustment. Our previous studies have focused on the development of the Intercultural Adjustment Potential Scale (ICAPS; Matsumoto, LeRoux, Bernhard, & Gray, 2001; Matsumoto et al., in press; Matsumoto, LeRoux, Ratzlaff et al., 2001), the only measure to date that can reliably and validly predict adjustment in a wide range of immigrants and sojourners. Across all studies the most important predictor of adjustment has consistently been shown to be emotion regulation (ER). We define ER as the ability of individuals to manage, modify, and use their emotions toward constructive outcomes. In fact we view ER as the "gatekeeper" skill of adjustment—that ER is a necessary component of adjustment because the utilization of it allows for the use of other knowledge, skills, and abilities to help people navigate the trials and tribulations of intercultural adaptation.

The importance of emotion regulation in intercultural adjustment raises the possibility that emotional intelligence (EI) is important for adjustment because ER is considered to be a single component of EI (Mayer, Salovey, Caruso, & Sitarenios, 2001). EI, which is "ability to recognize the meanings of emotions and their relationships and to use them as a basis in reasoning, problem solving and enhancing cognitive activities" (Mayer et al., 2001), is comprised of four skills; ER, emotion recognition in self and others, understanding of emotion, and utilization of emotion to facilitate thinking (Ciarrochi, Chan, & Bajgar, 2001; Ciarrochi, Chan, & Caputi, 1999; Mayer et al., 2001). These four skills form a hierarchy, with emotion recognition in the bottom forming the basis for the rest of the skills (Izard, 2001; Mayer et al., 2001). In other words, the other three skills are only possible when emotion recognition is first achieved. Therefore, emotion recognition ability (ERA) is conceptually a more primary construct than emotion regulation, because people need to recognize emotions before they can engage in emotion regulation.

Based on this notion, and based on the knowledge from previous studies that ER predicts intercultural adjustment, we hypothesized that ERA should predict intercultural adjustment also. If it does, we subsequently hypothesized that ERA mediates the relationship between ER and adjustment.

To test these notions we recruited 63 international students at San Francisco State University within the first month of their first semester at the university. They completed six subjective measures of intercultural adjustment that included the Beck Anxiety Inventory (BAI; Beck & Steer, 1993), the Beck Depression Inventory (BDI; Beck, Steer, & Brown, 1996), the Beck Hopelessness Scale (BHS; Beck & Steer, 1988), the Culture Shock Questionnaire (CSQ; Mumford, 1998), the

Homesickness and Contentment Scale (HCS; Shin & Abell, 1999), and the Satisfaction with Life Scale (SWLS; Diener, Emmons, Larsen, & Griffin, 1985). In addition, they completed the ICAPS and the neuroticism scale of the Big Five Inventory (John, 1989) to measure ER. ERA was measured by using the Japanese and Caucasian Brief Affect Recognition Test (JACBART), in which expressions of seven universal emotions (anger, disgust, fear, happiness, sadness, surprise, and contempt) are presented for 1/5 of a second embedded within a one second neutral expression of the same individual (Matsumoto et al., 2000).

The results confirmed our hypotheses. We performed a series of hierarchical multiple regressions on each of the adjustment scales, entering demographic variables that significantly predicted each adjustment scale on the first step (thus eliminating the effects of noncultural demographic variables), and then JACBART ERA scores on the second. ERA added significant and unique variance to the prediction of four adjustment scales above and beyond that already predicted by demographics: ERA of contempt predicted the BAI, ERA of sadness and disgust predicted culture shock, ERA of contempt predicted homesickness, and ERA of sadness predicted contentment.

Because ERA was correlated with ER and ER was correlated with all adjustment indices, we next examined the degree to which ERA mediated the relationship between ER and adjustment by computing another series of hierarchical multiple regressions, entering demographics on the first step, significant ERA scores on the second, and then ER scores on the third. ER contributed unique variance to the prediction of all four adjustment scores predicted by ERA. Comparison of the effect sizes associated with the predictive validity of ER on adjustment with and without ERA in the equation indicated that ERA accounted for between 9.09 and 19.26% of the association between ER and adjustment.

These results are the first to demonstrate that ERA can reliably predict adjustment in immigrants and sojourners and are significant in their own right. Moreover because ERA is a trainable skill these findings open the door to the possibility that the potential for positive adjustment outcomes may improve if immigrants and sojourners receive such training early on in their sojourns. We sincerely hope that future applied research may investigate these, and other, possibilities.

CONCLUSION

The goal of this chapter was to encourage cross-cultural research on applied nonverbal behaviors to take root, grow, and blossom, and to provide some of the basic information that could form some of the important nutrients that would allow this to occur. We first discussed a conceptual understanding and definition of culture, and then how culture influences the encoding and decoding of nonverbal behaviors. We then discussed several methodological issues concerning cross-cultural research that researchers should be aware of. Immediately above we briefly describe an example of an applied study of nonverbal behaviors from our laboratory.

Cross-cultural research in applied settings, like any good research in applied settings, is definitely not easy. Yet the potential rewards in information and knowledge and the possibilities of intervening positively in many people's lives, not only in one culture but in many, seem to be a benefit that far outweighs those difficulties. We sincerely hope that the information we have provided in this chapter will encourage researchers in the field to conduct such studies in the future. As the world becomes increasingly smaller and the need for people across cultural lines to get along better becomes more and more apparent, the role of such research becomes increasingly larger.

REFERENCES

Adamopoulous, J., & Lonner, W. J. (2001). Culture and psychology at a crossroad: Historical perspective and theoretical analysis. In D. Matsumoto (Ed.), *The Handbook of Culture and Psychology* (pp. 11–34). New York: Oxford University Press.

Bachman, J. G., & O'Malley, P. M. (1984). Black-white differences in self-esteem: Are they affected by response styles? *American Journal of Sociology, 90*(3), 624–639.

Beck, A. T., & Steer, R. A. (1988). *Beck Hopelessness Scale*. San Antonio, TX: The Psychological Corporation.

Beck, A. T., & Steer, R. A. (1993). *Beck Anxiety Inventory*. San Antonio, TX: The Psychological Corporation.

Beck, A. T., Steer, R. A., & Brown, G. K. (1996). *BDI-II: Beck Depression Inventory Manual* (2nd ed.). San Antonio, TX: The Psychological Corporation.

Berry, J. W., Poortinga, Y. H., Segall, M. H., & Dasen, P. R. (1992). *Cross-cultural psychology: Research and applications*. New York: Cambridge University Press.

Biehl, M., Matsumoto, D., & Kasri, F. (in press). Culture and emotion. In U. Gielen & A. L. Communian (Eds.), *Cross-cultural and international dimensions of psychology*. Trieste, Italy: Edizioni Lint Trieste S.r.l.

Bond, M., & Tedeschi, J. (2001). Polishing the jade: A modest proposal for improving the study of social psychology across cultures. In D. Matsumoto (Ed.), *The Handbook of Culture and Psychology* (pp. 309–324). New York: Oxford University Press.

Brislin, R. (1970). Back translation for cross-cultural research. *Journal of Cross-Cultural Psychology, 1,* 185–216.

Buss, D. M. (1988). The evolution of human intrasexual competition: Tactics of mate attraction. *Journal of Personality & Social Psychology, 54*(4), 616–628.

Buss, D. M. (1989). Sex differences in human mate preferences: Evolutionary hypotheses tested in 37 cultures. *Behavioral & Brain Sciences, 12*(1), 1–49.

Buss, D. M. (1991). Evolutionary personality psychology. *Annual Review of Psychology, 42,* 459–491.

Buss, D. M. (2000). The evolution of happiness. *American Psychologist, 55*(1), 15–23.

Buss, D. M. (2001). Human nature and culture: An evolutionary psychological perspective. *Journal of Personality, 69*(6), 955–978.

Ciarrochi, J., Chan, A. Y. C., & Bajgar, J. (2001). Measuring emotional intelligence in adolescents. *Personality and Individual Differences, 31*(7), 1105–1119.

Ciarrochi, J. V., Chan, A. Y. C., & Caputi, P. (1999). A critical evaluation of the emotional intelligence construct. *Personality and Individual Differences, 28*(3), 539–561.

Diener, E., Emmons, R. A., Larsen, R. J., & Griffin, S. (1985). The satisfaction with life scale. *Journal of Personality Assessment, 49,* 71–75.

Ekman, P. (1999). Basic emotions. In T. D. a. T. Power (Ed.), *The handbook of cognition and emotion* (pp. 45–60). Sussex, United Kingdom: John Wiley and Sons, Ltd.

Ekman, P., & Friesen, W. (1969). The repertoire of nonverbal behavior: Categories, origins, usage, and coding. *Semiotica, 1,* 49–98.

Greenfield, M. P. (1997). You can't take it with you. *American Psychologist, 52,* 1115–1124.

Izard, C. E. (2001). Emotional intelligence or adaptive emotions? *Emotion, 3,* 249–257.

Jahoda, G. (1984). Do we need a concept of culture? *Journal of Cross-Cultural Psychology, 15*(2), 139–151.

John, O. (1989). *The BFI-54.* Unpublished test; Institute of Personality and Social Research, Department of Psychology, University of California, Berkeley.

Keating, C. (1976). Nonverbal aspects of communication. *Topics in Culture Learning, 4,* 12–13.

Koopmann, B., & Matsumoto, D. (2003). *American-German Differences in Emotional Display Rules.* Paper presented at the 2003 Western Psychological Association Annual Convention. Vancouver, British Columbia, Canada.

Kroeber, A. L., & Kluckholn, C. (1952/1963). *Culture: A critical review of concepts and definitions.* Cambridge, MA: Harvard University.

Linton, R. (1936). *The study of man: An introduction.* New York: Appleton.

Linville, P. W., & Jones, E. E. (1980). Polarized appraisals of out-group members. *Journal of Personality and Social Psychology, 38,* 689–703.

Malinowski, B. (1927, 1961). *Sex and repression in a savage society.* Cleveland, OH: World Publishers.

Malinowski, B. (1944, 1960). *A scientific theory of culture and other essays.* New York: Oxford University Press.

Marin, G., Gamba, R. J., & Marin, B. V. (1992). Extreme response style and acquiescence among Hispanics: The role of acculturation and education. *Journal of Cross-Cultural Psychology, 23*(4), 498–509.

Masters, R. D., & Sullivan, D. G. (1989). Nonverbal displays and political leadership in France and the United States. *Political Behavior, 11,* 123–156.

Matsumoto, D. (1990). Cultural similarities and differences in display rules. *Motivation & Emotion, 14*(3), 195–214.

Matsumoto, D. (2001). Culture and emotion. In D. Matsumoto (Ed.), *The Handbook of Culture and Psychology* (pp. 171–194). New York: Oxford University Press.

Matsumoto, D. (2003). Cross-cultural research. In S. Davis (Ed.), *The handbook of research methods in experimental psychology* (pp. 189–208). Oxford, UK: Blackwell.

Matsumoto, D., Choi, J. W., Hirayama, S., Domae, A., & Yamaguchi, S. (2003). Culture, display rules, emotion regulation, and emotion judgments. *Manuscript currently submitted for publication.*

Matsumoto, D., Consolacion, T., Yamada, H., Suzuki, R., Franklin, B., Paul, S., Ray, R., & Uchida, H. (2002). American-Japanese cultural differences in judgments of emotional expressions of different intensities. *Cognition & Emotion, 16*(6), 721–747.

Matsumoto, D., Grissom, R., & Dinnel, D. (2001). Do between-culture differences really mean that people are different? A look at some measures of cultural effect size. *Journal of Cross-Cultural Psychology, 32*(4), 478–490.

Matsumoto, D., LeRoux, J. A., Bernhard, R., & Gray, H. (2001). Personality and behavioral correlates of intercultural adjustment potential. *Manuscript submitted for publication.*

Matsumoto, D., LeRoux, J. A., Iwamoto, M., Choi, J. W., Rogers, D., Tatani, H., & Uchida, H. (in press). The robustness of the Intercultural Adjustment Potential Scale (ICAPS). *International Journal of Intercultural Relations.*

Matsumoto, D., LeRoux, J. A., Ratzlaff, C., Tatani, H., Uchida, H., Kim, C., & Araki, S. (2001). Development and validation of a measure of intercultural adjustment potential in Japanese sojourners: The Intercultural Adjustment Potential Scale (ICAPS). *International Journal of Intercultural Relations,* 1–28.

Matsumoto, D., LeRoux, J. A., Wilson-Cohn, C., Raroque, J., Kooken, K., Ekman, P., Yrizarry, N., Loewinger, S., Uchida, H., Yee, A., Amo, L., & Goh, A. (2000). A new test to measure emotion recognition ability: Matsumoto and Ekman's Japanese and Caucasian Brief Affect Recognition Test (JACBART). *Journal of Nonverbal Behavior, 24*(3), 179–209.

Matsumoto, D., Takeuchi, S., Andayani, S., Kouznetsova, N., & Krupp, D. (1998). The contribution of individualism-collectivism to cross-national differences in display rules. *Asian Journal of Social Psychology, 1,* 147–165.

Mayer, J. D., Salovey, P., Caruso, D. R., & Sitarenios, G. (2001). Emotional intelligence as a standard intelligence. *Emotion, 1*(3), 232–242.

Miller, J. G. (1984). Culture and the development of everyday social explanation. *Journal of Personality and Social Psychology, 46,* 961–978.

Morris, D., Collett, P., Marsh, P., & O'Shaughnessy, M. (1980). *Gestures: Their origins and distribution.* New York: Scarborough.

Mumford, D. B. (1998). The measurement of culture shock. *Social Psychiatry and Psychiatric Epidemiology, 33,* 149–154.

Neuliep, J. W. (1997). A cross-cultural comparison of teacher immediacy in American and Japanese classrooms. *Communication Research, 24,* 431–451.

Oetzel, J., Ting-Toomey, S., Masumoto, T., Yokochi, Y., Pan, X., Takai, J., & Wilcox, R. (2001). Face and facework in conflict: A cross-cultural comparison of China, Germany, Japan, and the United States. *Communication Monographs, 68*(3), 238–253.

Peng, K., Nisbett, R., & Wong, N. Y. C. (1997). Validity problems comparing values across cultures and possible solution. *Psychological Methods, 2,* 329–344.

Pipher, M. (1998). *Another country: Navigating the emotional terrain of our elders.* New York: Putnam.

Poortinga, Y. H. (1989). Equivalence of cross-cultural data: An overview of basic issues. *International Journal of Psychology, 24,* 737–756.

Poortinga, Y. H. (1990). *IACCP presidential address: Towards a conceptualization of culture for psychology*. Tilburg, The Netherlands.

Rohner, R. P. (1984). Toward a conception of culture for cross-cultural psychology. *Journal of Cross-Cultural Psychology, 15*, 111–138.

Ross, L. (1977). The intuitive psychologist and his shortcomings: Distortions in the attribution process. In L. Berkowitz (Ed.), *Advances in experimental social psychology* (Vol. 10, pp. 174–221). New York: Academic Press.

Saarni, C. (1979). Children's understanding of display rules for expressive behavior. *Developmental Psychology, 15*(4), 424–429.

Seligman, M. E., & Hager, J. (1972). *Biological boundaries of learning*. New York: Appleton-Century-Crofts.

Shin, H., & Abell, N. (1999). The homesickness and contentment scale: Developing a culturally sensitive measure of adjustment for Asians. *Research on Social Work Practice, 9*(1), 45–60.

Shweder, R. A., & Bourne, E. J. (1984). Does the concept of the person vary cross-culturally? In R. A. Shweder & R. A. LeVine (Eds.), *Culture theory: Essays on mind, self, and emotion* (pp. 158–199). Cambridge, England: Cambridge University Press.

Singelis, T., Bond, M., Sharkey, W. F., & Lai, C. S. Y. (1999). Unpackaging culture's influence on self-esteem and embarassability. *Journal of Cross-Cultural Psychology, 30*, 315–341.

Tooby, J., & Cosmides, L. (1992). Psychological foundations of culture. In J. Barkow, L. Cosmides, & J. Tooby (Eds.), *The adapted mind* (pp. 19–136). New York: Oxford University Press.

Triandis, H. C. (1972). *The analysis of subjective culture*. New York: Wiley.

Triandis, H. C. (1994). *Culture and social behavior*. New York: McGraw Hill.

Triandis, H. C., McCusker, C., & Hui, C. H. (1990). Multimethod probes of individualism and collectivism. *Journal of Personality and Social Psychology, 59*(5), 1006–1020.

Von-Raffler Engel, W. (1981). Developmental kinesics: How children acquire communicative and non-communicative nonverbal behavior. *Infant Mental Health Journal, 2*(2), 84–94.

Wittgenstein, L. (1953). *Philosophical investigations*. New York: Macmillan.

About the Authors

Peter Blanck is the Charles M. and Marion Kierscht Professor of Law, and Professor of Psychology and of Public Health at the University of Iowa. He received his PhD in psychology from Harvard University and his JD from Stanford Law School, where he served as President of the *Stanford Law Review*. Blanck is the Director of the Law, Health Policy & Disability Center at the Iowa College of Law. Blanck has written over 100 articles and books on the ADA, received grants to study disability law and policy, represented clients before the United States Supreme Court in ADA cases, and testified before Congress. His work has received national and international attention. Blanck's recent books in the area include: *The Americans with Disabilities Act and the Emerging Workforce* (1998); *Employment, Disability, and the Americans with Disabilities Act* (2000). Blanck is a former member of the President's Committee on Employment of People with Disabilities, and has been a Senior Fellow of the Annenberg Washington Program in which capacity he explored the implementation of the Americans with Disabilities Act ("ADA"). He has been a Commissioner on the American Bar Association Commission on Mental and Physical Disability Law, chair of the American Psychological Association's Committee on Standards in Research, and President of the American Association on Mental Retardation's Legal Process and Advocacy Division. He has been a Fellow at Princeton University's Woodrow Wilson School, and a Mary Switzer Scholar.

Andrew Christensen is Professor of Psychology in the Department of Psychology at the University of California, Los Angeles. He received his PhD from the University of Oregon and did his internship at

Rutgers University Medical School. He studies couple conflict and couple therapy and has published widely on these topics. He is co-author of the influential scholarly work, *Close Relationships* (Freeman, 1983, reprinted in 2002). For therapists, he authored *Acceptance and change in couple therapy: A therapist's guide for transforming relationships* (1998, Norton) with Neil S. Jacobson. He also completed a trade book for couples, *Reconcilable differences* (2000, Guilford) with Jacobson. His therapy approach and research have been cited in the New York Times, Newsweek, Time Magazine, U.S. News and World Report, USA Today, and other magazines and newspapers.

Steve Duck received his BA and MA from Oxford University and his PhD (1971) from Sheffield University. He is the Daniel and Amy Starch Distinguished Research Chair in the College of Liberal Arts and Sciences at the University of Iowa. Duck is the Founding Editor and was Executive Editor (1984–1998) of the *Journal of Social and Personal Relationships* and a past President of the International Network on Personal Relationships. He co-founded the International Conferences on Personal Relationships (1982 onwards). Duck has published 35 books on issues such as personal relationship growth and breakdown, TV production techniques, the development of social psychology, and social support. His research interests are to enhance interdisciplinary scholarship, to promote the study of relationship processes, and to develop the careers of junior scholars and graduate students.

Judith A. Feeney received her PhD from the University of Queensland in 1991 and is currently Associate Professor of Psychology at that University. Her areas of research include adult attachment, emotion regulation, conflict in couple and parent-adolescent relationships and hurt feelings. She has published extensively in the area of adult attachment and in personal relationships more generally. Her publications include *Attachment style as a predictor of adult romantic relationships* (Feeney & Noller, 1990), *Attachment style and affect regulation: Relationships with health behavior and family experiences of illness* (Feeney & Ryan, 1994), and *Adult attachment and emotional control* (Feeney, 1995).

Howard S. Friedman is Distinguished Professor of Psychology at the University of California, Riverside. He is Editor of the *Journal of Nonverbal Behavior* (Kluwer), Editor-in-chief of the *Encyclopedia of Mental Health* (Academic Press), and directs a large project on health and longevity long funded by the National Institute on Aging. Friedman is a thrice-elected Fellow of the American Psychological Association (in Personality and Social Psychology, Health Psychology, and in Media Psychology) and an elected Fellow of the AAAS (Science) and the Society of Behavioral Medicine. Friedman is author of over 100 influential scientific articles and chapters in leading books and journals and was named a "most-cited psychologist." He has written a textbook on *Health Psychology* (Prentice Hall, 2002) and one on *Personality* (Allyn & Bacon, 2003) and has edited various scholarly volumes. He also wrote the comprehensive trade analysis entitled *The self-healing personality: Why some people achieve health and others succumb to illness* (1991/2000). Professor Friedman has received the *Distinguished Teaching Award* from the University of California, Riverside, and the Western Psychological Association's *Outstanding Teaching Award.*

Al Goethals is Chair of the Department of Psychology and Chair of the Program in Leadership Studies at Williams College. He graduated from Harvard College in 1966 and received his PhD from Duke University in 1970. In addition to his teaching duties, Professor Goethals has served Williams as Acting Dean of the Faculty, 1987–1988, and as Provost, 1990–1995. He has co-authored several textbooks on basic psychology, social psychology and the psychology of adjustment and has published numerous articles on attitude change, social perception, and self-evaluation. His current research interests concern how college students educate each other and the ways leadership is enacted and perceived.

Monica J. Harris is Associate Professor of psychology at the University of Kentucky. She obtained her BA from the University of California, Riverside, in 1983, and her PhD in Social Psychology from Harvard University in 1987. She has published widely on the topic of the nonverbal mediation of interpersonal expectancy effects, and she is currently serving as Associate Editor for the *Journal of Nonverbal Behavior.*

Charles Kornreich is Professor at the Free University of Brussels, Belgium. His main interests lie in psychiatry, emotion, alcoholism, and cravings. A part of the Service of Psychiatry and Medical Psychology at the Free University of Brussels, his recent work there is the clinical and experimental study of the expression of the emotions in the separated alcoholic, in particular in his relationships to the processes of craving. he has published several works in his scholarly career.

Marianne LaFrance is Professor of Psychology and Women's and Gender Studies at Yale University. She received her MA and PhD from Boston University. She is a Fellow of the American Psychological Association and the American Psychological Society. Her interests are at the intersections of gender, power and nonverbal communication. LaFrance strives to determine why facial expressions, like smiling, or linguistic strategies like apologizing, reveal clear gender differences. She also focuses on the effects of being the target of seemingly innocuous prejudice conveyed through humor, slights, or small provocations. She seeks to understand how subtle and implicit messages reveal, justify, and preserve unequal social structures.

Samantha Mann is a Research Fellow at the University of Portsmouth. Her PhD, 'Suspects, lies and videotape,' which she completed at the University of Portsmouth in 2000, examined the differences in behavior of suspects when telling the truth and when lying. In addition she investigated police officers' ability to detect these differences. She is currently working on a project designed to improve police officers' ability to detect deception.

Leslie R. Martin, PhD, is a social/personality psychologist specializing in health-related issues. Her primary research interests are in psychological factors that affect health and longevity and in physician-patient communication—areas in which she has worked for the past 12 years. Dr. Martin is on the editorial board for the *Journal of Nonverbal Behavior*. In addition to her full-time position as Associate Professor of Psychology at La Sierra University, she also holds a faculty position at Loma Linda University and a research appointment at the University of California, Riverside.

David Matsumoto is Professor of Psychology and Director of the Culture and Emotion Research Laboratory at San Francisco State University. He has studied culture, emotion, social interaction and communication for twenty years, and has written over 250 works in these areas. His books include well-known titles such as *Culture and psychology: People around the world* (Wadsworth, translated into Dutch and Japanese), *The Intercultural adjustment potential of Japanese* (Hon no Tomasha) and *The handbook of culture and psychology* (Oxford University Press, translated into Russian). His most recent book, *The new Japan* (Intercultural Press), has received national and international acclaim. He is the recipient of many awards and honors including being named a G. Stanley Hall lecturer by the American Psychological Association.

Patricia Noller received her PhD from the University of Queensland in 1981 and is currently Emeritus Professor of Psychology at that University. For seven years, she was Director of the University of Queensland Family Centre. She has published extensively in the area of marital and family relationships, including twelve books and over eighty journal articles and book chapters. She received an Early Career Award from the Australian Psychological Society and is a Fellow of the Academy of the Social Sciences in Australia, and a Fellow of the National Council on Family Relationships (USA). She has served on the editorial boards of the *Journal of Social and Personal Relationships*, *Journal of Personality and Social Psychology*, *Journal of Nonverbal Behavior*, *Human Communication Research*, the *Journal of*

Family Studies, and the *Journal of Family Communication*. She has served as associate editor of the Australian Psychologist and was appointed as foundation editor of *Personal relationships: Journal of the international society for the study of personal relationships*, which position she held from 1993–1997. She was President of that society from 1998 to 2000.

Maureen O'Sullivan is a Professor of Psychology at the University of San Francisco. She received her PhD at the University of Southern California, and has studied non-verbal behavior, deception and emotional intelligence for more than 20 years. Her recent research on expert lie detectors was featured in a lengthy New Yorker article about Paul Ekman in August, 2002. She has identified a rare group of people (about one in a thousand) who are expert lie detectors. This group includes cops, counter-terrorists, arbitrators, artists and therapists. Her presentation will describe some of the similarities and some of the differences that characterize this intriguing group of people.

Thierry H. Pham is a PhD psychologist from the Catholic University of Louvain (1996). He has worked as a prison psychologist for the Belgian Department of Justice for more than 15 years. He is currently the director of the Centre of Research in Social Defense in Tournai, Belgium and associate researcher at the Philippe Pinel Institute of Montreal. He is also associate professor of forensic psychology at the Mons-Hainaut University in Belgium and at the University Trois-Rivières in Quebec. He is mainly interested in the cognitive-emotion correlates of psychopathy and on risk assessment procedures among forensic populations.

Pierre Philippot is Professor of Psychology at the University of Louvain at Louvain-la-Neuve and Research Associate of the Belgian National Science Foundation. His teaching and research domains cover emotion (with special interests for cognitive regulation of emotion and autobiographical memories, respiratory feedback in emotion, and emotional facial expression recognition) and psychotherapy, especially CBT and emotion focused approaches. Pierre Philippot is past president of the Belgian French-Speaking CBT Association: Association pour l'Etude, la Modification et la Thérapie du Comportement (AEMTC). He founded and is presently directing a psychology clinical center specialized in the treatment of emotional disorders in the psychology department of his home university. Together with Robert S. Feldman he has edited volumes such as *The social context of nonverbal behavior* (Cambridge University Press), *Nonverbal behavior in clinical settings* (Oxford University Press), and *The regulation of emotion* (Lawrence Erlbaum Associates). More information and reprints can directly be obtained on line at www.ecsa.ucl.ac.be/ personnel/philippot

Ronald Riggio is the Henry R. Kravis Professor of Leadership and Organizational Psychology at Claremont McKenna College. He received his MA, 1979, and PhD, 1981, from University of California, Riverside in Social and Personality Psychology. His research interests include nonverbal communication skills, leadership, Industrial/Organizational Psychology, and higher education/outcome assessment. He served as editor for the Journal of Nonverbal Behavior from 1997–2002 and is also affiliated with the Academy of Management, the American Psychological Society, the Western Psychological Association, and the Society of Personality and Social Psychology. Riggio was honored with the *Outstanding Teacher Award* from Western Psychological Association in 1993.

Nigel Roberts completed his PhD at the University of Queensland in 1998. His educational focus is on violence in couple relationships. Roberts's doctoral thesis involved the use of physiological measures, observational coding and time-series analysis. He has a number of publications on observation of couple interaction, attachment and violence in couples, and emotion and violence in couples.

Robert Rosenthal is Distinguished Professor of Psychology at the University of California at Riverside and Edgar Pierce Professor of Psychology, Emeritus, Harvard University. His research has centered for over 40 years on the role of the self-fulfilling prophecy in everyday life and in laboratory situations. Special interests include the effects of teachers' expectations on students' performance, the effects of experimenters' expectations on the results of their research, and the effects of clinicians' expectations on their patients' mental and physical health. He also has strong interests in sources of artifact in behavioral research and in various quantitative procedures. In the realm of data analysis, his special interests are in experimental design and analysis, contrast analysis, and meta-analysis. His most recent books and articles are about these areas of data analysis; he is Co-Chair of the Task Force on Statistical Inference of the American Psychological Association. Rosenthal received the *Donald Campbell Award* of the Society for Personality and Social Psychology, the *Distinguished Scientist Award* of the Society of Experimental Social Psychology, and the *James McKeen Cattell Award* of the American Psychological Society. More recently he was awarded the *Samuel J. Messick Distinguished Scientific Contributions Award* of APA's Division 5—Evaluation, Measurement, and Statistics, *APA's Distinguished Scientific Award for Applications of Psychology*, and the *Gold Medal Award for Life Achievement in the Science of Psychology* of the American Psychological Foundation.

Michael (Mike) Searcy is a doctoral candidate in Communication Studies at the University of Iowa. He currently holds a MAR (Research) from Saint Louis University in Communication and a BA from Saint

Louis University. He has extensive experience in consulting within such fields as speech, training, sales, and business start-ups and has engaged himself in this work since 1996. As a founding member of Communication Resource Consultants, Searcy has taught in various higher educational institutions since 1997 in areas ranging from computers to communication. He currently conducts research in interpersonal, nonverbal, small group, and organizational communication.

Aldert Vrij is Professor of Applied Social Psychology at the University of Portsmouth, United Kingdom. His research interests are verbal and nonverbal cues to deception; people's beliefs about cues to deception; people's ability to detect deceit; and possible ways of improving this ability. He has published approximately 250 articles and book chapters and six books, about these and other issues. His book *Detect lies and deceit: The psychology of lying and the implications for professional practice*, published by Wiley and Sons in 2000, is a comprehensive review of verbal, nonverbal and physiological correlates of truth telling and deception. He regularly gives workshops and seminars to police officers about deception in several countries and regularly acts as an expert witness in criminal and civil court cases. He is Associate Editor of *Legal and Criminological Psychology*.

Julie A. Woodzicka received her PhD in Social Psychology from Boston College in 2000. She is an Assistant Professor in the Psychology Department at Washington and Lee University. Her research focuses on the impact of everyday instances of prejudice such as that conveyed through sexist jokes and subtle gender harassment, and White and male privilege. She has published several works such as *Gender and power: The role of sexual harassment* (2000), presented at the Society for the Psychological Study of Social Issues; *Real vs. imagined sexual harassment* (in press), featured in the *Journal of Social Issues*; and *No laughing matter: Women's verbal and nonverbal reactions to sexist humor* (pp. 61–80), in *Prejudice: The target's perspective* (1998).

Author Index

A

Abbey, A., 140, 148, 153
Abell, N., 273, 277
Ackerman, K., 27, 35
Adamopoulous, J., 258, 274
Aesop, 234, 248
Afifi, W., 196, 212, 229, 249
Aguinis, H., 125, 132
Aguirre, M., 131, 137
Akehurst, L., 65, 67, 68, 72, 76, 84, 90
Akert, R. M., 218, 248
Albrecht, T. L., 10, 12, 15
Alibali, M. W., 172, 183, 189, 191
Allen, L. Q., 158, 184, 186
Allwood, C. M., 78, 84
Altman-Weber, D., 25, 26, 36
Alton, A. O., 233, 253
Amador, M., 83, 86
Ambady, N., 7, 12, 12, 13, 49, 58, 126, 134, 247, 250
Amir, N., 20, 21, 33, 34
Amo, L., 273, 276
Andayani, S., 271, 276
Anders, S. L., 197, 207, 213
Andersen, J. F., 160, 166, 186
Andersen, P., 196, 212
Andersen, P. A., 121, 125, 132, 211
Anderson, A. H., 130, 136
Anderson, D. E., 81, 84
Anderson, E. D., 236, 248

Anderson, K., 209, 213
Anderson, K. L., 208, 209, 213
Ansfield, M. E., 236, 248
Antes, T. A., 184, 186
Anthenelli, R. M., 28, 37
Anton, R. F., 27, 33
Apple, W., 107, 108, 115
Araki, S., 272, 276
Archer, D., 6, 15, 132, 138, 218, 237, 248, 249, 252
Argyle, M., 43, 58
Arther, R. O., 70, 71, 89
Arvey, R. D., 122, 132
Ashkanasy, N. M., 126, 127, 132
Asmundson, G. J. G., 20, 34
Awamleh, R., 125, 132

B

Babad, E., 174, 181, 182, 186, 187, 191
Bachman, J. G., 268, 274
Back, A. L., 9, 14
Baer, B. A., 29, 35
Baert, Y., 26, 31, 36
Baeyens, C., 36
Baird, J. E., Jr., 141, 153
Bajgar, J., 272, 275
Baker, D. D., 143, 153
Baldry, A. C., 74, 84
Ballif, B., 18, 34
Barber, J. D., 104, 114

Subject Index

A

Advertising, 129
Affect Blend Test (ABT), 219
Affective learning, 161, 163
Alcoholics
emotional communication deficits, 24
facial decoding deficits, 19, 25–29, 32
interpersonal difficulties, 19, 23–25, 28–29
relapse predictors, 29
training programs for, 29–30
Alexander the Great, 100
Anchoring, 233–234
Anger
alcoholics and, 24, 29
facial expressions, 93n6
Angry withdrawal, 200
Anxiety
arousal and, 206
cognitive models of, 20
relationship-centered, 203, 207–208
see also Social phobics
Apple-orange comparisons, 70
Archer, Jeffrey, 65
Arm movements, 68, 70, 71, 72t, 227
Arousal, 92n3, 206
Attachment security, 197, 202–204, 207–208

Attentional bias, 19, 20–21, 32
Attorneys, expectations of, 45
Availability heuristic, 76, 233
Avoidance
alcoholics and, 25
social phobics and, 20, 21
withdrawal and, 200
Awareness, of nonverbal cues, 243–244

B

Back translation, 268
Beck Anxiety Inventory (BAI), 272
Beck Depression Inventory (BDI), 272
Beck Hopelessness Scale (BHS), 272
Bedside manner, 8
Behavior
complementary, 96
controlling, 67, 68
interpersonal, 96–98
patterns, 70
self-awareness of, 66
Behavioral consistency, 53
Behavioral intentions, 161, 163
Behavioral learning, 161
Biases
attentional, 19, 20–21, 32
cognitive, 233–234, 244–245
in cross-cultural research, 263–264
deception, 233

301